THE BROSS PRIZE . . . 1905

THE PROBLEM OF THE OLD TESTAMENT

CONSIDERED WITH REFERENCE TO RECENT CRITICISM

BY

JAMES ORR, D.D.

PROFESSOR OF APOLOGETICS AND SYSTEMATIC THEOLOGY
UNITED FREE CHURCH COLLEGE, GLASGOW

"*Nubecula est, quae cito evanescet.*"

CHARLES SCRIBNER'S SONS
NEW YORK 1911

TO

THE PRESIDENT, TRUSTEES, AND FACULTY

OF

LAKE FOREST COLLEGE

This Volume is Gratefully Dedicated

BY

THE AUTHOR

THE BROSS FOUNDATION

IN 1879, the late William Bross of Chicago, lieutenant-governor of Illinois in 1866–1870, desiring to make some memorial of his son, Nathaniel Bross, who had died in 1856, entered into an agreement with the "Trustees of Lake Forest University," whereby there was finally transferred to the said Trustees the sum of Forty Thousand Dollars, the income of which was to accumulate in perpetuity for successive periods of ten years, at compound interest, the accumulations of one decade to be spent in the following decade, for the purpose of stimulating the production of the best books or treatises "*on the connection, relation, and mutual bearing of any practical science, or history of our race, or the facts in any department of knowledge, with and upon the Christian Religion.*"

In his deed of gift the founder had in view "*the religion of the Bible, composed of the Old and New Testaments of our Lord and Saviour, Jesus Christ, as commonly received in the Presbyterian and other evangelical churches.*" His object was "*to call out the best efforts of the highest talent and the ripest scholarship of the world, to illustrate from science, or any department of knowledge, and to demonstrate, the divine origin and authority of the Christian Scriptures; and, further, to show how both Science and Revelation coincide, and to prove the existence, the providence, or any or all of the attributes of the one living and true God, infinite, eternal, and unchangeable in His being, wisdom, power, holiness, justice, goodness and truth.*"

At the close of the Trust Agreement, the donor expressed the hope that, by means of this fund, the various authors might, "*every ten years, post up the science of the world and show how it illustrates the truth of the Bible, and the existence of God,*" and that thereby "*the gospel of our blessed Saviour, Jesus Christ, and the glories of His sacrifice and plan of salvation,*" might be preached "*to the end of time.*"

The books or treatises procured by either of the methods described below are to be published as volumes of what is to be known as "The Bross Library."

The gift thus contemplated in the original agreement of 1879 was finally consummated in 1890. The first decade of the accumulations of interest having closed in 1900, the Trustees of the Bross Fund began at that time the administration of this important trust.

The Trust Agreement prescribes two methods by which the production of books of the above-mentioned character is to be stimulated:—

A. The Trustees of the Bross Fund are empowered to select able scholars, from time to time, to prepare books, upon some theme within the terms of the Trust Agreement, that would "illustrate" or "demonstrate" the Christian Religion, or *any* phase of it, to the times in which we live.

Ordinarily, the authors of these books are requested to deliver the substance of such books in the form of lectures before Lake Forest College, and any of the general public who may desire to attend them, such courses to be known as The Bross Lectures.

In pursuance of the first method, two writers have already been specially appointed:—

(1) The Reverend President Francis Landey Patton, D.D., LL.D., of the Princeton Theological Seminary, whose lectures on "Obligatory Morality," delivered in Lake Forest in May, 1903, are being revised and enlarged by the author and will be published in due time by the Trustees of the Bross Fund;

(2) The Reverend Professor Marcus Dods, D.D., of New College, Edinburgh, whose lectures on "The Bible: Its Origin and Nature," delivered in May, 1904, have already been published as a volume of the Bross Library.

B. The second method for securing books for the Bross Library is as follows: —

One or more premiums or prizes are to be offered during each decade, the competition for which was to be thrown open to "*the scientific men, the Christian philosophers and historians of all nations.*"

Accordingly, in 1902, a prize of Six Thousand Dollars ($6,000) was offered for the best book fulfilling any of the purposes described in the foregoing extracts from the Trust Agreement, the manuscripts to be presented on or before June 1, 1905.

The following were appointed a Committee of Judges to make the award: the Reverend George Trumbull Ladd, D.D., LL.D., Professor of Moral Philosophy, Yale University; Alexander Thomas Ormond, Ph.D., LL.D., Professor of Philosophy, Princeton University, and the Reverend George Frederick Wright, D.D., LL.D., Professor of the Harmony of Science and Revelation, Oberlin College.

The authorship of the various essays was not known to the judges until after the award was made, the undersigned having been the custodian of the sealed envelopes containing the names of the writers of the respective manuscripts.

The Committee of Judges has unanimously awarded the Bross Prize of 1905 to the essay entitled "The Problem of the Old Testament," which is now issued as Volume III of the Bross Library.

The next Bross prize will be offered about 1915, and will be announced in due time by the Trustees of the Bross Fund.

The Trust Agreement requires that once in every thirty or fifty years (according as the Trustees of the fund may decide at the time) the entire sum of simple interest accumulated during the previous decade is to be offered as a single premium or prize for a competition similar to the one which has just been completed.

RICHARD D. HARLAN,
President of Lake Forest College.

LAKE FOREST, ILLINOIS,
NOVEMBER, 1905.

PREFACE

THE thanks of the author are due, in the first place, to the Trustees of Lake Forest College, and to the adjudicators acting on their behalf, who, in their generosity, have awarded to this book the munificent prize at their disposal from the Bross Fund. It is right, however, to say, that, although the present volume has been so fortunate as to obtain the Bross Prize, it was not for the Bross Prize, or with thought or knowledge of the same, that the book was written. But for a long-standing promise to the English publishers, it is doubtful if it ever would have been written at all. The book was sent to press in the beginning of this year, and the delay in its publication has been due principally to the afterthought of submitting it in proof to the judgment of the Bross Prize arbiters. The author is deeply sensible of the courtesy of the publishers in so readily meeting his wishes in this matter at inconvenience to themselves.

The book in one sense is not new, but represents, as will probably be evident from its perusal, the gathering up of thought, reading, and formation of opinion on its subject, going as far back as the days of the old Colenso and Samuel Davidson controversies, and of the appearance of Graf's work in 1866, when the author's interest in these questions was first thoroughly aroused—an interest which has never since flagged. Much water had flowed under the bridge in the interval, and the author entered on the task of putting his book into shape with many misgivings. Still, now that the work is done, and apart altogether from the material reward which has so unexpectedly come to him, he does not regret having undertaken it. The time is past when the discussion of Old Testament questions can be left wholly to professional experts, who represent one, but only one, of the many points of view necessary to be taken into account in considering this subject. The conclusions of the critics, of whom personally the author would speak only with respect, force themselves on every-one's attention, and it is a matter, no longer of choice, but of necessity, to pay regard to their opinions. Especially for one engaged in the teaching of theology, in whatever department, it is absolutely indispensable to possess some acquaintance with the methods and results of Old Testament study, and to try to come to some understanding with himself in regard to the theories of Old Testament religion and literature which he finds prevailing around him. The judgment of such an one may not be of the highest value; but, if it is his own, and has been reached at the cost of prolonged thought and study, the expression of it, and the exhibition of the grounds on which it rests, may not be without help to others working their way through similar perplexities.

The standpoint of the present book can be readily understood from a survey of the Table of Contents, or from reading the sketch of its scope at the close of the first chapter. Those who expect to find in it a wholesale denunciation of critics and of everything that savours of criticism will be disappointed. The author is not of the opinion that much good is accomplished by the violent and indiscriminating assaults on the critics sometimes indulged in by very excellent men. The case which the critics present must be met in a calm, temperate, and scholarly way, if it is to be dealt with to the satisfaction of thoughtful Christian people. On the other hand, those who come to the book expecting to find in it agreement with the methods and results of the reigning critical schools will probably be not less disappointed. The author has here no option. With the best will in the world to accept whatever new light criticism may have to throw on the structure and meaning of the Old Testament, he has to confess that his study of the critical developments—now for over thirty years—has increasingly convinced him that, while Biblical students are indebted to the critics, and to Old Testament science generally, for valuable help, the Graf-Wellhausen hypothesis now in the ascendant is, neither in its methods nor in its results, entitled to the unqualified confidence often claimed for it. He is persuaded, on the contrary, that it rests on erroneous fundamental principles, is eaten through with subjectivity, and must, if carried out to its logical issues — to which, happily, very many do not carry it — prove subversive of our Christian faith, and of such belief in, and use of, the Bible as alone can meet the needs of the living Church. Only, if this is to be shown, it must, as far as one's knowledge enables him to do it, be done thoroughly, and with due regard for all really critically-ascertained facts.

Being designed specially for an English-reading public, the book is purposely cast in a form as little technical as the nature of the subject permits. Hebrew words and minute philological discussions are, as a rule, avoided, and where English translations of foreign books exist, references are usually made to these. The customary form of the divine name, "Jehovah," is retained; but in quotations authors have been allowed to use their own various spellings of the name. If, throughout, a seemingly disproportionate space is given to German writers, this is simply due to the fact that at least nine-tenths of the "Higher-Critical" theories now in vogue had their origin and elaboration in Germany, and in Britain and America are largely of the nature of importations. One early learns that, if these theories are to be dealt with satisfactorily, it can only be by going at first hand to the sources—tapping the stream, as it were, at the fountain-head. At the same time the Indexes will show that representative writers of English-speaking countries, of different schools, have by no means been overlooked.

In so immense a field, it is hardly necessary to say that no attempt whatever is made at a complete or exhaustive treatment of Old Testament questions. That would have been impossible in the space, even had the author possessed the knowledge or ability qualifying him to undertake it. Some aspects of the Old Testament—the Wisdom Literature, for example—have had to be left altogether untouched. The idea has been, as far as practicable, to concentrate attention on really crucial points, and to make these the pivots on which the discussion of other questions turns (see Appendix to first chapter). In handling so large a mass of material, and copying and re-copying so many references, it is inevitable that, with the utmost care, slips and mistakes should occur. The author can only hope that these will not prove in any case to be of such magnitude as seriously to affect the main argument.

Since the book went to press in the spring, no small amount of literature has appeared to which it would be interesting to refer. Allusion may here only be made to the appearance of a valuable work by Professor W. Lotz, of Erlangen, entitled *Das Alte Testament und die Wissenschaft*, with which, in parts, the treatment in these pages may be compared. It would be endless to specify articles and pamphlets. Professor James Robertson, of Glasgow, has contributed to the May and June numbers of the periodical *Good Words* two interesting papers on "The Beginnings of Hebrew History and Religion"; and Professor R. D. Wilson, of Princeton, has completed in July and October his valuable articles on "Royal Titles" in the *Princeton Theological Review.* The October article is specially devoted to the statements of Dr. Driver on the use of royal titles in the books of Ezra and Nehemiah. Three papers by Professors Driver and Kirkpatrick on *The Higher Criticism* have been published, aiming at the removal of misconceptions. In his *Biblische Theologie des Alten Testaments* Stade has re-stated his views on the religion of Israel in more systematic form.

With these remarks, the book must be left to its own mission. The author entertains no over-sanguine expectations as to its effect on general conviction, but he is not without hope that it may at least rouse to reflection some who have given too easy an assent to current theories, simply because they are the theories of the hour. He has no wish to be ultra-dogmatic on any point. Time may not justify all his conclusions; but he has the strong persuasion that, when the day for summing-up comes—if ever such arrives—the positions into which men's minds will be disposed to settle will be found much nearer those advocated in these pages than they will be to those of the advanced Wellhausen school. The future will show.

The volume, it will be observed, has been amply fitted with Tables of Contents, Indexes, and cross-references in footnotes. These should make the task of consulting its pages comparatively easy, and should lighten somewhat the impression of abstruseness created by certain of its chapters. The author's thanks are specially due to the Rev. J. M. Wilson, B.D., Highbury, London, and to George Hunter, Esq., Glasgow, for valuable aid in the correction of the proofs.

GLASGOW, *October* 1905.

CONTENTS

CHAPTER I

INTRODUCTORY: THE PROBLEM STATED.—*Pp.* 1-24.

CHAPTER III

CHAPTER IV

THE OLD TESTAMENT AS AFFECTED BY CRITICISM—I. THE HISTORY: COUNTER-THEORIES TESTED.—*Pp.* 83-116.

CHAPTER V

CHAPTER VI

THE OLD TESTAMENT AS AFFECTED BY CRITICISM—II. RELIGION AND INSTITUTIONS: ARK, TABERNACLE, PRIESTHOOD, ETC.—*Pp.* 149–190.

1. The *fundamental law* in Ex. xx. 24.
Professor W. R. Smith on freedom of worship.
Law does not give *unrestricted* liberty.
"Recording" of God's name covers cases of special revelation (Gideon, Manoah, etc.).
2. Unity of sanctuary *the ideal for Israel* from beginning.
"An altar" in fundamental law.
One "house of God" in Book of Covenant.
One sanctuary in wilderness.
The altar *Ed* in Josh. xxii.
Worship at one centre in Judges.
3. Deuteronomy does not demand *immediate* realisation of the law of unity.
Postponement of full realisation till land had "rest."
Settled state first with David and Solomon.
4. Allowance necessary for *irregularities* in times of unsettlement and disorganisation.
Period of confusion specially after capture of ark—"a religious interregnum."
Samuel's relation to worship.
Spirit of law above its letter.
5. Religious attitude to "high places."
Paucity of early notices.
Worship till Solomon mainly to Jehovah.
Idolatry in later reigns.
Attitude of prophets to "high places."
VI. The Aaronic Priesthood and the Levites.
A Levitical priesthood attested, but further questions.
1. Was the priesthood *Aaronic*?
Wellhausen's theorisings on tribe of Levi.
Denial of Aaronic "high priest" before exile.
Testimony to Aaronic priesthood—Aaron to Eli.
"High priest" seldom in Priestly Code.
2. *Priests and Levites.*
Alleged conflict of PC with Deuteronomy and early practice.
A relative contrast granted.
(1) Examination of *phraseology*.
"The priests the Levites" in earlier history.
"Priests *and* Levites" not in law.
"Levites" used also in wide sense in P.
"Sons of Aaron" in PC not a universal designation, and disappears later.
Change in designation with choice of tribe of Levi.
Nomenclature follows fact.
(2) Functions of priesthood attributed to *whole tribe* of Levi in Deuteronomy.
Even Urim and Thummim of priesthood.

APPENDIX TO CHAPTER VI

CHAPTER VII

DIFFICULTIES AND PERPLEXITIES OF THE CRITICAL HYPOTHESIS: I. THE JE ANALYSIS.—*Pp.* 193-239.

APPENDIX TO CHAPTER VII

CHAPTER VIII

DIFFICULTIES AND PERPLEXITIES OF THE CRITICAL HYPOTHESIS: THE QUESTION OF DEUTERONOMY.—*Pp.* 245–284.

CHAPTER IX

DIFFICULTIES AND PERPLEXITIES OF THE CRITICAL HYPOTHESIS: THE PRIESTLY WRITING.

I. THE CODE.—*Pp.* 285–329.

CHAPTER X

APPENDIX TO CHAPTER X

CHAPTER XI

CHAPTER XII

PSALMS AND PROPHETS: THE PROGRESSIVENESS OF REVELATION.—*Pp.* 431–478.

Psalms and prophets the soul of Old Testament revelation.

PART I

DAVID AND THE PSALTER

Value of psalms independent of their dates.
Yet dates important in history of revelation.

I. THEORY OF THE POST-EXILIAN ORIGIN OF THE PSALTER.
Post-exilian origin of psalms a dogma of Wellhausen School.
Wellhausen's estimate of the psalms.
1. Theory *is not and cannot be proved.*
There *are* post-exilian, possibly Maccabæan, psalms.
No proof that most, or all, of the psalms are post-exilian.
The theory conflicts with tradition.
2. Post-exilian period mostly *a blank* to our knowledge.
Opening for groundless theorising.
3. Age *not productive* of literature.
No record of itself.
Return from captivity an incentive to psalm-composition.
But bulk of psalms show no post-exilian marks.
Many psalms *demand* an earlier date.
Psalms about king, etc.
4. Traditional *connection of psalms with David.*
Presumption in favour of pre-exilian psalms.
Positive evidences of pre-exilian psalmody.
Temple "singers" at return.
References to temple praise.
"Songs of Zion"; quotations, etc.
Ascription of psalms to David in titles.
Chronicler traces temple singing and music to David.

II. THE HISTORICAL POSITION OF DAVID AS PSALMIST.
Critical view of David: untrue to history.
1. David's *career* surveyed:—
(1) As *young man*: early piety and skill.
(2) At *Saul's Court*: behaviour irreproachable.
(3) As *exile*: relations to his men; mode of life; relations with Saul, etc.
(4) As *king*: services to country and religion; foreign conquests; project of temple and promise.
Blots on life and reign: Bathsheba.
Estimate of character.

NOTES TO CHAPTERS

CHAPTER I

Introductory: The Problem Stated

"I have been obliged to bestow the greatest amount of labour on a hitherto entirely unworked field, the investigation of the inner constitution of the separate books of the Old Testament by the aid of the Higher Criticism (a new name to no Humanist)."—EICHHORN.

"It is true that the present destructive proceedings in the department of Old Testament criticism, which demand the construction of a new edifice, are quite fitted to confuse consciences and to entangle a weak faith in all kinds of temptation. If, however, we keep fast hold in this labyrinth of the one truth, *Christus vere resurrexit*, we have in our hands Ariadne's thread to lead us out of it."—DELITZSCH.

Wellhausen "has identified himself with that 'so-called criticism' (Ewald's phraseology) which has 'given up Moses and so much that is excellent besides,' and which leads on directly to the contemptuous rejection of the Old Testament, if not also of the New (again, Ewald's phraseology)."—CHEYNE.

"Erroneous criticism cannot be corrected by dogmatic theology, but only by a better, more searching, and less prejudiced criticism."—OTTLEY.

CHAPTER I

INTRODUCTORY: THE PROBLEM STATED

WHEN we speak of a problem of the Old Testament, what do we mean? What is the problem, and how does it arise? A consideration of these questions will form a suitable introduction to the subsequent discussions.

It can hardly be necessary for us, in opening our inquiry, to define what is meant by the Old Testament, though on this point also, as between Protestants and Roman Catholics, a few questions might arise. By the term is here understood, in brief, that collection of Scriptures which now forms the first part of our ordinary Bibles,[1]—which the Jews technically divided into "the law, the prophets, and the (holy) writings,"[2]—which our Lord and His apostles spoke of as "the Scriptures,"[3] "the Holy Scriptures,"[4] "the oracles of God,"[5] "the sacred writings,"[6] and uniformly treated as the "God-inspired"[7] and authoritative record of God's revelations to, and dealings with, His ancient people.[8] This yields a first regulative position in our study. It may be laid down as axiomatic that, whatever they may be for others, these ancient Scriptures can never have less value for the Christian Church than they had for the Church's Master—Christ

[1] This excludes the Apocrypha. On the name itself Bishop Westcott says: "The establishment of Christianity gave at once a distinct unity to the former dispensation, and thus St. Paul could speak of the Jewish Scriptures by the name which they have always retained since, as the 'Old Testament' or 'Covenant' (2 Cor. iii. 14). . . . At the close of the second century the terms 'Old' and 'New Testament' were already in common use."—*The Bible in the Church*, p. 5.

[2] Cf. Luke xxiv. 44: "In the law of Moses, and the prophets, and the psalms."

[3] Matt. xxi. 42; Luke xxiv. 27.

[4] Rom. i. 2.

[5] Rom. iii. 2.

[6] 2 Tim. iii. 15.

[7] 2 Tim. iii. 16. Cf. 2 Pet. i. 21.

[8] Matt. v. 18; xv. 3, 6; xxii. 29, 31, 32; Luke xxiv. 27; John x. 35, etc. See Note A on the Jewish Canon.

Himself. Believing scholars of all standpoints may be trusted to agree in this.[1]

But what is meant by the problem of the Old Testament? Naturally there are many problems, but our title indicates that the problem we have now in view is that which arises peculiarly from the course of recent criticism. That problem will be found large and complex enough to occupy us in this volume, and, as going to the root of a believing attitude to the Scriptures of the Old Covenant, will probably be allowed to be, for the present moment, the fundamental and essential one. In this chapter we shall seek to convey as clear an idea as we can of where we conceive the *crux* of this Old Testament problem to lie, and shall indicate generally the lines to be followed in the handling of it.

I. The Problem Twofold: Religious and Literary

The problem of the Old Testament, then, as it presses on the Church from various sides at the present hour, may be said to be twofold. First, and most fundamentally, the question raised by it is—How are we to conceive of the *religion* which the Old Testament embodies, and presents to us in its successive stages, as respects its nature and origin? Is it a natural product of the development of the human spirit, as scholars of the distinctively "modern" way of thinking—Kuenen, Wellhausen, Stade, and the like[2]—allege; or is it something more—a result of special, supernatural revelation to Israel, such as other nations did not possess? Then second, How are we to conceive of the *literature* itself, or of the books which make up the Old Testament, as respects their age, origin, mode of composition, trustworthiness, and, generally, their connection with the religion of which they are the monuments?

At first sight it might seem as if the second of these questions had no necessary relation to the first. Nothing, it may be plausibly argued, depends, for the decision of the supernatural origin of the religion, on whether the

[1] Professor G. A. Smith says: "The Bible of the Jews in our Lord's time was practically our Old Testament. For us its supreme sanction is that which it derived from Christ Himself. . . . What was indispensable to the Redeemer must always be indispensable to the redeemed."—*Modern Criticism*, p. 11.

[2] See below, pp. 12 ff.

Pentateuch, as we have it, is from the pen of Moses, or is made up of three or four documents, put together at a late date; or at what period the Levitical law was finally codified; or whether the Book of Isaiah is the work of one, or two, or of ten authors; or whether the Psalms are pre-exilic, or post-exilic, in origin. Yet, as will be seen more fully later,[1] the dependence of the literary criticism on the religious theory is really very close. For, if it be true, as every fair mind must admit, that there are many scholars who succeed, to their own satisfaction, in combining the acceptance of the main results of the critical hypothesis of the Old Testament, even in its advanced form, with firm belief in the reality of supernatural revelation in Israel, and in the culmination of that revelation in Christ; it is equally true that, in the case of others, and these pre-eminently, in Dr. Cheyne's phrase, "The Founders of Criticism," the decisions arrived at on purely literary questions,—the date of a psalm, *e.g.*, the genuineness of a passage, or the integrity of a book,—are largely controlled by the view taken of the origin and course of development of the religion; and, with a different theory on these subjects, the judgments passed on the age, relations, and historical value, of particular writings, would be different also. This dependence of many of the conclusions of criticism—by no means, of course, all—on the religious and historical standpoint is practically admitted by Wellhausen, when he declares that "it is only within the region of religious antiquities and dominant religious ideas — the region which Vatke in his *Biblische Theologie* had occupied in its full breadth, and where the real battle first kindled—that the controversy can be brought to a definite issue."[2]

It is the perception of this fact and of its results which affords the explanation of the very genuine disquiet and perplexity which undeniably exist in large sections of the Church as to the tendency and outcome of recent develop-

[1] See below, pp. 16 ff.

[2] *Hist. of Israel*, p. 12. On Vatke, see below, p. 18. Graf also, the pioneer of the new movement (see below, pp. 199 ff.), in his chief work, lays stress on the fact that Pentateuch criticism was bound to remain "unclear, uncertain, and wavering," till it grasped the fact of the post-exilian origin of the Levitical legislation. To attempt to decide its problems on mere literary grounds was to move in a "vicious circle."—*Geschicht. Bücher*, pp. 2, 3.

ments in Old Testament criticism. From the popular point of view—the light in which the matter presents itself to the average Christian mind—the problem of the Old Testament is simply one of how we are to regard the Bible. It is not merely, as the instinct of the humblest is quick enough to perceive, the dates and authorship of books that are in dispute in these critical theories: it is the whole question of the value of the Bible as an inspired and authoritative record of God's historical revelation to mankind. Has God spoken, and does this book convey to us His sure word for our salvation and guidance? Have the Scriptures of the Old Testament any longer the value for us which they had for Christ and His disciples? Or are we to concede to the writers of the school above mentioned, that, as the result of the critical discussions of the past century, the historical foundations of Old Testament revelation have in the main been subverted? Must man's changing and erring thoughts about God henceforth take the place of God's words to man? Are the erewhile "lively oracles" of God simply the fragmentary remains of a literature to which no special quality of divineness attaches, and is the supposed history of revelation largely a piecing together of the myths, legends, and free inventions of an age whose circle of ideas the modern spirit has outgrown? These and like questions, that extensive body of opinion which arrogates to itself the title "modern" would answer with an unhesitating "Yes"; it need not occasion surprise if the great mass of believing opinion in the Church, on the other hand, meets such a challenge with an emphatic "No."

It is to be admitted that the position of those who, at the present time, occupy a believing standpoint, yet are strongly repelled by the rationalism which seems to them to inhere in much of the prevailing criticism, is one of peculiar difficulty. On the one hand, they feel keenly the seriousness of the issues by which they are confronted. They seem to themselves to be called to give up, not only those ideas of the Bible in which they have been nurtured, and with which their tenderest associations are entwined, but the view of the Bible that appears to them to arise from an impartial study of its contents and claims. They see the disintegrating processes which have wrought such havoc, as they regard it, with the Old Testament, extended to the New, and with like results.[1] On the other hand, they are met by the assertion that practically all competent scholarship—believing and unbelieving alike—is agreed in the acceptance of those critical conclusions about the Old Testament which so greatly disturb them. What, in the "storm and stress" of this conflict and confusion of opinion, are those who hold fast by the Bible as the Word of Life for their souls to do? General assurances, such as are sometimes given, that, when they have parted with the greater part of what they have been accustomed to regard as the historical substance of revelation, they will find the Bible a diviner book to them than ever, do not yield the desired comfort. Is it to be wondered at if, in their perplexity and resentment, many who feel thus should round on "Higher Criticism" itself, and uncompromisingly denounce it as the prolific parent of all the mischief—an invention of the Evil One for the destruction of the unwary?

Nevertheless, this attitude of unreasoning denunciation of what is called "Higher Criticism" is also manifestly an extreme; and the problem we have to deal with, if it is to be profitably discussed, requires a clearer discrimination of issues. In particular, it cannot too early be recognised that this is not, at bottom, a question simply, as is too commonly assumed, between "Higher Critics" and "Non-Higher Critics." Questions of criticism, indeed, enter deeply—far more deeply, to our thinking, than many are disposed to allow—into the dispute; but it is only to confuse the issue, and is a gratuitous weakening of the believing case, not to recognise that the real cleft goes much deeper—viz., into a radical contrariety of view as to the natural or supernatural origin of the religion of Israel, and that on this fundamental issue those whom we call "critics" are themselves sharply divided, and found ranged in opposing camps. There are, one must own, few outstanding scholars at the present day on the Continent or in Britain—in America it is somewhat different—

[1] As examples reference may be made to the articles of Schmiedel in the *Encyc. Biblica*, and to such works, among many others, as O. Holtzmann's *Life of Jesus*, and Wernle's *Beginnings of Christianity*, recently translated. Cf. below, p. 478.

who do not in greater or less degree accept conclusions regarding the Old Testament of the kind ordinarily denominated critical;[1] yet among the foremost are many whom no one who understands their work would dream of classing as other than believing, and defenders of revealed religion. Such, among Continental scholars, recent or living, are Delitzsch, Riehm, Dillmann, König, Kittel, Köhler, Strack, Oettli, Westphal, Orelli; in Britain, Dr. Driver, the late Dr. A. B. Davidson, Professor G. A. Smith, and many others: all more or less "critics," but all convinced upholders of supernatural revelation. This is not a reason for unquestioning acceptance of their opinions; as critics it will be found that they are far enough from agreeing among themselves. But the attitude to criticism of so large a body of believing scholars may at least suggest to those disposed to form hasty judgments that there is here a very real problem to be solved; that the case is more complex than perhaps they had imagined; that there are real phenomena in the literary structure of the Old Testament, for the explanation of which, in the judgment of many able minds, the traditional view is not adequate, and for which they seem to themselves to find a more satisfactory solution in some form or other of the critical hypothesis.[2]

[1] This is true even of so cautious a scholar as Professor James Robertson, of Glasgow, whose works, in a conservative spirit, have done such excellent service. It is Dillmann, himself a pronounced critic, but decided in his opposition to what he calls the "Hegel-Vatke" view of religious development, who speaks of Professor Robertson's *Early Religion of Israel* as "hitting the nail on the head" (*Alttest. Theol.* p. 59). Yet, as will appear, the views of Professor Robertson, and those, say, of Dr. Driver, on such subjects as the Mosaic authorship of the Pentateuch, the gradual growth of legislation, the origin of Deuteronomy, etc., are not *in principle* so far apart as might appear, though Professor Robertson's results are somewhat more positive, and the *accent* falls differently. Cf. *Early Religion*, pp. 332 ff., 382, 420–27.

[2] An interesting example of how the leading results of criticism may be accepted by a devout and intensely evangelical mind is furnished by the Rev. G. H. C. Macgregor, a favourite teacher of the "Keswick" school. See his tribute to Professor W. R. Smith in the *Biography* by his cousin (p. 100), and the frequent references to critical positions in his *Messages of the Old Testament*, with Preface by Rev. F. B. Meyer. It is significant also that the productions of critical writers of believing tendency, such as König and Kittel, are now being translated and reproduced in conservative quarters, in refutation of the theories of the more rationalistic school. Cf. below, pp. 79, etc., on Kittel's pamphlet, *Babylonian Excavations and Early Bible History*, published, with Preface by Dr. Wace, by the London Society for Promoting Christian Knowledge.

The truth is, and the fact has to be faced, that no one who studies the Old Testament in the light of modern knowledge can help being, to some extent, a "Higher Critic," nor is it desirable he should. The name has unfortunately come to be associated all but exclusively with a method yielding a certain class of results; but it has no necessary connection with these results. "Higher Criticism," rightly understood, is simply the careful scrutiny, on the principles which it is customary to apply to all literature, of the actual phenomena of the Bible, with a view to deduce from these such conclusions as may be warranted regarding the age, authorship, mode of composition, sources, etc., of the different books; and everyone who engages in such inquiries, with whatever aim, is a "Higher Critic," and cannot help himself. The peculiar distribution of the names of God in Genesis, *e.g.*, is a fact to be recognised, whatever account may be given of it,[1] and the collation and sifting of evidence, with a view to the obtaining of a satisfactory explanation, is, so far, a critical process. There is nothing in such scholarly examination of the Bible, even though the result be to present some things in a new light, which need alarm anyone. As the world of nature presents a different aspect to the man of science, still more to the metaphysician, from that which it does to the common view of sense, yet is the *same* world; so the Bible may present a somewhat different aspect to the eye of the trained critical scholar, yet is the *same* Bible, for edification, devotion, and instruction in the way of righteousness.

That we may discharge our debt to criticism, even of the rationalistic sort, once for all, let us acknowledge that, with all its attendant evils, its course has been productive, under the providence of God, of many benefits, which in large measure counterbalance, if they do not outweigh, these evils. Some of the positive advances in its course it will be our business to notice hereafter.[2] It is assuredly not for nothing that, for more than a century, the light of the best European scholarship has been keenly directed on every page, verse, line, and even word, of the sacred record. Many of the leaders of criticism, however defective in their apprehension of the full truth of revelation, have been

[1] See below, p. 196. [2] See below, Chap. VII. pp. 196 ff.

men of fine literary gifts, wide culture, acute critical faculty, and genuine appreciation of the nobler elements in the religious and ethical teaching of the prophets; and the result of their labours, as everyone must own, has been, in modern times, a wonderful freshening of interest in the historical, poetical, and prophetical parts of the Old Testament, and an immensely better understanding of its textual meaning and historical setting. What student of Old Testament history or prophecy, *e.g.*, would willingly part with the aid afforded by the works of Ewald?[1] What most rabid opponent of criticism is not ready to own his indebtedness, on the linguistic side, to that dry old rationalist, Gesenius? There is a yet greater gain. It is not too much to say that one direct result of the application of the strictest historical and critical methods to the Old Testament has been to bring out, as never before, the absolutely unique and marvellous character of the religion of Israel.[2] With the best will in the world to explain the religious development of Israel out of natural factors, the efforts of the critics have resulted, in the view of many of themselves, in a magnificent demonstration of the immense, and, on natural principles, inexplicable difference between the religion of this obscure people and every other.[3] Some may regard this as a small result; to us it presents itself as something for which to be devoutly grateful.

II. The Fundamental Issue: Attitude to the Supernatural

Still the deep cleft remains between what we have called the believing and the unbelieving views of the Old Testament,—between the view which admits, and the view which denies, the properly supernatural element in the history and religion of Israel,—and it is not in our power,

[1] "From another side," wrote Principal John Cairns, "a great scholar like Ewald redressed the unfairness of Schleiermacher to the Old Testament, and, with many and great drawbacks of his own, asserted in his own way the historical greatness and necessity of the Bible revelation."—*Unbelief in the Eighteenth Century*, p. 230.

[2] See next chapter.

[3] This is the argument pursued, on critical lines, in Lecture IV., on "The Proof of a Divine Revelation in the Old Testament," of Professor G. A. Smith's *Modern Criticism*, etc.

neither is it our wish, to minimise it. We must now approach the subject more closely, and endeavour to fix with greater precision where the dividing-line between the two views lies.

In certain external respects, as in temple, priesthood, sacrifices, the religion of Israel necessarily presents a resemblance to other religions. To the eye of the outward observer, it is simply one of the great historical religions. If at the same time it presents differences, this does not of itself establish more than a relative distinction between it and others. Every religion has not only a certain resemblance to every other, arising from the fact that it *is* a religion, but has, moreover, a definite character or physiognomy of its own, resulting from the different genius of the people, from the individuality of its founder, or from the circumstances of its history. If now, however, we go further, and affirm that, in the midst of all resemblances, this religion of Israel presents features which not only differentiate it from every other, but differentiate it *in such a way* as to compel us to ascribe to it an origin in special, supernatural revelation, we obviously take a new step, which we must be prepared to justify by the most cogent reasons. It will not be enough to show that the religion of Israel is a *better* religion than others—or even taking into account its fulfilment in Christianity, that it is the *most perfect* of existing religions: for conceivably it might be that, yet have essentially no higher origin than they; just as one people may be endowed with the artistic, or philosophic, or scientific genius beyond others,—the Greeks, for instance, among ancient peoples, in art and philosophy,—without its being necessary to postulate for this a supernatural cause. Most critics, even of the rationalistic order, will admit that Israel had a genius for religion, and was the classical people of religion in antiquity; will not hesitate to speak also of its providential mission to humanity, even as Greece and Rome had their vocations to mankind. It is a proposition different in kind when the origin of the religion of Israel is sought in a special, continuous, authoritative revelation, such as other peoples did not possess. Here we touch a real contrast, and, with reservation of a certain ambiguity in the word "revelation,"[1] obtain a clear issue.

[1] See below, pp. 19 ff.

For now the fact becomes apparent,—there is, indeed, not the least attempt to disguise it,—that, to a large and influential school of critical inquirers—those, moreover, who have had most to do with the shaping of the current critical theories—this question of a supernatural origin for the religion of Israel is already foreclosed; is ruled out at the start as *a priori* inadmissible. The issue could not be better stated than it is by the Dutch scholar Kuenen in the opening chapter of his work, *The Religion of Israel.* The chapter is entitled "Our Standpoint," and in it the principle is expressly laid down that no distinction can be admitted in respect of origin between the religion of Israel and other religions. "For us," he says, "the Israelitish religion is one of those religions; nothing less, but also nothing more."[1] This is, in the style of assumption too usual in the school, declared to be "the view taken by modern theological science."[2] "No one," he says, "can expect or require us to support in this place by a complete demonstration the right of the modern as opposed to the ecclesiastical view."[3] It is an "ecclesiastical" view, it appears, to assume that any supernatural factor is involved in the history or religion of Israel: the "modern" view rejects this. If any ambiguity could attach to these statements, it would be removed by his further explanations, which, in so many words, exclude the idea that the Jewish and Christian religions are derived from "special divine revelation," or are "supernatural" in their origin.[4] He puts the matter with equal frankness in his work on *Prophets and Prophecy.* "Prophecy is," he tells us, "according to this new view, a phenomenon, yet one of the most important and remarkable phenomena, in the history of religion, but just on that account a human phenomenon,

[1] *Religion of Israel*, i. p. 5. [2] *Ibid.* p. 6.
[3] *Ibid.* p. 7.
[4] *Ibid.* pp. 5, 6. In a Life of Kuenen in the *Jewish Quarterly Review*, vol. iv., by Mr. Wicksteed, the Dutch "modern" movement, of which Kuenen was a principal leader, is thus described. "It was an attempt of singular boldness and vigour to shake the traditions of Christian piety free from every trace of supernaturalism and implied exclusiveness. . . . It involved the absolute surrender of the orthodox dogmatics; of the authority of the Scriptures; of the divine character of the Church as an external institution; and of course it based the claims of Jesus of Nazareth to our affection and gratitude solely upon what history could show that He, as a man, had been, and had done for men" (p. 596).

proceeding from Israel, directed to Israel."[1] And later: "So soon as we derive a separate part of Israel's religious life directly from God, and allow the supernatural or immediate revelation to intervene in even one single point, so long also our view of the whole continues to be incorrect. . . . It is the supposition of a natural development alone which accounts for all the phenomena."[2] Quite similar to the standpoint here avowed by Kuenen is that of a wide circle of leading scholars — of Duhm, Wellhausen, Stade, Smend, Gunkel, and a multitude more in the front ranks of the modern critical movement. We noted above Wellhausen's declaration of his identity in standpoint with Vatke — Vatke being a thorough-going Hegelian rationalist in the first half of last century. Shortly after in his book we have the express acknowledgment: "My inquiry comes nearer to that of Vatke, from whom indeed I gratefully acknowledge myself to have learned best and most."[3]

This, then, quite unambiguously stated, is the issue to which the religion of Israel—and with it Christianity, for in this connection the two very much stand or fall together—is brought at the present day. Yet the contrast drawn by Kuenen in the above passage between the "modern" and the "ecclesiastical" view, which he announces as the ruling principle of his treatment, is, it need hardly be said, a flagrant *petitio principii*.[4] To assume beforehand, in an inquiry which turns on this very point, that the religion of Israel presents no features but such as are explicable out of natural causes,—that no higher factors are needed to account for it,—is to prejudge the whole question; while to assume this to be the only view held by "modern" scholars—in other words, to exclude from this category men of the distinction of those formerly enumerated, who, with

[1] *Prophets and Prophecy in Israel*, p. 4.

[2] *Ibid.* p. 585. Dr. John Muir, at whose instance the work was undertaken, contributed an Introduction to the English translation. In the course of this he thus states Dr. Kuenen's position: "Israelitish prophecy was not a supernatural phenomenon, derived from divine inspiration; but was a result of the high moral and religious character attained by the prophets whose writings have been transmitted to us" (p. xxxvii). From a published letter of Kuenen's we learn the interesting fact, otherwise attested to us, that Dr. Muir subsequently changed his opinions, and recalled from circulation the volume he had been instrumental in producing.

[3] *Hist. of Israel*, p. 13.

[4] Cf. the remarks of Ladd, *Doct. of Sac. Scripture*, i. p. 371.

their critical views, take strong ground on the subject of revelation—is to contradict fact, and degrade the term "modern" to the designation of a clique. If, on impartial consideration, it can be shown that the religion of Israel admits of explanation on purely natural principles, then the historian will be justified in his verdict that it stands, in this respect, on the same footing as other religions. If, on the other hand, fair investigation brings out a different result,—if it demonstrates that this religion has features which place it in a different category from all others, and compel us to postulate for it a different and higher origin,[1]—then that fact must be frankly recognised as part of the scientific result, and the nature and extent of this higher element must be made the subject of inquiry. It will not do to override the facts—if facts they are—by *a priori* dogmatic assumptions on the one side any more than on the other. Thus far we agree with Kuenen, that we must *begin* by treating the religion of Israel exactly as we would treat any other religion. Whatever our personal convictions—and of these, of course, we cannot divest ourselves—we must, in conducting our argument, place ourselves in as absolutely neutral an attitude of mind as we can. We must try to see the facts exactly as they are If differences emerge, let them be noted. If the facts are such as to compel us to assume a special origin for this religion, let that come to light in the course of the inquiry. Let us frankly admit also that it is no slight, recondite, contestable, or inferential differences, but only broad, obvious, cumulative, indubitable grounds, which will suffice as basis of a claim to such special origin. If such do not exist, we concede that candour will compel us to fall back on the naturalistic hypothesis.

It is perfectly true that it is impossible in any inquiry to dispense with guiding principles of investigation, and with presuppositions of some kind, and there is no criticism on earth that does so—certainly not that of Kuenen and Wellhausen. Only these should not be allowed to warp or distort the facts, or be applied to support a preconceived conclusion. The scientist also finds it incumbent on him to "anticipate nature" with his interrogations and tentative hypotheses, which, however, have to be brought to the test

[1] This is the argument in Chap. II.

of experimental verification. We find no fault with these writers, if they are persuaded that their view of Israel's religion is the true one, for endeavouring, with all the skill at their command, to show that it is so. It is even well that such experiments should be made. The case, in short, is one of competing interpretations of the Old Testament, and, assuming Israel's religion to be divine, the effect of the most searching application of critical tests can only be to bring out this divineness into stronger relief. No Christian, therefore, who has confidence that God, who spoke to the fathers by the prophets, has in these last days spoken to us by His Son,[1] need shrink from any trial to which criticism exposes the Bible. It is the Nemesis of a wrong starting-point in every department of inquiry that those who adopt it find themselves plunged, as they proceed, into ever-deepening error and confusion; while a right guiding-idea as infallibly conducts to a view marked by simplicity and truth. If Kuenen and those who think with him are right in their first principles, they will find their theory work out easily and naturally in its application to the phenomena of Scripture:[2] if they are wrong, their hypothesis will inevitably break down under its own weight, as did that of Baur in the sphere of the New Testament half a century ago. The ultimate test in either case is fitness to meet the facts. It has already been pointed out that the result of a searching inquiry has been to produce in many minds the conviction that Israel's religion can *not* be explained on mere natural principles.

III. The Literary Problem: Its Dependence on the Religious

Thus much on the more fundamental part of our problem; it remains to be asked how far the conclusions reached on this point affect the questions raised, in the field of literary discussion, on the age, authorship, structure,

[1] Heb. i. 1.

[2] This is their own claim. Professor W. R. Smith, *e.g.*, in his Preface to Wellhausen, says: "In the course of the argument it appears that the plain, natural sense of the old history has constantly been distorted by the false presuppositions with which we have been accustomed to approach it."—Pref. to *Hist. of Israel*, p. viii. The implication is that Wellhausen's view gives the "plain, natural sense."

and historical value of the Old Testament *books*—especially of the Pentateuch, or "five books" traditionally attributed to Moses. What is the interest of Christian faith in these discussions, or has it any? Abstractly considered, of course, as already said,[1] questions of age, authorship, and historical genesis are, in comparison with those we have now been considering, of secondary importance. The later age, or composite structure, of a book is no necessary disproof of its truth. Freeman's *History of the Norman Conquest, e.g.*, though written in the nineteenth century, does not give us a less just or vivid idea of the series of events to which it relates, than the contemporary monkish chronicles, etc., on which it is based. The age, authorship, and simple or composite character of a book are matters for investigation, to be determined solely by evidence, and it is justly claimed that criticism, in its investigation of such subjects, must be untrammelled: that faith cannot be bound up with results of purely literary judgments. It will be urged, further, that, as we have admitted, the denial of the supernatural in the Old Testament history or religion in no way necessarily follows from any theory of the dates or relations of documents. All this is true; still the matter is not quite so simple as this rather superficial way of presenting the case would picture it. There *is*, as was before hinted, a very close connection between critical premises and critical results, and it is necessary in the present discussion that this connection should be kept carefully in view.

It has already been explained that it is no part of the design of these pages to cast discredit on the function of criticism as such. It is not even contended that the critical theories at present in vogue are constructed wholly in the interest of rationalism: far from that. If they were, we may be sure that so many believing men would not be found accepting or advocating them. To account for such acceptance we must assume that they are felt by candid minds to answer in some degree to real facts, to rest on a basis of real evidence, to afford an explanation of real phenomena, to possess a plausibility and reasonableness which constrain a genuine assent.[2] On the other hand, it can as little be doubted that the critical hypothesis, in the

[1] See above, p. 5. [2] See below, Chap. VII. pp. 195–6.

form into which it has gradually crystallised, shows, in many of its features, a marked dependence on rationalistic presuppositions. There is no gainsaying the fact that, historically, it was in rationalistic workshops, mainly, that the critical theory was elaborated, and that, from this circumstance, a certain rationalistic impress was stamped upon it from the first.[1] From Eichhorn and those who followed him—Von Bohlen, Vatke, De Wette, and the rest—the critical treatment of the Pentateuch received a "set" in the direction of naturalism which it has to some extent retained ever since. Most of all is it true of the type of theory which is at present the dominant one—the theory which, to indicate the line of its origin, we might describe as the Vatke-Graf-Kuenen-Wellhausen-Stade one—that it is rationalistic in its basis, and in every fibre of its construction. Yet it is this theory which, chiefly through the brilliant advocacy of Wellhausen, has for the time won an all but universal recognition in critical circles on the Continent and in English-speaking countries. Its arguments are adopted, its conclusions endorsed, its watchwords repeated, with almost monotonous fidelity of iteration, by a majority of scholars of all classes—in Churches and out of Churches, High Church, Broad Church, and Low Church, sceptical and believing. This says much for the plausibility of the theory, but it suggests also a grave problem. The critical hypothesis must, of course, be considered on its merits; but is there not, on the face of it, a supreme improbability that a theory evolved under the conditions we have described should be, in that form, a theory adequate to Christian faith, or with which Christian faith can ultimately be content? Is it such a theory as Christian faith would ever have evolved from its own presuppositions? Can it ever be purged of its rationalistic leaven, and adapted to the use of the Christian Churches, without a complete re-casting on

[1] The statement of the late Dr. Green may need qualification as respects later scholars, but is in the main true of the originators of the critical movement: "The development of critical hypotheses inimical to the genuineness and the truth of the books of the Bible has from the beginning been in the hands of those who were antagonistic to supernatural religion; whose interest in the Bible was purely literary, and who refused to recognise its claims as an immediate and authoritative revelation from God."—*Higher Criticism*, p. 177. Cf. Dr. Cheyne on the indebtedness of the German critical movement to English Deism (*Founders of Criticism*, pp. 1, 2). **See also below, p. 58.**

principles which are the direct antitheses of those which obtain in the schools in which it originated? We take leave to doubt it. Christian scholars are no doubt entirely serious in their acceptance of its conclusions, but there must grow up, we are persuaded—if there is not already growing up—a perception of the incompatibility of their belief, as Christians, in a historical revelation, culminating in the Incarnation,[1] with a set of results wrought out on the basis of a purely naturalistic view of Israel's history and religion—which, in fact, as will be discovered, reduces the bulk of that history to ruins![2]

Criticism, it is granted, must be untrammelled; also, the results complained of do not *necessarily* follow from the reigning critical hypothesis. This last remark we must admit to be true, for part of our own argument in a future chapter is built upon it.[3] Still it cannot well be denied that, if all the results do not necessarily follow from the theory, a good many of them do very easily and naturally follow; that the way is logically open for them, as it would not be on another theory; and that the reason why the stronger conclusion is not drawn often is simply that the believing critics are less logical than their fellows. A theory may not always be *followed* to its conclusions, where these, nevertheless, very logically *follow*. It could not be otherwise, when regard is had to the presuppositions under the influence of which the theory was formed. Everything, as Rothe said, can be laid hold of by two handles; and where the case is one, as before remarked, of competing interpretations of the same facts, while it is true as ever that both will not be found equally suitable to the facts, and that no ingenuity can make them so, the room left for the play of subjective considerations is still very large. In this connection, questions of age and authorship are far from being always of secondary moment. The true inwardness of many of these will appear after in the course of our discussion. It will be forced upon us when we observe how frequently the dating does not arise from purely literary considerations, but is determined by critical assumptions, or by congruity with an *a priori* scheme of development, and when we see the *use* to which the dating is put, viz., to lower the dates of other

[1] See Ottley below, p. 22.
[2] Cf. Chap. III. pp. 56 ff.
[3] Chap. III.

writings, or subvert the credibility of the history.[1] The late date of the documents composing the Pentateuch, *e.g.*, may be employed to support the contention that the narrative of the Pentateuchal books is wholly, or in great part, legendary; the post-exilian date of the Levitical laws may be used to destroy the connection of the laws with Moses; the low date assigned to the psalms may be really a corollary from a particular theory of Israel's religious development, and may be used, in turn, to buttress that theory. In other ways the literary criticism, not intentionally perhaps, but really and effectively, may be put at the service of the theory. Books may be divided up, or texts manipulated and struck out, till the writing is made to speak the language which the critic desires. The hyper-analysis of documents may result in the dissipation of everything of grandeur, not to say of consistency and truthfulness, in a narrative. Whether this is an over-colouring of the character of the critical procedure, in the hands of many of its representatives, will be better judged of in the sequel.

IV. Attitude of Criticism to "Revelation"

A little may be said before closing this chapter on a line of remark sometimes met with, to the effect that the contrast we have sought to indicate between the believing and the "modern" ways of regarding the Old Testament is, after all, less important than it seems. Partly, it may be urged, we have unduly narrowed the scope of the words "revelation" and "supernatural"; partly, we have not done justice to the high views of God and of His providential government which even rationalistic critics allow that the prophets of Israel ultimately attained. Professor W. R. Smith, in his lectures on *The Prophets of Israel*, may be taken as representing this latter standpoint. Referring to that "large and thoughtful school of theologians" which yet "refuses to believe that God's dealings with Israel in the times before Christ can be distinguished under the special name of revelation from His providential guidance of other nations," he observes that "in one point of view this departure from the usual doctrine of Christians is perhaps less fundamental than it seems at first sight to be."

[1] See Appendix to Chap. X. pp. 378–9.

He goes on: "For, as a matter of fact, it is not and cannot be denied that the prophets found for themselves and their nation a knowledge of God, and not a mere speculative knowledge, but a practical fellowship of faith with Him, which the seekers after truth among the Gentiles never attained to."[1] The idea seems to be that, these high views of God and of religion in the prophets being acknowledged to be there, it is not necessary to burden the argument with too curious questions as to how they got to be there,—whether by supernatural revelation, or in the way in which spiritual truth is grasped by thinkers of other nations. Enough that we now have them.

This appears to us, however, to be very fallacious reasoning; the more that Professor Smith admits that behind "there appears to lie a substantial and practical difference of view between the common faith of the Churches and the views of the modern school,"[2] and proceeds to give very cogent reasons for assuming a more direct and special revelation.[3] Not only, on the view described, is the prophet's own consciousness of the source of his message denied, and the higher character of his knowledge of God left without adequate explanation; but the results in the two cases are not the same. The ideas of the prophets on God, on the naturalistic hypothesis, cannot be allowed, at best, to rise higher than man is capable of attaining by the reflection of his own mind on his natural and providential environment, *i.e.*, to certain general truths about God's existence, unity, ethical character, and universal providence. Even this, it might be shown, assumes much more than the premises of the system will warrant, and, like the "natural religion" of the eighteenth century Deism, implies an unacknowledged debt to revelation. In any case it does not yield an authoritative revelation of God's purpose, and saving will for man, derived immediately from Himself: it lacks, even in what it does yield, in certitude; and in both respects falls short of what is demanded by the full Christian faith. It is further apparent that on such a view justice cannot be done to the earlier stages of the religion of Israel. The temptation of the critic who proceeds on these lines—if, indeed, he has any alternative—is to lower the character of the religion to suit the conditions of its hypothetical development; to give

[1] *Prophets of Israel*, p. 9. [2] *Ibid.* p. 10. [3] *Ibid.* pp. 11, 12.

a mean view of its origin and early manifestations; and to contend against the recognition of a divine redemptive purpose manifesting itself from the first in its history.

With respect to the usage of the words "revelation" and "supernatural," we have gladly acknowledged that there are few scholars of the present day—among serious investigators probably none—who would deny that Israel had a unique vocation, or would refuse to recognise, in some degree, a "providential guidance" in its history. Thus Duhm makes the quite general statement that, objectively regarded, there is no alternative to "the necessity of accepting a providential guidance in the actual stages of the development of religion."[1] Most, however, in recent years go further, and freely use the word "revelation" to express the peculiarity of Israel's religion. Thus Gunkel, one of the most radical of critics, says: "The conviction remains irrefragable that, in the course of the Israelitish religion, the power of the living God reveals itself";[2] and elsewhere: "Israel is, and remains, the people of revelation."[3] When the matter is inquired into, however, it is found that the term "revelation" is here used in a sense which does not in reality cover more than Kuenen's "natural development," or Duhm's "providential guidance." That which, on the human side, is natural psychological development, is, on the divine side, interpreted as God's revelation of Himself to man.[4]

Whichever formula is employed, the advocates of this type of theory find themselves in an obvious difficulty. God's "guidance" is recognised, but the guidance is of so faulty a character that it results in a set of ideas as to a *super*natural government of the world, and *super*natural dealings of God with Israel, wholly alien to the actual state of the facts as the critics represent it. If "revelation" is affirmed, the revelation is held to be compatible with an abundance of error and illusion, and results, again, on the part of the prophets, in a total misreading of the past history of the nation, and in views of God, His purpose, and living relations with men, which, if true, would cut the

[1] *Theol. d. Propheten*, p. 89.
[2] *Schöpfung und Chaos*, p. 118.
[3] *Israel und Babylonien*, pp. 37–38.
[4] Gunkel says: "The history of revelation transacts itself among men according to the same psychological laws as every other human event."—*Ibid.* p. 37. Cf. the whole passage, pp. 34–38.

ground from under the rationalistic theory. The elements, in either case, which the critics permit themselves to extract from the prophetic teaching do not, as said, rise above a vague theism, and the announcement of an ethical ideal. "Revelation," in the specific, supernatural sense, is not, and cannot be, admitted on this view, either in the process or in the goal. Not in the process, for there is nothing there, confessedly, transcending natural conditions; and not in the goal, for Jesus, with all these writers, while reverenced as the highest type—for us the pattern—of spiritual religion, is nothing more:[1] least of all is He the Son of God incarnate. Our distinction between natural and supernatural in the history of Israel, therefore, remains. Even with regard to those—and they are many—who do in some form admit "supernatural" revelation, it cannot be too constantly borne in mind that it is not any and every kind of admission of the supernatural which satisfies the Christian demand. It is Christ Himself in the full revelation of His glory as the only-begotten Son who is the touchstone and measure of the supernatural for faith; and only that view of revelation in Israel is adequate which finds its necessary culmination in His Person and redemption.[2]

It is now proper that a sketch should be given of the general course to be followed in the discussions in the succeeding chapters.

First, a brief preliminary survey will be taken of the witness which the Old Testament itself bears, in its structure, and in the uniqueness of its history and religion, to its own authority and inspiration as the record of God's revelation to His ancient people (Chap. II.). Thus far critical questions are held over.

[1] See on Kuenen above, p. 12.

[2] Ottley says: "If Jesus Christ were merely the last and most eminent of a line of prophets, there would be more to be said for that familiar type of criticism which represents Israel's religious development as a purely natural phenomenon, having its starting-point and controlling principle not in any intervention of a gracious and loving God, not in any supernatural revelation imparted to elect souls at different epochs in Israel's history, but in fetishism, or totemism, or polytheism, whence by a slow process of purely natural evolution it passed to its final stage in ethical monotheism."—*Aspects of O.T.*, p. 13. Ottley, in this work, with his belief in the Incarnation and in miracle, admits too much not to admit more. His positive Christian beliefs fit badly into the frame of Wellhausenism.

The next four chapters will be devoted to the consideration of the question—How far is this view which the Old Testament gives of itself affected by the results of modern criticism? At this stage the ordinary analysis of the Hexateuch (JE, D, P)[1] will be provisionally accepted, and the aim will be to show that, even on this basis, the essential outlines of the patriarchal and Mosaic history (Chaps. III., IV.), and the outstanding facts of the religion and institutions of the Old Testament (Chaps. V., VI.), are not sensibly affected,—that they are not, and cannot be, overturned. The way being thus cleared for consideration of the critical hypothesis on its own merits, the four succeeding chapters are occupied with a somewhat careful examination of that hypothesis in its fundamental positions and several parts. In this examination attention is concentrated on the points which are thought to be most crucial.[2] These chapters (VII.–X.) set forth the reasons which prevent us yielding our assent to the current critical hypothesis, except under conditions which essentially transform its character and bearings. The chapters may, if the reader likes, be viewed as setting forth our "sceptical doubts" on that hypothesis, though in many respects they are really more than doubts. It is sought to be shown how precarious and arbitrary are many of the grounds on which the critical hypothesis rests, and how strong are the reasons for challenging its principal postulates, and some of what are regarded as its most "settled" results. This is argued particularly in respect of:

1. The alleged distinction of the documents J and E, and the dates assigned to these (Chap. VII.).

2. The origin of Deuteronomy in the age of Josiah or Manasseh (Chap. VIII.).

3. The post-exilian origin of the so-called Priestly Code (Chaps. IX., X.). Chap. IX. deals with the Code and Chap. X. with the document.

The question of the divine names is discussed in Chap. VII.

With respect to the Priestly writing (P), it is contended that, whilst it is distinct in stylistic character from JE, there

[1] For explanation of these symbols see **Chap. III. pp. 65–66, and Chap. VII.** pp. 196 ff.

[2] Cf. Appendix at end of chapter.

is no evidence of P ever having existed as an independent document; that, on the contrary, it stands in the closest relations with the other elements in the narrative, and is most appropriately regarded as (at least in Genesis) the "framework" in which the JE narrative is set, with slight working over of the latter. Reasons are given for carrying back both books and legislation to a much earlier date than the critical hypothesis allows, and for recognising in both a substantially Mosaic basis.

A glance is taken at the later historical books in an Appendix to Chap. X.

The conclusions reached in the preceding discussions receive corroboration in a chapter on the bearings of Archæology on the Old Testament (Chap. XI.).

A closing chapter deals with the age of the Psalter, the reality of predictive prophecy, and the progressiveness of divine revelation (Chap. XII.).

APPENDIX TO CHAPTER I

CRUCIAL POINTS IN THE CRITICAL THEORY

IT is interesting to note what the critics themselves regard as the crucial points in their theory. Here are a few utterances on the subject.

Westphal says: "We shall take Deuteronomy as Ariadne's thread in the labyrinth into which the historical problem of the Pentateuch introduces us."[1]

Delitzsch says: "Since then [Graf's time] the Book of Ezekiel has become the Archimedean point on which the Pentateuchal criticism has planted itself, and from which it has lifted off its hinges the history of worship and literature in Israel as hitherto accepted."[2]

Wellhausen says: "The chapters xl.–xlviii. (in Ezekiel) are the most important in his book, and have been called by J. Orth, not incorrectly, the key of the Old Testament."[3]

Smend also says: "The decisive importance of this section for the criticism of the Pentateuch was first recognised by George and Vatke. It has been rightly called the key of the Old Testament."[4]

Wellhausen in another place says: "The position of the Levites is the Achilles heel of the Priestly Code."[5]

Elsewhere he emphasises the centralisation of the cultus as containing his whole position. "I differ from Graf," he says, "chiefly in this, that I always go back to the centralisation of the cultus, and deduce from it the particular divergences. My whole position is contained in my first chapter" (on "The Place of Worship.")[6]

Kuenen also has his Achilles heel. Speaking of Graf's original division of the priestly history and legislation (see

[1] *Sources du Pent.* ii. p. xxiv.
[2] Luthardt's *Zeitschrift*, 1880, p. 279.
[3] *Hist. of Israel*, p. 421.
[4] *Ezechiel*, p. 312.
[5] *Hist. of Israel*, p. 167.
[6] *Ibid.* p. 368.

below, p. 200), he says: "I saw clearly that his division of the *Grundschrift* was the Achilles heel of his whole hypothesis: the solution of Graf could not be the true one: it went only half-way."[1]

In the argument in the present book special weight will be found to be attached to the following facts:—

1. The "pre-prophetic" character of J and E, as involved in their admitted priority to Amos and Hosea.

2. The admittedly "parallel" character of J and E, and their marked stylistic resemblance.

3. The admitted priority of J and E, and of the "Book of the Covenant," to Deuteronomy.

4. The admitted priority of J and E to P (in reversal of the older view), and the fact that P is throughout parallel to, and presupposes, JE (Wellhausen).

5. The admission by many critics (*e.g.*, Driver, Baudissin, Ryle) of the priority of the Levitical collection known as the "Law of Holiness" to Ezekiel.

The turning points in the discussion are those indicated in the text:—

1. Are J and E two documents, or one?
2. The Josianic origin of Deuteronomy.
3. The post-exilian origin of the Levitical Code.

The critical positions on these three points are traversed and the rejection of them is shown to involve as its only tenable alternative (middle views as Nöldeke's and Dillmann's being cut out by the Wellhausen polemic) the essential Mosaicity of the Pentateuch.

[1] *Theol. Tijdschr.* 1870, p. 410.

CHAPTER II

The Old Testament from its own Point of View

"Israel has the idea of teleology as a kind of soul."—DORNER.

"Behind it all is the mystery of race and of *selection*. It is an ultimate fact in the history and government of the world, this eminent genius of one tiny people for religion. We know no more: and, in M. Renan's own terms, the people was 'selected,' just as, in words more familiar, Israel is 'the chosen people.'"—ANDREW LANG.

"When we say that God dealt with Israel in the way of special revelation, and crowned His dealings by personally manifesting all His grace and truth in Jesus Christ the incarnate Word, we mean that the Bible contains within itself a perfect picture of God's gracious relations with man, and that we have no need to go outside the Bible history to learn anything of God and His saving will towards us,—that the whole growth of the true religion up to its perfect fulness is set before us in the record of God's dealings with Israel culminating in the manifestation of Jesus Christ."—W. R. SMITH.

"If the first three chapters of Genesis are taken out of the Bible, it is deprived of the *terminus a quo*: if the last three chapters of the Apocalypse are taken away, it is deprived of the *terminus ad quem*."—MENKEN.

CHAPTER II

THE OLD TESTAMENT FROM ITS OWN POINT OF VIEW

OUR subject of study, then, is this book of history, of laws, of prophecy, of psalms, of wisdom literature, which we call the Old Testament. Before, however, entangling ourselves in the thorny brakes into which the critical study of this older collection of Scriptures conducts us, it is desirable that we should look for a little at the book by itself, in the form in which we have it, and allow its own voice to be heard on its character and place in the economy of revelation.

There are obvious advantages in this course. No slight is intended to be cast on criticism: but it may be gravely questioned whether this constant discussion going on *about* the Bible,—this minute dissection and analysis of it, and perpetual weighing of its parts in the nice scales of a critical balance,—has not at least one harmful effect, that, viz., of coming between men and the devout, prayerful study of the Bible itself, out of which alone can grow that sense of its harmony and proportion, and experience of its saving and sanctifying power, which yield the best proof of its divine origin. The dissecting chamber is necessary; but it is not exactly the best place for acquiring a sense of the symmetry and beauty of the living human body, or for cultivating reverence for it. It is hardly less difficult to grow into a spiritual appreciation of Scripture, when we are not permitted to make acquaintance with a Biblical book till it has first been put upon the critic's table, and there sliced, severed, and anatomised, till all the palpitating life has gone out of it, and we are left, as chief result, with dry lists of the sections, verses, or parts of verses, supposed to belong to the different narrators or editors![1] The Bible has a character and power of impression which belong to it as a living book; it is right that these should have justice done to them before the process of disintegration begins.

We would here indicate, therefore, at the outset, what precisely it is we propose to do, and what we do not propose to do, in the present chapter. We propose, then, treating the Old Testament for the time as part of the general organism of Scripture, to take the Bible just as it is,—just as it lies before us,—and to ask what kind of a book it is, what sort of an account it gives of itself, and what kind of impression of its origin and source grows out of this first-hand acquaintance with it. We shall have little or nothing to say at this stage of theories of criticism—these will come after; nothing of questions of age, authorship, or genuineness; little of theories of revelation or inspiration. There may be gain, for once, in leaving these things for a short while aside, and permitting the Bible to speak for itself—to utter its own unconstrained testimony—to produce on the mind its own immediate effect, without reference to outside controversies. The Bible may prove in this way, as it has often proved before, to be its own best witness, and it is this aspect and evidence of its divineness which, it seems to us, it is necessary at the present time, in the difficulty and uncertainty in which many are involved, most of all to emphasise.

I. The Organic Unity of the Book

We take up the Bible, then, in the way suggested, and the first thing, we think, that must strike us in connection with it, is, that this book is, in a remarkable sense, *a unity*. From another point of view, of course, the Bible is not one book, but a collection of books: as Jerome named it, "a divine library." It comes to us "by divers portions and in divers manners."[2] The writings that compose it are spread over at least a thousand years. Yet the singular fact is that, when these writings are put together, they

[1] In illustration, the reader may consult, *e.g.*, the tabular summations which are the chief outcome of the (otherwise able) article on "Exodus" in Hastings' *Dict. of the Bible* (i. pp. 806 ff.). The sensation is like chewing glass.

[2] Heb. i. 1.

constitute, structurally, one book; make up a "Bible,"[1] as we call it, with beginning, and middle, and end, which produces on the mind a sense of harmony and completeness.

This peculiarity in the Bible, which is not essentially affected by any results of criticism—since, indeed, the more the critic divides and distributes his material, the outcome in the book as we have it is only the more wonderful[2]—is best illustrated by contrast. For Christianity is not the only religion in the world, nor is the Bible the only collection of sacred books in existence. There are many Bibles of different religions. The Mohammedan has his Koran; the Buddhist has his Canon of Sacred Scriptures; the Zoroastrian has his Zendavesta; the Brahman has his Vedas. On the basis of this very fact, comparative religion groups a number of religions together as "book-religions." These sacred books are made accessible to us by reliable translations, and we can compare them with our own Scriptures. But, not to speak of the enormous superiority of the Bible to these other sacred books, even in a literary respect,—for few, we presume, capable of judging, would think of comparing even the noblest of the Babylonian or Vedic hymns, or of the Zoroastrian Gathas, in power or grandeur, with the Hebrew psalms; or would liken the few really lofty passages on God in the Koran with the sustained sublimity of the Hebrew prophets; or would draw a parallel between the wild extravagances of the Buddhist *Lalita Vistara* and the simplicity, beauty, and self-restraint of the Christian Gospels,[3]—we would fix attention only on this one point—the contrast in respect of unity. We seek in vain in these ethnic Scriptures for anything answering to this name. The Koran, for instance, is a miscellany of disjointed pieces, out of which it is impossible to extract any order, progress, or arrangement. The 114 Suras or chapters of which it is composed are arranged chiefly according to length—the longer in general preceding the shorter.[4]

[1] Originally *Biblia*, "The Books," then "in the thirteenth century, by a happy solecism," says Westcott, "the neuter plural came to be regarded as a feminine singular, and 'The Books' became, by common consent, 'The Book,' in which form the word has passed into the languages of modern Europe."—*Bible in the Church*, p. 5.

[2] See below, Chap. III.

[3] See Note A on the Bible and other Sacred Books.

[4] They were originally, as given by Mohammed, written on pieces of stone, bone, leather, palm-leaves, or whatever material was available, and

It is not otherwise with the Zoroastrian and Buddhist Scriptures. These are equally destitute of beginning, middle, or end. They are, for the most part, collections of heterogeneous materials, loosely placed together. How different everyone must acknowledge it to be with the Bible! From Genesis to Revelation we feel that this book is in a real sense a unity. It is not a collection of fragments, but has, as we say, an organic character. It has one connected story to tell from beginning to end; we see something growing before our eyes; there is plan, purpose, progress; the end folds back on the beginning, and, when the whole is finished, we feel that here again, as in the primal creation, God has finished all His works, and, behold, they are very good. This is a very external way, it may be granted, of looking at the Bible, yet it is a very important one. It puts the Bible before us at the outset as a unique book. There is nothing exactly resembling it, or even approaching it, in all literature.[1] To find its explanation, it compels us to go behind the fragmentariness of the parts, to the underlying unity of thought and purpose in the whole. The unity of the Bible is not something factitious—*made*. It grows out of the unity of the religion and the history, and points to that as its source.

II. Fulfilment of the Old Testament in the New

To deepen our impression of this unity of the Bible, and at the same time carry us a step further into the heart of our subject, we notice again that the Bible consists of two parts—*an Old Testament and a New,*—and would observe *how the second of these parts folds back upon the first.* The Old Testament is one group of writings, mostly in Hebrew, and the New Testament is another group of writings, in Greek, with centuries between them. Yet how manifestly is the latter the counterpart and completion of the former! The argument from prophecy has often been overdriven, and may easily be run into exaggeration and triviality; but if

thrown into a chest; thence, after Mohammed's death, they were taken out and copied. Some were preserved only by memory.

[1] "No other literature is linked into one whole like this, instinct with one spirit and purpose, and, with all its variety of character and origin, moving forward to an unseen yet certain goal."—Kirkpatrick, *Divine Library of the O.T.*, p. 92.

we take the Bible's own way of putting it, "The testimony of Jesus is the spirit of prophecy,"[1] it is difficult for any candid mind to deny that the spirit of the Old Testament fulfils itself in the New. This, again, is a result largely independent of critical discussions. Take, for example, that wonderful picture of the suffering Servant of Jehovah in the 53rd chapter of Isaiah, which the Church has always, and rightly, regarded as Messianic.[2] Dismissing for the moment all critical considerations as to age, authorship, or original reference, let anyone steep his mind in the contents of that chapter, then read what is said about Jesus in the Gospels, and, as he stands under the shadow of the Cross, say if there is not the most complete correspondence between the two. In Jesus of Nazareth, alone in all history, but in Him perfectly, has this prophecy found a fulfilment. The meekness, the pathos of undeserved suffering, the atoning function, the final triumph, will suit no other.[3]

The result is not different if we enlarge our view to the consideration of the religion of Israel as a whole. The religion of Israel has been called a religion of hope. Its face is always to the future.[4] The system of things in the Old Testament presents itself prevailingly as something provisional, temporary, incomplete. There is growth in the Old Testament—from the patriarchal stage to the Mosaic; from the Mosaic to the prophetic; but it is like the plant developing from stalk to bud, and from bud to flower, there is a final stage yet to come—that of the ripened fruit.[5]

[1] Rev. xix. 10.

[2] Cf. Dr. A. B. Davidson, *O.T. Prophecy*, pp. 411, 427, 445. "There is not one," he says, "of the better class of critics who does not recognise the pertinence of the question, In whom are the features of the Servant to be recognised? or who does not give the same answer to the question as the orthodox theologian" (p. 411).

[3] Bleek, quoted by Dr. Davidson, says: "What the prophet here says as yet in general, in reference to the Servant as such, as it were *in abstracto*, has received its complete fulfilment in the One, who was the only holy and perfectly sinless among the human race, and therefore the only one whose sufferings had such a character that, not being due to His own individual transgression in any way, they can be regarded as serving for the atonement of the sins of men."—*O.T. Prophecy*, p. 411; cf. Orelli, *O.T. Prophecy*, pp. 387 ff.

[4] *E.g.*, Gen. xii. 3.

[5] Dillmann says: "This religion of the ancient people of Israel everywhere points beyond itself, exhibiting itself as a work begun, which lacks its final perfection, and so compels us in the nature of the case to apprehend

The old covenant is to give place to a new,—a more inward and spiritual,—when the law of God shall be written on men's hearts;[1] the old national forms are to break up, and Jehovah is to become the God of the whole earth;[2] in their deepest abasement and humiliation the people of Israel never lose the assurance that from them the light is to go forth which shall illumine the darkness of the whole world—that the Gentiles shall come to their light, and kings to the brightness of their rising.[3] These things are not to be brought about without instrumentality, and here we find, trait after trait, the figure of the Messiah shaping itself,—the King who is to reign in righteousness,[4] the Immanuel-Child, with the wondrous fourfold name, who is the guarantee for the perpetuity of the throne and kingdom of David,[5] the Servant of Jehovah, who is to bear the people's sins,[6] the Branch who is to build again the temple of Jehovah.[7] The Spirit will be poured out upon all flesh,[8] and the kingdom of God will come.

Now, let anyone open his New Testament, and say if there is no counterpart to, and completion of, all this there. Something higher, grander, diviner, no doubt, than even the prophets could imagine; yet bringing to pass in every essential respect all that they foretold, all that lay in the bosom of that old covenant waiting its realisation.[9] May we not say that the Christian Church itself is a living proof of the truth of these predictions? Is it not Israel's God we worship? Is it not Israel's faith that beats in our hearts? Israel's Messiah we trust in for salvation? Israel's privilege to which we are admitted? Every time we sing these old Hebrew psalms, which are to this hour so marvellous an expression of the faith, and hope, and aspirations of the soul seeking after God, do we not declare that we

it in relation to Christianity, as that in which essentially it is perfected."—*Alttest. Theol.* p. 8.

[1] Cf. Deut. xxx. 6; Jer. xxxi. 31-4; xxxii. 39, 40; Ezek. xi. 19, 20; xxxvi. 26, 27.

[2] Num. xiv. 21; Isa. xlv. 22, 23; Zeph. ii. 11; Hag. ii. 6, 7.

[3] Isa. lx., etc.

[4] Isa. xxxii. 1; xxxiii. 15, 16.

[5] Isa. vii. 14; viii. 8, 10; ix. 6, 7; cf. Mic. v. 2, 3.

[6] Isa. liii.

[7] Zech. iii. 8; vi. 12; cf. Isa. iv. 2; Jer. xxiii. 5.

[8] Joel ii. 28, 29. On these passages see the works on O.T. Prophecy by Davidson, Delitzsch, Riehm, Orelli, etc., and cf. below, Chap. XII. p. 460.

[9] Cf. the suggestive sections in Riehm's *Mess. Prophecy* (E.T. 1876), pp. 33 ff.

belong to the same spiritual city as the men who wrote them?[1] When, accordingly, the New Testament gathers up all these types and prophecies of the Old Testament, and sees them fulfilled in Christ,[2]—calls Him, for example, the "Lamb of God, which taketh away the sin of the world,"[3] the "chief corner stone, elect, precious," which God has laid in Zion,[4] identifies Him with that Servant of whom it is declared that the Spirit of Jehovah was upon Him, to preach good tidings to the meek, to bind up the broken-hearted, to proclaim liberty to the captives, and the opening of the prison to them that are bound,[5]—do we not feel that it is justified in so doing? When the writer of the Epistle to the Hebrews sees all the old rites and institutions glorified in the light of the new religion, and represents them as types and shadows which have fulfilled their function, and pass away now that the reality has come,[6]—do we not recognise that he is giving us the truest *rationale* of that old economy? When the Book of Revelation tells of Paradise restored, and figures the tree of life growing in the midst,[7] do we not feel that the end of revelation, in very truth, looks back to its beginning, and that here the ruin of Eden is repaired, and the curse of man's first disobedience, which "brought death into our world, and all our woe," finally abolished? There is again nothing mechanical in this relation of the Old and New Testaments. The connec tion is vital, not external, but is on that account all the more wonderful, and without parallel.

III. Teleological Character of the History

We have seen that this surprising unity which characterises the Bible is only to be explained by going back to the *history* and the *religion* which the Bible makes known

[1] Cf. Ps. lxxxvii. (R.V.).

[2] Kuenen allows that this fulfilment was claimed by Jesus and His disciples, and says "it is impossible for us to form too high an estimate of the importance of the application of these passages."—*Prophets and Prophecy*, pp. 522 ff. But he holds that the interpretation is unwarranted. Yet how singular that these representations should admit of "being merged in one grand figure," if nothing of the kind was intended.

[3] John i. 29.

[4] 1 Pet. ii. 6; cf. Isa. xxviii. 16.

[5] Isa. lxi. 1; cf. Luke iv. 18. It is Jesus Himself who makes this identification.

[6] Heb. ix. 9; x. 1.

[7] Rev. ii. 7; xxii. 2.

to us, in which the real mystery or wonder lies. The Bible is a unique book, because it is the record and literature of a unique religion. We turn first to the *history*, and here are at once arrested by what may be described as its *teleological* character. "Israel," says Dorner, "has the idea of teleology as a kind of soul."[1] Its history, that is, is dominated by the idea of purpose. It is this which gives unity to the history and to the books which contain it. The purpose is not always consciously apprehended by the actors in the events; still less, as we shall see hereafter, is it something which exists only in the minds of the authors of the books, and is by them *put into* the history.[2] It lies in the facts themselves, and reveals itself with increasing clearness as the history proceeds, till at length the mystery "hid from all ages and generations"[3] is fully unveiled in Christ and His salvation. This teleological character of the history is recognised by every writer of genuine insight into the spiritual nature of Israel's religion,[4] and is allowed to stamp the religion with a uniqueness which absolutely distinguishes it from every other.

But the fact lies on the face of the history itself. This is readily seen by a glance at the development. The basis is laid in the account of the creation of the world, and of the culmination of that creation in man. From this the narrative goes on to recount man's fall, and to trace the development of the race in the lines of piety and impiety through Seth and Cain respectively, till the growing corruption of the world brings upon it the judgment of the flood. A new start is made in the covenant with Noah, from whom the repeopling of the world, and the distribution of its races, proceed. The growing spread of godlessness, and lapse of the nations into heathenism, leads to the next step in the unfolding of the divine purpose in the call of Abraham, and in the promises made to him and

[1] *Syst. of Doct.* i. p. 274.

[2] See this discussed below, Chap. III. pp. 62–64.

[3] Col. i. 26; cf. Eph. iii. 3, 9.

[4] Schultz, *e.g.*, in his *O.T. Theol.* p. 2, says: "We mean to describe, not various forms of religion, which have merely an external connection of place or time, but a *single* religion in the various stages of its development, which stages consequently have an organic inner connection. Hence in such a presentation each member must be properly linked to its fellow. A common ligament of living growth must bind all the parts together. The presentation must be, not merely historical, but *genetic.*"

to his seed. The promise of blessing, beginning in Eden,[1] afterwards restricted to the line of Shem,[2] is now, in the Abrahamic covenant, definitely associated with this patriarch and his posterity—not, however, in the spirit of a narrow particularism, but with a view to the ultimate blessing of mankind.[3] Already appears at this early stage of the history that law of election,—of gracious purpose working along a defined line for an ultimate larger good,—which is so marked a feature of the history throughout. The line of promise still further narrows itself—for limitation and definiteness here are essential to success—in Abraham's sons, in the election of Isaac, not Ishmael; in Isaac's sons, in the choice of Jacob, not Esau; in Jacob's sons, in the designation of Judah as the royal tribe.[4] The patriarchal age, with its renewals of the covenant, its prophetic announcements, its singular providences, its preparation in the elevation of Joseph for the descent into Egypt, ends with the removal to that country, where the people had room and opportunity to multiply, till, with change of dynasty, the fiery trial overtook them by which they were finally welded into a nation.

The Mosaic age, which succeeds the patriarchal, is closely linked with the preceding through the promises to the fathers, of which it brought the fulfilment. Allusion need only be made to the series of events which marks this beginning of Israel's national life—the birth and call of Moses, the Exodus, the covenant at Sinai, the discipline of the wilderness, the settlement in Canaan, the land before promised to Abraham. The vicissitudes and disorganisation of the time of the Judges and of Samuel lead up to the rise of the monarchy, and to the new hopes and promises attached to the line of David.[5] The rending of the kingdom, and the backslidings and often wholesale lapses into idolatry of the people, might seem to portend the ruin of these hopes, and the frustration of the divine purpose. But the singular—the unexampled—thing in the history of this people is that the purpose of God in the history is *not*

[1] Gen. iii. 15. Ottley says that this passage "strikes at the outset of redemptive history the note of promise and of hope."—*Hist. of Hebs.* p. 11. Cf. Driver, *Genesis*, pp. 49, 57.

[2] Gen. ix. 26.

[3] Gen. xii. 3; cf. xviii. 18; xxii. 18.

[4] Gen. xlix. 10. On the interpretation, cf. Driver, *Genesis*, pp. 385, 410–14; Orelli, *O.T. Prophecy*, pp. 118–23, etc.

[5] 2 Sam. vii.

defeated by outward failure; rather, it is in the depth of adversity and seeming defeat that it asserts itself most clearly, enlarges, purifies, and spiritualises itself, and is never, in the prophets, more confident of victory than when, to the eye of sense, the cause of the kingdom of God appears hopelessly lost.

We need not pursue this proof of a teleological character in the history of Israel further. The same result would be obtained if, starting with the completed revelation, we looked at the history retrogressively. Not only does the Gospel of the kingdom which Jesus proclaimed unfold itself from the bosom of the Jewish community, but the whole consciousness of Jesus roots itself in the older revelation,—presupposes it, moves in the circle of its ideas, claims to be the fulfilment of it. It was not the prophets only that Jesus came to fulfil, but "the law and the prophets,"[1]—the whole Old Testament revelation. If we go back to the prophetic age, we find the prophets as uniformly basing their message on the covenant relation of Israel to Jehovah which the earlier history attests.[2] The national consciousness of Israel connects itself unalterably with Moses and the Exodus, and with the laws and statutes it then received from Jehovah; yet with not less distinctness it declares that the national stage in its history was not the earliest, but was preceded by the patriarchal, and by the covenants with the fathers. Israel's God was the God of Abraham, of Isaac, and of Jacob. The starting-point in its covenant history was not Moses, but Abraham.[3] There is thus displayed throughout the whole of these Old Testament Scriptures a historical continuity, a firmness and coherence of texture, a steadily evolving, and victorious, self-fulfilling purpose, which has nowhere, even in the remotest degree, its parallel in the history of religions.

IV. Unique Ideas of the Religion

Thus far we have looked at the *book* and at the *history* of Israel's religion, and have found in both a character for

[1] Matt. v. 17.

[2] *E.g.*, Amos ii. 4, 10; iii. 1, 2; Hos. viii. 1; xi. 1–4; Mic. vi. 4; Isa. i. 2; v. 1–7; xi. 16; li. 1, 2, 10; Jer. ii. 17, etc.

[3] Isa. xxix. 22; li. 1; Jer. xxxiii. 26; Ezek. xxxiii. 24; Mic. vii. 20. See on this below, pp. 94 ff.

which no proper parallel can be discovered elsewhere: we now advance a stage further, and inquire whether the *religion itself* does not present a similar uniqueness. Only those who have not truly entered into its spirit, or appreciated its relation to other forms of belief, will dispute the proposition that the religion of Israel is unique. It is not the fact of its uniqueness, but whether the uniqueness is of such a kind as to require us to postulate a special, supernatural cause for its explanation, which is matter of controversy. We shall see immediately what the Old Testament itself has to say on that point.

1. A unique religion will display its character equally by what it has and by what it wants. There are, on the *negative* side, many things absent in Israel's religion which we should expect to find there, if it was simply one among other religions. Resemblances, as before remarked, in outward respects, there necessarily are. In the religion of Israel we have a sanctuary, priesthood, altars, sacrifices, ritual—much more that has its counterpart in other cults. When, however, from this outward vesture of the religion, we come to its heart and essence, it is not the resemblances, but the contrasts, which impress us. We are not disposed to be stinted in our acknowledgment of the better elements in the ethnic religions; but, whatever place may be given to these, the fact remains that, in their historical forms, the higher elements are hardly visible, while the foreground is occupied by an idolatrous worship, an extravagant and often immoral mythology, customs and usages debasing to the last degree. We need only recall the spirit-worship and magic of Babylonia; the animal-worship and ancestor-worship of Egypt; the stone-worship, and tree-worship, and serpent-worship, the human sacrifices, the lustful rites, the self-immolations, which enter so deeply into most non-Biblical religions. How great the contrast when we come to the religion of Israel! We do not enter into details at present, for we shall have to return to the subject in dealing with the very different theory of the critical school, that Israel began practically on the same level, and with much the same beliefs and practices, as its heathen neighbours, and only late in its history, in the days of the prophets, attained to higher

conceptions.[1] It will not be contended, at least, that this is the view of things that meets us on the *face* of the religion. Few will be bold enough to maintain that tree-worship, stone-worship, serpent-worship, image-worship, and similar superstitions, are conspicuous features on the Bible page. These things, we grant, or some of them, are found in the Bible history—in patriarchal and Mosaic times in sparse traces; later, in times of general declension, when the people fell away into the idolatries and vices of the nations around them, more abundantly; but they are no proper part of Israel's religion, and are invariably resisted, denounced, and condemned, as apostacy from Jehovah. Idolatry is sternly condemned in the oldest code of laws:[2] divination, necromancy, consulting with familiar spirits, are prohibited;[3] the instances in which contrary practices appear, as Rachel's teraphim,[4] Micah's images,[5] Saul's consulting of the witch of Endor,[6] etc., are sporadic and occasional, and appear either as survivals of older superstitions, or as violations of fundamental principles of the religion, such as are met with in every age and country.[7]

2. We do not dwell longer on these negative features of Israel's religion, but turn to the *positive* side, in which, naturally, the clearest proof of its uniqueness must lie. Here it may be sufficient to fix attention on *three great fundamental ideas,* in which, perhaps, the contrast between it and other forms of religion is most distinctly to be traced.

(1) We take, first, what meets us on the surface—the *monotheism* of this Israelitish religion. This of itself is much, if we think of the polytheism and idolatry which everywhere else overspread the earth. We look to the religions of ancient Babylonia, Assyria, and Egypt, or

[1] See Chaps. IV. p. 86; V. pp. 133 ff. [2] Ex. xx. 4, 5; xxiii. 4.

[3] Deut. xviii. 9-14.

[4] Gen. xxxi. 34 (stolen from her father Laban, ver. 30).

[5] Judg. xvii.

[6] 1 Sam. xxviii. The fact that Saul had put down all witches and wizards is proof of the law.

[7] Kuenen objects that the current conceptions of Israel's religion are drawn, not from the facts, but from the general reviews of the Hebrew historians.—*Nat. Religions,* etc. (Hibbert Lectures), pp. 69 ff. Professor Robertson aptly replies that, if we turn to these reviews, "they are precisely in the tone of the prophets Amos and Hosea, the very earliest witnesses to whom we are allowed to appeal."—*Early Rel. of Israel,* p. 116.

to those of Israel's own kinsfolk and neighbours in and around Palestine;[1] and, while recognising higher elements in these religions, ever, however, becoming dimmer as we recede from their source, we find them, one and all, in historical times, grossly, growingly, and incurably, polytheistic and corrupt. In Judah alone was God known. In no single case, moreover, was this polytheism ever thrown off by inherent effort. Even, therefore, were the theory, favoured by modern critics, that "ethical monotheism" was only attained by Israel in the age of the great prophets, allowed to be established, the fact would still remain to be accounted for that Israel, alone of all nations, *did* attain to it, and became the teacher of the rest of the world. We do not, however, give our adherence to the view that this monotheism of the religion of Israel was a late development of the time of the prophets. As will be shown more fully in a subsequent chapter,[2] the Old Testament knows of no time when the people of Israel were without the knowledge of the one God as the Creator and providential Ruler of the whole world. Monotheism is not the doctrine of one part of the Old Testament, and not of another. Its oldest parts—those which the critics allow to be the oldest[3]—have this doctrine of the unity of God as well as the latest. In these oldest parts, we have as fundamental ideas the creation of the world by God, the unity of the human family as descended from a first pair, made by God, the destruction of the whole race by a flood on account of sin, the promises to Noah, embracing the whole earth,[4] a new descent and distribution of the race from Noah, the recognition of God by Abraham as the Judge of the whole earth,[5]—all laying the foundation for the call of Abraham, the covenants with the patriarchs, the growth of Israel into a nation, its redemption from bondage, and formation into a people for God's glory. While, therefore, it is not contended that there was no advance in the ideas of God,—no deepening, purifying, or spiritualising of these ideas,—from the days of Abraham and Moses, it may very confidently be maintained that, in the Old Testament as we

[1] As respects the Semitic peoples, cf. Professor G. A. Smith's *Modern Criticism*, pp. 111–29.

[2] Chap. V. pp. 123 ff.

[3] The J and E histories, see pp. 65–66.

[4] Gen. viii. 20, 21; ix.

[5] Gen. xviii. 25.

have it, the unity of God is present as a basal conception from the first.

(2) The monotheism of Israel, however, is not the whole, is not even the main thing, in this religion. It is not so much, after all, in its declarations of what God is in Himself, or of the unity of God, as in what it tells us of *the relations of God to man*, and of *His purposes of grace to the world*, that the peculiarity of the religion of the Old Testament lies.[1] No religion exalts man so high as the religion of the Bible, in representing him as made in the image of God, and capable of knowing, loving, and serving God; and no religion abases man so low, in picturing the depths of his apostacy from God, and his inability to deliver himself from the guilt and bondage in which that apostacy has involved him. But it is the glory of the religion of the Bible—this in both Old Testament and New—that over against the picture it gives of the developing sin and corruption of the race, there appears almost from its first page the developing plan and purpose of God for man's salvation.[2] The history of the Bible is essentially, what Jonathan Edwards called it, "the history of redemption." If the malady is aggravated, the remedy provided is adequate to cope with it, even on the Bible's own showing of its evil. In Paul's language, "Where sin abounded, grace did abound more exceedingly."[3] This again brings us to the idea of teleology, but now shows us more precisely in what the teleology consists. It is the unfolding in its successive stages of God's gracious counsel for man's salvation.[4] It is this which gives its unity to the Bible; which is the golden thread running through history, psalm, prophecy, Gospel, epistle, and binding all together. There is nothing, again, which even remotely resembles this in any other religion. The partial exception is the Zoroastrian, which, in a dim, mythological way, has the idea of a conflict of the good principle with the evil, and of a final triumph of the

[1] Cf. Kirkpatrick, *Divine Library*, p. 93.

[2] See below, pp. 61–62.

[3] Rom. v. 20.

[4] Cf. Ottley, *Aspects of O.T.*, pp. 55 ff.: "The Old Testament is to be studied, in the first place, as a record of the history of redemption. It contains the account of a continuous historical movement of which the originating cause was the grace of God, and the aim the salvation of the human race." On p. 93: "In the Pentateuch and the historical books, the two most prominent ideas are those of redemption and revelation."

good. But, apart from the fact that, as was inevitable on a dualistic basis, good and evil are in Zoroastrianism largely physical conceptions, the idea receives no development, is the subject of no history, is embodied in no plan which is historically carried out. The uniqueness of the Biblical religion appears only the more strikingly from the contrast.

(3) The aim of God's salvation, of His entire work of grace in humanity, is, that man shall be made *holy*.[1] This brings us to a third marked feature in the religion of the Old Testament, as of the Biblical religion generally—*the indissoluble relation it establishes between religion and morality*. Religions can readily be found which have no close connection with morality; we are familiar also with a morality which would fain make itself independent of religion. In few of the higher religions, however, is this relation between religion and morality altogether obscured. Throughout history there is generally some dim perception that the gods will protect and reward the good, and will not fail to punish the evil-doer. The peculiarity of the Biblical religion is that in it this idea of the connection of religion with morality is the all-dominating one. To minds awakened to the significance of the moral it may now appear self-evident that a religion has no real worth which does not ally itself with moral ends,—which, going beyond even external guardianship and sanction of duties, does not take morality up into itself as the expression of the will and character of God, and count moral obedience an essential part of His service. But it should not be forgotten that this was not always the view taken of religion, and that it is largely through the influence of the religion of the Bible, purifying and ennobling our conceptions, that we have now come to perceive even this truth as clearly as we do. Already in its first pages—before the word "holy" is yet met with—the Old Testament sets itself against sin in heart and deed.[2] God accepts and vindicates righteous men like Abel, Enoch, and Noah; overwhelms with His judgments a world corrupted by sin; destroys wicked cities like Sodom and Gomorrah. He requires that Abraham shall walk before Him and be perfect; Abraham's assurance

[1] Cf. Dillmann, *Alttest. Theol.* p. 42.
[2] See below, pp. 114–15.

about Him is that the Judge of all the earth will do right.[1] As revelation advances, the indissolubleness of this connection of religion and morality becomes only clearer. The ethical was never so exalted; the ideals of conduct were never raised so high; religion and duty were never so completely fused together, as in the pure and sublime precepts of psalms and prophets. "He hath showed thee, O man, what is good, and what doth Jehovah require of thee, but to do justly, to love mercy, and to walk humbly with thy God."[2] A religion of this kind, so high in its views of God, so true to the needs of man, so adequate in its provisions for man's deliverance, so holy in its spirit, so exalted in its moral demands, never emanated, we may be sure, from man's own devisings. It is too high for him; he could not attain to it. Even if he could have conceived the idea of it, he could not have translated it into fact and history as is done in the Scriptures.

V. Claim to an Origin in Revelation

This, accordingly, is the next thing which impresses us in our study of the Old Testament,—the consciousness which everywhere pervades it that this religion, the historical stages of which it unfolds to us, is not the creation of man's own spirit, but is a product of *special divine revelation.* The tendency of the modern mind, it was before seen, is to substitute psychology for revelation. Instead of God's word to Isaiah, or John, or Paul, it gives us the thoughts of Isaiah, or John, or Paul about God. Even where the word "revelation" is used, it is with this purely psychological connotation.[3] This, however, is not the Bible's own point of view. The Bible is not primarily a record of man's thoughts about God, but a record of what God has done and revealed of Himself to man. Its basis is not, "Thus and thus thinks man," but, "Thus and thus saith Jehovah," or, "Thus and thus Jehovah has done." It records, indeed, man's thoughts about God—his prayers, struggles, hopes, meditations, aspirations—but these spring always out of what God has made known of Himself in word and deed. The Bible is not a mere revelation of

[1] Gen. xvii. 1, xviii. 25, etc.
[2] Mic. vi. 8.
[3] See above, p. 21.

abstract, or what Lessing would call "eternal," truths about God, but above all a discovery of the way in which God has revealed His loving will to man in word and deed in history. "He made known His ways unto Moses, His doings unto the children of Israel."[1] It is this, we would here observe, which makes the historical element in Scripture so indispensable and precious, and warns us against the tendency to speak slightingly of it, as if myth and legend would serve the purposes of revelation equally with fact.[2] Everyone feels that this is not the case with the history of Christ in the Gospels; but in the Old Testament also it is in great measure true that it was not from inward intuition, or reflections of their own, that prophets and psalmists, or the ordinary pious Israelite, derived their knowledge of God, and assured confidence in Him, but from what God had revealed of Himself in the past history of the people.[3] The *acts* were the source, the medium, the authorisation of the knowledge; and, if these were taken away, the knowledge would disappear with them. Accordingly, we find that, in the highest point which the saint of the Old Testament can reach in the apprehension of this revelation, he still feels that it transcends him, is infinitely above him, in a way which anything proceeding from his own thoughts could not be. Thus: "Many, O Jehovah my God, are Thy wonderful works which Thou hast done, and Thy thoughts which are to us-ward: they cannot be set in order unto Thee: if I would declare and speak of them, they are more than can be numbered."[4] Or again: "My thoughts are not your thoughts, neither are your ways My ways, saith Jehovah. For as the heavens are higher than the earth, so are My ways higher than your ways, and My thoughts than your thoughts."[5]

Here, then, we strike on another great peculiarity of Israel's consciousness — the sense, viz., that it was the

[1] Ps. ciii. 7.

[2] Thus, *e.g.*, Schultz, *O.T. Theol.* i. pp. 17–23: "In fact, legend must be regarded as fitted in a higher degree than history to be the medium of the Holy Spirit." Would Schultz apply this to the history of Jesus in the Gospels? See Note B on Mythology and History in the Old Testament.

[3] Cf. W. R. Smith, *Prophets*, pp. 10–14; Ladd, *Doct. of Sac. Scripture*, i. pp. 737 ff.; Bruce, *Chief End of Revelation*, pp. 57 ff. This connecting of revelation with *acts* of God is the strong point made in Rothe's *Zur Dogmatik*.

[4] Ps. xl. 5.

[5] Isa. lv. 8, 9.

possessor and guardian of a quite peculiar revelation from God, and in this respect occupied a perfectly unique position among the nations of the earth. The answer to this, we know, is thought to be simple. It is often said by those who believe all religions to be equally a natural growth: "Every nation in the beginning of its history has its wonderful stories to tell of miracles, revelations, apparitions of the gods: all religions in this respect are much the same: the Jewish and Christian religions are just like the rest." But we would take the liberty to reply: That is not quite the case. There *is* no other nation on earth which has such a story to tell of the beginnings of its religion—even as a story, we mean—as the Israelite had to tell of his, and the Israelite was perfectly conscious of this absolutely unique character of his history. Mythologies, fables, legends of appearances of the gods there are in abundance; but no such orderly, coherent history, charged with great ideas, as that which meets us in the Bible. This consciousness of the absolutely exceptional character of the history is brought out very strikingly in one passage in the Book of Deuteronomy. Moses there speaks: "For ask now of the days that are past, which were before thee, since the day that God created man upon the earth, and from the one end of the heaven unto the other, whether there hath been any such thing as this great thing is, or hath been heard like it? Did ever people hear the voice of God speaking out of the midst of the fire, as thou hast heard, and live? Or hath God assayed to go and take Him a nation from the midst of another nation, by temptations, by signs, and by wonders, and by war, and by a mighty hand, and by a stretched-out arm, and by great terrors, according to all that Jehovah your God did for you in Egypt before your eyes? Unto thee it was shewed, that thou mightest know that Jehovah He is God: there is none else beside Him."[1] If this be true of the origin of the religion of Israel, it is still more true of the origin of Christianity; for, assuredly, no other religion is founded on such a history as that of Jesus Christ,—on the character, claims, work, life, death, and resurrection, of such a Person as Jesus Christ is,—no, not in all the world!

The truth is, it is vain to attempt to find a parallel for

[1] Deut. iv. 32–35; cf. vers. 6–8.

this wholly unique phenomenon of the religion of Israel. Take again the two points already mentioned: the monotheism of this religion, and the indissoluble connection it establishes between religion and morality. It is not uncommon to hear this monotheistic faith spoken of as if it were a stage which, given only favourable conditions, every nation was bound to reach in the course of its development.[1] Man begins, it is supposed, by worshipping spirits, or ghosts of ancestors, or something of the kind; then mounts to the conception of a tribal deity; then extends the power of this deity, or blends the deity with others, till he is viewed as the sole ruler of the world. But, unfortunately, the facts do not bear out this ingenious theory. It has frequently been pointed out that there are, even yet, only *three* monotheistic religions in the world—the Jewish, the Christian, and the Mohammedan, which, in this respect, is derived from the other two. That is to say, all the monotheistic religion there is in the world is derived from the religion of the Bible. It is not meant that, beneath and behind the polytheism of older religions, there are not many indications of a purer monotheistic consciousness, or that there have not often been, in individuals and schools, very remarkable approximations to the truth about the unity, power, wisdom, goodness, and providence of God.[2] In that sense God has never left Himself without witness. But it is a well-understood truth that philosophical speculations have never founded, or can found, a religion; and it is simple fact of history that no monotheistic religions—religions, that is, based on the unity and spirituality of God as fundamental articles—have ever arisen, except those above mentioned.

Or take the other point—the indissoluble blending of morality and religion. Where, again, do we find anything corresponding to this outside the Biblical revelation? One of the early fathers of the Church gives us a description of an Egyptian temple—lofty, spacious, gorgeous, inspiring the worshipper by its grandeur with solemn awe. You

[1] Kuenen, *e.g.*, says: "To what we might call the universal, or at least the common rule, that religion begins with fetishism, then develops into polytheism, and then, but not before, ascends to monotheism—that is to say, if this highest stage be reached [a very important proviso]—to this rule the Israelites are no exception."—*Rel. of Israel*, i. p. 225.

[2] See p. 128 below.

enter the precincts of the temple, but when the priest, with grave air, draws aside the veil that hides the inner shrine, you behold—what? A cat, a crocodile, a serpent, or other animal, rolling on a purple couch.[1] Visit now the temple of Jehovah at Jerusalem. Here, too, you have a gorgeous building; here, too, a priesthood, altars, a shrine hidden by a veil. Within the veil stands the ark of the covenant, covered by the mercy-seat, sprinkled with blood of atonement, and shadowed by the golden cherubim. Let that covering be lifted, and within that ark, in the very core and centre of Israel's religion, in its most sacred place, you find—what? *The two tables of the moral law.* There, in a word, is the contrast of the two religions. There is the declaration of the truth that, before and above all things else, Israel's is an ethical religion. For these are "the tables of the testimony"[2]—the basis and bond of the nation's covenant with God—and all the ritual of ceremonial institutions is but a scaffolding to protect this ethical core from injury, or a means of restoring the worshipper to favour when sin has disturbed his fellowship. It will be remembered that, when Jesus came, He did not cut Himself off from that older revelation, but declared that on its two commandments of love to God and love to man hung all the law and the prophets.[3]

VI. Revelation in Relation to its Record

If we thus let the Bible—Old Testament and New—speak for itself, and compare it part with part: still more if we yield ourselves to its power, and strive faithfully to follow its directions, the conviction will irresistibly grow upon us that it is right when it claims to be based on divine revelation. Out of that revelation, the *literature of revelation*, which we call the Bible, grows. If this fact be firmly apprehended, particular questions about the dates or placing of books will not much trouble us. The revelation is there, and no changes in the dates or placing of books—none at least that are likely to be permanently brought out—can do anything to alter its fundamental outlines. *If* a revelation has been given, it is surely the most natural thing in

[1] Clem. Alex. *Pæd.* iii. 2.
[2] Ex. xxxii. 15. See below, Chap. VI. pp. 152 ff.
[3] Matt. xxii. 40.

the world to expect that a record should be made or kept of the stages of that revelation, either by its original recipients, or by those who stood within the circle of revelation, and possessed in an eminent degree its spirit.[1] *That* such a literature exists, adequate in every respect for making known to us the revelation, animated and penetrated by its spirit, though in varying degrees,—for the strictest upholder of inspiration will hardly place the Books of Chronicles on the same level with the Gospel of St. John, —fitted as a whole infallibly to accomplish its great end of making men wise unto salvation through faith in Jesus Christ, and of completely furnishing the man of God unto every good work,[2]—*that* such a literature exists, the only ultimate proof that can be given is the existence of the book itself; and such a book, as we have seen even from this brief inspection of its character, we have in the Bible. The simple fact that in this sacred volume, so marvellous in its own structure, so harmonious and complete in the view it gives of the dealings of God with man, so rich and exhaustless in its spiritual content, so filled with the manifest presence and power of the Spirit of God, we have everything we need to acquaint us fully with the mind and will of God for our salvation, and to supply us for all the ends of our spiritual life, is sufficient evidence that the revelation which God has given is, in every essential particular, purely and faithfully embodied in it. No more than the revelation from which it springs, is the Bible a product of mere human wisdom, but has God for its inspiring source!

This, as we understand it, is the Bible's own test of its inspiration, alike in Old Testament and in New,[3] and by it, without nearer definition, we are content, for our present purpose, to abide. The subject is taken hold of by its wrong end, when the test of inspiration is sought primarily

[1] "What would be the conceivable nature of revealed religion, without a record of facts? The briefest consideration convinces us, that either the whole nature of revelation must be essentially changed, or else a record of its historic process must somehow be preserved. To be sure, the fact of ultimate and supreme importance is the fact of revelation itself. But the very nature of revelation, if it is to take the form of an historic process, is such as to demand a record of that process. The foundations of Christianity are historically laid," etc.—Ladd, *Doct. of Sac. Script.* i. p. 737.

[2] 2 Tim. iii. 15–17.

[3] Cf., *e.g.*, Deut. xxx. 10–16; Josh. i. 7, 8; Pss. i., xix. 7–14, cxix.; John xiv. 26; xx. 31; Rom. xv. 4, etc.

in minute inerrancy in external details, as those of geography, or chronology, or of physical science. Inspiration does not create the materials of its record: it works upon them.[1] The crucial question is—Do the qualities which inspiration is expressly declared to confer on Scripture—*e.g.*, in such a classical passage as 2 Tim. iii. 15–17—really belong to it? We think it will be difficult for any candid mind to deny that they do. Who, coming to this sacred book, with a sincere desire to know God's will for the direction of his life, will say that he cannot find it? Who, desiring to be instructed in the way of salvation "through faith which is in Christ Jesus," will consult its pages, and say it is not made plain to him? Who, coming to it for equipment of his spiritual life, will say that there are still needs of that life which are left unprovided for? Who, seeking direction in the way of the life everlasting, can doubt that, if he faithfully obeys its teaching, he will reach that goal? The Scripture fulfils the ends for which it was given; no higher proof of its inspiration can be demanded.[2]

VII. Relation of the Old Testament to Christ

There is but one further remark we would make in closing this chapter. It relates to the place which Christ holds in Scripture, and ought to have in our study of every part of it. If what has been said of divine revelation is true, it follows that everything else in Scripture has its centre and point of connection in Him. If the Bible is a structure, Christ is the corner stone in that structure. All else in it is designed to lead up to Him, while in knowing Him, in learning to see in Him the image and revelation of the Father, in being drawn into sympathy with His

[1] See Note C on Inspiration and the Materials of the Record.

[2] Cf. Westcott, *Bible in the Church*, p. 14: "The Bible contains in itself the fullest witness to its divine authority. If it appears that a large collection of fragmentary records, written, with few exceptions, without any designed connection, at most distant times and under the most varied circumstances, yet combine to form a definite whole, broadly separated from other books . . . if in proportion as they are felt to be separate they are felt also to be instinct with a common spirit; then it will be readily acknowledged that, however they were united afterwards into the sacred volume, they are yet legibly stamped with the divine seal as 'inspired of God' in a sense in which no other writings are."

Spirit, in tasting the grace of His salvation,—in coming to know that in Him we possess "the true God and eternal life,"[1]—we gain the key which sets all else in Scripture in its true light. Without this key we are bound to miss our way in the search for its secret. No learning, no cleverness, will enable us to find it out. In vain do we go to the Old Testament, or to any part of Scripture, for the satisfaction of a mere intellectual or literary curiosity. It was not for this it was given, but to conduct us into the presence of Him who, of God, is made unto us wisdom, and righteousness, and sanctification, and redemption.[2] What the closing verse of the 20th chapter of John's Gospel says of that book: "But these are written, that ye may believe that Jesus is the Christ, the Son of God, and that believing ye may have life through His name,"[3] may with equal truth be applied to the Bible as a whole. Christ is the central sun in that firmament: only when we are brought within the range of His beams have we the light of life.

[1] 1 John v. 20. [2] 1 Cor. i. 30. [3] John xx. 31.

CHAPTER III

The Old Testament as affected by Criticism—I. The History: Argument from Critical Premises

"The Bible is through and through of historical nature and spirit."—Ewald.

"For what is the Old Testament from the Christian point of view—and from no other point of view can it be rightly understood—but the record of God's gradual revelation of Himself to Israel in His purpose of redeeming love with a view to the establishment of His universal kingdom? The Incarnation was to be the culminating point of that revelation and that purpose."—A. F. Kirkpatrick.

"On the other hand, writers of the liberal school in Germany take so completely for granted,—either on mere *critical* grounds, or because they assume from the first the utter impossibility of miracles or supernatural revelations,—the unhistorical character and non-Mosaic origin of the greater portion, at least, if not the whole, of the Pentateuch, that they do not generally take the trouble to test the credibility of the story, by entering into such matter-of-fact inquiries as are here made the basis of the whole argument."—Colenso.

"We nevertheless firmly maintain that the preceding history of Israel, from the Elohistic account of the creation to the history of Joseph, was written in ancient pre-exilian times."—Delitzsch.

"Kuenen's name for the book [JE] with which we are dealing, viz., the 'Prophetic' narrative, is scarcely happy. Some of its most remarkable elements are, as Kuenen himself points out, pre-prophetic. . . . The two books evidently proceeded in parallel lines of narrative, and it is often hard—nay, impossible—to say whether a particular section of the Hexateuch belongs to the Jahvist or the Elohist."—Addis.

CHAPTER III

THE OLD TESTAMENT AS AFFECTED BY CRITICISM —I. THE HISTORY: ARGUMENT FROM CRITICAL PREMISES

LONG ere this point is reached, loud protests will have been raised against the flagrantly "uncritical" character of our procedure, as shown in our ignoring of those well-established results of scholarship which have had the effect of shivering the supposed unity of the Old Testament, and of destroying the credibility of its narratives, especially of those which have had most weight attached to them in the history of revelation. We shall now do what we can to remove this reproach by proceeding to inquire how far the view of the Old Testament to which we have been led by the consideration of its own structure is overthrown or modified by the application of a really scientific criticism. Further, that no undue advantage may be taken, or cause given for complaint that the strength of the critical position is overlooked, we propose, in the first instance, as indicated in the preliminary sketch, to discuss the questions of the history, and of the religion and institutions, of Israel, on the basis of the critical theory itself, that is, with provisional assumption of the correctness of the ordinary critical analysis and dating of books. The canvassing of the critical theory on its merits will come after. But it is well at the outset to see what follows, even if the generally-accepted critical analysis, to its full extent, is admitted. In this chapter and the next we shall deal with the *history*.

It is not necessary to repeat the caution formerly given, that all critics are not offhand to be classed as of the same mind on this and other subjects. There are, as we shall constantly have occasion to see, more radical and more moderate schools of criticism. But it has also in justice to be recognised that it is largely the methods and conclusions of the *most* radical school—the Graf-Kuenen-Wellhausen school—which, without always the adoption of its anti-supernaturalistic premises, have been imported into English-speaking countries, are actively propagated under the name "Higher Criticism," and chiefly rule the current representations of Old Testament history and religion.[1] The late Professor W. R. Smith already claimed in 1885: "Almost every younger scholar of mark is on the side of Vatke and Reuss, Lagarde and Graf, Kuenen and Wellhausen"[2]—an ominous utterance for the Old Testament. This is our justification, if one is needed, for treating the radical school as representative.

I. Critical Assault on Old Testament History

We begin by looking at the general attitude of this advanced school to the history of the Old Testament.

1. It does not put the matter too strongly, then, to say that, to the more radical school of critics, the Old Testament is in the main *unhistorical*. Not necessarily, of course, that there is not in parts—some would acknowledge in considerable parts—a historical substratum. Everyone may not go so far, at one end of the history, as Stade, who doubts whether Israel as a people was ever in Egypt at all;[3] or, at the other end, as Kosters, who denies the return from the exile at Babylon under Zerubbabel.[4] But the books as they stand are, for all that, held not to be, at least till the days of the kings, and even then only very partially, genuine history.

[1] Cf. above, pp. 12, 17. In proof we may refer generally to the Old Testament articles in Hastings' *Dict. of Bible* (with exceptions) or Cheyne's *Encyc. Biblica*; to Addis and Carpenter on the Hexateuch; to the volumes on Joshua, etc., in "Polychrome Bible"; to those on Numbers, Judges, Samuel, etc., in the "International Crit. Commentary"; to Professor H. P. Smith's *O.T. History*, in the "International Theological Library," and many other works of the same class.

[2] Preface to Wellhausen's *Hist. of Israel* (E.T.), p. vi.

[3] *Geschichte*, i. pp. 129–30.

[4] In his *Het herstel van Israel* (1894). H. P. Smith adopts his theory, *O.T. Hist.* chap. xvi. According to the latter writer, "the decree of Cyrus is impossible," and "the theory of a return, of an interruption of the work, of any interference by Darius, is contradicted by Haggai and Zechariah" (p. 353). Of Ezra, if he existed, "we know nothing" (p. 396). See below, Chap. IX. p. 295.

To illustrate: the Book of Genesis, we are told, is "a book of sacred legend, with a mythical introduction."[1] It yields us "no historical knowledge of the patriarchs, but only of the time when the stories about them arose in the Israelite people: this later age is here unconsciously projected, in its inner and outer features, into hoar antiquity, and is reflected there like a glorified mirage."[2] The "descriptions of the Exodus from Egypt, the wandering in the desert, and the conquest and partition of Canaan . . . to put it in a word, are *utterly unhistorical*."[3] "Briefly described, then, the Book of Joshua is an historical romance. . . . We must lose much of the religious value the Book of Joshua possesses while we treat it as history, and, indeed, until we treat it as what it is—romance."[4] "The narrative gives us exactly what did not occur at the conquest."[5] The Jehovistic writer in the Hexateuch (J) "feels himself in an ideal fairy land in which no wonders are surprising."[6] The unfortunate Priestly writer (P), on the other hand, has neither historical nor literary merit, and is refused credence on all hands. Nöldeke, we are told, made an end of him "once for all"; but "Colenso is properly entitled to the credit of having first torn the web asunder."[7] His names, numbers, and precise details, which imposed even on such good critics as Bleek, Hupfeld, and Knobel, "are not drawn from contemporary records, but are the fruit solely of late Jewish fancy, a fancy which, it is well known, does not design nor sketch, but counts and constructs, and produces nothing more than barren plans."[8] In brief: "We have no really historical knowledge of a patriarchal period preceding Israel's conquest of Canaan. The individuals, Abraham,

[1] Schultz, *O.T. Theol.* i. p. 31.

[2] Wellhausen, *Hist. of Israel*, pp. 318–19.

[3] Kuenen, *Hexateuch*, p. 42 (italics his). It is of this writer's work that Professor W. R. Smith permitted himself to say: "His [Kuenen's] discussions of the more complicated questions of Pentateuch analysis are perhaps the finest things that modern criticism can show."—Preface to Wellhausen, p. viii.

[4] Professor G. B. Gray, in a review of Bennett's *Joshua* ("Polychrome Bible"), 1899.

[5] H. P. Smith, *O.T. Hist.* p. 332.

[6] F. H. Woods, art. "Hexateuch" in *Dict. of Bible*, ii. p. 372. Cf. with Dr. Driver's statement in his *Genesis*, p. xlv, quoted below, p. 105: "The patriarchal narratives are marked by great sobriety of statement and representation," etc.

[7] Wellhausen, *Hist. of Israel*, p. 347. [8] *Ibid.* p. 348.

Isaac, and Jacob, are eponyms—personifications of clans, tribes, or ethnological groups—and they are nothing more."[1]

As respects the later books, a basis of political history is necessarily recognised, but the books as we have them are declared to be throughout unreliable and misleading. "In Judges, Samuel, and Kings," we are told, "we are not presented with tradition purely in its original condition: already it is overgrown with later accretions. . . . To vary the metaphor, the whole area of tradition has finally been uniformly covered with an alluvial deposit by which the configuration of the surface has been determined."[2] Here are a few examples. On 1 Sam. vii.: "The mere recapitulation of the contents of this narrative makes us feel at once what a pious make-up it is, and how full of inherent impossibility."[3] On 1 Sam. xix. 18–24: "We can scarcely avoid the suspicion that what we have before us here is a pious caricature; the point can be nothing but Samuel's and David's enjoyment of the disgrace of the naked king."[4] On the Deuteronomic revision of Kings: "The most unblushing example of this kind, a piece which, for historical worthlessness, may compare with Judges xix.–xxi., or 1 Sam. vii. *seq.*, or even stands a step lower, is 1 Kings xxii."[5] On editorial additions: "These valuable notes commence even with Solomon, though here they are largely mixed with anecdotic chaff."[6] Chronicles, of course, so far as it does not embody extracts from older works, is regarded as past redemption. It is the product of a "law-crazed" fancy, which effects "a complete transformation of the original tradition."[7] "His work must not be called history."[8] In the irreverence of much of this, one is forcibly reminded of what Dr. Cheyne says of the indebtedness of the newer criticism to eighteenth century English Deism.[9] The atmosphere into which we are brought back is that of Morgan, and Bolingbroke, and Hume, and the impression produced is correspondingly painful.[10]

[1] H. P. Smith, *O.T. Hist.* p. 48.
[2] Wellhausen, *Hist. of Israel*, p. 228.
[3] *Ibid.* p. 248.
[4] *Ibid.* p. 268.
[5] *Ibid.* p. 285.
[6] *Ibid.* p. 286.
[7] *Ibid.* pp. 195, 224.
[8] H. P. Smith, *O.T. Hist.* p. 5.
[9] *Founders of Criticism*, pp. 1, 2.
[10] We have not taken notice of the older mythological theories, *e.g.*

2. It will not be disputed, we think, that these extracts, taken almost at random, fairly represent the views and spirit of the majority of the books and articles written from the newer critical standpoint,—certainly those of the most influential representatives of the school,—but, as already said, there are critics also of *more positive tendency,* who contest these deductions of the extremer party, and take much firmer ground on the historicity of the patriarchal and Mosaic periods. Such, *e.g.*, on the Continent, are König, Strack, Kittel, Oettli, and many more.[1] In England, Dr. Driver, in his reverence and moderation of tone, represents the mediating position of many believing scholars, though he is obviously hampered by his adherence to the Wellhausen basis. He argues for a historical "core" in the patriarchal narratives, thinks, even, that there are "reasonable grounds for concluding that the narratives are *in substance* historical"; but comes in the end to the rather lame conclusion, that "it is still, all things considered, difficult to believe that *some* foundation of actual personal history does not underlie the patriarchal narratives."[2] The main stream of the critical movement, however, is not to be held in by these feeble barriers, and continues to spread itself over the entire field of patriarchal and Mosaic history in a broad flood of scepticism.

3. What are the *grounds* on which this sweeping indictment against the Old Testament history, and specially the

those of Goldziher in his *Mythology among the Hebrews,* who takes the characters in Genesis and Judges to be sun-myths; or of the newer extravagances of Winckler, whose theories are favourably regarded by Dr. Cheyne (*Nineteenth Century*, Dec. 1902). See Note A on Critical Extravagances.

[1] In his *Neueste Prinzipien* König combats the views of Stade, Guthe, and others, who would resolve the patriarchs into "personifications" of tribes (see below, pp. 88 ff.); Kittel defends the earlier history in his lecture (translated) on *The Babylonian Excavations and Early Bible History*, etc. Dillmann, in his posthumously published *Alttest. Theol.* (pp. 77–78, 82–83), says: "We have no right to explain these Genesis narratives as pure fiction, as so many now do. . . . We mistake if we do not recognise that they rest *in essentials* on sound historical recollection. . . . Even if none of their names had been handed down to us, we would require to postulate such revelation-figures as we have in Abraham and those who followed him. . . . The facts, therefore, afford rational justification for the picture of the course of events given in Genesis, at least in its main features (*im grossen und ganzen*)." Even Dillmann, however, concedes a good deal more than is necessary.

[2] *Genesis*, pp. xlv, xlvii, lvii. Canon Cheyne, on the other hand, is seriously disturbed at what he thinks to be the halting attitude and spirit of compromise in Dr. Driver's *Introduction*. He thinks "his fences are weak, and may at any moment be broken down."—*Founders of Criticism*, pp. 251 ff.

earlier part of it, is based? They are, as we shall see, various: the late date of composition, the manifest legendary character of the narratives, assumed variations and contradictions in the sources, supposed incompatibility with the rudimentary state of religious belief in early times, and the like. The historicity of the early narratives, it is held, cannot be maintained in view of the fact, which criticism is said to have established, that the Pentateuch (or with Joshua, the Hexateuch) is composed of documents of late date, based on tradition many centuries old—in the case of the Exodus at least 500 or 600 years, in the case of the patriarchs 1000 to 1300 years—which, therefore, cannot be supposed to preserve accurately the memory of such distant events.[1] Kuenen, who here may be taken as representative, gives four special reasons for rejecting the patriarchal narratives. They are: the religious ideas which are ascribed to the patriarchs, insoluble chronological difficulties, the familiar intercourse of the deity with the patriarchs ("we are not in the habit of accepting as history the legends which afford evidence of that belief"), and, "the principal cause of hesitation," the persons who appear as actors in the narratives "are all progenitors of tribes."[2] We wonder how many readers of the Bible feel these "obstacles" to be as "insurmountable" as they were to Dr. Kuenen.[3] Much of all this, in any case, as we shall soon discover, is undiluted assumption: the criticism rests on the theory, not the theory on the criticism. How obviously, *e.g.*, does the argument from "religious ideas"[4] rest on a certain assumption as to the stage of religious knowledge of the patriarchs—an assumption which has no warrant save in the critic's own theory of the course of the development.[5]

[1] Cf. Kuenen, *Rel. of Israel*, i. pp. 16, 17; Driver, *Genesis*, p. xliii; H. P. Smith, *O.T. Hist.* i. p. 7.

[2] *Rel. of Israel*, i. pp. 108–9. Cf. below, pp. 88 ff.

[3] Cf. Ladd, *Doct. of Sacred Scripture*, i. p. 362.

[4] Dr. Driver also argues for an "idealisation" of the narratives, on the ground that "in the days of the patriarchs religion must have been in a relatively rudimentary stage" (p. lx). It is shown later (p. 115), however, that it is not the case, as Kuenen argues, that the patriarchs are represented as "not inferior to the prophets of the eighth century B.C., in pureness of religious insight and inward personal piety."

[5] Hommel says: "When we find that a whole school of evangelical theologians do not hesitate to declare that a passage was composed at a later date or interpolated, simply because they are unwilling to recognise the existence of any high moral teaching or lofty conception of the Godhead prior

Postponing meantime, however, the discussion of these objections, we propose to proceed in more constructive fashion, in setting forth, first, the grounds of our belief in the substantial trustworthiness of the Old Testament history, even under the limits prescribed by the critical hypothesis.

II. Ignoring of Teleological Element in the History

The critical treatment breaks down the Biblical narratives, disintegrates them, causes them to crumble to pieces. But there are features in the narratives which resist this treatment, and constitute a standing protest against it. In the previous chapter we laid stress on the singular character of "teleology" in the Hebrew history. It is history dominated by the idea of purpose, and that a purpose of *grace*—of redemption. There is little, if any, recognition of this in the writers we have chiefly in view, though, to do them justice, they do not seek to get rid of the impression of the extraordinary and unique in Israel's history. Still the necessity of explaining the development out of purely natural factors causes a very different picture to be given from that which the Old Testament itself sketches.[1] One looks in vain in Kuenen, or Wellhausen, or Stade, or Gunkel, or in such an *Old Testament History* as that of Professor H. P. Smith, for any perception of the deeper ideas that lie in the Genesis narratives, or of their organic relation to the rest of Scripture. To a developing purpose of salvation they seem altogether blind. In this their criticism is already self-condemned; for what they fail to see is discerned by many others, as keenly critical as themselves. An example or two may be cited from such critical writers, if only to show that this idea of purpose is no hallucination of our own fancy, which we are seeking perversely to import into the narratives. Dr. Kautzsch, of Halle, in a lecture on *The Abiding Value of the Old Testament*, thus writes: "The abiding value of the Old Testament lies above all in this, that it guarantees to us with absolute certainty the fact and the process of a divine plan and way

to the time of the prophets of the eighth or seventh centuries B.C., then, in view of the facts adduced in the present volume, we cannot but regard their attitude as a deplorably mistaken one, and hope that it may soon become a thing of the past."—*Anc. Heb. Trad.* pp. 291–92.

[1] See below, pp. 86, 133 ff.

of salvation, which found its conclusion and fulfilment in the new covenant, in the Person and work of Jesus Christ."[1] Dillmann likewise sees in the Old Testament the development of God's redemptive "plan." "So soon," he says, "as man becomes untrue to his original idea, and, forsaking the attitude of obedience to God, begins his self-seeking way, there comes also to manifestation the saving activity of God directed to this apostacy of the creature. . . . So soon as, and so long as, sin is in the world, there is also a saving activity of God."[2] Dr. Driver says of the narrator J: "The patriarchal history is, in his hands, instinct with the consciousness of a great future: Abraham, Isaac, and Jacob are vouchsafed in succession glimpses of the divine plan."[3] Kautzsch, again, just quoted, says of his (two) J writers: "Both relate the primeval history from the standpoint of a history of redemption."[4]

To all this, so far as it is admitted, the reply which comes from the side of the criticism that seeks to get rid of the teleological element in the history is, that the Biblical representation is an unreal and artificial one: not a development in accordance with the actual history, but an *imaginary* development, the result of a reading back into the primitive legends of the ideas of the prophetic age. The appearance of development is superimposed on the historical tradition by the manner in which its materials are manipulated. Grant, it is said, the critical scheme—its analysis and partition of documents—and the illusion of teleology in the Old Testament story disappears; so far at least as any extraordinary cause is required to account for it. In the words of Professor Robertson: "What they maintain is, that the scheme of the Biblical writers is an afterthought, which, by a process of manipulation of older documents, and by a systematic representation of earlier events in the light of much later times, has been made to appear as if it were the original and genuine development."[5]

[1] *Die Bleibende Bedeutung des A. T.*, p. 28.

[2] *Alttest. Theol.* p. 411. See whole section.

[3] *Genesis*, p. xxi; cf. pp. lxx ff.

[4] *Lit. of O.T.*, p. 38. See also Ottley's *Aspects of the O.T.*, pp. 56 ff.; McFadyen's *Messages of the Prophetic and Priestly Historians*, pp. 27 ff. on "The Progress of the Divine Purpose in the Book of Genesis."

[5] *Early Religion*, p. 30. Most critics agree with the above view, so far as the reading back of prophetic ideas into the narratives is concerned.

Now we do not wish to shirk any real difficulty: we do not really feel that there is any difficulty here that needs to be shirked. We shall not even at this stage, as before said, raise any objection to the currently-accepted critical view. We are prepared to assume provisionally that, within reasonable limits, that view is correct. But we ask—Is it the case that, if the general critical hypothesis be granted, this organic unity of the history, with the remarkable teleological character which we have seen to belong to it, disappears, or is shown to be an illusion? It is there in the Old Testament as it stands:[1] can it be got rid of by any skilful dividing up, or re-dating, of documents, or snpposed later touching-up, interpolation, or re-editing? We answer that question very confidently in the negative.

1. For, in the first place, this teleological character we speak of is not a thing upon the *surface* of the Biblical history,—not a thing that could be produced by any number of editorial touchings and interpolations, and ingenious piecing together of fragments,—but is ingrained into the very substance of the history, is part of its texture, is, to use the happy figure of Bushnell about the image of Christ in the Gospels, like a watermark in paper, which cannot be destroyed without destroying the paper itself. It is not the ingenuity of the writer in arranging his materials, but the facts of the history and development of the people, which work out this plan for us. It makes little difference how far we multiply the parts; the singular thing is that, when the parts are put together, this remarkable appearance of teleology should present itself. If the critic persists: "That depends on your way of arranging the materials: let me arrange them *my* way, and this appearance of development will be destroyed"; it is a fair reply to make that, if the Biblical way of arranging the materials brings out a manifest divine design, whereas his yields only confusion, this of itself is a good reason for thinking that the Biblical way is probably the right one. Take an illustration. The pieces of a child's puzzle map are put together to form, say, the map of Europe. "Oh," says a bystander, "that is because you have put the bits together in a particular way.

[1] Wellhausen himself, we shall find, allows: "There is no primitive legend, it is well known, so well-knit as the Biblical one," and he speaks of "the linked unity" of the narrative.—*Hist. of Israel*, pp. 285, 318.

Let *me* arrange them in another way, and you will have no map at all." Possibly; but the fact that the pieces, when so put together, form the map is the best proof that this was the contriver's intention. But the map of Europe is a small matter compared with this purpose of God wrought out in the history of Israel from patriarchal times, and culminating in Christ.

2. A second reason for our answer is, that, if the plan inwrought into the history of Israel is an artificial or invented one, we *have to find the mind* capable of inventing it. If anyone can bring himself to believe that the teleology we meet with in Scripture—the divine plan of grace which forms its connecting thread—is of so simple and superficial a character that it would readily and naturally occur to any casual collector of legends, or prophetically-minded man, in the ninth or eighth century B.C., so that he could sit down and work it into a whole history, and give it an appearance of naturalness there, we can only say of such an one that he has a very large faith,—a faith nearly as great as that of the theorists who suppose that the portrait of Jesus in the Gospels was created by a Church gathered promiscuously out from Jews and Gentiles, working on the legendary reminiscences of a good and wise teacher, when the real image of Jesus had been forgotten! The difficulty is tenfold enhanced if we accept the descriptions furnished us by the Wellhausen school of the state of prophetic orders in the age when the narratives are supposed to have originated; and further assume, with the newer critics, that the authors of these narratives were not, as formerly believed, individuals, but were "schools" of writers.[1] This is how Wellhausen speaks of the prophets before Amos: "In the time of Ahab and Jehu the *Nebiim* were a widespread body, and organised in orders of their own, but were not highly respected; the average of them were miserable fellows, who ate out of the king's hand, and were treated with disdain by members of the leading classes. Amos of Tekoa, who, it is true, belonged to a younger generation, felt it an insult to be counted one of them."[2] Truly a likely soil for the growth of such conceptions as we have in the Book of Genesis!

[1] On this, see below, pp. 206 ff.
[2] *History of Israel*, p. 293; cf. p. 461. See also Stade, *Geschichte*, i. pp. 476 ff.

III. Credibility of History on Premises of Critical Theory

It is possible, however, we believe, on the premises of the critical theory itself, to show that this "teleology" in the history of Israel is not an invented or manipulated thing,—an element which does not inhere naturally in the facts, but a conception unhistorically imported into them,—and to furnish strong reasons for belief in the essential trustworthiness of the narratives. This we shall now attempt to do. We confine attention to the Pentateuch, or Hexateuch, in which most will admit that the crucial part of the problem lies, and limit ourselves, at this stage, to absolutely essential outlines and most general agreements. The full discussion of particular points involved in the theory belongs to later chapters.

We take, then, the history of things that lies before us in our present Pentateuch, and ask what, on the critical theory, is the origin of this book. Setting aside Deuteronomy, commonly assumed to be a composition of the age of Josiah,[1] we have, on the currently-accepted view, three main strands of narrative in the Pentateuch, of which one—the Priestly Writing (P)—is understood, in its present form, and principal contents, to date from the time of the exile, or after. It furnishes the "framework" of the Book of Genesis,[2] and contains, in the middle books, the Levitical legislation, to which the slender thread of narrative and genealogy in the earlier part serves as introduction.[3] It is not supposed to be an independent historical source, but in its narratives —so Wellhausen thinks[4]—presupposes and runs parallel to the other and earlier history books, J and E, by that time united into one. Nothing is lost, therefore, by meanwhile leaving this P portion aside, and confining ourselves to the two older writings. The theory regarding these, in brief, is, that they were originally separate, probably independent productions, extending, with inclusion of the Book of Joshua, to the conquest of Canaan, but latterly were combined with

[1] Cf. Chap. VIII. [2] Dillmann, *Genesis*, i. p. 16. See below, pp. 215, 340 ff.
[3] See Wellhausen, *History of Israel*, p. 332, quoted below, p. 342.
[4] *Ibid.* pp. 295, 318. See below, p. 107. The P narrative up to Ex. vi. is given by Wellhausen, pp. 327–32.

each other into something like the form in which we now find them in the Pentateuch. They are allowed to be works extremely similar in character, and largely parallel in contents;[1] but are marked, the one by the use of the divine name Jehovah,[2] the other by the use of the divine name Elohim (God).[3] Hence the designations J and E applied to them respectively. One of these histories (J) is commonly thought to have originated in the Southern Kingdom of Judah; the other (E) in the Northern Kingdom of Israel.[4] How far they were the fixing of mere oral tradition, or how far they rested on older written material, is a moot question, to which different answers are given. It is further a point in dispute which of these assumed narratives, J or E, is the earlier;[5] but it is agreed that, in the words of Dr. Driver, "both belong to the golden period of Hebrew literature."[6] The stylistic and other differences between them are slight; whereas both present a strong contrast to P, which is distinguished by marked peculiarities of style and method.[7]

What are the dates of these books? On the current view, we may say roughly, not later in their independent form than the ninth and eighth centuries, or from 850 to 750 B.C.; in combination a century or two later. Dr. Driver may be usefully quoted on this point. "On the relative date of E and J," he says, "the opinions of critics differ. Dillmann, Kittel, and Riehm assign the priority to E, placing him 900–850 B.C., and J *c.* 750 (Dillmann), 830–800 (Kittel), or *c.* 850 (Riehm). Wellhausen, Kuenen, and Stade, on the other hand, assign the priority to J, placing him 850–800 B.C., and E *c.* 750 B.C." In a footnote to the

[1] See below, pp. 218 ff.

[2] Variously spelt by the critics, in its original form, Yahweh, Yahveh, Jahweh, Jahveh, Yahve, etc. The form "Jehovah," arising from the combination of the Hebrew consonants with the vowels of the name "Adonai" (see below, p. 228), was first introduced by the Franciscan friar Petrus Galatinus, in 1518 A.D. It is, therefore, quite modern.

[3] E is supposed to begin in Gen. xx.: according to some, earlier (chap. xv.). See below, p. 217.

[4] See Chap. VII. pp. 208 ff.

[5] See Chap. VII. pp. 204 ff.

[6] *Introd.* p. 124: Wellhausen also says that JE "dates from the golden age of Hebrew literature."—*History of Israel*, p. 9.

[7] J is described as vivid, flowing, anthropomorphic: E as slightly less [illegible], more elevated, etc. P, on the other hand, is pragmatic, formal, precise, statistical, genealogical, juristic, and abounds in words and phrases peculiar to himself. See below, Chap. X. pp. 330 ff.

first of these sentences, he adds: "So most previous critics, as Nöldeke (J *c.* 900), Schrader (E 975–950; J 825–800), Kayser (*c.* 800), Reuss (J 850–800; E 'perhaps still earlier')." And in a second note: "H. Schultz, *O.T. Theology*, i. pp. 66 ff. (J to the reign of Solomon: E 850–800)."[1]

Accepting provisionally this account of the documents, we proceed to inquire what inferences may be deduced from it as to the trustworthiness of the history.

1. And, first, we invite the attention of the reader to the important fact, that, according to the dates given, these writings *antecede the age of written prophecy*, and embody the traditions which the Israelitish people possessed of its history *prior* to that age. We do not ask at present whether this tradition was oral, or was already in any degree written. It was there, and these writings are the literary depository of it, in somewhat the same way as the Synoptic Gospels are the records of the oral teaching about Christ in the apostolic age. It is customary to speak of J and E as the reduction to writing of the popular *legends* of the Israelites about their own past. Be it so: the essential point is that they are at least not histories invented or doctored by prophets in the interests of a later theory of the religious development. The more *naïve* the consciousness they exhibit, the less can they be regarded as the products of reflective manipulation. In any case they antecede the period of written prophecy.[2] They cannot, therefore, as regards their general character, be reasonably assumed to be influenced, modified, or transformed, by the ideas of that period. Their authors—the unknown J and E—we are entitled to suppose, put faithfully down the tradition as they found it in circulation among their people. They might select according to predilection from the material furnished to them, but they did not consciously falsify or invent. It is a contradiction, in one breath to speak of these writers as giving literary form to the current

[1] *Introd.* p. 123. Further dates of interest are given below, pp. 73–74.

[2] "The general conclusions," says Dr. Driver, "to which a consideration of all the facts has led critics . . . are that the two sources, J and E, date from the early centuries of the monarchy, J belonging probably to the ninth and E to the early part of the eighth century B.C. (*before* Amos or Hosea)."—*Genesis*, p. xvi. See below, p. 97. It will be seen after, however, that this theory has come to be greatly modified in the interests of later dating (see pp. 205 ff).

traditions of their nation, and in another to represent them as elaborating and transforming the narratives to make them the vehicles of the ideas of an age which, on the hypothesis, had not yet come.

It could be wished that critical writers showed themselves a little clearer here as to the implications of their own admissions as to the dates of these J and E narratives. Two representations cross and mingle continually in their pages: one, that the writers of these narratives were simple "collectors of legends,"[1] as Grimm might collect the folk-tales of Germany; the other, that they were consummate literary artists, altering, embellishing, and idealising their material at pleasure: one, that the narrators are "*pre-prophetic*,"[2] that is, antecede the age of the great writing prophets, when, we are told, "ethical monotheism" was first introduced; the other, that they were *prophetic* narrators, instinct with the prophetic spirit, dominated by prophetic ideas, and adepts in recasting their narratives to make them express these ideas.[3] Manifestly the critics cannot have it both ways: on the one hand holding the low views of Wellhausen, Kuenen, and Stade, on the state of people and prophets in "pre-prophetic" Israel, and regarding "pure Jahvism" as the "creation" of Amos and Hosea;[4] and on the other, picturing the ninth and eighth centuries as already penetrated with lofty prophetic ideas, bringing to the birth, and giving exquisite expression to, the elevated conceptions which we find in Genesis and Exodus—writing histories "from the standpoint of redemption." A choice must be made, and either the books be brought down to an age when prophetic ideas were in the ascendant, which involves the abandonment of the given dates, or the contention be surrendered that these higher ideas first entered

[1] "The Jahvist and the Elohist," says Addis, "were historians, or rather collectors of national myths and legends, which passed for history." —*Hex.* p. lxvi.

[2] "Both belong," says Bennett, "to the pre-Deuteronomic, pre-prophetic stage of the religion of Israel."—*Primer*, pp. 11, 15. Cf. Wellhausen, *Hist. of Israel*, p. 32; Addis, p. liii; Driver, *Genesis*, p. xlviii, etc.

[3] Thus, *e.g.*, Kautzsch, *Lit. of O.T.*, pp. 35 ff.; McFadyen, *Messages* etc., pp. 25, 26 ("Prophetic Documents"): Kuenen likewise uses this designation (*Hex.* pp. 138 ff., 232 ff.), but regards J and E as undergoing extensive changes in a later "Judæan edition" (p. 248).

[4] Or, with Duhm, Micah and Amos. "Micah and Amos," he says, "first raised religion out of the sphere of nature into that of morality: thence it could develop higher."—*Theol. d. Proph.* p. 103.

with Amos and Hosea. The natural course would seem to be to regard the writings as, indeed, "pre-prophetic" in the sense of anteceding written prophecy, but at the same time as faithfully recording the ancient tradition,[1] in which prophetic ideas were already present.

2. The fact thus conceded of the "pre-prophetic" character of the narratives yields several weighty results.

(1) We deduce from it, first, as just said, that the internal unity and teleological character so conspicuous in these narratives formed *an integral part of the tradition*, and was not put into it by later prophetic manipulation. It was part of the tradition as early as the ninth century, when at least one of these narratives took written shape. If here, again, anyone is content to think of what he finds in the J and E histories as answering to the idea of loose, popular legend, he must be allowed to retain his opinion, but we cannot share it. Legend does not usually assume this character of depth, coherence, developing purpose; does not embody ideas, transactions, promises, such as we find in these narratives,—the protevangelium, for instance, the call of Abraham, the covenants, the revelations at the Exodus,—containing in them the germs of a long future. If these things are there in a "pre-prophetic" narrative, they clearly formed part of the original tradition, and were not *put* there by a later prophetic hand.

(2) We deduce, next, that this tradition, at the time of its being written down by J and E, must already have assumed a *quite developed and settled form*. When we look at the range of this J and E history in the Pentateuchal books—at its rich content, at its well-developed biographies, with their wealth of characterisation, finished dialogue, connection with specified localities and situations, at its

[1] On this point of the faithful recording of the tradition, on which much hinges, we have such testimonies as the following:—

Dillmann says that E "preserves unchanged in its narrations the manner, tone, and colour of the living legendary lore of the people."—*Genesis*, p. 9.

Gunkel says: "The legends of J and E are taken over by the collectors *essentially as they found them*."—*Genesis*, Introd. p. lvi.

Driver says: "J and E give us pictures of the traditions as they were current in the early centuries of the monarchy."—*Genesis*, p. lviii. He speaks of the indications "that these narrators were keeping themselves within the limits of a tradition which they had received, rather than freely creating ideal pictures of their own" (p. xlv).

articulated unity from beginning to close, it seems clear as day that it is no floating, Protean legend we have to deal with, but a legend—if the critic will have it so—already firmly fixed in outline and in the bulk of its contents, already clothed with flesh and blood, already as definite in substance, if not in form, as a written narrative itself could be. The loose way in which many speak of J and E giving literary shape to floating, popular legends, as one might write down countryside fairy tales, shows that they have never clearly apprehended what kind of history this in the JE narrative is, or what it is needful to presuppose as the condition of such a history being there to write. If the ideas in these writings were elaborated in any early prophetic workshop, how profoundly spiritual, how deep-seeing, the minds in that workshop must have been! How explain the presence, or prevalence, of such ideas in the age of Elijah and Elisha, on Wellhausen's theory of the religious development and of the state of the prophetic orders?[1]

(3) There is a yet weightier consideration—one based directly on the critical hypothesis—which we do not see how anyone can easily get over. It is the fact that, on this theory, we have *not one only*, but *two* histories of early times to reckon with. Here, as the critics tell us, are two lengthy and practically independent[2] histories, one emanating from the South, the other from the North, at a time when (on the hypothesis) the kingdoms were already divided, and separate in interests. Both cover the same ground, and give the history of the people for the same period. But now comes the startling thing about them, that, while two in authorship, place of writing, and perhaps tendency, these histories are, in nearly every other respect, almost identical. The substance of the narrative is the same, or varies only in trifling details. They record the same incidents, follow nearly the same order, tell their story

[1] Elijah was, in Wellhausen's view, the first to grasp the idea "that there exists over all but one Holy One and one Mighty One, who reveals Himself not in nature, but in law and righteousness, in the world of man."—*Hist. of Israel*, p. 462. But Elijah's idea was not generally shared.

[2] Addis says that Hupfeld made it plain "that each of these documents had once been an independent work."—*Hex.* p. xxix. Gunkel strongly affirms the independence of the documents (*Genesis*, p. lvii). Other critics suppose partial dependence of one on the other. See below, p. 204.

in almost the same language. They are parallel narratives in the fullest sense. The proof of this lies in the fact that, on the critical view, these narratives have subsequently been combined, and in the union, not only is sometimes the section of one, sometimes the section of another, taken into the record, but in many chapters the two narratives are blended line by line, clause by clause, with such minuteness, somewhat after the fashion of a Harmony of the Gospels, or are so completely fused together, that the keen-scented critics often declare themselves baffled to separate them, and differ widely in their attempts to do so.[1] The reader has only to examine the analysis offered of such chapters as Gen. xxvii., xxviii., xxx., xxxvii., to be convinced of the truth of what we state.

So striking a class of phenomena naturally suggests the question whether we are really dealing with two documents at all.[2] Keeping, however, meanwhile to the critical hypothesis as given, we ask—What follows from it? Two things very plainly. In the *first* place, such phenomena put an effective check on any theorist who would contend that the J and E writers did not, as we have supposed, faithfully reproduce the tradition, but wrought it up artistically in a new form of their own, as Shakespeare might work up the old stories of Macbeth or King Lear, or Tennyson the legends of King Arthur. If that were admissible for one writer, it plainly would not be admissible for two, working independently. The fact that two writers—one Northern, the other Southern—give the same cycle of stories in much the same way, is proof that both are reproducing, not inventing. But, *second*, it proves also the truth of what has been said above of the fixed character of the tradition. Here, *ex hypothesi*, we have two writers setting down the traditions current in their respective localities and circles; and these, when compared, are found to be, in the words of

[1] On the parallelism of the narratives, see below, Chap. VII. pp. 218 ff. Wellhausen, as already noted, extends the parallelism to P; see below, p. 107. Testimonies as to the closeness of the resemblance, and intimate union, of the JE narratives are found in every writer. Dillmann says: "It is often very difficult or impossible to make a complete separation between them, where their narratives have been worked into each other by later editors, and material criteria are wanting."—*Genesis*, p. 14. Cf. Gunkel, *Genesis*, pp. lx ff.; and see below, pp. 219 ff.

[2] The question is discussed in Chap. VII. pp. 216 ff., and there answered in the negative.

Klostermann, "throughout parallel."[1] The slight discrepancies that are alleged are quite outweighed by the substantial agreement. Criticism, therefore, if its division of these documents could be trusted, would furnish us with a powerful corroboration of the genuineness and fixed character of the tradition at a period not later than the ninth century B.C. It would give us two witnesses instead of one.[2]

IV. Stepping-Stones to Earlier Date of Tradition

The above results are obtained from the simple considerations that our assumed documents antedate the age of written prophecy, and that they are two in number. From the vantage-ground thus gained, we may now push our inquiry into the value of the Hebrew tradition a good way further back. Obviously there is need for doing this. Grant that we have a rich, and in the main coherent, tradition as a possession of the people of Israel in North and South as early as the ninth or eighth century, it will be felt that we are still a long way from the events themselves to which the tradition relates,[3] and the question may properly be asked whether an earlier date can be assigned to the tradition than that which we have yet reached? Conjecture here is of little value; but there are some very definite stepping-stones, to which we may, we think, trust ourselves with great confidence.

1. It is first to be noted that the *facts already ascertained* about the tradition *of themselves carry us a good way* beyond the dates assumed for the reduction of the tradition to writing. The point here is, that, whatever the date of authorship of the supposed documents, the tradition itself, from its fixed and settled character in both branches of the kingdom, must be much earlier. The tradition which J and E found did not come into existence in that year, or that century. It had a definite, stable form, which it

[1] *Der Pentateuch*, p. 10; see below, pp. 218–19, 345.

[2] Cf. Kittel, *Hist. of Hebs.* i. p. 168; Driver, *Genesis*, p. xliv; Westphal, *Les Sources du Pent.* i. Pref. p. xxviii.

[3] Kuenen asks in regard to these narratives: "Do we arrive at the certainty of which we are in search with regard to Israel's former history?" and he answers: "To begin with, we obtain nothing but the idea which was entertained of that history in the eighth [or ninth] century B.C."—*Rel. of Israel*, i. p. 103.

must have possessed for a considerable time before, and which took a much longer time to grow into its settled shape. It must have had substantially the shape in which we find it before the division of the kingdom,—only thus can we account for its being found in practically the same form in both North and South,—and for the absence of all allusions to the division.[1] This means that it was the possession of Israel in the days of Solomon and David: there is no great stretch of imagination in saying, even in the days of Samuel. If it be urged that this is incompatible with its mode of transmission by vague popular repetition, it may with great cogency be replied that the coherence, consistency, and persistence of the tradition may be itself a proof that it was *not* left to depend entirely on this mode of transmission, but already existed, in some form, in written shape, or was at least the subject of careful and continuous instruction.[2]

2. With this has to be taken into account another fact of great importance. We have hitherto, in deference to prevailing views, accepted the ninth and eighth centuries as the periods of the composition of the J and E narratives. These dates, however, it is now necessary to remind the reader, are at most the *termini ad quem* for the writing of these histories. They were not *later* than 850–750 B.C., but it does not follow that they were not much earlier. "The *terminus a quo*," says Dr. Driver, "is more difficult to fix with confidence: in fact, conclusive criteria fail us."[3] The statement that J and E originated at about the dates named has settled down into a kind of commonplace in the critical schools; yet it is far from being a secure result of criticism: we should be disposed to say it is one of the most insecure. If the reader will consult the list of dates formerly given, he will see that critics like Dillmann, Riehm, Kittel, carry back the date of E as far as 900–850 B.C.; Schrader to 975–950 B.C.; Nöldeke puts J about 900 B.C.; Schultz puts J in the reign of Solomon, etc. Writers of older standing went back still further. Bleek, *e.g.*, put the Jehovist in the

[1] Stade, indeed, thinks that the Jacob-Joseph legend supposes the divided kingdom (*Geschichte*, i. p. 128). This is a good specimen of the style of argument.

[2] Cf. Gen. xviii. 19; Ex. xii. 26, 27; Deut. vi. 7, 20–25; xi. 19; Ps. lxxviii. 3, 4.

[3] *Introd.* p. 123.

reign of David; Colenso, in the age of David and Solomon.[1] But many recent writers also uphold a very early date. König, *e.g.*, thinks that E can be placed with greatest certainty in the time of the Judges; J is put by him in the reign of David.[2] Köhler gives similar dates: E in the time of the Judges (*c.* 1100 B.C.) and J in the reign of David (*c.* 1000 B.C.).[3] Klostermann, from an independent standpoint, attributes to the old Pentateuchal history a very high antiquity, the upper limit of which cannot be determined.[4]

If, in surprise, the reader asks on what grounds the dates have undergone so remarkable a lowering in the Wellhausen school, the answer is not far to seek. It is not that any new and revolutionary discoveries have been made as regards the language, text, or contents of the books. The really determining factor will be found generally to lie in *a new theory of religious development*,[5] combined with assumptions as to the reflections of later events (*e.g.*, the wars of Syria with Israel) in the patriarchal stories.[6] But here again, as we shall see more fully below, the newest school of all—that of Gunkel—comes in with a weighty caveat. Gunkel argues strongly for the "pre-prophetic" character of the narratives; finds the formation of patriarchal legends concluded as far back as 1200 B.C.; is clear that their after working-up is not later than the early kings; rejects the mirroring of the Syrian wars, and (with one exception due to later addition) can discover

[1] *Pent.* Pt. vi. p. 536. It is to be remembered that all these older writers put the Elohist writer (including P) still earlier than J. Ewald, *e.g.*, places his "Book of Origins" under Solomon; Colenso assigns his Elohistic narrative in Genesis to the age of Saul and Samuel (*Pent.* Pt. vi. App. p. 116).

[2] *Einleitung*, p. 205.

[3] Hauck's *Realencyc.* art. "Abraham," i. p. 102.

[4] *Pent.* pp. 77, 219–20. There have, of course, always been those also who defended a direct Mosaic authorship.

[5] Dr. Driver says: "We can only argue upon grounds of probability derived from our view of the progress of the art of writing, or of literary composition, or of the rise and growth of the prophetic tone and feeling in ancient Israel. . . . For estimating most of which, though plausible arguments, on one side or the other, may be advanced, a standard on which we can confidently rely scarcely admits of being fixed."—*Introd.* pp. 123–24.

[6] *E.g.*, "In the story of Jacob and Laban, again, the contemporary background shines through the patriarchal history very distinctly."—Wellhausen, *Hist. of Israel*, p. 323; cf. Addis, *Hex.* i. p. 62; Driver, *Genesis*, p. lix. See below, pp. 111, 209.

no indication of political conditions after 900 B.C.[1] It need not be said that if dates such as those preferred by the above-mentioned writers be admitted, the whole state of the question is revolutionised, and we are brought within measurable distance of a period from which sound tradition could easily be preserved. The argument from the firmness and consistency of the tradition acquires in that case enhanced importance.

3. The supposition is made above that the J and E histories, if the dates assigned to them by the critics are correct, were not based wholly on oral tradition, but may rest on *older written material* as well. Is this entirely conjecture? Let us see.

(1) The history of the *language* affords the best grounds for believing that the history of the people must have existed in some earlier written form. We have argued that the existence of the tradition in a fixed and settled form in the ninth and eighth centuries implies its existence at a long anterior period. But what shall we say of the works J and E themselves, and of the language in which they are written? That language belongs, as we have seen, "to the golden age of Hebrew literature."[2] It was a fully-formed literary language—a language with the finest capabilities of historical narration already developed. How did that language come into being? Whence did it derive its literary capabilities? Whence the literary art and skill to produce these books we are dealing with? These are questions which seem often strangely ignored. The language of Shakespeare was not Shakespeare's creation; neither was the language of Chaucer, Chaucer's creation. But here are two historians—according to some, "schools" of historians—expert to the highest degree in the use of the pen. The men who wrote the 24th chapter of Genesis—that "charming idyll, the captivating picture of the wooing and bringing home of Rebekah"[3]—the story of Joseph, the dramatic scenes between Moses and Pharaoh, the narrative of the crossing of the Red Sea, were authors of the first rank. How were they created? On what models did they work? **Is it not** necessary to assume earlier literature, and that,

[1] *Genesis*, pp. lxi, lxii. See below, pp. **111, 209.**
[2] Driver, Wellhausen, see above, p. 66.
[3] Delitzsch, *Genesis*, ii. p. 104.

too, of a highly developed kind,—not songs merely, or dry court chronicles, but historical compositions,—to explain the existing productions?

(2) But here, again, it is important to note, we are not left wholly to inference or conjecture. The productions of J and E are *not*, on the current view of their dates, the earliest specimens of Hebrew literature we possess.[1] We need not go further than the pages of Dr. Kautzsch, whose devotion to criticism will not be doubted, in proof of this statement. According to this authority, the language was already highly developed, and the art of writing disseminated among the common people,[2] in the time of the Judges. The Song of Deborah in Judges v.—"a poem of priceless worth," "genuine, splendid poetry"—is ascribed by him to about 1250 B.C., and the fable of Jotham (Judg. ix. 7 ff.), the artistic finish of which, he says, is so high, and the delicate satire so great, "as again to suggest the conjecture that this form of composition must have been long and diligently cultivated, is referred to the same period."[3] Between this and the reign of David fall other pieces, as the Song of Miriam, the poetical fragments in Numbers, the address to the sun and moon in Joshua. To David's reign (1020–980 B.C.) belong the elegies of David on Saul and Abner, and to the same age, or that of Solomon, a number of other highly finished productions.[4] The speech of Solomon at the dedication of the temple, 1 Kings viii. 12 ff. (how much?) is held to be "an authentic monument

[1] It would scarcely be necessary to emphasise this, but for the suggestion in a remark of Wellhausen's, that in the interval between Elijah and Elisha and Amos, "a non-literary had developed into a literary age."—*Hist. of Israel*, p. 465.

[2] *Lit. of O.T.*, p. 10; cf. Judg. viii. 14 (R.V.). Many critics carry literary composition much further back. Ewald, *e.g.*, supposes Gen. xlix. 22–26 to go back to the times before Moses (written?).—*Revelation: its Nature and Record* (E.T.), p. 323. Delitzsch thinks the Song and Blessing of Moses may have been written by him.—*Genesis*, i. p. 45, etc.

[3] *Ibid.* pp. 4, 5. Kautzsch thinks it probable, however, "that we must come down to the time of David for the writing out of the products of those earlier days" (p. 10. Why?). Stade also says the Song of Deborah bears traces of having been composed under the immediate impression of the victory it records. See the remarkable list of testimonies on this point in König's art. "Judges," in *Dict. of Bible*, ii. p. 813. Professor Robertson thinks the Song "may have come down in writing from that period."—*Early Religion*, p. 79.

[4] He includes here the Blessing of Jacob, and the original form of the Balaam-Discourses.

of the reign of Solomon."[1] Then we come to the so-called "Hero-Stories" of the Book of Judges, and to the "Jerusalem-Stories," the "David-Stories," and the "Saul-Stories," which make up a large part of the Books of Samuel. These are placed between 933–911 B.C.—the "Saul-Stories" a few years later.[2] The "Jerusalem-Source" is assigned "to the period immediately after Solomon,"[3] and is described as "one of the most complete, truthful, and finished products of historical writing which have come down to us from the Hebrews, and indeed from the whole ancient world."[4]

Here then we have the language nearly in its prime carried back to the thirteenth century B.C., with a long cultivation necessarily preceding,—are brought, in short, almost to the verge of the Exodus. Are we to suppose that all this while nothing was done to produce some records of the people's history, of the events of the Exodus, which admittedly so deeply moved them,[5] and, beyond that, of the traditions of the fathers? To us this appears so incredible, that, even if no literature existed which seemed to require such records for its explanation, we should be forced to suppose that they once existed, but had unfortunately become lost. Much more are we driven to assume them, if regard is had to the mass of the tradition, and to the clearness, coherence, and religious importance of its contents, so different from what forms the staple of popular oral legend. It is not a conclusive answer to this to say that we have no direct evidence of the existence of such records. If the essential parts of such records are incorporated in the works we have, it can readily be understood why they should drop out of memory and use;[6] or it may turn out in the end that the so-called J and E are themselves such records,—that is, we may be compelled by the internal character of the history to antedate its written

[1] *Lit. of O.T.*, p. 12; cf. p. 177. See below, p. 102.

[2] *Ibid.* pp. 178–79. [3] *Ibid.* p. 27.

[4] *Ibid.* p. 25. Dr. Driver says of this narrative (2 Sam. ix.–xx.): "The abundance and particularity of detail show that the narrative must date from a period very little later than that of the events related. The style is singularly bright, flowing, and picturesque."—*Introd.* p. 183.

[5] See below, pp. 100 ff.

[6] Thus the voluminous records which underlie the historical books (Samuel, Kings, Chronicles, etc.) have perished: so also the early attempts at the composition of written Gospels (Luke i. 1).

form, and to revise our conceptions of the literary capabilities of an earlier age.[1]

(3) A third consideration under this head remains. The use of earlier records in the composition of J and E is not a hypothesis opposed to critical science: it is one to which adherents of the critical school in perhaps increasing number are coming back. Not to speak of others more conservative, such writers as Delitzsch always insisted on the use of ancient material, part of it Mosaic, in the Pentateuch; but, as representing a newer position, we may instance Kittel. "Certain it is," this writer says, "that such sources, probably even in documentary form, to some extent, lay before E as well as J. . . . In many cases it seems demonstrable that E worked in accordance with sources that were ancient, and in part very ancient. And further, where this cannot now be discerned, we may accept his descriptions as resting on older material, oral or written, except where there are conclusive reasons of a special kind to the contrary."[2]

V. Corroborative Evidence of Early Date of Sources

There are, we would say in concluding, three things which strongly corroborate the positions we have laid down.

1. The first is the enormous increase of light which recent discovery has cast on the *very early, and indeed common, use of writing*, and *high development of literature* in the ancient East. We return to this subject in a later chapter,[3] and only here anticipate the general result. The discoveries amount to a revolution in old beliefs, and, as scholars are beginning to recognise, alter the perspective of everything that relates to arts, laws, and letters in the early parts of the Old Testament. Culture and writing are carried back in Babylonia to an almost fabulous antiquity—millenniums

[1] This, it will be seen after, is what we take to be the true solution. The classic period of the JE writings does not then come after, but, as seems most reasonable, lies behind the flourishing age of Kautzsch's "Jerusalem-Source." Can it be thought likely that such skill should be bestowed on the reign of David, while the whole wonderful past of the nation stood neglected?

[2] *Hist. of Hebs.* i. pp. 90, 95.

[3] Chap. XI., where details are given.

before the days of Abraham, and the age of Abraham itself is shown by the Code of Hammurabi and the contract tablets of the same age to have been one of highly-developed civilisation and general enlightenment. In Egypt we find that the hieroglyphic system was already complete by the time of Menes, founder of the first dynasty (*c.* 4000 B.C.); in Canaan, as the Tel el-Amarna tablets discover to us, epistolary correspondence was freely carried on about 1400 B.C., in the Babylonian language and cuneiform character;[1] Crete is proved to have been the abode of an advanced culture long before the age of Moses: if Dr. Glaser's speculations are correct,[2] the inscriptions of the kingdom of Maon in South Arabia are possibly as old as the Exodus. It cannot be denied that this wholly unexpected light on the all but universal diffusion of letters in the ancient world[3] puts the problems of the patriarchal and Mosaic times in an entirely new setting.[4] It is no longer sufficient to reply that a nomad people like the Hebrews was an exception to the general rule. The nomad theory rests on the critic's own assumptions, and is of no force against the indications of the history itself.[5] Moses was not a nomad, but is figured as "learned in all the wisdom of the Egyptians."[6] Joseph and his family were not nomads, and the position of the Hebrews in Egypt under Joseph's *régime* must have been one of great honour and influence.[7]

2. The progress of discovery, again, has brought to light

[1] Dr. Sayce goes so far as to say of Canaan: "Schools and libraries, in fact, must have existed everywhere, and the art of reading and writing must have been as widely spread as it was in Europe before the days of the penny post."—*Higher Crit.* p. 57; cf. his *Early Israel*, Introduction.

[2] Cf. Sayce, *Higher Crit.* pp. 39 ff.

[3] Sayce says: "From one end of the civilised ancient world to the other men and women were reading and writing and corresponding with one another; schools abounded and great libraries were formed, in an age which the critic only a few years ago declared was almost wholly illiterate."—*Monument Facts*, p. 42.

[4] "According to all analogy," says Professor Kittel, "we may henceforth expect that in the case of Biblical science also, the stakes may be pushed further forward and the cords much further lengthened than anxious minds were prepared for, and that, too, without leaving the ground of the historically possible and admissible. If in the case of Hellas and the Islands the second millennium before Christ is no longer absolutely a *terra incognita*, in all probability the presumably older culture-field of Syria and Palestine will be still less so."—*Babyl. Excavs.* pp. 17, 18.

[5] See below, pp. 104, 154.

[6] Acts vii. 22.

[7] Gen. l. 7–11. Cf. Hommel, *Ancient Heb. Trad.* p. 229.

so much *minutely confirmatory of the historical, geographical, and ethnographical data* of the early parts of the Old Testament, that the assumption of early records seems indispensable to explain how such knowledge—often antiquarian and obsolete—has been preserved. Such, *e.g.*, is the light thrown on the historical conditions in the account of the expedition of Chedorlaomer in Gen. xiv.; or on the remarkable statements in Gen. x. as to the origin and relations of the most ancient peoples; or on the vivid picturing of Egyptian life and customs in the history of Joseph, and in the narratives of Moses and the Exodus.[1]

3. Lastly, there is the *evidence of the Biblical narratives* themselves as to the early use of writing in Israel. Thus far we have refrained from drawing on the Biblical history, but, in an inquiry of this kind, its evidence cannot in fairness be disregarded. It is not to be thought of, that, while every scrap of testimony from profane sources is welcomed, and made the most of, the Scriptures alone are to be treated like criminal suspects, whose every word is to be doubted, unless hostile cross-examination fails to shake it, or independent confirmation of it can be produced.[2] Like other witnesses, the Biblical writers are entitled to be heard with a *prima facie* presumption of their honesty. It is the case, then, that writing and written records are frequently referred to in the Pentateuchal narratives. Not, indeed, in the patriarchal narratives—an internal mark of their truthfulness[3]—but in the age of Moses and Joshua. Repeatedly things are said to be written, or are commanded to be written. Writing is implied in the name of the "officers" (*Shoterim* = scribes)[4] set over the Israelites in their bondage. No inconsiderable amount of written matter is directly ascribed to Moses, creating the presumption that there was more, even when the fact is not directly stated. Moses wrote "all the words of Jehovah" in the "Book of the Covenant."[5] He was commanded to write in a

[1] See below, Chap. XI. pp. 413 ff.

[2] Cf. Ladd, *Doct. of Sac. Scripture*, i. p. 345. Ladd quotes Lessing on the N.T.: "If now Livy and Dionysius and Polybius and Tacitus are treated so frankly and nobly that we do not put them to the rack for every syllable, why not also Matthew and Mark and Luke and John?"

[3] Cf. Delitzsch, *Genesis*, i. p. 3. But see below, p. 375. The argument from silence is precarious, and Babylonian analogy would suggest that writing would be used in such a contract as that in Gen. xxiii.

[4] Ex. v. 6, 14, etc.

[5] Ex. xxiv. 4, 7.

(the) book the decree against Amalek.[1] He wrote "the goings-out" of Israel from Egypt, "according to their journeyings."[2] There was a written register of the seventy elders.[3] He wrote "the words of this law" at Moab, "in a book until they were finished,"[4] and also wrote his "Song," and "taught it to the children of Israel."[5] "All the words of this law" were to be written on stones at Mount Ebal,[6] and the Book of Joshua records that this was done.[7] Joshua assumes, in conformity with Deut. xxxi. 24–26, the existence of a "book of the law," and it is said of Joshua's own address to the people that "he wrote these words in the book of the law of God." All this, as we now know, is in keeping with the state of culture at the time,[8] and lends support to the view that much first-hand material from the Mosaic age is substantially preserved in the books which refer to this period.

The conclusion we draw from the whole discussion is, that the view is untenable which regards the Biblical history of Israel's early condition and religious development as a projection back on patriarchal times of the ideas of the prophetic age. Even accepting the critical premises—in part by help of them—we are warranted in the belief to which we were led by the consideration of the organic and purposeful character of the Old Testament narrative itself, that it is a faithful representation of the actual course of the early history of the people. This conclusion will obtain confirmation from the detailed examination which follows.

[1] Ex. xvii. 14.
[2] Num. xxxiii. 2.
[3] Num. xi. 26.
[4] Deut. xxxi. 9, 24, 26.
[5] Deut. xxxi. 19, 22.
[6] Deut. xxvii. 8.
[7] Josh. viii. 30–35. See below, p. 263.
[8] Referring to the Tel el-Amarna discoveries, Professor Robertson says: "We need no longer, therefore, wonder that among the towns taken by Joshua was one called Kirjath-Sepher, *Book-town* (Josh. xv. 15; Judg. i. 11), or Kirjath-Sannah [*City of Instruction*] (Josh. xv. 49); or that a lad caught at the roadside was able to write down the names of the chief men of Succoth in the time of the Judges (Judg. viii. 14, R.V.)."—*Early Religion*, p. 78. See further on Hebrew writing in Chap. X. below, pp. 374–5.

CHAPTER IV

The Old Testament as affected by Criticism—I. The History: Counter-Theories Tested

"The characteristic of the Israelitish mind was an outlook into the future. . . . Was the case different with Abraham? If he was anything like that character which these early histories describe him to have been, nothing would seem more natural than that he should be made to know what the goal was to be to which his history looked. One can scarcely explain how Israel came to direct its attention to Canaan when it escaped from Egypt, unless it had some tradition of its destiny alive in it."—A. B. Davidson.

"Abraham in that early dawn of history, with polytheism and idolatry all around him, saw his own creed triumphant in the world; he predicted its triumph, and the prediction has as a matter of fact come true. It is triumphant. The creed of Abraham has become the creed of the civilised world. The patriarch's creed has been victorious over the idolatry of the human race, and grown from a deposit in the breast of one man into a universal religion."—Mozley.

"There are certain points which all the sources take for granted as firmly established by tradition: namely, that Moses, of the tribe of Levi, was the first to proclaim Jahweh as the God of the whole people of Israel, and as their Deliverer from the bondage of Egypt; that at Sinai he brought about the conclusion of a 'covenant' between Jahweh and Israel; that he at least laid the foundation of the judicial and ceremonial ordinances in Israel, and that he left behind him more or less copious notes on all this."—Kautzsch.

CHAPTER IV

THE OLD TESTAMENT AS AFFECTED BY CRITICISM —I. THE HISTORY: COUNTER-THEORIES TESTED

It is necessary now to widen our argument, and look more closely at the construction of the history which the radical criticism opposes to the Biblical—to test its grounds, and weigh the force of the considerations which are thought to be fatal to the latter. This will afford us opportunity of reinforcing our previous conclusions, and will prepare the way for the discussion, in succeeding chapters, of the bearing of critical principles on religion and institutions.

I. Rival Constructions as Dependent on their Presuppositions

It was pointed out in the first chapter[1] that nearly everything in the critical discussion of the history and religion of the Old Testament depends on the presuppositions with which we start. If the Old Testament is read in the light of its *own* presuppositions,—which, surely, in the first instance, is not an unfair thing to ask,—its contents present a very different aspect from what they do if read in the light of principles which contradict these presuppositions. Let one assume, and hold fast by the idea, that there has really been a great scheme of historical revelation extending through successive dispensations, and culminating in the Incarnation in Jesus Christ, and many things will appear natural and fitting as parts of such a scheme, which otherwise would be rejected as incredible, or be taken account of only to be explained away.

It need not surprise us, therefore, that, rejecting the Biblical presuppositions, the more radical criticism rejects

[1] See above, p. 14.

of necessity the history which depends on these, and, for the picture of the origins of Israel, and of Mosaic times, given in the Old Testament, substitutes another and very different one, evolved from its own assumptions. For it, the unhistorical character of the Biblical narratives is decided before the inquiry begins. Israel, on its view, emerges from the dim past as a loose aggregation of tribes; polytheists, or at least monolaters; not a people chosen and called of God, with the memory of a past, and the consciousness of a future, but a horde of semi-barbarians, sharing the ordinary Semitic ideas, customs, and superstitions, and indebted for what rudiments of culture they ultimately came to possess to the more advanced Canaanites. There was no revelation; everything happened by natural development. It is obvious that such a people could not have had the history which the Bible ascribes to it. With such a theory in the background of his mind, and consciously or unconsciously used as the standard of his judgments, the critic has no alternative but to regard the stories he is dealing with as a bundle of legends. The sole question he has to ask himself is, How did such legends come to be formed? What tribal reminiscences may be supposed to shimmer through them? The paradoxical thing is, when his conclusions are taken over by those who do not share his presuppositions, and receive endorsement as the results of the latest critical scholarship!

When, however, as just said, the standpoint is reversed, and we look at the matter from the Bible's own point of view, things appear very differently. Assume, for instance, what is the Bible's own assertion, that God did really call this man Abraham, and make His covenant with him, —assume that this was a grave, serious transaction, of the utmost moment to Abraham himself, to his posterity, and to mankind, and was felt to be so,—assume that it was required of him that he should diligently train his children and his household after him in the knowledge of it,[1]—then, can it be doubted that the utmost pains would be taken to preserve and transmit faithful accounts of these doings, till such time as a permanent record could be made of them; and does not the patriarchal history, with its rich

[1] Cf. Gen. xviii. 18, 19.

biographies, and impregnation with covenant-ideas, present precisely the character we might expect in such a record? Assume, again, that the Exodus really took place in some such way as the Bible relates,—that Jehovah, the covenant-keeping God of the fathers, really revealed Himself to Moses, and really brought the people out of Egypt with wonderful manifestations of His power and grace,—we have only to ask the question, Could the people ever forget it? to see how impossible is the supposition. We shall then cease to wonder at the graphic narratives which have come down to us from that soul-stirring time, and will be ready to see in them a faithful reflection of the consciousness of the period.

All this, naturally, is folly to the newer critical school; for does it not imply those higher religious ideas, and that "familiar intercourse of the Deity with the patriarchs,"[1] which Kuenen tells us are conclusive marks of the un-historical character of the narratives? We are not without hope that a different impression may be produced by a candid examination of the grounds of his objections.

The foregoing, it should be noticed, yields us the right point of view for answering the question sometimes asked —In what sense do we speak of "history" in these early parts of the Bible? So far we must agree with the critics when they remind us that the history in the Bible is *religious* history—that is, not bare narratives of outward occurrences, as an ancient chronicler, or modern newspaper reporter, might set them down, but history written from a religious standpoint, for purposes of edification, and reflecting in its story the impression on the mind of the beholder and on the writer, as well as the objective fact. As respects the early periods, it follows from what has been said, and is evident of itself, that what we have to do with is, for the most part, not contemporary narration, but history in the form of *carefully preserved tradition*,—not, indeed, as the critics will have it, mere floating folk-lore, but sacred tradition of real events and transactions in the lives of real men, and of God's revelations and dealings with them—tradition on which we can rely as faithfully conveying to us the contents of God's message to them and to ourselves — yet still *tradition*, having the rounded,

[1] *Rel. of Israel*, i. p. 108. See above, p. 60.

dramatic character which narratives naturally assume as the result of repeated telling,[1] and recorded in the form in which they finally reached the literary narrator. Such transmission may not exclude a measure of "idealisation," and reflection of later ideas and conditions; but this, we are persuaded, to a far smaller extent than many—even believing writers—suppose. The view of the history thus indicated we now proceed to vindicate.

II. Theory that Patriarchs were not Individuals, but "Personifications"

An interesting light is thrown on the method of unproved assumption and arbitrary hypothesis by which, as we think, much of the work of this newer criticism is done, in what Kuenen adduces as his "principal cause of hesitation" in accepting the patriarchal narratives, viz., that the actors in them "have one characteristic in common—they are all *progenitors of tribes.*" He infers from this "that the narratives in Genesis present us, not with real historical personages, but with personifications."[2] Since the days of Ewald the theory of personification has been a favourite one with critical writers, though generally there has gone with it, as in the case of Ewald himself, the recognition of a basis of real personal history in the narratives. Wellhausen, Stade, and the more thorough-going members of their school, however, make no such reservations. With them all historical reality is given up,—logically enough, for, if individual progenitors of tribes are admitted *at all*, a main foundation of the theory is destroyed,—and only collective names, and reflections of tribal relations and characteristics remain.[3] Wellhausen actually thinks that Abraham was a compara-

[1] Dr. John Smith, in his *Integrity of Scripture*, p. 38, speaks of the Pentateuch, which he upholds as "a credible and substantially contemporary record of a true revelation of God to Moses, and through Moses to Israel," as "incorporating the sacred family traditions of earlier revelations."

[2] *Rel. of Israel*, i. pp. 109–112.

[3] Cf. Kuenen, *ut supra*; Wellhausen, *Hist. of Israel*, pp. 318 ff.; Stade, *Geschichte*, pp. 28 ff.; Gunkel, *Genesis*, Introd.; Guthe, art. "Israel," *Ency. Bib.* (also arts. on Patriarchs); Cornill, *Hist. of Israel*; H. P. Smith, *O.T. Hist.* pp. 38 ff., etc. For criticism of the theory, cf. König's *Neueste Prinzipien*, pp. 35 ff.; Köhler, art. "Abraham" in Hauck's *Realencyc.*; Robertson's *Early Rel.* pp. 121 ff., etc.

tively late "free creation of unconscious art";[1] others can persuade themselves that even Amos and Hosea did not regard the patriarchs as individual persons.[2] It is well that Kuenen should tell us that this is his strongest proof, for, in testing his chain in its firmest link, we are better enabled to judge of its strength as a whole.

The theory, then, is, that the patriarchs were not actual individuals, but "personifications" of tribes. To the critic's mind nothing could be simpler or more demonstrable. "To the Oriental," says Professor H. P. Smith, "it is natural to speak of the clan as an individual. . . . The common method of our Hebrew writers was to personify clans, tribes, nations, or geographical divisions, and treat them as individuals."[3] No shade of doubt is held to rest on this conclusion. "What interests us here is the fact that the patriarchs cannot be taken as individuals. If individuals Reuben, Gad, and Judah never existed, it is plain that individuals Jacob, Esau, and Abraham cannot have any more substantial reality. We have to do here with figures of the poetic or legend-building imagination."[4] Let us look at the reasons by which these confident assertions are supported.

1. The theory has its starting-point in the statement that the *names of the patriarchs* in the history are not individual, but tribal. But this, to begin with, is only partially true. Of the majority of the progenitors of tribes (*e.g.*, Dan, Gad, Naphtali), little is recorded save the names; of a few (Judah, Simeon, Reuben), only special incidents; of the three great patriarchs—Abraham, Isaac, and Jacob—on the other hand, and of Joseph, we have full and detailed biographies. But, as has often been pointed out, neither Abraham nor Isaac[5] gave their names to tribes; Joseph, also, did not do so directly, but only through his sons, Ephraim and Manasseh. Lot is not the name of any tribe, though this "weak-kneed saint," as Wellhausen calls him,

[1] *Hist. of Israel*, p. 320.

[2] H. P. Smith says: "Amos and Hosea at anyrate had little idea of the patriarchs as individual men."—*O.T. Hist.* p. 38. So Guthe, etc.

[3] *Ibid.* pp. 38, 39.
[4] *Ibid.* p. 42.

[5] In Amos vii. 16 the designation "house of Isaac" is used, but for the whole nation, and plainly with reference to the Biblical statements as to the relation of Isaac to Jacob. No light is thrown from the history of the tribes on the origin of the name.

is the father of the Moabites and Ammonites. Neither does Esau give his personal name to his descendants, the Edomites. Even of Jacob, whose names (Jacob, Israel) became, quite naturally and reasonably on the Biblical view, those of the nation, it is to be noted that he is regarded, not as the founder of a special tribe, but as the progenitor of the individual tribes from whose union the nation was formed. His name and character, therefore, can hardly have been a mere abstraction from the nation collectively. There seems, indeed, to be now evidence that both his name, and those of Abraham and Joseph (with Ishmael, and others) were proper names in use in Babylonia and Palestine from early times.[1]

Abraham, as might be expected, is a special difficulty to the theory. He is, as Wellhausen owns, "a little difficult to interpret."[2] We have just seen that his name is not a designation of either tribe or nation: neither is Isaac's. The critic is therefore driven, as above hinted, to suggest that he is "a free creation of unconscious art";[3] later than Isaac.[4] But then how explain these long and detailed biographies, which bear so inimitable a stamp of reality, yet have so little to suggest the reflection of the features of a later age? For here again the theory is in difficulty. "It is remarkable," confesses Wellhausen, "that the heroes of Israelitish legend show so little taste for war, and in this point they seem to be scarcely a true reflection of the character of the Israelites, as known from their history. . . . The patriarchs, Abraham, Isaac, and Jacob, are all peace-loving shepherds, inclined to live quietly beside their tents, anxious to steer clear of strife and clamour. . . . Brave and manly they are not,[5] but they are good fathers of families,"[6] etc. There are evidently knotty problems still

[1] In a list of Thothmes III. (*c.* 1480 B.C.) there occur the names Jacob-el and Joseph-el (the latter doubted by some), as those of places in Central Palestine. Much earlier, in Babylonian contract tablets (*c.* 2200 B.C.), are found the names Jacob, Jacob-el, and the name Abe-ramu, similar to Abraham. See below, Chap. XI. pp. 409–10.

[2] *Hist. of Israel*, p. 320. The idea that Abraham was the name of a "god" has been very generally abandoned, but is now revived by Winckler; see above, p. 59.

[3] *Ibid.*

[4] Professor Robertson pertinently remarks: "One would like to know how much of the story of Isaac, as a popular legend, would be comprehensible without reference to that of Abraham."—*Rel. of Israel*, p. 125.

[5] See below, p. 109.

[6] *Hist. of Israel*, pp. 320–21.

unsolved on the theory that the history is simply a form of "ethnographic genealogy."

2. A special proof of the personifying tendencies of the Hebrew writers is sought in the forms of some of the *Scripture genealogies.* These, it is pointed out, are frequently ethnographical, not individual. A familiar example is the "table of nations" in Gen. x. When, *e.g.*, one reads there: "The sons of Ham; Cush, and Mizraim, and Phut, and Canaan. . . . And Mizraim begat Ludim, and Anamim, and Lehabim, and Naphtuhim. . . . And Canaan begat Sidon his first-born, and Heth, and the Jebusite, and the Amorite, and the Girgashite,"[1] etc., everyone readily perceives, that not individual persons, but nations or tribes, are meant. The genealogies bear their ethnographic character upon their face. But all genealogies are not of this nature; and the existence of such tables no more proves that Abraham and Sarah, Isaac and Rebekah, Esau and Jacob, Joseph and his brethren, Moses and Aaron, were not real persons, than it proves, say, that Elkanah was not the father of Samuel, or Eli of Hophni and Phinehas, or Jesse of David, but that in all these cases we are dealing only with tribal abstractions. We do not suppose, *e.g.*, that when we read, "Salmon begat Boaz, and Boaz begat Obed, and Obed begat Jesse, and Jesse begat David,"[2] we have before us a scrap of "ethnographic genealogy," because elsewhere it is said that Canaan begat the Jebusite and the Amorite. When we find richly-developed biographies like those of Abraham and Jacob attached to such names as "Mizraim," or "Ludim," or "the Girgashite," it will be time to consider the analogy.[3]

3. The crowning support for the personification theory is sought by Kuenen, Stade, Guthe, and others, in *an assumed law of the growth of societies.* "New nations," Stade says, "never originate through rapid increase of a tribe; new tribes never through derivation from a family propagating itself abundantly through several generations."[4] To which König aptly replies: "Often as I have read these sweeping statements, I have always missed one trifle: I never found a proof of this thesis."[5] Such a proof, in fact, is not to be

[1] Gen. x. 6, 13, 15, 16. [2] Ruth iv. 21, 22.
[3] See further illustration in Note A—König on the Personification Theory.
[4] *Geschichte*, i. p. 28. Cf. Kuenen's *Rel. of Israel*, i. p. 110.
[5] *Neueste Prinzipien*, p. 36.

found; for none can be offered which does not, as in the present case, assume the thing to be proved. As a general *dictum* on the origin of society, its truth would be disputed by many far better entitled to be listened to on the subject than Stade. H. S. Maine, for instance, in his book on *Ancient Law: its Connection with the Early History of Society*, maintains the directly opposite thesis. To him the "patriarchal theory" of the origin of society is the one which best accords with all the facts. Jurisprudence, he affirms, is full of the clearest indications that society in primitive times was not a collection of individuals, but *an aggregation of families.* "The unit of an ancient Society was the Family. . . . The elementary group is the Family, connected by common subjection to the highest male ascendant. The Aggregation of Families forms the Gens or House. The Aggregation of Houses makes the Tribe. The Aggregation of Tribes constitutes the Commonwealth."[1] Allowing, however, what is probably the truth, that society does not follow everywhere the same law of growth, we are still in no way shut up to the conclusion that it was not thus that the Hebrew nation, under its peculiar conditions of call and destiny, did develop. The development from the one chosen individual into the many,[2] in fulfilment of promise, is the most natural thing imaginable, provided the nation's own account of its antecedents and mission to the world is accepted. The history here is in complete harmony with itself. From the earliest period to which we can trace back the Hebrew tribes, they are "the sons of Israel," and of what that title meant they believed themselves to have the clearest historical recollection. Why should that recollection not be trusted, and designations like "house of Jacob," "house of Isaac," "seed of Abraham," not be allowed to mean what they obviously suggest, and were always believed to mean—that the people were historically descended from these patriarchs, instead of being twisted into proofs that these progenitors of the race never existed?

The result to which we are thus far led is that the newer criticism is unsuccessful in its attempt to make out the patriarchs to be "not persons, but personifications." The

[1] *Ancient Law*, pp. 126, 128.

[2] Isa. li. 1, 2: "When he was but one, I called him, and I blessed him, and made him many."

patriarchs, in the Biblical view, are *both* persons and progenitors of tribes, and there is no necessary contradiction between the two things. It is to be anticipated that ancestral traits will reappear in the descendants, and it is not inadmissible to suppose that characteristics of the descendants, to some degree, will be found, designedly or unconsciously, reflected in the portraiture of the progenitor —as, for instance, in the cases of Ishmael and Esau.[1] In this sense there may be an element of "idealisation" in the narratives, as there is, in fact, in every good painting, or every good biography, of a person who has become historical. This does not detract from the fidelity of the history, but enhances it by interpreting its inner significance, and investing it with the charm of literary art.

III. Witness of Israel's National Consciousness: The Patriarchs

There is another branch of the critical method on which it is proper that something should now be said. This relates to the point just touched on—*the testimony of the national consciousness of Israel to its own past.*

It was seen above that exception is taken to the high religious ideas ascribed to the patriarchs, and to the stories of the divine communications made to them. The question of the early religion of Israel will be investigated in next chapter. Meanwhile it may be permitted to remark on Kuenen's *dictum* that "at first the religion of Israel was polytheism," that *that* can hardly be a sure result of criticism which many of the most distinguished critics of both past and present times energetically repudiate. Ewald was free enough in his treatment of the history, but he had no doubt of the existence of the patriarchs, or that they "thought and spoke monotheistically."[2] Dillmann, and Delitzsch, and Riehm were critics, but none of them would assent to the propositions of the Kuenen school about the religion of early Israel. As little would König, or Kittel, or Baethgen, or Klostermann, or Oettli, or the late Dr. A. B. Davidson, or many others that might be named. Dillmann may be quoted in this connection as an example. "If anyone," he says, "desires to maintain that this representation rests

[1] Cf. Gen. xvi. 11, 12; xxvii. 40.

[2] *Hist. of Israel*, i. p. 320.

only on an idealising conception of later writers, and is not to be accepted as historical, it must be contended in opposition that not merely Genesis, but the whole Old Testament, speaks of a covenant, of a peculiar relation in which God stood with the fathers, Abraham, Isaac, and Jacob; that Moses attached himself with his work to the God of the fathers; that without this attachment his work would be incomprehensible; that, therefore, even if Genesis had said nothing on the subject, we should be compelled to postulate a certain acquaintance of these fathers with the living God, a higher faith in God."[1]

This deep consciousness which the Israelites possessed throughout their history of their origin from Abraham, Isaac, and Jacob, and of the peculiar favour of God to these fathers of their race in making His covenant with them, might be deemed an irrefragable argument for the truth of the Biblical representations. So in reality it is; but it is essential to the modern critical view that the argument should be deprived of its force, and the method by which this is sought to be accomplished is an excellent example of the arbitrariness we complain of in the critical procedure. The aim is to show that the references to the patriarchs and their doings—even to Moses—are *so late* as to deprive them of all value, and the means employed for this end is the summary excision from the text of all passages that speak to the contrary as later additions. It is a method beautiful in its simplicity, easily worked, and, when applied with sufficient courage, as it is in both history and prophets, never fails in silencing all opposing witness.[2]

1. We begin by giving two examples of the application of this method to the *prophets*. "A striking fact is," says Professor H. P. Smith, "that none of the prophets allude to Abraham till we come to Ezekiel. The weight of this in an inquiry into the historicity of the patriarchs can hardly be

[1] *Alttest. Theol.* p. 82; cf. pp. 414–15. Cf. Klostermann's *Geschichte des Volkes Israel*, pp. 28 ff. Klostermann rejects as an "absolutely irrational opinion" the view that the patriarchs are mythical forms, and contends that only grounds of real tradition could have led the people to see, not in Moses, who actually formed them into a nation, but in fathers, sharply distinguished from Moses, and living in quite other times and relations, the founders of their monotheistic religion.

[2] It need scarcely be said that our remarks are not intended to apply to soberly-directed attempts to correct errors or corruptions in the Hebrew text, which reliable evidence shows to be really such. See Note H to Chap. X.

over-estimated."[1] Wellhausen, who, as we saw, is disposed to regard Abraham as "a free creation of unconscious art," similarly writes: "The later development of the legend shows a manifest tendency to make Abraham the patriarch *par excellence*, and cast the others into the shade. In the earlier literature, on the other hand, Isaac is mentioned even by Amos. Abraham first appears in Isa. xl.–lxvi."[2] The two statements, it may be observed, are not quite in harmony, for Ezekiel, in which the one critic allows a reference to Abraham, is at least earlier than the date assumed by Wellhausen for Isa. xl.–lxvi., where, on his showing, Abraham first appears. The passage in Ezekiel (chap. xxxiii. 24) reads: "Abraham was one, and he inherited the land." Even on the meagre footing of these passages, it might be urged, we would not be without important witnesses to the singular place occupied by Abraham in the Israelitish tradition.

But are the facts as stated? If we take the Hebrew text as it stands, they certainly are not. We go back to Jeremiah, and there read, chap. xxxiii. 26: "I will take of his seed to be rulers over the seed of Abraham, Isaac, and Jacob." We go back a stage further, to the *earlier* Isaiah, and there read, chap. xxix. 22: "Jehovah who redeemed Abraham." We turn to Isaiah's contemporary, Micah, and read, chap. vii. 20: "Thou wilt perform the truth to Jacob, and the mercy to Abraham, which Thou hast sworn to our fathers from the days of old." Here, then, are passages which directly contradict the categorical assertions of the critics: how are they dealt with? In the simplest possible fashion, by denying that they should be there. Thus, to *his* statement that no prophet prior to Ezekiel alludes to Abraham, Professor H. P. Smith calmly appends the footnote: "The present text shows two passages, Micah vii. 20 and Jer. xxxiii. 26, but both are confessedly (?) late additions to the prophetic text."[3] Wellhausen is equally summary:

[1] *O.T. Hist.* p. 49; cf. p. 38. [2] *Hist. of Israel*, p. 310.

[3] As above. The whole passage Jer. xxxiii. 14–26 is omitted in the LXX, which otherwise takes extensive liberties with the text. But no good ground exists for its rejection from the Hebrew text. Graf defends it, and Ewald says: "Nothing is so perverse and groundless as to find in this passage, or generally, in chaps. xxx.–xxxiii., additions by a later prophet."—*Die Propheten*, ii. p. 268. The remaining passages are in the LXX as well as in the Hebrew.

"Micah vii. 20," he says, "belongs to the exile, and the words 'who redeemed Abraham' in Isa. xxix. 22 are not genuine: they have no possible position in the sentence." To which it may be as summarily replied, that there is no convincing reason for changing any of the passages,—if reason at all, except in the critic's own caprice. Even Kuenen, in his *Religion of Israel*, accepts as genuine the passages to which Wellhausen takes exception.[1] Gunkel, one of the newest and most radical of critics, enters a much-needed protest against the whole system of procedure. "The author," he says, "at this point cannot conceal his conviction that the reigning school of literary criticism is all too zealous to explain as not genuine the passages which do not exactly fit in with its construction of the history, or which are hard to be understood by the modern investigator, and that a powerful reaction must follow on the period of this criticism."[2]

2. It is now to be remarked, however, that even if the critics were right in their assertion that there are no express allusions to Abraham in the prophets prior to the exile, *no such dire results* would follow for the historicity of the patriarchs as the authorities we have quoted imagine. Direct allusions in the prophets are, after all, only a fraction of the evidence, and hardly affect the force of the argument from the national recollection of Israel. In the first place, it is to be observed that where allusions to Abraham *do* occur, it is always as to a person well known, and enshrined in the highest honour in the memory of the people. It is no stranger that is being introduced to them. Israel is "the seed of Abraham My friend."[3] They are exhorted to look to Abraham their father, and to Sarah that bare them, and are reminded for their encouragement, how, when he was but one, God called him, and blessed him, and increased him.[4] He was one, and he inherited the land.[5] It is declared that God will perform the truth to Jacob, and the mercy to Abraham, which He had sworn to their fathers from the days of old.[6] But further, these patriarchs appear

[1] *Rel. of Israel*, i. p. 101. Another historical passage in Micah, chap. vi. 3, 4, declared by some to be late, is also accepted by Kuenen in this work (p. 113).

[2] *Genesis*, p. 113. Gunkel's own methods, as will be seen after, are sufficiently arbitrary.

[3] Isa. xli. 8; cf. lxiii. 16.

[4] Isa. li. 1, 2.

[5] Ezek. xxxiii. 24.

[6] Mic. vii. 20.

as figures in a connected history, and whatever in the prophets implies acquaintance with *part* of that history may fairly be regarded as implying knowledge of the rest, at least in its main features. The admitted allusions to Isaac and Jacob, for instance, and to incidents in the life of the latter,[1] inferentially imply some knowledge of Abraham as well.

But this is by no means the whole. Nothing is surer in criticism, as was shown in the last chapter, than that, by the time of Amos and Hosea—*i.e.*, long before the time of the exile—written histories of the patriarchal period existed, and were in circulation, embodying the current tradition of the nation,[2] in which Abraham plays so prominent a part. "When stories were told of Isaac and Ishmael, and Lot and Esau," says Wellhausen himself, speaking of a time when, as he thinks, the stories only circulated orally, "everyone knew at once who these personages were, and how they were related to Israel, and to one another."[3] Is it credible that the same should not be true of Abraham? What stories of Isaac, or Ishmael, or Lot, could be in currency in the days of the monarchy, which did not imply a knowledge of that patriarch? Or what stories could be told of Joseph which did not bring in Jacob, and Judah, and Reuben, and Benjamin, and the patriarchs generally?[4] Then what of the Book of Deuteronomy?—a prophetic book, on the theory of the critics, yet based upon, and saturated with allusions to, this whole earlier history, including the Abrahamic covenant and promises.[5] Is not this book before Ezekiel, or Isa. xl.–lxvi., as the critics date the latter? What, in view of such facts, becomes of Professor H. P. Smith's "can hardly be over-estimated" in relation to the historicity of the

[1] *E.g.*, Amos vii. 9, 16 (Isaac); Hos. xii. 3–5, 12.

[2] Professor W. R. Smith says that the story of the patriarchs "is still recorded to us as it lived in the mouths of the people. . . We still read it very much as it was read or told in the house of Joseph in the days of Amos and Hosea."—*Prophets*, pp. 116, 117.

[3] *Hist. of Israel*, p. 333.

[4] Professor Bennett says: "The story of Joseph may be taken as the account of events which really happened to a historical individual, Joseph, who really existed. Such history might be supposed to be accurate in every detail by those who held the strictest theory of verbal inspiration."—*Genesis*, p. 47. But how much of the remaining history is involved in that of Joseph? If he is historical, Jacob, Judah, Reuben, etc., are no longer "personifications."

[5] Deut. i. 8, vi. 10, etc.

patriarchs,—because, as he alleges, nothing is heard of Abraham before Ezekiel? Does not the use of such language recoil rather on himself as showing his singular lack of perspective in dealing with the subject?

IV. Moses and the Exodus

To the testimony which the prophets and related writings bear to the period of the patriarchs falls to be added that of the later historical books, and of the psalms.[1] Here, however, we prefer to cast a glance at the *Mosaic* period, to which objections of the same kind are made, and to which the same general considerations, based on the immovable certainty of the consciousness of the nation as to its own past, apply. Attention is naturally concentrated in this connection on two things—the personality of Moses, and the great deliverance of the Exodus.

1. If there is one personage in Hebrew history about whose character and doings it might be supposed without doubt that every Israelite had some knowledge, that person is *Moses.* Yet in regard to Moses also we have occasionally the suggestion that the earlier prophets knew little or nothing about him;[2] and particularly it is argued that only in the latest period is he definitely connected with a code of laws. Thus in an authoritative work we read: "The indications of subsequent literature suggest that Moses was only gradually connected by tradition with the production of a continuous body of legislation. . . . Even to the author of Isa. lxiii. 11 Moses is the heroic leader under divine guidance to whom Israel owed its liberty rather than its laws. Malachi is the first of the prophets to refer to a Mosaic code (iv. 4)."[3]

This appears to us, in the light of admitted facts, to be remarkable reasoning. We go back again to the Book

[1] Pss. xlvii. 9, cv. 9, 42, etc. On the Psalms, see Chap. XII.

[2] Mic. vi. 4, with its explicit reference to Moses, Aaron, and Miriam, is declared to be an interpolation. Ghillany, an older writer, cannot find Moses named in the prophets before Malachi. Cf. König's *Hauptprobleme*, pp. 15, 16. Yet besides Mic. vi. 4, which Kuenen accepts as genuine, there is Isa. lxiii. 11, and the reference to Moses in Hos. xii. 13. Even Kautzsch, however, who, on the whole, stands up for a higher conception of Moses, arbitrarily declares the passage in Hosea to be an interpolation ("Rel. of Israel," *Dict.* p. 625).

[3] Carpenter, Oxf. *Hex.* i. p. 19.

of Deuteronomy, alleged by critics to be a work of "prophets," which, in any case, came to light in the days of Josiah. This book, in point of form, is a repromulgation by Moses in the steppes of Moab of the commandments, statutes, and judgments received by him thirty-eight years before from God in Horeb, and by him then communicated to the people. In it, it will hardly be denied, Moses appears pre-eminently as the lawgiver. But the book itself, it is now well recognised, presupposes the older code of laws in the "Book of the Covenant" of Ex. xx.–xxiii. Moreover, not only are the laws Mosaic, but both the "Book of the Covenant," and the "law" of Deuteronomy, are declared to have been *written* by Moses.[1] What then does the writer of the above-quoted passage mean by saying that "for the pre-exilian seers there was no fixed and definite 'law' recorded in precise and definite form"?[2] Was Deuteronomy not a law-book? The Mosaic authorship of Deuteronomy and of the "Book of the Covenant" may be disputed; but can it be denied that "tradition" at any rate had by that time come to regard Moses as a lawgiver, and in the fullest and most "definite" way ascribed the laws of the nation to him, or to God through him? There is the further argument from the JE histories. Already in these histories, which antecede the time of written prophecy, and extend, in the view of the critics, to the conquest, there is embodied the whole history of the Exodus, of the lawgiving at Sinai, of the covenant, of the events of the wilderness, of the entrance into Canaan. How then could any Israelite or prophet of that or any subsequent time possibly be ignorant of the *rôle* of Moses as a lawgiver? How could the writer of Isa. lxiii. 11 be ignorant of it? It is amazing that the critics do not see more clearly the force of their own admissions in these matters. If Deuteronomy was promulgated in the reign of Josiah; if the JE histories existed a century and a half earlier; it is a strange inconsequence to talk of the paucity of references in the prophets before Malachi as showing that Moses was not

[1] Ex. xxiv. 4; Deut. xxxi. 24. See below, Chap. VIII. pp. 262 ff.

[2] As above. Kautzsch says: "Over against this [scanty mention] must be set the fact that, throughout the Old Testament, *all* the various legislations . . . are said to have been introduced, and in part even written down by him."—"Rel. of Israel," *Dict.* p. 626.

connected in the Israelitish mind with the work of legislation.[1]

The basis of the argument is greatly strengthened, if, from the references to legislation, we extend our view to the related history. Here, again, it is to be remembered, the history goes in a piece. The people who knew of the Exodus, of the Red Sea deliverance, and of the wilderness journeyings, knew also of Sinai, of the covenant of their nation with God, and of the commandments and laws on which the covenant was based. It seems futile to contend, with Professor W. R. Smith, that "the early history and the prophets do not use the Sinaitic legislation as the basis of their conception of the relation of Jehovah to Israel, but habitually go back to the deliverance from Egypt, and from it pass directly to the wilderness wanderings and the conquest of Canaan."[2] The Levitical legislation, if that is meant, the history and prophets do not use,—*no* part of Scripture uses the Levitical law as the basis of God's relation to Israel,—but it is hard to see how anyone can imagine that either prophets or people could be familiar with the Exodus and the wilderness wanderings, and leave out of view, or be indifferent to, that which forms the kernel of the whole history,—the covenant which God made with the nation through Moses; when, as Jeremiah says, He "brought them out of the land of Egypt, from the iron furnace, saying, Obey My voice, and do them [the words of the covenant], according to all which I command you";[3] or when, as Hosea expresses it, He espoused the nation to Himself in the wilderness, in the days of its youth.[4] Are we to suppose that the prophets (even Jeremiah) were ignorant of the recapitulation of the law of Horeb in Deuteronomy?

2. It is true, nevertheless, that the great fact in which the consciousness of Israel ever rooted itself, as that which first gave the nation its freedom, and *made* it a nation, was the ***Exodus***, with which is constantly associated the deliverance at the Red Sea. It was remarked at the beginning that we have only to reflect on the nature of such an event as the

[1] The position of Moses as legislator is further discussed in Chap. VI. Cf. pp. 151 ff.

[2] *Prophets*, p. 111.

[3] Jer. xi. 4.

[4] Hos. ii. 15; cf. viii. 1. The passages are among those cited by Professor Smith himself. See Note B on the Covenant with Israel.

Exodus to see that, if it really happened, it could never again be forgotten by the people whose redemption it was. Some things in a nation's history may be forgotten; of others the memory is indelible. Could the English people ever forget the Normans and the Conquest; the Scottish, Bannockburn or Flodden, or the events of their Reformation; Americans, Bunker's Hill or the Declaration of Independence? Yet these are small matters compared with what the Exodus, and the events which followed it, were to the Israelites. When we turn, accordingly, to the poetical and prophetical books of the Old Testament, we find that, amidst all the vicissitudes in their fortunes, the memory of the Exodus, with its attendant circumstances, never was obliterated, but remained fresh and green in the minds of the people as long as their national life lasted. In song, and psalm, and prophecy, the echoes of this wonderful deliverance in Egypt and at the Red Sea ring down their history till its close.[1] The same difficulty meets us here, indeed, as before, that the historical and prophetical books are not allowed to be used as witnesses till they have been critically adjusted, and, in the multitude of editors and redactors among whom their contents are parcelled out, it is never hard to find a way of getting rid of an inconvenient testimony. Apart, however, from the direct narratives, which, in their freshness, force, and dramatic power, speak so unmistakably to the liveliness of the impression under which they were composed, the literature *en bloc* is a witness to the vivid recollection of the essential facts. An old monument is the Song of Miriam at the Red Sea, in Ex. xv., the genuineness of which there are no good grounds for disputing.[2] Joshua and Samuel go back on these facts in rehearsing the great deeds of God for their nation.[3]

[1] Cf. Ex. xv.; Josh. xxiv. 4–7; 1 Sam. xii. 6 ff.; 1 Kings viii. 16, 51–53; Pss. xliv. 1, lxxvii. 12–20, lxxviii., etc.; Amos ii. 9, 10; Hos. xi. 1; xii. 13; Isa. li. 9, 10; Jer. ii. 6, etc.; Deut. iv. 34; xvi. 3, 6, 12; xxvi. 5, etc.

[2] Dr. Driver says: "Probably the greater part of the Song is Mosaic, and the modification or expansion is limited to the closing verses; for the general style is antique, and the triumphant tone which pervades it is just such as might naturally have been inspired by the event which it celebrates."—*Introd.* p. 30.

[3] References as above. Josh. xxiv. is usually ascribed by the critics to E, with later touches. 1 Sam. xii. 6 ff. is attributed by Kautzsch to his Saul-Source in the tenth or ninth century B.C. H. P. Smith, on the other

Solomon dwells on them in his speech and prayer at the dedication of the temple.[1] They appear as the motive to obedience in the Decalogue,[2] in the discourses and legislation in the Book of Deuteronomy, and in the Levitical Code known to critics as the "Law of Holiness,"[3] assigned by very many to an early date. Amos, Hosea, Jeremiah, and the other prophets appeal to them; and they inspire many of the psalms. These recollections of the nation we can fully trust. "No nation," as Professor Kautzsch says, "ever gratuitously invented the report that it had been ignominiously enslaved by another; none ever forgot the days of its deliverance. And so through all the centuries there survived in Israel the inextinguishable recollection that it was once delivered out of Egypt, the house of bondage, by Jahweh, the God of its fathers, with a strong hand and outstretched arm; that specially at the passage of the Red Sea it experienced the mighty protection of its God."[4] This knowledge dwells, not as a vague reminiscence, but as a strong, definite, historical assurance, in the heart of the nation, and it is as inconceivable that Israel should be mistaken about it, as that a grown man should forget the scenes of his boyhood, or episodes of his early life that burned themselves into his very soul.

The confidence which the dramatic vividness and tone of reality in the Mosaic history beget in us is not dissipated by the often far-fetched criticism to which its details are subjected by writers like Colenso, in search of arithmetical and other "contradictions" and "impossibilities." This criticism will come before us for consideration after;[5] meanwhile it would be well if those who urge these objections to the

hand, holds it to be exilian. Driver, following Budde, ranks it as pre-Deuteronomic, etc. See below, p. 386.

[1] Kautzsch says that "in his speech dedicatory of the temple, 1 Kings viii. 12 ff., we have an authentic monument of the time of Solomon." He apparently attributes, however, vers. 14–43 to the "Deuteronomist" (*Lit. of O.T.*, pp. 12, 241). The LXX derives vers. 12, 13 from "the book of the Song."

[2] Ex. xx. 2; Deut. v. 6, 15.

[3] Lev. xix. 36; xxii. 33; xxiii. 43; xxv. 55, etc. On this Code see below, pp. 308 ff.

[4] *Lit. of O.T.*, p. 9; cf. his "Rel. of Israel," *Dict.* p. 631. It is the more unaccountable that, acknowledging the essential facts, Kautzsch should sit so loosely to the history as given. He rejects, *e.g.*, the upbringing of Moses at the court of Pharaoh.

[5] See below, Chap. X. pp. 362 ff.

truth of the history would reflect a little on the difficulties which, on the other side, attach to their own too hasty rejection of it. After all, these things which the Mosaic books record were not, any more than the events in Christ's life, to which Paul appealed before Agrippa, "done in a corner."[1] They were public events, in the fullest sense of the term. Does it involve no strain on belief to say that an event so extraordinary as, in any case, the Exodus of Israel from Egypt must be admitted to have been,[2] happened in the full light of one of the most brilliant civilisations of the time, and yet that the people who came out, with a leader like Moses at their head, did not know, or could not remember, or could ever possibly forget, *how* it happened? The Israelites themselves, as we have seen, did not believe they did not know. They had but one story to give of it all down their history—the same story which, in circumstantial detail, is embodied in these old books. If this is not how the Israelites got out of Egypt, will the critic, in turn, furnish us with some plausible explanation of how they *did* get out? It is here as in the discussion of the origins of Christianity. It is not enough to discredit the Gospels and the Acts; the critic must be prepared to show how, if these are rejected, Christianity *did* originate. So, in the case of the Exodus, it is not enough to discredit the one history we have of that event; the critic has to show how, if the whole history was different from that which we possess, it came about that no echo of it was preserved in Israel, and that this lifelike, vivid, detailed narration came to take its place. It is admitted, with few extreme exceptions, that the people of Israel were once in Egypt; that they were in bitter bondage; that Egypt at the time was ruled over by one or other of its powerful monarchs; that they came out, not by war, but peaceably; that they were at least tolerably numerous, with women, children, and cattle; that they found their way, under pursuit,—so Wellhausen allows,—across the Red Sea. Is it unfair to ask—How did they make their way out? Theories of course there are: ingenuity, when freed from

[1] Acts xxvi. 26.

[2] Cf. Wellhausen, *Hist. of Israel*, pp. 432–33: "His design was aided in a wholly unlooked-for way, by a marvellous occurrence, quite beyond his control, and which no sagacity could possibly have foreseen."

the necessity of respecting facts, is equal to anything. But have they warrant, or even verisimilitude?[1] It is easy to pen sentences about an "escape" of nomadic tribes on the border, in whom the despotic policy of the Pharaoh had awakened "the innate love of freedom";[2] or to hazard the conjecture that there was a slipping away of the tribes one by one;[3] but such speculations, alongside of which the Egyptian story of an expulsion of lepers is respectable, conflict with tradition, and break on the hard facts of the situation. For the Israelites were no loose conglomeration of tribes on the border.[4] According to every testimony, they occupied a wide territory, dwelt in houses, were the victims of a systematic oppression,[5] were engaged in forced labour, were broken-spirited, under strict *surveillance* of tyrannical overseers, etc. How, in these circumstances, was furtive escape possible? Where is there analogy for such a horde of "runaway slaves" finding their way out of bondage, and defying the power of a mighty king to bring them back? It is a simple method to reject history as we have it, and evolve hypotheses, but the process is not always as satisfactory as it is simple. There is need in this case for the "strong hand" and "stretched-out arm."

V. Internal Character of Narratives a Guarantee for Historicity

Attention may now be given to the *internal character* of the narratives, and to the bearings of this on their credibility.

It sounds paradoxical, yet it is the case, that internal evidence of truthfulness is sometimes such as to outweigh in value even external evidence, and to support confidence in a narrative where external evidence is lacking or disputed. Had we, for instance, no external evidence for the Gospels,—did they come to us for the first time from

[1] See Note C on Theories of the Exodus.

[2] Thus Kuenen; cf. Colenso, *Pent.* Pt. vi. p. 600.

[3] This theory is thought to find support in indications of the presence of the tribes of Asher (W. Max Müller; cf. Hommel, *Heb. Trad.* p. 228) and Judah (Jastrow) in Palestine prior to the Exodus. The facts probably really point to an earlier date for the Exodus. Cf. below, Chap. XI. pp. 422 ff.

[4] Cf. above, p. 79.

[5] Note the recurrence of "house of bondage" in history, law, prophecy.

unknown hands,—it might still be possible to argue that the holy and gracious Personage portrayed in them was no invention, but a drawing from a divine Original. In like manner it may be contended that there are internal marks which support our confidence in the patriarchal and Mosaic histories, apart from all reasoning as to the age of documents, or mode of transmission of the traditions. Something has already been said of the teleological character of the narratives; the argument may, however, now be widened to include a number of other features, hardly less remarkable. We draw our illustrations chiefly from the patriarchal age.

1. A first question relates to the *general credibility* of the patriarchal narratives. Discussion of alleged historical and chronological "contradictions" can stand over; but what of the credibility of the narratives as a whole? Here we willingly avail ourselves of the well-weighed judgment of a moderate critic like Dr. Driver. "The patriarchal narratives," Dr. Driver says, "are marked by great sobriety of statement and representation. There are no incredible marvels, no fantastic extravagances, no surprising miracles; the miraculous hardly extends beyond manifestations and communications of the Deity to the earlier patriarchs, and in the case of Joseph there are not even these:[1] the events of his life move on by the orderly sequence of natural cause and effect. There is also a great moderation in the claims made on behalf of the patriarchs." He goes on to ask: "Do the patriarchal narratives contain intrinsic historical improbabilities? Or, in other words, is there anything intrinsically improbable in the lives of the several patriarchs, and the vicissitudes through which they severally pass?" And he answers: "Though particular details in them may be improbable (*e.g.*, Gen. xix. 31 ff. [?]),[2] and though the representations may in parts be coloured by the religious and other associations of the age in which they were written, it cannot be said that the biographies of the first three patriarchs, as told in JE, are, speaking generally, historically improbable: the movements and personal lives of Abraham, Isaac, and Jacob, are, taken on the whole, credible."[3]

[1] Cf. Professor Bennett on Joseph, above, p. 97.
[2] See below, p. 115.
[3] *Genesis*, pp. xlv, xlvi. Exception is taken by Dr. Driver, however, to

The witness here borne is true. Nothing is more striking to an impartial mind than the sobriety of tone and sparingness of miracle in the Book of Genesis, where, on the legendary theory, one would expect a superabundance of marvels. To say, as is done, for instance, in the article, "Hexateuch," in Hastings' *Dictionary*, that, "in J the most wonderful phenomena appear quite natural, the writer feels himself in an ideal fairy land in which no wonders are surprising,"[1] is to convey a quite misleading impression. Apart from the theophanies to the patriarchs and a few instances of revelations in dreams, there is but *one* recorded miracle in the whole long period from Abraham to Moses—the destruction of the cities of the plain, and even this, like the Noachian deluge, is connected with physical causes. If the birth of Isaac is reckoned another, there are two. This, as one has said,[2] is a frugal provision of signs and wonders for the first foundation of an economy by which all families of the earth were to be blessed. In this respect the patriarchal period presents a marked contrast to the period of the Exodus, which *is* distinguished by the number, frequency, and stupendous character of its miracles. All the remaining miracles of the Old Testament, in fact, are scarcely so numerous and striking as those which are crowded into this single generation. But this again is intelligible from the nature of the case. It is characteristic of the miracles of the Bible that they are never mere prodigies, or aimless displays of power, but stand in intimate connection with, and strict subordination to, the ends of revelation. It need stagger no one that the Exodus took place, and the foundations of the covenant with Israel as a nation were laid, amidst surpassing manifestations of divine power and grace, designed to produce an indelible impression on the minds of the beholders, and burn into their hearts a grateful sense of their indebtedness to Jehovah. And this end, as we saw from the history, was effectually attained.

2. As another point in the argument from internal character, which powerfully supports belief in the historicity

the chronology "as it stands." A particular example from an article by Dr. Driver in the *Contemporary Review*, lvii, p. 221, is considered in Note D, on the Patriarchal Chronology.

[1] *Dict of Bible*, ii. p. 372.

[2] Birks.

of the patriarchal narratives, we may note the *unity* of the picture of the patriarchs in the various sources. There are, we are assured, three main strands of narrative, at least, in Genesis,—in the case of Abraham there are *four*, for Gen. xiv. is allowed to be a source by itself,—yet it is the same personages, the same environment, the same doings, the same idiosyncrasies, essentially, which we have in each. "There is," as Wellhausen himself declares, "no primitive legend so well-knit as the Biblical one."[1] Nor is this simply a matter of artificial arrangement. "This connection," he says, "is common in its main features to all the sources alike. The Priestly Code runs, as to its historical thread, quite parallel to the Jehovist history."[2] Again: "In the history of the patriarchs also, the outlines of the narrative are the same in Q [=P] and in JE. We find in both, Abraham's immigration into Canaan with Sarah and Lot, his separation from Lot, the birth of Ishmael by Hagar, the appearance of God for the promise of Isaac, Isaac's birth, the death of Sarah and Abraham, Ishmael, Isaac's marriage with Rebekah, Jacob and Esau, Jacob's journey to Mesopotamia, and the foundation of his family there, his return, Esau, Joseph in Egypt, Jacob in Egypt, Jacob's blessing on Joseph and his sons, his death and burial."[3]

Closer observation discovers that the case for unity is even stronger than Wellhausen represents it. The sources specified not only presuppose the same persons and the same history, but are so interwoven as to constitute a compact single narrative of which the several parts imply, and depend on, each other. *E.g.*, the change of the names of Abram and Sarai in Gen. xvii. into Abraham and Sarah governs the rest of the story,[4] and there are continual similar interlacings. Wellhausen, in fact, overstates the matter when he says that all the above details are found in each of the three sources. It is not the case, *e.g.*, that the birth of Ishmael, or the death of Abraham, is mentioned in JE.[5] The separation of sources only makes the problem

[1] *Hist. of Israel*, p. 295.
[2] *Ibid.* By "Jehovist" Wellhausen means the *combined* J and E.
[3] *Ibid.* p. 318.
[4] This is assumed to be the work of a redactor. See below, p. 220.
[5] Wellhausen points out (*Compos. d. Hex.* pp. 27, 28) that Abraham disappears from view in Gen. xxiv., and (quite arbitrarily) conjectures that originally ver. 67, "Isaac was comforted after his mother's death," may

harder; for the unity which exists in the book as it is disappears when its parts are sundered. Abundant illustration is given in later chapters,[1] and only an example or two need be cited here. Thus, Haran is assumed in JE as the place where Abraham received his call,[2] but, with the elimination of Gen. xi. 31, xii. 4*b*, 5, assigned to P, the reference to Haran in the story of Abraham's migrations disappears. So no explanation is given in J of "the land" which Abraham, chap. xii. 6, is said to have passed through: it is P, in ver. 5, who tells us it was "the land of Canaan." It has been mentioned that the death of Abraham is not recorded in JE. But, strangely enough, it is in P alone, on the current analysis, that an account is found of the deaths of *any* of the patriarchs.[3] In JE the account of Jacob's funeral is actually given before any allusion to his decease.[4] This had preceded in P. Apart, however, from such details, which might be indefinitely multiplied, the entire picture of the patriarchs, alike in their personal characters, their attitude to God, the promises made to them, and of the persons connected with them in the story, as Sarah, Lot, Hagar, Ishmael, Esau, is identical throughout, and leaves essentially the same impression on the mind in all the supposed sources. Thus, in the P narrative of Abraham's dealings with the sons of Heth in Gen. xxiii., he appears as "a mighty prince" (ver. 6); with this agrees the picture of him in chap. xiv—a separate source—as the possessor of 318 trained servants, born in his own house.

3. This leads us to remark that *the figure of Abraham* might almost be adduced as of itself a guarantee of the historicity of the narrative in which it is embodied. It is difficult, indeed, in our familiarity with the story, rightly to estimate the nobility and grandeur of the personality that here presents itself. To speak of Abraham's faith is to touch the central and most conspicuous point in his greatness; yet it must not be overlooked that this faith is only the highest expression of a largeness of soul which manifests

have read, "after his father's death." Addis actually adopts this conjecture into his *text*!

[1] Cf. Chaps. VII., X.

[2] Gen. xxiv. 4, 7, 10; cf. xxvii. 43.

[3] Gen. xxv. 7–10; xxxv. 28, 29; xlix. 28–33; l. 12, 13.

[4] Gen. l. 15.

itself in all the aspects of his character. As instances of this magnanimity, with which is joined a rare meekness, peaceableness, and unselfishness, together with a never-failing courtesy and politeness, we need only refer to his dealings with Lot about the choice of a settlement,[1] his relations with the king of Sodom and with Melchizedek,[2] and his negotiations with the sons of Heth about a burying-place for his dead.[3] But this is only one side of his character. Wellhausen was never further astray than when he spoke of this patriarch as unmanly. With his gentleness and reasonableness of disposition were united, as the rescue of Lot showed, the most conspicuous courage and decision. Abraham was no mere wealthy sheikh; no mere stay-at-home watcher by the sheepfolds. His was a strong as well as a meek nature. Sarah, his wife, though in many respects a noble woman, worthy of such a husband, is a far inferior character. She moves throughout on a lower level. Steadfast and loyal in her affection to her lord, and moved by a true religious feeling, she has not Abraham's strength of faith, tends to be haughty, imperious, and impatient, can brook no rival, is stung by Hagar's conduct, though she was herself to blame for putting the girl in her false position, complained petulantly to Abraham, treated her maid with intolerable harshness, and finally would be content with nothing but the expulsion of Hagar and Ishmael from the household. In comparison with her, the strong, patient, much-enduring Abraham appears greater than ever.

Yet there is no attempt to picture Abraham as faultless. It is, indeed, difficult to understand how a man whose faith was uniformly so strong should so far yield to fear as twice, according to the history, to stoop to falsehood or evasion to conceal his true relation to his wife. It was not a casual lapse, but seems to have been part of a settled policy, that Abraham should pass off Sarah as his sister, when travelling in dangerous parts.[4] One can only say of it, that, by whatever excuses Abraham may have sought to justify his behaviour to himself, it was a course of conduct unworthy of him, indefensible even with such moral knowledge as he possessed, inexcusable in the eyes of God, and certain to

[1] Gen. xiii. [2] Gen. xiv. [3] Gen. xxiii.
[4] Gen. xx. 13. On this incident, see below, Chap. VII. pp. 237 ff.

involve him, as it actually did, in much danger and unhappiness.

The highest point of view, however, in which to consider Abraham in these narratives is in his connection with the plan and purpose of revelation. Alike on the divine and the human sides, we are here in presence of transactions unsurpassed in the Old Testament in interest and importance. The call of Abraham—the covenant made with him—is the beginning of a new era in the religious history of mankind.[1] The faith with which Abraham responded to that call, and, in prompt and unhesitating obedience to the divine word, left home and kindred to go to a land which yet he knew not; his patient waiting, in spite of apparent natural obstacles, for the fulfilment of the promise of a son; his disinterested and lofty intercession for Sodom; above all, the great act of surrender of Isaac on the altar at Moriah, in undoubting confidence, apparently, that God was able to give his son back to him, even if from the dead,[2]—in general, his habitual enduring as seeing Him who is invisible,—all show the magnificent greatness of this man, as, to the end of time, the Father of the Faithful! It is this unique and profoundly significant character which the revolutionary criticism would dissipate into unsubstantial myth or legend. But the thing cannot be done. What legend can effect for the life of Abraham is sufficiently evidenced by the fables and stories in Jewish, Mohammedan, and Persian sources. The history of Abraham in the Bible stands, from internal evidence alone, on an entirely different footing from these. In its simple, coherent, elevated character, its organic unity with the rest of revelation, its freedom from the puerility and extravagance which mark the products of the myth-forming spirit, it approves itself as a serious record of important events, the knowledge of which had been carefully preserved—*possibly* at an early age had been written down[3]—and the essential contents of which we may safely trust.

[1] Cf. the fine remarks of Mozley on Abraham, *Ruling Ideas*, etc., pp. 21 ff.

[2] Heb. xi. 17–19; cf. Mozley, p. 60.

[3] Cf. Hommel, *Ancient Hebrew Tradition*, pp. 277, 296; and see below, p. 375.

VI. Fidelity of Narratives to Patriarchal Conditions

One of the most pronounced internal signatures of the truth of the patriarchal history is undoubtedly found in its primitive character, and its simplicity of ideas and worship, as compared with later stages of revelation.

1. This appears on the surface in the fact that the patriarchal history moves in *primitive conditions*, and keeps true to these throughout. The patriarchs have a character of their own, and are not modelled after the pattern of heroes, and prophets, and warriors of a later time.[1] They live their own free life under the open heaven, moving from place to place, building their altars, and calling on the name of Jehovah. Their thoughts, hopes, interests, outlook into the future, are all relatively simple. They are untroubled by the problems and mental conflicts of later times,—the problems met with in Job, for instance, or in some of the psalms,—even their temptations, as in the command to sacrifice Isaac, are those of a primitive age. It is generally agreed, therefore, that it would not be possible to assign a late date to the narratives in Genesis on the ground of that book alone.[2] Many critics, no doubt, think otherwise, and fancy they can see in the narratives in question reflections of almost the whole political history of Israel,—the revolt of Moab, the contempt for the wild Arabs on the south-west border, the subjection and revolt of Edom, the Syrian wars,[3] the prosperity and pride of the Northern Kingdom, etc.[4] But it may safely be affirmed that most of these supposed mirrorings of later conditions are imaginary. Gunkel recently has cogently argued that the narratives in Genesis —"legends" as he calls them—are far more distinguished by contrast to the later period than by resemblance. With

[1] Cf. Robertson, *Early Religion*, p. 126.

[2] "The Book of Genesis," says Kuenen, "may here be left out of account, since the picture it contains of the age of the patriarchs gives us no unequivocal indications of the period at which it was produced"—*Hex.* p. 42. "The question of the *dates* of the sources of which the Book of Genesis is composed," says Dr. Driver, "cannot be properly answered from a consideration of this book alone," etc.—*Genesis*, p. xv. See below, Chap. X. p. 273.

[3] See above, p. 74.

[4] A large collection of these may be seen in the Introduction to Mr. Fripp's book on *The Composition of Genesis*, written from the standpoint of Stade.

one exception, that of the revolt of Edom (regarded by him as a later addition),[1] he can find no trace of reflection of political events after 900 B.C., and the narratives themselves he takes to be much older—completed by the time of the Judges. He points out that there is no trace of the sanctuary at Jerusalem, of the kingdom of Saul, of the conflict of Saul with David, of the kingdom in its united form under David and Solomon, of the division and wars of the separate kingdoms, of the frightful Syrian wars, etc. As little, he argues, is there any trace of the later conflicts of the prophets against image-worship, Asherahs, *maççebas* (pillars), high places; the worship of the patriarchs, on the contrary, is *naïve* and free, and betrays no sense of the existence of these bitter contests.[2] Gunkel's own theory of the origin of the patriarchal stories is, we grant, as untenable as any which he criticises;[3] but he is surely right, at any rate, in his defence of their relative antiquity.

2. We observe next, in partial anticipation of subsequent discussion, that the *religious ideas*, and *forms of worship*, in the patriarchal history, are those which suit an early stage of revelation, and would not be in place later. The patriarchs worship one God—there is no trace of any other in Genesis[4]—but their worship is of the simplest order: prayer and sacrifice. There are no temples or fixed sanctuaries. The only ceremonial rite is circumcision; the one suggestion of Levitical prescriptions is in the distinction of clean and unclean animals, and this is found in J,[5] not in P. The form of revelation is not, as in the prophetic age, internal, but is predominatingly objective—by dream, vision, theophany, or through the Mal'ach, or "Angel of Jehovah." This last mode of revelation is one deserving of special attention. The doctrine of angels generally is undeveloped in these earlier books. The critics note it as a mark of P that he does not introduce angels; but even in J and E angels are brought in very sparingly. In E they are only

[1] On Edom, see below, p. 209.

[2] *Genesis*, Introd. pp. lxi–lxiii. Cf. Note E on Gunkel's Theory of Patriarchal History.

[3] It is surprising that Gunkel does not see that his argument is as cogent against the *late writing down* of the narratives in their present form (ninth and eighth centuries) as against their *composition* in or near that age. The "mirrorings" are a chief reason for the later dating.

[4] See below, p. 124.

[5] In the story of the flood, Gen. vii. 2, 8; viii. 20.

introduced twice, and then collectively—in Jacob's dream at Bethel,[1] and again at Mahanaim, when "the angels of God"—"God's host"[2]—met him. J mentions "angels," in forms of men, at the destruction of Sodom.[3] The apparent exception to this reticence, the appearances of the "Angel of Jehovah," or "Angel of God," is really a striking confirmation of our argument. For this form of revelation is one almost peculiar to the earlier periods—patriarchal and Mosaic—and stands by itself. "The Angel of Jehovah" is not an ordinary angel, like those in the above passages, but is a peculiar manifestation of Jehovah in the creaturely sphere, for purposes of revelation. Jehovah's name is in him; he is distinct from Jehovah, yet again mysteriously identified with Him; in address his name is interchanged with that of Jehovah; he is worshipped as Jehovah.[4] How came so remarkable a conception to be there in this early age, and how came it to be confined to this age? It is certainly no creation of the prophetic mind, and can only be explained as the tradition of a well-known form of revelation of the older time.

3. The *idea of God* Himself in these narratives is appropriate to that early age, and is readily distinguishable from the more developed conceptions of later epochs of revelation. Without discussing at present the divine names as the basis of a theory of documents,[5] we can at least say that the names of God proper to the patriarchal history—El, Elohim, El Elyōn, El Shaddai—are those which represent God under the most general forms of His being and manifestation, and in this respect stand in contrast with the name Jehovah, as, in its fullest significance, the covenant-name of the God of Israel. El, the most generic of all, is the only name that enters into the composition of proper names in Genesis. It corresponds with the Babylonian Ilu, but is not ordinarily used without some predicative designation—El Elyōn (God Most High), El Olam (God Everlast-

[1] Gen. xxviii. 12. [2] Gen. xxxii. 1, 2.
[3] Gen. xix. 1, 15.
[4] Cf. Gen. xvi. 7, 11, 13; xxi. 17 ff.; xxii. 12, 14, 15; xxxi. 11–13; xlviii. 15, 16; Ex. iii. 2, 6; xiii. 21; xiv. 19, 24; xxiii. 20 ff., etc. On the views taken of these appearances and their significance, see the works on O.T. Theology of Oehler, Schultz, Dillmann, Smend, etc. (Oehler, i. pp. 183 ff., has good remarks); art. "Angel" by Dr. A. B. Davidson in *Dict. of Bible*, etc.
[5] See below, pp. 221 ff.

ing), etc. Elohim, a plural form with a singular sense, is peculiar to Israel, and is likewise general in signification. It denotes God as the God of creation and providence. El Shaddai, again, marks a distinct stage in patriarchal revelation,[1] but seems still, like the two former names, to be connected with the idea of power.[2] The fuller manifestation of the divine attributes implied in, or to be historically connected with, the name Jehovah, lay yet in the future. It is true that in the sections of Genesis ascribed by criticism to J the name Jehovah is carried back into the days of the patriarchs—is put even into the mouth of Eve.[3] Even there, however, careful observation of the phenomena will suggest that while, in the view of the narrator, the name Jehovah was not unknown in earlier times, it is used by him sparingly and with discrimination in comparison with other designations—often is used simply proleptically.[4] Its absence in proper names is a testimony to this discrimination in its use.

The ideas of the divine *attributes* suggested by these names, though high, are yet in many respects undeveloped, relatively to later stages of revelation. What later Scripture means by the holiness, righteousness, wrath against sin, condescending grace, and covenant-keeping faithfulness of God, is, indeed, everywhere implied. God is the Judge of all the earth, doing right. He accepts and saves the righteous, and overwhelms a sinful world, or sinful cities, like Sodom and Gomorrah, with His judgments. Yet the terms "holy," "righteousness," "wrath," "love," are not yet found. The word "holy" first appears in connection with the revelations at the Exodus.[5] Schultz, in his *Old Testament Theology*, speaks of "the impression of the terrible God of the Semites" in earlier times, and says "the ancient Hebrews, too, tremble before a mysterious wrath of God."[6]

[1] Gen. xvii. 1; xliii. 14; xlix. 25; cf. Ex. vi. 3.

[2] The etymology of this, as of the other names, is uncertain, but probably the root-idea is power (God Almighty). The power denoted by El Shaddai is power exercised within the sphere of revelation, *e.g.*, in the promise of a son to Abraham. Cf. Driver on "The Names of God" in *Genesis*, pp. 402 ff.; Ottley, *Aspects of O.T.*, pp. 181 ff.; also Oehler, *O.T. Theol.* i. pp. 128 ff.

[3] Gen. iv. 1 (LXX, however, has "God").

[4] See Note F on the Name Jehovah in the Patriarchal Age, and Note B to Chap. V.

[5] Ex. iii. 5; xv. 11.

[6] *O.T. Theol.* ii. p. 175.

He strangely forgets that, on his own hypothesis, the passages he cites in proof are all from the *very latest* parts of the Pentateuch—from P. The Book of Genesis has no mention of the "wrath," any more than of the "holiness," of God—a fact the more striking that the writers are familiar with these ideas in Exodus.[1] But the limits of the earlier revelation are in the former book carefully preserved.

4. As it is with the idea of God, so, we observe lastly, it is with the *ethical conceptions* of the patriarchs. These again, as already seen, are relatively high, yet fall short in many respects of the ethical standards of the period of the prophets. Abraham marries his half-sister; Jacob marries two sisters, Leah and Rachel; the custom is recognised of the childless wife giving a handmaid as concubine to the husband for the purpose of obtaining children by her—a custom now so singularly attested by the provisions of the Code of Hammurabi as belonging to that age.[2] The conduct of the daughters of Lot in Gen. xix. 30 ff., and that of Judah in chap. xxxviii., shock our moral sense, but are in keeping with the degrading offer made by Lot of his daughters to the men of Sodom. The patriarchs Abraham and Isaac fail in a due sense of the sin involved in their conduct about their wives. With all the religious and ethical elevation we must ascribe to the patriarchs, therefore, Kuenen is not borne out in his formerly-quoted remark that Abraham, Isaac, and Jacob are pictured as "not inferior to the prophets of the eighth century B.C., in pureness of religious insight and inward spiritual piety."[3]

When we advance to Exodus, we are conscious of a great progress. The writers are, on the theory, the same, and the history is the continuation of the preceding. Yet everything is on a changed and grander scale. The ideas are deeper; the scene is larger and more imposing; the forces at work are more titanic; the issues are more

[1] Cf. arts. "Anger" and "Love," in *Dict. of Bible*. A similar line of argument is developed in Dr. Watson's little work, *The Book Genesis a True History*, which we had not seen before writing this. Dr. Driver singularly misses the point of Dr. Watson's argument in supposing it to prove only that the narratives reached their present form before the age when Amos, Hosea, etc., "began to emphasise and develop beliefs and truths such as those referred to" (*Genesis*, p. xlviii). Dr. Watson's argument turns on the contrast of *Genesis* with *Exodus*, which was likewise prior to that age, yet has these ideas.

[2] *Code* (Johns' edition), sects. 144–47.

[3] See above, p. 60.

tremendous. The hour has come for Jehovah to fulfil His promises to the fathers. The instrument is prepared; the yoke of bondage is to be broken; the people are to be led forth to breathe the air of liberty in the desert, and, as redeemed, to make voluntary dedication of themselves to their Deliverer. With this access of religious enthusiasm, and unparalleled experience of divine grace, goes of necessity an immense uplifting both in the religious ideas and in the standard of ethical obligation. The people have now given them "statutes and judgments" which are to serve as the norm of moral conduct. The ideal set before them is nothing less than the holiness of Jehovah Himself. They are to be a "holy" people to Him,[1] and are to prove their fidelity by obedience to His voice. The scenes in this great drama are depicted with a realism and fresco-like vividness of colouring which irresistibly suggest that the narratives were written under the recent impression of the events which they record: when, at least, the vividness of that impression had not yet faded from the memory and heart of the nation. The strands of the story may be multiple,—that is yet to be inquired into,—but we cannot admit that they are diverse. Moses and Aaron are the central figures in the history, but, as in the case of the patriarchal narratives, the portraits of the two are the same in J, E, P, D alike. It is one and the same Moses, with one and the same Aaron beside him, who appears in all the so-called "sources," and mediates, under God, the freedom and covenant-organisation of the nation.

[1] Ex. xix. 6.

CHAPTER V

The Old Testament as affected by Criticism—
II. Religion and Institutions: God and His Worship

"The πρῶτον ψεῦδος, historically considered, of Graf, Kuenen, and all their followers, consists in this: that they make use of the variety of material afforded them for positively constructing a history of ancient Israel, only to destroy the possibility of such a history. This they appear to do, not so much because of the discrepancies which exist in the materials, as because of their predetermination to reject as untrustworthy all the materials which partake largely of the Hebrew belief in the supernatural."—LADD.

"The view of Israel's early history, offered by any writer, will largely depend upon his thought of Israel's God."—J. E. CARPENTER.

"We must first firmly assert that, while there have been different forms of monotheism in many peoples and at various times, nevertheless Israel is and remains the classical people of monotheism; of that monotheism which we confess, or, more strictly, which is the precursor of ours; and in Israel this monotheism is of native origin: we know the history of its origin very well."—GUNKEL.

"God, in creating, theomorphises man; man, therefore, necessarily anthropomorphises God."—JACOBI.

CHAPTER V

THE OLD TESTAMENT AS AFFECTED BY CRITICISM —II. RELIGION AND INSTITUTIONS: GOD AND HIS WORSHIP.

It will be evident from the preceding discussions that the real leverage of the newer criticism is found in its theory of the religious development in ancient Israel: to this subject, therefore, special attention must now be given. It is not disputed that difficult problems have to be faced on any theory of the Israelitish religion and institutions. Questions exceedingly hard of solution arise in regard to laws, institutions, and practice, and it is the service of criticism to have set these in the clearest light. We are far from persuaded, however, that the methods which have come into vogue with the radical school hold out the promise of a satisfactory solution of these difficulties. On the contrary, these methods seem to us eaten through with an arbitrary subjectivism which vitiates their application at every point. Stade and Budde are conspicuous examples of this fault; but few of the other best-known writers of the school are far behind in their wilful setting aside, or mutilation, of the Biblical accounts, and substitution for these of an imaginary history, built up from ingenious conjectures, and brilliant combinations on the line of what the critic thinks the history *should* have been.

I. Fault of the Critical Method

It may be useful, before entering on the main discussion, to offer one or two examples of what we regard as the radical vice of the newer critical method—its continual substitution of arbitrary conjecture for the facts of the history as given.

We take the following from Budde, who prides himself—be it said—on his *respect* for the history.[1] After propounding the extraordinary thesis that "the tradition claims that it was *not* Israel's *own* God who performed these great deeds" at the Exodus, "but a God up to that time completely unknown to the Israelites, whose name even they then learned for the first time"[2] (the statement that the forefathers had known Yahweh is a later "palliating addition"),[3] he proceeds to explain how this God became transformed into the Yahweh of a later period by the absorption of "other gods" into Himself. "Yahweh had not expelled or annihilated them (the Canaanitish gods), but had made them subject; He had divested them of their personality by absorbing them into His own person."[4] Then, with charming frankness: "*To be sure, neither the law, nor the historical narratives, nor the prophets, say a word of all this*, yet it can be proved," etc.[5] Nearly anything, we imagine, could be proved in the same manner.

Budde's respect for the history does not allow of his agreeing with those who, "while relinquishing everything else, have tried to save the Ten Commandments, the 'Mosaic' moral law, for these oldest times." For, "the Ten Commandments base all their demands on the nature of the God of Israel. If, then, they really did come from this period"—we may ask the reader to note what, in Budde's view, is involved in the acceptance even of the Decalogue—"it appears that there existed, even in the earliest times, a conception of God so sublime that hardly anything could have remained for the prophets to do. This of itself should suffice to show the impossibility of the Mosaic origin of the Ten Commandments." Then, with the same engaging frankness: "It is, therefore, in the highest degree improbable that Yahweh demanded at Sinai the exclusive veneration of His own Godhead. *True, this is the unvarying testimony of Old Testament tradition.* It is to this day the generally accepted view, and is held even by advanced specialists. But it can hardly be maintained," etc.[6]

[1] "Thus treated," he says, "the Biblical tradition, even of the oldest times, has proved itself to me to be, in its main features, trustworthy—I speak of the history of Israel as a nation, not of the stories of primeval and patriarchal times in Genesis."—*Rel. of Israel*, p. 8.

[2] *Ibid.* p. 14. [3] *Ibid.* p. 15. [4] *Ibid.* p. 41.

[5] *Ibid.* (italics are ours). [6] *Ibid.* p. 59.

We quote these passages because they are typical. Delitzsch has said: "If history is critically annihilated what is left but to fill the *tabula rasa* with myths?"[1] This we take, as said, to be the primary vice of the prevailing theory—*either*, the arbitrary setting aside of the Biblical narrative in favour of some novel, no doubt highly ingenious, construction of the critic's own; *or*, the persistent reading into the history, in the interest of some fancy, of a meaning which it cannot be made to bear. A main difficulty, in fact, in the discussion, is, that, in the multitude of hypotheses, and unbounded liberty claimed by the critic to accept or reject as suits his convenience, it is impossible ever to feel that one has a sure hold on anything. The critic should at least, one would think, abide by his own assumptions; but he is far from doing so. How constantly, for instance, are Jephthah's words in Judg. xi. 24,[2] relied on in proof that, in the time of the Judges, Jehovah sustained the same relation to Israel as Chemosh did to Moab. Yet this section is declared by the critics not to belong to the older stratum of the Book of Judges, but to be a late insertion of uncertain date:[3] certainly, therefore, on the theory, no real speech of Jephthah's. Wellhausen cites it,[4] yet, as Dr. A. B. Davidson points out, "elsewhere regards the whole passage, with the allusion to Chemosh, as a later interpolation founded on Num. xxi. 29."[5] Similarly, the statement of David in 1 Sam. xxvi. 19, that his enemies had driven him out of Jehovah's inheritance, saying, "Go, serve other gods"—continually quoted in proof that to David Jehovah was only a tribal god[6]—is, with the chapter to which it belongs, assigned by Kautzsch, with others, to a comparatively late date:[7] is valueless, therefore, as a testimony to David's own sentiments. Is it desired, again, to prove an original connection between Jehovah and Moloch? Kuenen, to that end, accepts as "historical" the statement in Amos v. 26 that the Israelites carried about in the desert "the tabernacle of Moloch,"[8]

[1] *Genesis*, i. p. 9.
[2] See below, p. 131.
[3] Thus Kautzsch, Moore (*Judges*), Thatcher (*Judges*, "Cent. Bible"), etc.
[4] *Hist. of Israel*, p. 235.
[5] *Expositor*, 3rd Series, v. p. 49. "This pet passage," Dr. Davidson says, "figures of course in Wellhausen, as it does everywhere else since Vatke." He refers to Wellhausen's *Bleek*, p. 195.
[6] See below, p. 132.
[7] *Lit. of O.T.*, pp. 45, 237.
[8] *Rel. of Israel*, i. p. 250.

though the whole history of the wanderings, which, in its JE parts, is allowed to be *older* than Amos, is rejected by him. A proof of the bull-worship of Jehovah from ancient times is found by some in the story of the making of the golden calf in Ex. xxxii.; yet the story is rejected as unhistorical.[1] Others take it as a protest *against* bull-worship:[2] Kuenen, as will be seen below, thinks it glances at the fact that the idolatrous priests of the Northern Kingdom claimed descent from Aaron.[3]

To take only one other example, Professor W. R. Smith writes thus of the sacred pillars of the patriarchs: "In the Biblical story they appear simply as memorial pillars, without any definite ritual significance." "This, however, he goes on, "is due to the fact that the narratives are conformed to the standpoint of the law and of the later prophets, who look on the ritual use of sacred pillars as idolatrous."[4] The critic forgets, or ignores, that, on his own showing, these patriarchal stories anteceded the age of written prophecy, and that, according to him, in the days of Amos and Hosea, pillars were still thought to be legitimate.[5] Where then is the place for the conforming of the narratives to the ideas of "later prophets"? With the talismanic power which such instances exemplify of getting rid of unwelcome facts, and making a theory prove itself by employing it as a means to break down opposing testimony, it is not difficult for criticism to produce astonishing results.

Accepting for ourselves the historicity of the Biblical narratives, till at least their title to our confidence is disproved, we propose to invert the procedure of the schools, and, instead of sacrificing the history to *a priori* considerations, to inquire at every point whether reason is shown for setting it aside.

[1] Most writers see some connection with the bull-worship, *e.g.*, Stade, *Geschichte*, i. pp. 466–67. Addis dates the narrative later than the fall of Samaria (722 B.C.) on the ground that only then "the old worship of Yahweh under the form of a calf, long maintained by kings and Levitical priests (Judg. xviii. 30), received its death-blow."—*Hex.* i. pp. 151–52. On this see below, pp. 143 ff.

[2] Cf. Kittel, *Hist. of Hebs.* i. p. 152.

[3] *Hex.* p. 245. See below, p. 211.

[4] *Rel. of Semites*, p. 186; *O.T. in J. C.*, pp. 241, 354.

[5] *Ibid.* pp. 186–87; *Prophets of Israel*, p. 116.

II. Early Israelitish Monotheism

We begin by contrasting the Biblical and the critical views of the early Israelitish conceptions of God.

1. It was formerly shown that, in the earliest tradition we possess of Israel's beliefs, there is no trace of any conception of God but one essentially *monotheistic*. There is but one qualification, which, in justice to the facts, it is necessary to make on this statement. It is not contended that, at any period of their history, the Israelitish people as a whole rose to, or maintained themselves at, the full height of the monotheistic conception: we know they did not. To many the conception of Jehovah was no doubt simply that of their national god; nor was it always, or perhaps even generally, clear, that some kind of inferior reality did not belong to the gods worshipped with so much pomp and ardour by the nations around them.[1] Even in apostolic and sub-apostolic times, Christian believers and Church fathers did not regard the idol-gods of the Gentiles as simple nonentities: paganism was to them a system of demon-worship.[2] Still harder would it be for Israel to rise to the height of the prophetic conception that the idols were "nothings" (*elilim*),[3] in a world where every people was polytheistic but themselves. But that the religion of Abraham, and Moses, and the other great leaders of the nation was at heart the worship of the one true God, recognised by them to be the Creator, Ruler, and Lord in providence of the whole world, we see not the smallest reason to doubt. This was the common view, prior to the advent of the Kuenen-Wellhausen school, among the critics themselves,[4] and, as the passage above cited from Budde acknowledges, is the view of leading

[1] It would be unsafe, however, to infer this from such expressions as, "Who is like Thee, O Jehovah, among the gods?" (Ex. xv. 11), for such expressions are found in prophets and psalms where the monotheistic consciousness is not doubted. See below, p. 438.

[2] 1 Cor. x. 20, 21; cf. Justin Martyr, *1 Apol.* 14, 54, 62, etc.

[3] Cf. Deut. xxxii. 21; Lev. xix. 4; Isa. ii. 8; Ps. xcvi. 4, 5, etc. In the last passage we read: Jehovah "is to be feared above all gods," but in ver. 5, "For all the gods of the peoples are nothings."

[4] So De Wette, Lengerke, Hitzig, Ewald, Bleek, Dillmann, etc. On the other hand, the views of Vatke, and of writers like Daumer, Ghillany, etc., met with little countenance. Cf. König's *Hauptprobleme*, pp. 7 ff.

Old Testament specialists still.[1] It is the view also, we are persuaded, which answers to the natural reading of the facts.

The Book of Genesis, originating, it is to be remembered, as respects at least its JE parts, in the "pre-prophetic" age, is, as before pointed out,[2] throughout a monotheistic book.[3] God is the Creator of the world and of man: destroys the whole human race by a flood; is present and active in all lands—Babylonia, Mesopotamia, Egypt; works out a gracious purpose in the lives of men. The difficulty in Genesis is not its recognition of God as supreme,—that appears in every part,—but its almost entire ignoring of what we nevertheless know to be the fact, the existence of polytheism and idolatry in tribes and nations outside the patriarchal circle. The God worshipped by the patriarchs is the *only* God whose existence, presence, and working are recognised in it. We read nothing of gods of Canaan or Egypt. Melchizedek is, like Abraham, a worshipper of El Elyōn—"God Most High,"[4] and even Abimelech and Pharaoh speak generally simply of "God."[5] The single glimpse we get to the contrary is in the "strange gods" (teraphim) which Jacob's household brought with them from Mesopotamia, and which Jacob required them to put away.[6] In Exodus and the remaining Pentateuchal books it is different. There we have a sharp contrast drawn between Jehovah and "the gods of Egypt";[7] the people are stringently forbidden to worship "other gods";[8]

[1] See above, p. 120; and Chap. IV. p. 93. [2] Cf. above, p. 41.

[3] This is very generally admitted of the Book of Genesis as we have it. H. P. Smith, *e.g.*, says of the early part, where anthropomorphism is most marked: "What J has preserved he was able to bring into harmony with the strictest monotheism. For the Yahweh of our account, anthropomorphic as He is, is yet the Supreme God."—*O.T. Hist.* p. 16. Cf. Wellhausen, *Hist. of Israel*, p. 304. Gunkel acknowledges this "monotheistic trend" of Genesis, and carries it back to an early date.—*Genesis*, p. xlvii; see also his *Israel und Babylonien*, p. 29.

[4] Gen. xiv. 18–22. It is not easy to say how far polytheism had advanced in Canaan in the time of Abraham. The Tel el-Amarna tablets speak of Baalat of Gebal (frequently), Asherah, Milku (Moloch), Ammon (? Amon), Samas, Dagon, etc., but do not give much definite light.

[5] Cf. Gen. xxi. 22 ff. (in chap. xxvi. 27, 28, "Jehovah"); Gen. xli. 39, etc.

[6] Gen. xxxi. 19, 30; xxxv. 2, 4.

[7] Ex. xii. 12 (P); xv. 11. It will not be claimed that P, in the former passage, writes other than monotheistically.

[8] Ex. xx. 3; xxiii. 32.

they are enjoined to keep themselves apart from, and to root out, the idolatry of the Canaanites.[1] But Jehovah is still regarded as exalted above all these other gods in nature, dignity, and power, as the God of the whole earth—its Creator, Ruler, and Lord. He is the One who says of Himself, "All the earth is Mine."[2] Budde, we have seen, acknowledges that this is the view of God involved in the Decalogue. While, therefore, Kuenen is right when he sums up Israel's religion in the formula, "Yahweh Israel's God and Israel Yahweh's people,"[3] this does not in the least imply that Jehovah was simply to Israel a tribal or national god. He was the God of their fathers—the God of heaven and earth[4]—who of His condescending love had chosen them to be a people for Himself, with a view to the ultimate larger blessing of mankind. The keynote in these early books is precisely the same as in Amos—the alleged introducer of the "ethical monotheism": "You only have I known of all the families of the earth."[5]

What is here said of early monotheism is not contradicted by the anthropomorphisms attributed peculiarly to the J writer in the Genesis narratives. The anthropomorphisms are *naïve* and popular enough;[6] yet, beneath them, the conception of Jehovah as the Creator and Ruler of the world is never lost sight of;[7] and the sublimity of the representations of God in other parts of the J narrative—in the revelation of God's name, *e.g.*, in Ex. xxxiii. 18, 19, xxxiv. 5–8[8]—shows clearly that no such paltry ideas of God as the critics ascribe to this writer were really his. The anthropomorphisms belong either to the older tradition the writer is dealing with, or to a vivid and personalising way of setting forth God's presence and interest in human

[1] Ex. xxiii. 24; cf. Deut. xii. 2 ff.
[2] Ex. xix. 5.
[3] *Nat. and Univ. Religions* (Hibbert Lectures), p. 105.
[4] Cf. Gen. xxiv. 3, etc.
[5] Amos iii. 2.
[6] "Jehovah *forms* men and beasts, *breathes* the breath of life into man's nostrils, *builds* a rib into a woman, *plants* a garden, *takes* a man and *puts* him into it, *brings* the beasts to the man, *walks* in the cool of the day, *speaks* (Gen. iii. 22) as though He were *jealous* of the man" (Knobel, in Dillmann).
[7] Cf. the narrative of the flood, the representations of God in Gen. xviii. 25, xxiv. 3. See H. P. Smith, quoted above.
[8] On the sole ground of this loftier character these passages are treated by certain critics as later insertions.—Cf. Oxf. *Hex.* ii. p. 134.

things,[1] such as is found in prophets and psalmists to the latest time.

2. Entirely different from this is the early Israelitish conception of God *imagined by the new critical school.* The guiding idea here is no longer "revelation," but "evolution." Man's oldest ideas of God being supposed to be his poorest, an original monotheism in this people is decisively rejected. "At first," says Kuenen, "the religion of Israel was polytheism."[2] "Monotheism," says Wellhausen, "was unknown to ancient Israel."[3] "The knowledge that there is a supreme spiritual Being, alone of His kind, Creator and Preserver of all things, is perfectly lacking to ancient Israel," is the first sentence in Stade's chapter on pre-prophetic religion in Israel.[4] If we ask what conception is to take the place of that which is discarded, we have first the general answer that "the relation in which Yahweh stands to Israel is the same as, for instance, that of Chemosh to the Moabites."[5] Beyond this, we are offered a wide choice of theories. Kautzsch, *e.g.*, can find nothing in the religion of pre-Mosaic Israel but a species of "polydemonism." "It is only in a very restricted sense," he thinks, "that we can speak of such a notion [as God] at all."[6] A connection is sought by Kuenen between Jehovah and Moloch, the fire-god, who was worshipped with human sacrifices.[7] A favourite theory at present, revived by Budde, is that Yahweh was originally the storm-god of Sinai, worshipped by the Kenites, from whom Moses borrowed the name and cult.[8] With these theories are blended by Stade and others

[1] Cf. Dr. A. B. Davidson, art. "God" in *Dict. of Bible*, ii. p. 198: "The language only testifies to the warmth and intensity of feeling of the writers"; *Theol. of O.T.*, pp. 108–9. Gunkel remarks: "In the Old Testament there are occasionally strong anthropomorphisms; but they are not so gross as is usual in Babylonia; Israel never said that Jehovah eats and drinks. Such anthropomorphisms are, in the Old Testament, archaisms," etc.—*Is. und Bab.* p. 32.

[2] *Rel. of Israel*, i. p. 223. He deduces this from the later practice of idolatry.

[3] *Isr. und Jud. Geschichte* (1897), p. 30. [4] *Geschichte*, i. p. 428.

[5] Kuenen, *Rel. of Israel*, p. 224; so Wellhausen, Stade, Budde, W. R. Smith, etc.

[6] Art. "Rel. of Israel" in *Dict. of Bible* (Extra), p. 623. Kautzsch severs himself from naturalistic theories when he comes to Moses. *His* idea of God, he thinks, can only have come from special revelation (p. 625). But it was not yet a monotheism: only a "monolatry."

[7] *Rel. of Israel*, i. pp. 226–28, 240, etc. On the similar theory of Daumer, etc., cf. König, *Hauptprobleme*, pp. 7 ff.

[8] The Kenite theory, on which see below, pp. 129 ff., is advocated by Budde,

a number of other elements drawn from fetishism, animism, ancestor-worship, totemism, etc.—of which more again. What are some of the grounds of these allegations, and of the rejection of the Biblical view?

(1) First, and perhaps deepest, of the reasons for this rejection is the *a priori* one, that such a conception of God as the Old Testament attributes to the patriarchs and to Moses was *impossible* for them at that stage of the history. It is too elevated and spiritual for their minds to have entertained. The idea of the unity of God has for its correlates the ideas of the world and of humanity, and neither of these ideas, it is asserted, was possessed by ancient Israel.[1] The idea of the world did not arise till the time of Amos, when it was introduced through the Assyrian invasions. These "introduced," says Wellhausen, "a new factor, the conception of the world—the world, of course, in the historical sense of that expression. In presence of that conception, the petty nationalities lost their centre of gravity, brute force dispelled their illusions, they flung their gods to the moles and to the bats."[2] Thus arose the universalism of the prophets: thus was brought about the transformation of Yahweh-worship from monolatry to monotheism.

This seems to us most singular reasoning; is, indeed, throughout, both as to the idea of the world, and the impossibility of framing a spiritual conception of God, again a huge *petitio principii*. Here is a people whose own traditions, with the best warrant, went back to Babylonia and Mesopotamia; who had lived for centuries in Egypt in the most brilliant period of its civilisation; a people of the age of the Tel el-Amarna tablets; who entered Canaan when it stood in connection with, and was the highway of,

Tiele, Stade, Cheyne, etc. It was favoured by Colenso, and some older writers. It is one of the conceits of Budde that originally the Israelites traced their descent to Cain! Cf. Delitzsch, *Genesis*, i. p. 192.

[1] Thus Stade, Kuenen, Wellhausen, etc. On the creation of the world, Wellhausen declares that "in a youthful people such a theological abstraction is unheard of, and so with the Hebrews we find both the word and the notion only coming into use after the Babylonian exile."—*Hist. of Israel*, p. 305. "The religious notion of *humanity* underlying Gen. ix. 6 is not ancient with the Hebrews any more than with other nations."—*Ibid.* p. 312.

[2] *Ibid.* p. 473. Wellhausen fails to show what other nations flung their gods to the moles and the bats as the result of the Assyrian conquests, or even that Israel did so as the result of these conquests, or till after the exile.

all the great empires of the world; who knew something of the vast power of the Hittites in the north; yet we are asked to believe that it had no conception of the world, or of anything larger than a petty state, till the days of Amos! The JE parts of the "table of nations" alone, in Gen. x., cry out against such a notion. As to the spirituality of God, how can it well be maintained, in view of the exalted conceptions of God now proved to have existed in both the Babylonian and the Egyptian religions in periods long anterior to Abraham and Moses,[1] that such conceptions were beyond the grasp of the greater spirits in these times? The Code of Hammurabi, in the simplicity and elevation of its idea of "God," as the One in whose name, or before whom, oaths were to be taken,[2] is a singular example of what thoughtful minds were capable of in the age of Abraham. In the Mosaic religion itself we have the powerful witness of the Decalogue. We agree with Budde in his testimony to the spirituality of the conception of God involved in the Ten Words,[3] but we do not, on that account, in face of the strongest historical improbabilities, deny these precepts to Moses. The First Commandment, indeed, "Thou shalt have no other gods before Me," might be interpreted in the sense of monolatry,[4] not of monotheism; but, in its actual setting, the obvious meaning of the precept is, that Jehovah alone is to be worshipped, because He alone is the living and true God.[5]

[1] On the pronounced monotheistic elements in the oldest Egyptian texts, cf. Renouf, *Hibbert Lectures*, 1879, pp. 89 ff. See also Note A, below.

[2] The formula in the Code is simply, "shall swear in the name of God," "shall recount before God," or the like. The language is nearly identical with that of the Book of Genesis. The difference is, that with this high conception of divinity, the Babylonians worshipped many special gods, while the Hebrews were forbidden to worship any but Jehovah. See Note A on Early Ideas of God.

[3] Wellhausen also speaks of "the actual monotheism which is undoubtedly presupposed in the universal precepts of the Decalogue."—*Hist. of Israel*, p. 440. We have thus the alternative of denying the Decalogue to Moses, or of admitting that a monotheistic conception of God lay at the foundation of the religion of Israel. See below, pp. 152 ff. Even Kuenen admits that, in its fundamental form, the Decalogue is Mosaic.

[4] Thus Kuenen, Kautzsch, etc. The theory on which this rests, viz., that "monolatry," or the worship of one sole (tribal) god, was the rule among surrounding peoples is open to the gravest doubts. Cf. Dr. A. B. Davidson, art. "God," in *Dict. of Bible*.

[5] Cf. Dr. A. B. Davidson on this precept in *Expositor*, 3rd Series, v. p. 44.

(2) The modern theory may be usefully tested by reference to its most prevalent recent form—the alleged *Kenite origin* of the Yahweh cult. The theory, in essence, is, as above stated, that Yahweh, whose name and worship Moses introduced into Israel, was originally the storm-god of the Kenites, believed by them to have his local seat on Mount Sinai. A connection is thought to be established by the facts that Moses was living among the Kenites, with Jethro, when Yahweh was revealed to him; that the abode of Yahweh is placed at Sinai; and that His presence there is associated with thunder, lightning, and storm. The classical passage in proof is Deborah's Song,[1] in which, according to Wellhausen, Yahweh is "summoned to come from Sinai to succour His oppressed people, and to place Himself at the head of His warriors."[2] Budde, it was seen, draws the conclusion that Yahweh was a God absolutely unknown to the Hebrews before the Exodus, and explains His intimate association with Canaan by the notion that He "absorbed" the Canaanitish deities into Himself!

The far-fetched and arbitrary character of this theory, which Budde allows to be contradictory of the uniform tradition of the Old Testament, can be judged of by the most ordinary reader. Not only does it lack real evidence, but it is directly in the teeth of the fact that the Jehovah who appeared to Moses is expressly identified in the oldest sources with the God of the fathers, and His interposition is represented as in fulfilment of His covenant promises to them.[3] This is independent of any theory we may form as to whether the sacred name was known earlier or not. In point of fact many of the critics now hold that it *was* known, if only in limited circles.[4] On the other hand, there is not the least proof, as Kittel points out, that Yahweh was the name of a Kenite deity.[5] When Moses, later, invited Hobab the Kenite, his brother-in-law, to come with the Israelites, it was that they might do *him* good, "for Jehovah hath spoken good concerning Israel," not that he, as an earlier worshipper of Yahweh, might do *them* good.[6] It is but a precarious hold which the theory finds

[1] Judg. v.
[2] *Hist. of Israel*, p. 344.
[3] Ex. ii. 23–25, iii. 13–16, etc.
[4] See Note B on the Antiquity of the Name Jehovah. **Many now trace it as far back as Babylonia.** See below, p. 409.
[5] *Hist. of Hebs.* i. p. 250.
[6] Num. x. 29.

in the Song of Deborah, especially when it is remembered that by the time of the Judges Jehovah's presence is beyond all question presupposed as in the midst of His people in Canaan.[1] How then should He require to be "summoned" from Sinai?[2] The bold, figurative language in the opening of the Song is most easily understood as a reminiscence of the manifestations of Jehovah's presence and power in the desert and at Mount Sinai, viewed as a pledge of present help.[3]

Stade has himself no little difficulty in maintaining his theory of a local and limited deity, whose seat was at Sinai. Yahweh, he allows, was "everywhere" present to His worshippers in Canaan, and could be worshipped "everywhere."[4] His presence and help are not confined to His own land: He accompanies His worshippers into foreign lands, and there guards and defends them. Thus He promises to Jacob at Bethel to be everywhere with him: He is with Joseph in Egypt, goes with Jacob down to Egypt, works miracles for Elijah at Zarephath, etc. He knows Sarah's thoughts; it is declared of Him that nothing is too hard for Him; He can help by many or by few; He destroys wicked cities; visits lands like Egypt with famine; and otherwise displays His universal might.[5] Stade speaks of these things as indications of a tendency to "break through" the old notion of God;[6] they are in reality a disproof of his theory of that notion. The Song of Deborah itself, rightly regarded, is evidence of a far higher conception of Jehovah in the time of the Judges than the modern theory will allow. How sublime the picturing of the majesty and omnipotence of God in the opening theophany; how irreconcilable with the idea of a local deity the resist-

[1] The whole book is evidence; but cf. Judg. i. 19, 22; or chap. xi. 11: "Jephthah uttered all his words before Jehovah in Mizpeh"; or the presence of the ark of Jehovah at Bethel and Shiloh.

[2] "The truth is," says Professor Robertson, "the Song says not a word about Jehovah being 'summoned' from Sinai on the occasion of the battle referred to."—*Early Rel.* p. 193.

[3] Cf. for parallels, Deut. xxxiii. 2; Hab. iii. 3 ff.; Pss. xviii. 7 ff., lxviii. 7 ff., etc. Kuenen himself says: "Of course, we do not deny that the pious among the Israelites, in using these expressions, were aware that they spoke in metaphors."—*Rel. of Israel*, i. p. 241.

[4] *Geschichte*, i. p. 446.

[5] *Ibid.* i. pp. 430–32. Cf. the references, Gen. xviii. 14; xxviii. 15 ff.; 1 Sam. xiv. 6; 2 Kings v. 15 ff., etc.

[6] *Ibid.* p. 430.

less presence of Jehovah in Seir, at Sinai, in Canaan;[1] how manifest the supremacy of this God in nature and providence, when even "the stars in their courses" fight against His enemies;[2] how distinct the assertion of Jehovah's righteousness;[3] how lofty and *spiritual* the closing strain—suggestive of the Second Commandment and of Deuteronomy—"Let them that love Him be as the sun when he goeth forth in his might!"[4] The theory as a whole thus fails of evidence, and we are not surprised that critics like König, Kittel, Kautzsch, Dr. A. B. Davidson,[5] and others reject it. The fact that Horeb is already spoken of in Ex. iii. 1 as "the mountain of God" is a very fragile buttress: the expression is probably used proleptically.

(3) We come back, then, in support of the theory that Jehovah was a "tribal" (or merely national) god to the *two passages* which, from their perpetual recurrence, may, without offence, be called the stock proofs of that hypothesis, viz., the words of Jephthah in Judg. xi. 24, and those of David in 1 Sam. xxvi. 19. But, impartially examined, what do these passages amount to? Jephthah says to the king of the Ammonites: "Wilt thou not possess that which Chemosh thy god giveth thee to possess? So whomsoever Jehovah our God hath dispossessed from before us, them will we possess." Even accepting the interpretation put upon the words, one may reasonably demur to the erecting of the utterance of this rude Gileadite chieftain, in a time of religious disorganisation, into a standard for the true idea of God in the Mosaic religion. That must be judged of on its own ampler evidence, apart from a passage like this. But even on the lips of Jephthah, rude soldier though he is, it is by no means clear that the words are intended as more than a form of speech in accommodation to the

[1] Judg. v. 4, 5.

[2] Ver. 20. "In the Song," says Dr. A. B. Davidson, "we observe Him regarded as ruling in heaven and on earth, commanding the stars in their courses, and the rivers as they flow."—*O. T. Prophecy*, p. 38.

[3] Ver. 11. In Budde's view, the Yahweh of Moses had not even moral character (*Rel. of Israel*, p. 30).

[4] Ver. 31. Dr. Davidson says here: "Had we a few more poems by prophetic minds such as this, and not the external histories of rude soldiers, such as unfortunately we possess alone [But see below, pp. 143, 384], we should, I believe, be able to form a higher idea even of the religious condition of the people under the Judges."—*Ibid.* pp. 37–38.

[5] Kautzsch speaks of it with respect, but does not accept it.—"Rel. of Israel," *Dict.* p. 62; cf. Davidson, *Theol. of O.T.*, pp. 50–52.

Ammonite point of view. The section seems based, as before said, on Num. xxi. 22 ff., where, it might be shown, a sufficiently high idea of God is implied. Jehovah, in any case, is obviously far more to Israel than Chemosh is to Ammon; is even, in ver. 27, invoked as "the Judge" to judge between them.[1] The second passage, in which David says, "They have driven me out this day that I should not cleave unto (or, have no share in) the inheritance of Jehovah, saying, Go, serve other gods," has, to our mind, even less probative force. Wellhausen entirely misrepresents its import when he speaks of David as "compelled to serve other gods,"[2] and Professor W. R. Smith not less when he says that David takes it for granted that a man who is excluded from the commonwealth of Israel "must go and serve other gods."[3] One desiderates here some more exact thinking. Does anyone—even Wellhausen—really suppose that when David crossed into Philistia he ceased to worship Jehovah, and served Dagon instead? or that Naomi worshipped Chemosh in Moab? or that Elijah served Baal at Zarephath? What, on this theory, would be the meaning of Naaman's apology for "bowing down" in the house of Rimmon?[4] We have learned from Stade himself, what all the history teaches, that Jehovah accompanied His servants in their wanderings: how could David imagine it would be otherwise with him? Taking the passage most literally, David is not speaking for himself, but declaring what *others* say; and he uses this bold mode of speech to emphasise his sense of the deprivation implied in being banished from Jehovah's immediate presence, and driven into a land where other gods are worshipped. The fact that precisely the same expression occurs twice in an undoubtedly monotheistic book like Deuteronomy should warn us against attaching too much weight to its presence here.[5]

[1] We may quote Dr. A. B. Davidson again: "The truth is that such references to Chemosh and other heathen gods prove nothing, because they would prove that even Jeremiah regarded Chemosh as a real divinity (Jer. xlviii. 7)."—*Expositor*, 3rd Series, v. p. 49. We may compare our own way of speaking of heathen gods. Even in the case of a monotheistic religion like Mohammedanism, we make a distinction between the Christian's God and Allah. Both are designations of the Supreme Being, yet the conceptions of God are so different that we hold them apart in thought, and give them different names.

[2] *Hist. of Israel*, p. 22. [3] *Prophets*, p. 54. [4] 2 Kings v. 18.

[5] Deut. xxviii. 36, 64. Wellhausen cites as another proof: "When

We conclude that no good ground has been shown for the view that "ethical monotheism" was first introduced by the prophets, beginning with Amos.[1] We have found monotheism already embedded in the narratives in Genesis, which, in their J and E parts, are, on the critic's own showing, "pre-prophetic." So far from monotheism being the creation of the prophets,—with, perhaps, Elijah as precursor,—these prophets, without exception, found upon, and presuppose, an older knowledge of the true God. They bring in no new doctrine, still less dream of the evolution from a Moloch or a Kenite storm-god,—as much the product of men's fancies as Chemosh or Dagon,—of the living, holy, all-powerful, all-gracious Being to whose service the people were bound by every tie of gratitude, but from whom they had basely apostatised. They could not have understood such evolution from an unreality into a reality. They were in continuity with the past, not innovators upon it. Dillmann speaks for a large class of scholars when he says, in decisively rejecting this theory: "No prophet is conscious of proclaiming for the first time this higher divine Principle: each reproaches the people for an apostacy from a much better past and better knowledge: God has a controversy with His people."[2]

III. Early Israelitish Worship

Budde stands nearly alone in denying an ethical element in the original Mosaic conception of God; but it is hardly possible to put lower than most writers of this school do the ideas entertained by the people in the pre-prophetic age of the proper mode of representing and worshipping the deity to whom they had attached themselves. Fetishism, animism, totemism, image-worship, ancestor-worship, tree- and stone-worship, human sacrifices, etc., all play their part

Cain is driven out of the land (Canaan), he is driven from the presence of Jehovah" (Gen. iv. 14, 16). Similarly Stade: "Cain, driven out of Palestine, and pleading for the alleviation of his punishment, is made to say," etc. (i. pp. 446–47). Cain, on this view, is supposed to have had his abode in Palestine. Wonderful is the power of criticism to make the text say what it pleases—even to the turning of it into nonsense!

[1] Cf. Duhm, quoted above, p. 68.

[2] *Alttest. Theol.* p. 56. Cf. Schultz against Stade in *O.T. Theol.* i. pp. 123–24. Baethgen maintains that the religion of Israel never was polytheistic: that its strange gods were imported.—*Beiträge*, p. 289.

here. Most writers are content to explain a religion by the help of one or two such principles—by fetishism, *e.g.*, or ancestor-worship, or totemism. It is reserved for Stade, in his picture of pre-prophetic religion, to blend *all* these forms of superstition in one grand *mélange*. We shall consider this subject under the general head of worship.

The simple elements of patriarchal worship, in the Biblical view, are prayer and sacrifice. The patriarchs build their altars, and call on the name of God. After the Exodus, worship is regulated by the Mosaic constitution. The fundamental laws of the covenant forbade the worship of God by images, required the extirpation of idolatry, denounced witchcraft, and condemned the practices of the Canaanites generally.[1] In the hands of the critics this picture of Israel's history undergoes a complete transformation. It was seen before that the Biblical history, on the face of it, does not lend support to the view that tree- and stone-worship, ancestor-worship, totem-worship, teraphim-worship, human sacrifices and the like, were prominent features of the religion of the patriarchs, or of the people who came out of Egypt with Moses.[2] How then is the theory made out? In the first place, as before, by rejecting the history we have, and substituting for it a construction evolved from a general theory of the origin of religion; in the next place, by reading back the disobediences and corruptions of the later history into the original form of the religion, and fastening on stray passages and incidents an interpretation contrary to the general impression of the narrative.[3] The method can best be illustrated by observing it at work.

1. The Book of Genesis gives us a clear and intelligible account of how *places* like Bethel, Hebron, Beersheba, Shechem, came to be regarded with peculiar veneration by the Israelites. They were places hallowed by the residence and worship of their fathers, and by the revelations of God. These stories form part of the patriarchal history, and we have sought to show that there is no reason for discrediting them. The newer criticism, however, cannot accept so

[1] Ex. xx. 4, 5, 23; xxii. 18, 21; xxiii. 24, 32, 33.

[2] See above, pp. 39, 40.

[3] Kautzsch says he "must emphasise very strongly that in almost every instance we have here to deal with hypotheses, and not with facts."—"Rel. of Israel" *Dict.* p. 613.

simple an explanation. It rejects the history, and assumes that these places were really *old Canaanitish sanctuaries,* which the Israelites adopted on their entrance into Canaan, and afterwards glorified by weaving around them this web of patriarchal legend.[1] If we ask for proof, none is forthcoming. We are thrown back on assertion, and on the assumption of the mythical character and non-historicity of the patriarchal narratives generally.

2. Stade gives the matter a further development. There were *graves* at some of these places (Hebron, Machpelah, Shechem). What is clearer than that the real origin of the sacredness of these sanctuaries was *ancestor-worship*? "Before the altars at Hebron and Shechem were altars of Yahweh, sacrifices were offered on them to the ancestral spirits of Abraham and Joseph, and we have here a proof" —the reader will note the stringency of Stade's ideas of proof—"that we are right in our conclusion that the worship of ancestors was a usage in ancient Israel."[2] The tribal system is thought to be connected with ancestor-worship,[3] and additional proofs are found in mourning customs.[4] Other writers amplify the suggestion. "The teraphim," Budde thinks, "belong to the extensive domain of ancestor-worship, which, in many lands and continents, even in the New World, has formed the oldest verifiable foundation of religion."[5] The yearly sacrifice of David's family in Bethlehem may be presumed to have been originally offered "to a deified eponymous hero."[6] The rule is a simple one—wherever you find mention of burial-places, be sure you are on the track of worship of ancestors.[7] Addis finds Jacob in Gen. xxxv. 14 "pouring out a libation

[1] Wellhausen, *Hist. of Israel*, pp. 18, 30, 325, etc.; Budde, *Rel. of Israel*, p. 107, etc. *E.g.*, Jacob's vow at Bethel is supposed to be meant as a sanction of the payment of tithes to the priests of the calf-worship at that place.

[2] *Geschichte*, i. pp. 451–52. [3] *Ibid.* p. 452.

[4] Mourning customs are supposed to have their rationale in the attempt, as Kautzsch says, "to render oneself *unrecognisable* by the spirit of the dead, and thus to escape its malign influence."—"Rel. of Israel," *Dict.* pp. 614–15. Kautzsch criticises the theory, and concludes that if ancestor-worship ever prevailed in the pre-Mosaic period, no consciousness of it survived to historical times.

[5] *Rel. of Israel*, p. 64. Max Müller subjects the theory of ancestor-worship to a historical examination in his *Anthropological Religion* (Lect. V.), and rejects it as based on totally mistaken data.

[6] *Ibid.* p. 65. [7] *Ibid.*

to the soul of the dead."[1] And these things, in all seriousness, are regarded as "scientific" treatment of the history.

3. Was *animism*, or belief in a spiritual presence in natural objects, a feature of the religion of ancient Israel? These writers have no doubt of it. Primitive peoples are accustomed to connect the presence of the deity with wells and trees.[2] Now there are "wells" mentioned in Genesis, at Beersheba and elsewhere.[3] It is true that there is no hint in the patriarchal narratives that the wells were valued for anything but the supply of water they yielded. But this is no obstacle to the belief that originally the wells were thought of as dwelt in by spirits, and that this was the real ground of the reverence paid to them.[4] So trees were wont to be regarded as manifestations of a divine life. And the patriarchs were fond of the shade of spreading trees, built altars near them,[5] sometimes even planted them. Abraham dwelt by the "oaks" or "terebinths" of Mamre;[6] he planted a tamarisk at Beersheba; Deborah, Rebekah's nurse, was buried under "the oak" at Bethel, which thenceforth was called "Allon-bacuth"—"the oak of weeping."[7] "The famous holy tree near Shechem," says Professor W. R. Smith, "called 'the tree of soothsayers,' in Judg. ix. 37, and 'the tree of the revealer' in Gen. xii. 6, must have been the seat of a Canaanite oracle."[8] Possibly; though there is in the statement the full measure of assumption usual in such matters.[9] But there is nothing to connect the patriarchs with these superstitions, or to indicate that they thought of a god as dwelling in these trees. The Canaanite

[1] *Hex.* ii. p. 226. Addis takes this verse from its place, and connects it with the death of Deborah.

[2] Cf. W. R. Smith, *Rel. of Semites*, pp. 151 ff.

[3] Gen. xvi. 7; xxi. 25, 30 ff.; xxiv. 16; xxvi. 15, 19 ff., etc.

[4] Stade, *Geschichte*, i. p. 456.

[5] Gen. xiii. 18.

[6] Gen. xiii. 18; xiv. 13; xviii. 1. The LXX has the singular, "oak."

[7] Gen. xxxv. 8. Stade would connect the very names of the trees—*Elah*, *Elon*, *Allon*—with the divine name El (i. p. 455). "This attempt," says Professor A. B. Davidson, "may be safely neglected."—*Dict. of Bible*, ii. p. 199.

[8] *Rel. of Semites*, p. 179.

[9] "The famous holy oak" has already a touch of such assumption. It is assumed that the "Moreh" in Gen. xii. 6 is not, like Mamre, a proper name (cf. Dillmann, *in loc.*), and that the identity of this tree is certain with the "oak of Meonenim" in Judg. ix. 37. Similarly, "the palm tree" under which Deborah sat and judged (Judg. iv. 4) is identified with "the oak" which marked the grave of Rebekah's nurse (Gen. xxxv. 8).

Asherahs, or tree symbols of Astarte, on the other hand,—another of the proofs,—were no doubt idolatrous; but they were from the first, and all down the history, absolutely condemned.[1]

4. The proofs offered of *fetishism* and of *stone-worship* in ancient Israel are equally numerous—and equally inconclusive. Only allusion need be made here to the ark of the covenant, which will form a subject of discussion by itself after.[2] The history speaks of an ark, the visible symbol of the presence of Jehovah among His people,[3] in which were deposited the two tables of the law.[4] Jehovah dwelt, not *in*, but above the ark, between (or upon) the cherubim."[5] This, however, in the view of the critics, is a mistake. Analogies are drawn from other religions to prove that "the ark of Yahweh" was really a fetish-chest; and the tradition that it contained tables of stone is to Stade the "most convincing" evidence that it had in it two stones in which Yahweh was believed to dwell.[6] The stones were probably "meteorites"—appropriate to the lightning-god.[7] "If the divinity of Sinai resided in a rock," says Professor H. P. Smith sagely,—"which from Arabian analogies seems very probable,—it would be natural for the people to secure His presence by providing such a chest in which to transport the fetish."[8] One feels sometimes that it would require

[1] Ex. xxxiv. 13; cf. Deut. xvi. 21.

[2] Cf. Chap. VI. pp. 161 ff.

[3] Num. x. 33 ff.; Josh. iii. 6.

[4] Hence the name "ark of the covenant." Cf. Deut. x. 1–6, 1 Kings viii. 9, with Ex. xxiv. 12 ff., xxv. 21. See below, p. 162.

[5] 1 Sam. iv. 4; 2 Sam. vi. 2. Cf. A. B. Davidson, *Theol. of O. T.*, p. 112. Kuenen says of these passages: "We must hold that the author wrote 'the ark of Yahweh,' and 'the ark of God,' nothing more."—*Rel. of Israel*, i. p. 259. Apart, however, from the omission of the words "of the covenant" in the LXX (Vat. Cod.) of 1 Sam. iv. 3–5, which is not decisive, the "must" is in his own theory. See below, p. 162.

[6] *Geschichte*, i. pp. 448–49, 457. "This conception," Stade says, "is what from the standpoint of the history of religion must be called fetishistic" (p. 448).

[7] *Ibid.* p. 458; cf. Kuenen, i. p. 233. Kautzsch adopts the "meteorite" theory.—"Rel. of Israel," *Dict.* p. 629. Bennett says: "According to early tradition, two sacred stones were preserved in the ark."—*Genesis*, p. 282. Tradition, however, says nothing of "two sacred stones," it speaks only and definitely of the two tables of the law.

[8] *O. T. History*, p. 71. Professor A. R. S. Kennedy, in art. "Ark" in *Dict. of Bible* (i. p. 150), dissociates himself from this view, "now generally adopted," he says, "by Continental writers." On the literature, see Kautzsch, as above.

the irony of an Elijah to deal fittingly with such hypotheses, but we are content to leave them to the reader's own reflections.

A more direct proof of stone-worship, however, is thought to be found in the setting up of sacred "pillars" or *maççebas* by the patriarchs and others—as by Jacob at Bethel,[1] by Jacob and Laban in Mount Gilead,[2] by Joshua at Shechem,[3] by Samuel at Ebenezer,[4] etc. It is true that, as Professor W. R. Smith admits, these pillars or stones are never represented in the narratives as anything but memorial pillars;[5] but it is insisted that the real idea underlying them is that God was actually present in the stone, or at least then took up His abode in it.[6] It is pointed out that, in the case of Jacob, not "the place," but the "stone" itself, is called "Bethel," in Gen. xxviii. 22,[7] and a connection is sought with the Greek word *βαιτύλια*, a name for sacred stones.[8] But there is not a vestige of evidence that there was ever a class of sacred stones in Israel called "Bethels,"[9] and it is surely obvious from the context that the *stone* is called "Bethel," merely as marking the site of the *place*. This ingenious hypothesis, in short, is simply a reading into the narrative of ideas which do not necessarily belong to it. "It cannot be inferred," Dillmann says justly, "from Gen. xxviii. 18, xxxv. 14, 15, xlix. 24, that the patriarchs worshipped holy stones: the stone of Jacob appears only as a symbol of a place, and monument of the experience of God's nearness; also in later times we read nothing of stone-worship among the people."[10] Neither, we may add, is there the slightest evidence that the prophets, in their later polemic against idolatrous *maççebas*, intended the least disrespect to such memorial pillars as were set up by Jacob or Joshua. In

[1] Gen. xxviii. 18, 22; xxxv. 14.

[2] Gen. xxxi. 45. Also in vers. 46–49, a heap or cairn.

[3] Josh. xxiv. 26, 27.

[4] 1 Sam. vii. 12.

[5] Cf. above, p. 122.

[6] Professor W. R. Smith distinguishes such dwelling in stones from fetishism proper (*Rel. of Semites*, p. 189).

[7] *Ibid.* p. 187.

[8] Cf. art. "Bethel" in *Dict. of Bible*, i. p. 218.

[9] As Schultz, *e.g.*, would seem to suggest, *O.T. Theol.* i. p. 207.

[10] *Alttest. Theol.* p. 90. So König in art. "Symbol" in *Dict. of Bible* (Extra), p. 170: "The *maççeboth*, again, were not set up on their own account. They were not meant to be dwelling-places of the deity, but were symbols, expressive of gratitude for a divine revelation," etc.

Isa. xix. 19 it is even predicted that "in that day there shall be an altar of Jehovah in the midst of the land of Egypt, and a pillar (*maççeba*) at the border thereof to Jehovah." It is a forced explanation of such a passage to say that, in Isaiah's time, pillars were not yet regarded as unlawful.[1] Memorial pillars never were so regarded: "pillars" on the other hand, connected with idolatrous worship were already condemned in the first legislation,[2] —far older, on any showing, than Isaiah.

5. Another form of superstition with which the religion of Israel is brought into relation is *totemism*, or belief in the descent of a tribe from a sacred animal. Professor W. R. Smith found in this the key to the clan system and sacrificial customs of the Semites—the Hebrews included.[3] Support is sought for the theory in Biblical names—in the name Caleb, *e.g.*, which means a dog,[4]—and Stade urges such facts as the "horns" of the altar, and the bull-worship of the Northern Kingdom.[5] The theory has not met with general acceptance, and hardly needs here fuller discussion.[6]

6. To the long list of heathenish practices asserted to belong to the religion of ancient Israel may be added—*human sacrifice.* Human sacrifice was a feature of Moloch-worship: the Israelites were acquainted with it; in times of religious declension even caused their children to pass through the fire to Moloch.[7] If, then, as Kuenen thinks, Yahweh was originally connected with Moloch,

[1] According to Vatke, Kuenen, Duhm, etc., the abolition of *maççebas* was included in the reforms of Hezekiah. Cf. König, *Hauptprobleme*, p. 68.

[2] Ex. xxiii. 24 (images=*maççebas*); cf. Isa. xvii. 7, 8; Mic. v. 13. Hosea, in chap. iii. 4, seems to group together lawful and unlawful objects.

[3] *Rel. of Semites*, pp. 117 ff., 130, 251 ff., 424 ff.; *Kinship and Marriage*, chap. viii.; "Animal Worship and Animal Tribes," *Jour. of Philology*, 1880.

[4] Cf. *Kinship and Marriage*, pp. 218 ff.: "The nomadic populations of Southern Palestine, which ultimately became incorporated with Judah, also present animal names, of which the most important is that of the Calebbites, or dog-tribe" (p. 219).

[5] *Geschichte*, p. 465. Stade mentions (p. 466) that W. R. Smith supposes the serpent to be the totem of the house of David.

[6] See Note C on Professor W. R. Smith's Theory of Sacrifice. Kautzsch criticises the totem-theory in "Rel. of Israel," *Dict.* p. 613. If the theory were as ingeniously applied to *British* personal (animal) names, symbols (*e.g.*, John Bull, British Lion), tavern signs (a large class), etc., it would bring out startling results.

[7] Cf. 2 Kings xvi. 3; xxi. 6; xxiii. 10; Jer. xxxii. 35, etc.

human sacrifice was to be expected in His service.[1] If, on the other hand, this abhorrent idea of the connection of Jehovah with Moloch is rejected, the chief basis of the theory is destroyed, and other proofs become of secondary account. No fair reader of the history of Israel can say that human sacrifice was at any time a legitimate or recognised part of the worship of the nation. Proofs drawn from Abraham's temptation (the moral of which is that such sacrifices were *not* desired by Jehovah),[2] from the destruction of the first-born,[3] Samuel's hewing of Agag in pieces before Jehovah,[4] the hanging of Saul's seven sons,[5] etc., are quite illusory, for none of the last-named cases answers properly to the idea of sacrifice. If Micah asks: "Shall I give my first-born for my transgression, the fruit of my body for the sin of my soul?"[6]—asks it only to reject the supposition—this no more proves that human sacrifice was a usual or recognised part of Jehovah's religion, than Paul's words, "If I give my body to be burned,"[7] prove that surrender to death by fire was a common form of devotion in the apostolic Church. There remains the case of Jephthah's sacrifice of his daughter in fulfilment of his rash vow.[8] The circumstances are unusual, and there is still doubt as to the manner in which Jephthah fulfilled his vow.[9] But, admitting that the maiden was actually slain as a sacrifice, and not simply devoted, we may be excused, as before, for not accepting the action of this very partially enlightened Gileadite, in a rude age, as a rule for judging of the true character of Israel's religion. How would it fare with Christianity, if it were judged by individual instances of misguided zeal, in contrariety with its own first principles, occurring, say, in the Middle Ages? We may safely apply to all human sacrifices

[1] Cf. *Rel. of Israel*, i. pp. 228, 237. Kuenen carries over all the things condemned by the prophets, including female prostitution, into the worship of Yahweh (cf. p. 72).

[2] Gen. xxii.

[3] Ex. xiii. 2, 11–12, etc. The redemption of the first-born is thought to have its origin in this practice. Cf. Kuenen, i. p. 290.

[4] 1 Sam. xv. 33.

[5] 2 Sam. xxi. 1–14. These are Kuenen's own instances (i. p. 287).

[6] Mic. vi. 7, 8.

[7] 1 Cor. xiii. 3.

[8] Judg. xi. 30, 31, 34–40.

[9] Cf. Sanday, *Inspiration*, p. 138; and see the full discussion in Köhler's *Bib. Geschichte*, ii. pp. 100–3.

what Jeremiah says of the sacrifices to Moloch: "Which I commanded them not, neither came it into My mind, that they should do this abomination, to cause Judah to sin."[1]

IV. Image-Worship in Israel

A more important question than any of the above is—Was *image-worship* an original or permissible part of Israel's religion? To most the Second Commandment would seem decisive on that point; but it is not so to the critics. The Decalogue is denied to Moses, and a principal reason for rejecting the precept prohibiting images is precisely that images are held to have been, in point of fact, worshipped.[2] That there was deplorable defection, and lapsing into idolatry, in the time of the Judges, and under the kings, no one, of course, denies; it is the assertion of the Bible itself, and the constant subject of the denunciation of the prophets. It is a different matter when it is maintained that the worship of Jehovah was originally, and all down the history, by images. The assertions of the critics here are of the most positive kind. Wellhausen says roundly: "The prohibition of images was during the older period quite unknown."[3] Professor H. P. Smith tells us that even the great prophets "no doubt conceived God as existing in human form."[4] It was not, however, in human form, but under the image of a bull, that Jehovah is supposed to have been worshipped from ancient times in Israel.[5] The support for this is chiefly drawn from the calf-worship set up by Jeroboam in Northern Israel, and confirmatory evidences are sought in the ephod of Gideon,[6] the images

[1] Jer. xxxii. 35. Another prophetic passage adduced by Kuenen is Hos. xiii. 2, with the reading, "Sacrificing men, they kiss the calves" (i. p. 75). Even so, the practice is only mentioned to be condemned. See Note D on Sacrifice of Children.

[2] See above, p. 120; and below, p. 153. Cf. Kittel, *Hist. of Hebs.* i. p. 248. Cf. Schultz, *O.T. Theol.* i. p. 210. Professor W. R. Smith says: "Even the principle of the Second Commandment, that Jehovah is not to be worshipped by images . . . cannot, in the light of history, be regarded as having so fundamental a place in the religion of early Israel."—*Prophets*, p. 63.

[3] *Hist. of Israel*, p. 439.

[4] *O.T. History*, p. 18. Kautzsch also thinks that the idea of Jehovah having bodily form continued *till* the prophetic age.—"Rel. of Israel," *Dict.* p. 637. Cf. Kittel, *Hist. of Hebs.* i. pp. 248 ff.

[5] Thus generally.

[6] Judg. viii. 27.

of Micah,[1] the brazen serpent of Moses.[2] It is allowed that there was no image of Jehovah in the temple at Jerusalem;[3] but it is urged that there were other visible symbols,[4] and that images were common among the people.[5] Nothing, in our view, could be more baseless than this contention, but it will be well to look at the subject more closely.

1. We are entitled to say that the *oldest periods* of the history afford no confirmation of this theory. The worship of the patriarchs, in the Book of Genesis, was without images. The only apparent exception, as before noticed, is in the "teraphim" of Laban's family.[6] What these "teraphim" were is obscure. They are probably correctly enough described by Kuenen as "images which were revered as household gods, and consulted as to the future."[7] They were at any rate not images of Jehovah, and were put away by Jacob at Shechem as incompatible with the pure worship of God.[8] In the cases of Abraham, of Isaac, of Jacob, of Joseph, or, indeed, of any of the patriarchs, image-worship is not so much as hinted at. "The worship of God in the house of Abraham," as Dillmann says, "was imageless."[9] Baudissin, indeed, would carry back the bull-worship even to Abraham;[10] but this is baseless conjecture. Again, in Mosaic times, and in the Book of Joshua, there is no suggestion of a lawful worship of images. The only recorded instance of image-worship is in the making of the golden calf at Sinai,[11] and this is denounced and punished as a flagrant transgression, which all but cost the people their covenant privilege. The prohibitions of image-worship, and of participation in the idolatry of the Canaanites, are, on the other hand, absolute. The brazen serpent erected by Moses was not an image of Jehovah, or an image for worship at all, though it became at a later time an object of worship to the Israelites, and was in consequence destroyed by

[1] Judg. xvii. 3, 4; xviii. 14, 20, etc.
[2] Num. xxi. 8, 9.
[3] Kuenen, *Rel. of Israel*, i. pp. 80, 289.
[4] The ark is held by Kuenen, Stade, etc., to have been such a symbol. The two brazen pillars in the temple of Solomon are alleged by Professor W. R. Smith to have been "doubtless symbols of Jehovah."—*Rel. of Semites*, p. 191.
[5] Kuenen, as above, p. 80.
[6] Gen. xxxi. 19, 30–35.
[7] *Rel. of Israel*, p. 246.
[8] Gen. xxxv. 2–4.
[9] *Alttest. Theol.* p. 90.
[10] Cf. König, *Hauptprobleme*, p. 58.
[11] Ex. xxxii.

Hezekiah.[1] Neither Moses nor Joshua — none of the leaders—showed the least tendency to image-worship. The first notice of idolatrous practices in the wilderness journeyings is in the prophet Amos—if even there.[2]

2. When we pass to the *Book of Judges*, it is different. We are now in a period expressly signalised as one of declension and sinful adoption of Canaanitish idolatries.[3] But even here we seek in vain in the greater part of the book for evidence of an image-worship of Jehovah. The sin for which the people are blamed is much more that of forsaking Jehovah, and serving "the Baalim and the Ashtaroth" (Astartes), "the Baalim and the Asheroth" (sacred trees or poles), of their heathen neighbours,—an undeniable violation of fundamental law, — than image-worship of their own God.[4] One clear example of the latter is in the case of the Ephraimite Micah, whose images were carried off by the Danites.[5] The other case usually cited is that of Gideon, who, after his victory over the Midianites, made from the spoils a golden "ephod," which, it is declared, became a "snare" to Gideon and his house.[6] On this mistaken act of a man whose zeal had been conspicuous against the Baal altars and the Asherahs,[7] a whole edifice of rickety conjecture is built up. It is first assumed that Gideon's "ephod" was an "image" of Jehovah; it is next taken for granted that the image was in the form of a bull;[8] lastly, it is concluded that bull-worship, or at least

[1] 2 Kings xviii. 4. Professor H. P. Smith, who sees in the brazen serpent a survival of primitive totemism in Israel, has some characteristic remarks on the subject. See Note E on H. P. Smith on the Brazen Serpent.

[2] Amos v. 25, 26. The interpretation of the passage is much disputed.

[3] Judg. ii. 11–14.

[4] Judg. ii. 11, 13; iii. 7; x. 6, etc. It is possible, however, to paint even this period of backsliding and disorganisation in too dark colours. It is, *e.g.*, an exaggeration to say with Mr. Thatcher: "There is no conception of spiritual worship or moral duty in our book."—*Judges* ("Cent. Bible"), Introd. p. 33. This is only true if first of all the higher elements (the repentances, etc.) are critically eliminated. The very absence of image-worship in so large a part of the book is a disproof of the statement. The Song of Deborah strikes a lofty, and at the end, spiritual note. Cf. above, p. 131; and see the remarks of König on this point in art. "Judges," *Dict. of Bible*, iii. p. 816 (cf. below, p. 384). Cf. also the Book of Ruth.

[5] Judg. xvii., xviii.

[6] Judg. viii. 27.

[7] Judg. vi. 28–32.

[8] Thus even Schultz, *O. T. Theol.* i. p. 149: "The molten image . . . is, according to the analogy of other passages (Judg. xviii. 30; 1 Kings xii. 28 ff.; Ex. xxxii. 4) to be thought of as the image of an ox." Cf. Kuenen, *Rel. of Israel*, i. p. 236.

image-worship, was common among the people. It may be observed that, even if it were true that Gideon made an image for worship, these sweeping inferences would not be justified. There would in itself be nothing more wonderful in this heroic man falling in his latter days into the sin of idolatry, than there is in Solomon, in his old age, building idolatrous shrines for his wives.[1] But the inferences are unwarranted on other grounds. What the text says is, not that Gideon made an "image," but that he made an "ephod"[2]—a massive and costly piece of work,[3] certainly, and not designed for actual use, but in some way suggestive of the high priest and his oracle. There is no indication that he meant the ephod for worship. Least of all is there any ground for the assertion that it was an image in the form of a bull.[4] The ephod is expressly declared to have become a "snare" to Gideon and his house: a condemnatory statement not to be got rid of by the too easy hypothesis of interpolation. There remains, therefore, as the single prop of the theory of an image-worship of Jehovah in the time of the Judges, the case of Micah, who made for himself "a graven image and a molten image," a sanctuary, "an ephod (here evidently distinguished from the images) and teraphim":[5] an undisputed instance of idolatry in the worship of Jehovah. We willingly make a present of this weak-minded, superstitious Ephraimite, and of the Danites who stole his images from him, to the critics; but decline to accept his behaviour as evidence of the fundamental law, or better religious practice, in Israel. It is more to the point to notice that even Micah does not appear to have had images till his mother suggested this use of the stolen silver to him.

3. The stronghold of the case for image-worship, how-

[1] 1 Kings xi. 4, 5.

[2] Kuenen, in a long note in his *Rel. of Israel* (i. pp. 260 ff.), "decidedly rejects" the opinion that the ephod was an image; but in his *Hibbert Lecture* he accepts it (p. 82).

[3] This is shown by the amount of gold used, about 70 pounds.

[4] The idea rests, as the passage from Schultz above cited shows, on the reading back into the time of the Judges of the calf-worship of Jeroboam. It has no basis in the Book of Judges itself. Even so extreme a rationalist as Dr. Oort contests this idea (cf. Kuenen, i. pp. 261–62).

[5] Judg. xvii. 3–6; xviii. 14, 20. Budde says of Micah's ephod, which he takes to be "a silver, oracular image," that "unfortunately we do not know its form."—*Rel. of Israel*, p. 80. See Note F on Dillmann on Image Worship.

ever, is in the *two calves of gold* which Jeroboam set up at Bethel and Dan, after the division of the kingdom. It is true that no hint is given that such images were known before in Israel, unless the words, "Behold thy gods, O Israel, which brought thee up out of the land of Egypt," be an allusion to the golden calf of Ex. xxxii.; but it is thought *unlikely* that Jeroboam would set up a symbol entirely new,[1] and it is pointed out—at least alleged—that no protest was made against the worship of the calves by prophets like Elijah and Amos.[2] The denunciations in the Books of Kings are regarded as representing a later point of view. Here, again, the history which we have is thrust aside and a new history invented which suits the critic's theory. No ingenuity, however, can give this new theory the semblance of probability. How strange, if this was an old and well-known custom in Israel, that absolutely no trace of it should be discoverable, or that it should need to be "revived"! How remarkable that nothing of this bull-worship should be known in Jerusalem, or in the temple, the seat of Jehovah's worship,[3] in which there was no image, or, apparently, in Judah generally, where it was universally regarded as an abomination! The narrator in the Book of Kings, who had access to old records, plainly regarded it as something new. The judgment of the prophets, when we turn to these, does not differ from that of the Book of Kings. Hosea, it is generally admitted, is unsparing in his denunciation of the calves,[4] and he was a prophet of Northern Israel. It is held, however, that his attitude in this respect is not that of his predecessors. "There is no feature in Hosea's prophecy," says Professor W. R. Smith, "which distinguishes him from earlier prophets so sharply

[1] A connection is conjecturally sought with the old sanctuary at Dan, Judg. xviii. 29–31.

[2] Thus Wellhausen, Kuenen, Stade, W. R. Smith, and generally. The suggestion may be made that Jeroboam got the idea from Egypt, where he resided from the time of his revolt against Solomon till the accession of Rehoboam (1 Kings xi. 40; xii. 1–3). Kuenen, however, rejects this, and says: "It is much more reasonable to suppose that the ten tribes who rebelled against Solomon's exactions, and his leanings towards foreign manners and customs, introduced a genuinely national and ancient Israelitish worship."—*Rel. of Israel*, i. p. 236.

[3] Are the "lions, *oxen*, and cherubim" that supported the "bases" in the temple (1 Kings vii. 29) thought to be an exception? They were certainly not objects of worship.

[4] Hos. viii. 5, 6; xiii. 2.

as his attitude to the golden calves, the local symbols of Jehovah adored in the Northern sanctuaries. Elijah and Elisha had no quarrel with the traditional[1] worship of their nation. Even Amos never speaks in condemnation of the calves."[2] This last sentence is astonishing. To the ordinary reader Amos and Hosea would seem to speak with precisely the same voice on the Northern calf-worship —Amos, if possible, with the greater vehemence of the two. "When I visit the transgressions of Israel upon him," says this prophet, "I will also visit the altars of Bethel."[3] "Come to Bethel," he exclaims, "and transgress."[4] He speaks of those "that swear by the sin of Samaria, and that swear, As thy god, O Dan, liveth."[5] Even Kuenen agrees that Amos speaks in the same way as Hosea of the calf-worship.[6]

With greater plausibility it may be maintained that there is no direct denunciation of the calf-worship by Elijah and Elisha. The argument from silence, however, is a peculiarly unsafe one here. In the only episodes in which Elijah is brought before us, he is engaged in a life-and-death struggle of another kind—the conflict between Jehovah and Baal arising from the introduction of the Tyrian Baal-worship into Samaria by Ahab and Jezebel.[7] It requires great faith to believe that a stern and zealous monotheist like Elijah could have any toleration for the calf-worship, which every other prophet of that age is represented as denouncing.[8] It is a sounder application of the argument from silence to observe that Elijah is never found as a worshipper in the neighbourhood of Bethel or Dan, and that he never drops a word indicative of recognition of that worship.[9] When he speaks despairingly of Jehovah's altars being thrown down,[10] he can hardly have included Bethel and Dan among their number, for these altars stood, and doubtless

[1] The reader will mark the *petitio* in the word "traditional." To Professor Smith also the calf-worship is as old as the days of the Judges (*Prophets*, p. 96).

[2] *Prophets*, p. 175.

[3] Amos iii. 14.

[4] Amos iv. 4; cf. v. 4, 5.

[5] Amos viii. 14.

[6] *Rel. of Israel*, i. pp. 73–74. Cf. the pungent remarks of Dr. A. B. Davidson, *Bib. Essays*, pp. 91, 120–22.

[7] 1 Kings xvi. 30–34.

[8] *E.g.*, Ahijah (1 Kings xiv. 7 ff.); the prophet from Judah (chap. xiii. 2); Jehu, the son of Hanani (chap. xvi. 1, 2).

[9] Elisha was mocked at Bethel (2 Kings ii. 23).

[10] 1 Kings xix. 10.

had their crowds of worshippers. We may suppose that to him they would be practically in the category of the Baal-altars. And does his threatening to Ahab, "I will make thine house like the house of Jeroboam, the son of Nebat,"[1] etc., convey no allusion to that by which peculiarly Jeroboam "made Israel to sin"?

A dispassionate review, therefore, of this long catalogue of superstitions alleged to belong to pre-prophetic religion in Israel fails to establish the theory of the critics that any one of these formed part of the genuine religion of Israel. They show abundant defection in particular periods from the pure norm of that religion; but the evidence is overwhelming that they were foreign to the true genius of the religion, were condemned by its laws and by the prophets, and at no time received countenance from its great representatives. The ideas on which the religion rested—the unity, holiness, universal providence, and saving purpose of God—were, as before shown, entirely distinct from those of other religions. As it is with the idea of God and with the adjuncts of His worship, so, we shall next see, it is with the institutions of the religion.

[1] 1 Kings xxi. 21-24.

CHAPTER VI

The Old Testament as affected by Criticism—II. Religion and Institutions: Ark, Tabernacle, Priesthood, etc.

"I believe that, alongside of the modern representations, which resolve the founders of the Old Testament religion into flitting shadows that elude the grasp, and throw overboard the solid mass of the Pentateuchal history, like unnecessary ballast from a ship, my attempt will still meet with sympathy, to find an intelligible meaning in the narrative of the Pentateuch, and to apprehend the religion of Abraham as the preliminary stage, and the proclamation of Moses as the foundation, of the Old Testament faith, thought, and life. The Bible remains: scientific attempts to represent the Biblical history come and go."—KLOSTERMANN.

"It [German criticism] has generally been wanting in flexibility and moderation. It has insisted upon knowing everything, explaining everything, precisely determining everything. . . . Hence complicated and obscure theories, provided with odd corners in which all the details may be sheltered, and which leave the mind little opening or leisure to observe the tendency of facts and the general currents of history."—DARMESTETER (in Ottley).

"In Wellhausen's review of the history, he has much to say of the gradual rise of feasts from the presentation of first-fruits, and of their annual observance at neighbourhood sanctuaries, and the growth of larger sanctuaries towards the close of the period of the Judges. . . . But the whole thing is spun out of his own brain. It is as purely fictitious as an astronomical map would be of the other side of the moon."—W. H. GREEN.

CHAPTER VI

THE OLD TESTAMENT AS AFFECTED BY CRITICISM —II. RELIGION AND INSTITUTIONS: ARK, TABERNACLE, PRIESTHOOD, ETC.

THE subject of laws and institutions in Israel is bound up with so many intricate critical questions as to dates and succession of codes, that it may seem scarcely possible to deal with it satisfactorily till the critical questions have been, at least in some provisional way, disposed of. On the other hand, it is to be observed that the discussion of laws and institutions does not *wholly* depend on the conclusions reached on such matters, say, as the age of Deuteronomy, or date of compilation of the Priestly Code; for, conceivably, these books, in their present form, might be late, yet the laws embodied in them might be very old.[1] It will be found, in fact, that the determination of the critical questions themselves depends in no small measure on the view we are led to take of the history and nature of the institutions.[2] There is room and need, therefore, for some preliminary consideration of the latter, so far as this can be done without begging any question not yet critically dealt with.

I. General Position of Moses as Lawgiver

We may first advert a little further than has yet been done to the general position assigned to Moses in tradition as the *lawgiver* of Israel.[3] This is a point on which the critics can hardly avoid involving themselves in some inconsistency. On the one hand, it is necessary to exalt

[1] This is the position taken up by some critics, as König.
[2] See Wellhausen above, p. 5.
[3] See above, Chap. IV. pp. 98–99.

the personality and work of Moses, in order to explain how it comes about that all the legislation in the Old Testament is connected with his name;[1] on the other hand, it is necessary to minimise his influence almost to vanishing point, in order to make it credible that he really gave to Israel no laws at all—none at least of which we have any knowledge. It will be recalled how we are told that "Malachi is the first of the prophets to refer to a Mosaic code."[2] This line of reasoning, as shown before, is fatuous. The JE history, put by the critics as early as the ninth or eighth century, gives the foremost place to Moses as a lawgiver. The Book of the Covenant, older than this history, and incorporated into it, is expressly ascribed to Moses as its author. The Book of Deuteronomy, again, whenever written, is evidence that Israel had but one tradition about Moses—that he gave and *wrote* laws for the nation. The force of this testimony is not in the least satisfied by supposing, with Wellhausen, W. R. Smith, and others, that the repute of Moses rested on such *oral* decisions as those referred to in Ex. xviii. 13–16, 26.[3] Budde will have nothing to do with this basing of the legislation of Moses on these oral *toroth* of Ex. xviii.,[4] and there is certainly something arbitrary in founding on this chapter as more historically trustworthy than its neighbours. If it is accepted, one must notice the evidence it yields of a high organisation of the people at the time of the Exodus.[5] What then are the reasons for refusing to Moses such legislation as the Old Testament ascribes to him?

1. If anything can be attributed with certainty to Moses, it surely is the *Decalogue*, which lies at the foundation of the whole covenant relation of Jehovah to Israel. Yet even this, which Delitzsch calls "the most genuine of genuine

[1] Cf. Wellhausen, *Hist. of Israel*, pp. 432 ff., 438 ff.; Kuenen, *Rel. of Israel*, i. pp. 272 ff. The latter says: "The collections of laws were fearlessly embellished with his name, because it was known that he had laid the foundations of all legislation" (p. 279). He thinks, indeed, that "this he could do without writing down a single precept."

[2] Carpenter, as above, p. 98. "The prophets of the eighth century," says Professor W. R. Smith, "never speak of a written law of Moses."—*O.T. in J. C.*, p. 302. To show this, he has to put a non-natural sense on Hos. viii. 12 (see below, p. 325). But at least the prophets knew of the Book of the Covenant, professing to be written by Moses.

[3] Wellhausen, *Hist. of Israel*, p. 439; W. R. Smith, *O.T. in J. C.*, pp. 304, 339.

[4] *Rel. of Israel*, p. 33.

[5] Ex. xviii. 21, 25.

productions,"[1] it has of late become almost universally the fashion to deny to the lawgiver. But on what subjective and arbitrary grounds![2] A main reason, as we have seen, is the prohibition of images in the Second Commandment[3]—a subject already discussed.[4] Apart from this, and the too elevated idea of God in the Decalogue as a whole, two special objections may be noticed: (1) the variation in the form of the Fourth Commandment in the Deuteronomic version,[5] and (2) the alleged occurrence of a second Decalogue in Ex. xxxiv. 12–26—a notion borrowed from Goethe. The first of these objections comes badly from those who see in Deuteronomy a free prophetic composition of the age of Josiah, and, apart from the supposition of an original shorter form, seems sufficiently met by Delitzsch's remark that "the Decalogue is there freely rendered in the flow of hortatory oratory, and not literally reproduced."[6] The variation may indeed be regarded as an incidental mark of genuineness in Deuteronomy, for hardly any other than the lawgiver would be likely to allow himself this liberty of change. The second objection derives some colour from a slight ambiguity or confusion in the language of Ex. xxxiv. 27, 28; but cannot overbear the clear connection of ver. 28, "And He [Jehovah] wrote upon the tables the words of the covenant, the ten commandments [words]," with ver. 1, "I will write upon the tables the words which were upon the first tables, which thou brakest," or the plain intention of the narrative as a whole. The so-called second Decalogue of J in Ex. xxxiv. 12–26, is, in fact, pretty much, as scholars are coming to see, a figment of the critical imagination. It is only by straining that the section can be made into a Decalogue at all,[7] and, with its mixed precepts, it has no

[1] *Genesis*, i. p. 29. Smend also formerly wrote: "The Decalogue, whose Mosaic origin no one can doubt."—*Stud. u. Krit.* 1876, p. 643. Cf. in defence of the genuineness, Riehm, *Einleit.* i. p. 166; Kittel, *Hist. of Hebs.* i. p. 244 ff. (in shorter form).

[2] For a summary by Addis, see Note A on Objections to the Decalogue. Cf. also Wellhausen, *Hist. of Israel*, pp. 392–93, 439 ff.; Smend, *Alttest. Religionsgeschichte*, p. 47.

[3] "There would be no valid reason," says Kautzsch, "for refusing to attribute to Moses himself a primitive, concise form of the Decalogue, were it not for the formidable difficulty presented by *the prohibition of the use of images*."—"Rel. of Israel," *Dict.* p. 633.

[4] See above, pp. 141 ff.

[5] Deut. v. 15.

[6] *Genesis*, i. p. 30.

[7] Scarcely two critics divide the precepts so as to make ten in precisely

suitability for taking the place of the historical "words" of the tables.[1]

2. If the Decalogue is allowed to be Mosaic, there is little reason for denying that the remaining laws ("judgments") of the *Book of the Covenant*, with which the "ten words" stand in so close a connection, also proceeded from Moses in *substantially* their present form.[2] The principal objection urged to this is that they imply a settled life and agriculture.[3] But, on the one hand, the laws in question are of a very primitive and simple character, probably resting on old usage;[4] and, on the other, the people were not the undisciplined horde the critics for their own purposes would make them out to be.[5] They had long had the experience of orderly and settled life, and were, moreover, on the point of entering Canaan. They were organised, and had "statutes of God" and "laws" given them in the wilderness.[6] What more likely in itself than that Moses, by divine command, should draw up for them a simple code, suited for present and prospective needs? How, indeed, could a people like Israel have been kept together, or have preserved its distinction from the Canaanites, without some such body of laws,—moral, civil, and religious,[7]—and this not simply in the form of floating

the same way, and the attempt to do so is now being pretty generally given up, even by advanced critics. Addis speaks of the division into ten as "mere guess-work." "Many critics," he says, "(*e.g.*, Wellhausen), adopting a suggestion of Goethe, have tried to disentangle ten 'words of the covenant,' answering to the Ten Words or Decalogue of the Elohist. This, however, is mere guess-work."—*Hex.* i. p. 157. Carpenter also does not favour the notion. Kittel says: "It requires the utmost arbitrariness even to find in it the number ten."—*Hist. of Hebs.* i. p. 198. Kautzsch rejects the second Decalogue.

[1] Cf. Kittel and Riehm, as above, in reply to Wellhausen.

[2] Thus Delitzsch, *Genesis*, i. p. 31.

[3] Thus Wellhausen, Kuenen, Addis, etc. Cf. Riehm in reply, i. pp. 170 ff.

[4] The Code of Hammurabi presents interesting ancient analogies. See for details art. in *Dict. of Bible* (Extra Vol.). One regrets to find Mr. Johns, in the section on comparison with Hebrew legislation, writing in the usual flippant style—"The current opinion of critics does not ascribe much of the Hebrew law to Moses. So his personality may be set aside" (p. 608).

[5] See above, pp. 79, 104.

[6] Ex. xviii. 16, 21, 25.

[7] Wellhausen himself points out that "when the Israelites settled in Palestine, they found it inhabited by a population superior to themselves both in numbers and in civilisation," yet "it never had the effect of making the Israelites Canaanites; on the contrary, it made the Canaanites Israelites. Notwithstanding their inferiority, numerical and otherwise

oral *toroth*, but in the shape of definite, authoritative "statutes and judgments," such as the history, the prophets, and the psalms, uniformly assume the nation to have possessed?[1] And if this was needed, can we suppose that a man of Moses' capabilities and prescient mind would have left the people without it? We have several codes of laws—"programmes"— which the critics assume to have arisen at various junctures in the history of the nation. But, as Dr. Robertson observes, "it is strange indeed that critical historians should postulate the putting forth of 'legislative programmes' at various later points in Israel's history, and should be so unwilling to admit the same for the time of Moses."[2] We seem fully entitled, therefore, in accordance with the whole tradition of Israel, to look on Moses as the fountain of both civil and religious institutions to his nation, and to consider without prejudice any statements attributing such institutions to his time. The question of ritual laws demands separate treatment.

II. The Sacrificial System and Ritual Law

The Book of the Covenant deals mainly with civil matters, and, except in the law of the altar,[3] and the ordinance about the three feasts,[4] has no properly religious enactments. This of itself creates a not unreasonable presumption that such will be found elsewhere. To most it will appear incredible that, in settling the constitution of Israel, Moses should not have given the people, among his other laws, at least *some* ordinances for religious worship. The critics, however, hold a directly contrary opinion. Not content with denying that Moses was the author of any ritual legislation, they go so far as to maintain that, till the time of the exile, no sacrificial or other ritual existed which was even *believed* to have Mosaic or divine sanction. The prophets, it is declared, show clearly by their denunciations that they know nothing of such a divinely-ordained ritual. "Thus it is," says Wellhausen, "that the prophets

they maintained their individuality, and that without the support of any external organisation. Thus a certain inner unity subsisted long before it had found any outward political expression: it goes back to the time of Moses, who is to be regarded as its author."—*Hist. of Israel*, p. 433.

[1] See below, pp. 308, 324.

[2] *Early Religion of Israel*, p. 337.

[3] Ex. xx. 24–26.

[4] Ex. xxiii. 14–19.

are able to ask whether then Jehovah has commanded His people to tax their energies with such exertions: the fact presupposed being that no such command exists, and that no one knows anything at all about a ritual *torah*."[1] The idea of a ritual which "goes back to Moses or to Jehovah Himself"[2] is said to be foreign to them. It first came in with the Priestly Code, which is so insistent on the Mosaic origin of lawful sacrifice that it carefully avoids, in the earlier history, ever ascribing sacrifice to the patriarchs.[3] Without at this stage entering into details, which will more properly come up when discussing the Code itself, we would make on these representations the following remarks:—

1. There is, to put it mildly, some absurdity in the often-repeated statement that "the Priestly Writer *knows nothing* of sacrifice by the servants of God before Moses."[4] We might ask—How often is sacrifice mentioned altogether in the Book of Genesis? And in how many instances does the meagre thread of narrative assigned to the Priestly Writer admit of the act of sacrifice being introduced? But there is a more obvious answer—one of which a good deal more will be heard as we proceed. The Priestly Writer knew at least about the patriarchal sacrifices all that the J and E histories had to tell him; for he had, on the newer theory, these histories before him, presupposes and founds upon them, if he does not actually furnish the frame in which their narratives are set.[5] He cannot, therefore, be supposed designedly to contradict them on this point of patriarchal sacrifices.[6] It is in truth no part of the theory

[1] *Hist. of Israel*, p. 56; cf. the whole section, pp. 52–59. Thus also Kuenen, *Hex.* pp. 176–77; W. R. Smith, *O.T. in J. C.*, pp. 293–95. "All this," says Professor Smith, "is so clear that it seems impossible to misunderstand it. Yet the position of the prophets is not only habitually explained away by those who are determined at any cost to maintain the traditional view of the Pentateuch," etc. We shall see immediately about the "explaining away."

[2] *Hist. of Israel*, p. 56.

[3] *Ibid.*

[4] Addis, *Hex.* p. li.

[5] See below, pp. 340, 360.

[6] Colenso, in combating Kuenen on this point, says: "Is it credible that he supposed the patriarchs to have offered no sacrifices *at all* before the delivery of the sacrificial laws at Sinai—more especially if he had before him the sacrifices mentioned in Gen. iv. 3, 4; viii. 20, 21; xxxi. 54; xlvi. 1, etc."; and in another connection: "It seems incredible that a later post-captivity writer, sitting down (as Kuenen supposes) with the J narrative before him, and of course known to him, and *now venerable by age*, should deliberately contradict it."—*Pent.* Pt. vi. pp. 126, 139.

of the Priestly Writer that sacrifices began with Moses. His own legislation gives no hint that up to that time these were unheard-of. Rather, in such phrases as, "If any man bring an offering to Jehovah," . . . "If his offering be a burnt offering of the herd,"[1] etc., it assumes that such sacrifices are well-known and customary.

2. As little can it be maintained, with any show of reason, that, up to the time of the exile, sacrifice in Israel was simply, as Wellhausen affirms, traditional custom, without divine sanction, or regulation of the *when*, the *where*, the *by whom*, the *how*.[2] The Book of the Covenant already makes a beginning in regulations about the altar, and the times and manner of sacrifice—"My sacrifice";[3] and the Book of Deuteronomy, "which still occupies the same standpoint as JE,"[4] has abundance of prescriptions and regulations about sacrifices—described as "all that I command you."[5] How can it be claimed that Jeremiah, whose mind is steeped in Deuteronomy—if he had not, as some of these writers think, to do with its production—is ignorant of these commands, or means to deny them, in his impassioned protestations that it was not about burnt offerings and sacrifices, but about obedience, that God commanded their fathers, when He brought them out of Egypt?[6]

3. The strong language of the prophets in *denunciation of outward ritual*,[7] while the ethical side of religion was neglected, admits of easy explanation: the one explanation it will not bear, it is safe to say, is that which the critics put upon it. This for a twofold reason. Probably, first, not one of these prophets could form the conception of a religion for a nation which had not its temple, priesthood, sacrifices, and outward order of worship, or ever dreamt of the abolition of these things; and, second, so far from regarding sacrifice as not well-pleasing to Jehovah, when the right spirit was present, there is not one of the greater prophets who does not include sacrifice in his own picture of the

[1] Lev. i. 2, 3, etc.
[2] *Hist. of Israel*, p. 54.
[3] Ex. xx. 24, 25; xxiii. 18, 19.
[4] Wellhausen, as above.
[5] Deut. xii. 11, etc.
[6] Jer. vii. 22, 24. Professor W. R. Smith nevertheless thinks "it is impossible to give a flatter contradiction to the traditional theory that the Levitical system was enacted in the wilderness."—*O. T. in J. C.*, p. 295.
[7] Amos iv. 4, 5; v. 21, 27; Isa. i. 10–15; Jer. vii. 22, 23, etc.

restored and perfected theocracy.[1] It is to be remembered that it is not sacrifice alone, but prayer, feast-days, Sabbaths, etc., that the prophets include in their denunciations; yet we know the importance they attached to prayer and the Sabbath in other parts of their writings.[2] In many places and ways, also, we see incidentally their recognition of the divine sanction of these outward ordinances, which, in other connections, viz., when made a substitute for heart-piety and moral conduct, they condemn. It was in vision of the temple of Jehovah that Isaiah received his call, and by the touch of a live coal from the altar that his lips were purged.[3] It is Jehovah's courts—"My courts"—that were profaned by the people's splendid but unholy worship;[4] just as in Hosea it is "the sacrifices of Mine offerings" which the people turn into "sacrifices of flesh."[5] If the 40th Psalm is relegated, as on the critical theory it must be, to post-exilian times, we read in it also: "Sacrifice and offering Thou didst not desire . . . burnt offering and sin offering hast Thou not required."[6] But who misunderstands these words?

4. Strange to say, all this, and a great deal more, is, in the end, *admitted* by the critics. Their argument means nothing, if it does not amount to a rejection by the prophets of a ritual worship of God absolutely. Yet we are told by Kuenen: "We must not assert that the prophets reject the cultus unconditionally. On the contrary, they too share the belief, for instance, that sacrifice is an essential element of true worship (Isa. lvi. 7; Zech. xiv. 16–19; Mic. iv. 1 ff.; Isa. ii. 1 ff.; xviii. 7; xix. 19 ff., etc. etc.). The context always shows that what they really protest against is the idea that it is enough to take part in the cultus," etc.[7] Only, it is argued, they did not allow this cultus to be of Mosaic or divine origin. It is precisely on this point that the proof fails. The proof was supposed to be found in the fact that the prophets condemned the cultus; now it is owned that they did not condemn it as in any sense incom-

[1] Cf. Isa. lvi. 6, 7; lx. 7; lxvi. 23, etc.; Jer. xvii. 24–27; xxxiii. 17–18, etc. (cf. p. 95); Ezek. xl. ff.

[2] Cf. Jer. xvii. 21–27; "As I commanded your fathers" (ver. 22); Isa. lviii. 13, 14.

[3] Isa. vi. [4] Isa. i. 12. [5] Hos. viii. 13. [6] Ps. xl. 6.

[7] *Hex.* p. 176; cf. Smend, *Alttest. Religionsgeschichte*, p. 168. See also Smend's article, referred to on next page.

patible with the belief that it was a lawful and necessary part of the service of Jehovah. If, further, we ask—What *kind* of cultus was it which existed in the days of the prophets? we get a number of surprising admissions, to which it will be necessary that we return later. It was a cultus "of very old and sacred usage,"[1] and highly elaborate in character. There were "splendid sacrifices . . . presumably offered in accordance with all the rules of priestly skill."[2] We have, in fact, only to analyse the passages in the prophets to see what a highly elaborate ritual system was already in operation in their day—as elaborate, practically, as in the Levitical Code itself. It is interesting to read what one of the ablest adherents of the Graf school—Rudolf Smend—had to say on this point at an earlier stage in his development. In his work *Moses apud Prophetas*, Smend discerns what he calls "Levitismus" peering out from the pages of the oldest prophets—Amos and Hosea. He says, even: "It is sufficiently evident that the cultus of Jehovah, as it existed in the time of the earlier prophets, and doubtless long before, is by no means at variance with the character of Leviticus. Whatever judgment may be formed of the age of this book, the opinion hitherto entertained of the birth, growth, and maturity of the religion of Israel will undergo no change."[3] In a valuable article contributed to the *Studien und Kritiken* in 1876, he reiterates these views, and concludes: "Accordingly, we do not know what objection can be made to the earlier composition of Leviticus on the ground of the older prophetical writings."[4] In such statements, supported by reasons which time has done nothing to refute, we are far enough away from the theory that nothing was known of a divine sanction of ritual ordinances till after the time of the exile.

To ourselves, as before said, it appears incredible that no ordinances for religious worship should have been given to the people by Moses, in settling the constitution of

[1] Wellhausen, *Hist. of Israel*, p. 59.

[2] *Ibid.* p. 55. See below, p. 303.

[3] P. 75.

[4] *Stud. und Krit.* 1876, p. 661. This important article was written ten years after the appearance of Graf's work (see below, p. 325), in criticism of Duhm, and from the standpoint that up to that time "a stringent proof" had not been offered "either for or against" Graf's hypothesis of the age of Leviticus, and that such "was not to be looked for in the near future" (p. 644).

Israel. If such *were* given, they must, in the nature of the case, have included regulations about priesthood, sacrifice, purification, and much else.[1] This does not prove the existence of the Levitical ritual Code; but such laws, if given, must have covered a large part of the ground of that Code. It does not prove even that the laws were written, but it is highly probable that they soon were.[2] If these laws are not incorporated in our present Levitical Code, it is certain they are not to be found anywhere else. We shall be better able to judge on this point, when we have looked at some of the more special institutions of the national worship.

We proceed now, accordingly, to consider how it stands with such institutions as the *ark*, the *tabernacle*, the *priesthood*, and, in connection with these, with the *unity of worship*, made by Wellhausen, as we shall see, the turning-point of his whole discussion.[3] Graf, with his thesis of the post-exilian origin of the Levitical Code, is the pioneer here, and we are not sure that the case for the new theory, as respects the above institutions, has been more plausibly presented anywhere than it is in his pages.[4] It is not denied by the Graf school that there was an ark, a tent to cover it, and priests of some sort, from early times, but it is contended with decision that these were not, and could not have been, the ark, tabernacle, and priesthood of the Levitical Code. All we read on these subjects in the Priestly sections is "unhistorical fiction" of exilic or post-exilic origin. Rejecting hypotheses, our duty will be to turn the

[1] We shall see below that Dillmann, in fact, supposes Lev. xvii.–xxvi. (mainly) to be a very old, and in basis Mosaic, code, which he thinks may originally have stood after Ex. xxiv. Cf. his *Exod.–Lev.* on Ex. xxv. and Lev. xvii., and see below, pp. 328, 376.

[2] See below, p. 329. Dillmann says in the Preface to his Commentary on Exodus–Leviticus: "That the priesthood of the central sanctuary already in ancient times wrote down their laws is the most natural assumption in the world, and can be proved from A, C, D [= P, J, D]: that the laws of the priesthood and of divine service were written down, not to say made, first of all in the exile and in Babylon, where there was no service of God, is contrary to common sense."

[3] *Hist. of Israel*, p. 368. See below, pp. 173 ff.

[4] On Graf and his place in the critical development, see next chapter (pp. 199 ff.). His principal work, *Die Geschichtlichen Bücher des Alten Testaments*, was published in 1866. His chief predecessors were Vatke and George, but their works had produced little impression, and were regarded as conclusively refuted. Cf. Delitzsch, Luthardt's *Zeitschrift*, 1880, pp. 57 ff.

matter round about, and try to look at the facts historically This will prepare the way for the later critical inquiry.

III. The Sacred Ark

It has been seen above what the critics think of the *original* ark which they allow to have existed. It was a sort of fetish-chest in which Jehovah, represented by two stones, probably meteoric, was thought of as carried about; or it was itself a fetish.[1] This may be met by observing that, while Jehovah's presence is conceived of as connected with the ark, the special *symbol* of His presence—the cloud, or pillar, or glory—is always distinguished from both ark and sanctuary: this in both JE and P sections.[2] The cloud, or pillar of cloud and of fire, is represented as *above* the tabernacle, or *over* the people, or as going *before* them in their journeyings. Jehovah descends in the pillar to commune with Moses at the tabernacle. He dwells upon or between the cherubim.[3] His presence, therefore, it is perfectly plain, was not identified with the ark, or with anything in it.

1. It is not denied, then, and it is a valuable admission, that there was an ark of Jehovah in Israel from the times of Moses. Where did it come from? The ark does not appear to have been with the people in Egypt: we may therefore conclude it to be a Mosaic institution. A first point of interest relates to the *making* of the ark. The only account we have of its construction is in the Priestly Code, Ex. xxv. 10 ff.; xxvii. 1 ff.; outside of P the first incidental notice is in the important passage, Num. x. 33–36, "And the ark of the covenant went before them," etc., where, however, its existence is firmly assumed. On the critical side it is said—indeed, is taken for granted as one of the things about which "no doubt" exists[4]—that originally the JE narrative also must have had an account of the making of the ark, now displaced by that of P.[5] Let this

[1] See above, p. 137.

[2] Cf. Ex. xxxiii. 9; xl. 34–38; Num. x. 34; xiv. 10–14; xx. 6; Deut. xxxi. 15, etc.

[3] Ex. xxv. 22; 1 Sam. iv. 4. etc.

[4] Addis says: "He [the J writer] no doubt also mentioned here the making of the ark, to which he refers shortly [where?] afterwards."—*Hex.* i. p. 155.

[5] Thus practically all the critics, as Wellhausen, Kuenen, Dillmann, Driver, Addis, Carpenter, Kennedy, etc.

be assumed: we discover from Deut. x. 1–5, which is supposed to follow this older account, that the ark of the JE story was an ark made "of acacia wood," and was the repository of the two tables of the law, which agrees perfectly with the history we have. Thus far, therefore, there is no contradiction. It remains to be seen whether any emerges in the further notices of the nature, uses, fortunes, and destination of the ark.

2. We pass to the *subsequent history* of the ark, and note on this the following interesting facts. Its familiar name is "the ark of the covenant."[1] It is connected with the presence of Jehovah among His people.[2] It goes before, or accompanies, the people in their journeys.[3] It is invested with the most awful sanctity: to touch it irreverently is death.[4] It is taken charge of, and borne, by Levitical priests, or by Levites simply.[5] It is found, in the days of the Judges, at Bethel, where Phinehas, the son of Eleazar, the son of Aaron, ministers before it.[6] In Eli's days it is in the sanctuary at Shiloh.[7] It is overshadowed by the cherubim.[8] After its captivity among the Philistines, and prolonged sojourn at Kirjath-jearim,[9] it is brought up by David with the greatest solemnity and the utmost rejoicings to Zion, and there lodged in a tent he had pitched for it.[10] Finally, it is brought into the temple of Solomon, when we are told it had nothing in it "save the two tables of stone, which Moses put there at Horeb."[11] Here, as it stands, is a very fair history of the ark from pre-exilian sources, and it requires some ingenuity to discover wherein the ark of these accounts differs, in structure, character, and uses, from the ark of the law in Exodus. That ingenuity,

[1] This name occurs in Num. x. 33; xiv. 44; Deut. x. 8; xxxi. 9, 25, 26; Josh. iii. (seven times); iv. 7, 9, 18; vi. 6, 8; viii. 33; Judg. xx. 27; 1 Sam. iv. 3–5 (see above, p. 137); 2 Sam. xv. 24; 1 Kings iii. 15; vi. 19; viii. 1, 6, etc. etc. In *all the cases in the older history* the words "of the covenant" *are simply struck out by the critics.* Cf., *e.g.*, Kuenen, *Hist. of Israel*, i. pp. 257–58; or Oxford *Hex.* on Josh. iii., iv. The passages then read "the ark of Jehovah" only. See Note at end of chapter.

[2] Num. x. 33, etc.

[3] Num. x. 33–36; cf. Ex. xl. 36, 37; Num. ix. 15–23 (P). On the position of the ark, see below, pp. 168–69.

[4] 1 Sam. vi. 19; 2 Sam. vi. 7.

[5] Josh. iii., iv; 2 Sam. xv. 24, 29; cf. Deut. xxxi. 9, 25.

[6] Judg. xx. 27, 28.

[7] 1 Sam. iii. 3.

[8] 1 Sam. iv. 4; 2 Sam. vi. 2.

[9] 1 Sam. vii. 1, 2.

[10] 2 Sam vi.

[11] 1 Kings viii. 1–11.

however, is not wanting. One point of alleged contradiction, viz., that in JE the ark is represented as borne at a distance *in front of* the host, while in P it is carried, with the tabernacle, *in the midst* of the host, is considered below in connection with the place of the tabernacle.[1] For the rest, the method is always at hand, and is freely resorted to, of getting rid of inconvenient testimony by the assumption of interpolation. This disposes, as noted above, of the words "the covenant," and also of the mention of the "cherubim,"[2] and gets rid of the notices of "Levites" as bearing the ark, in distinction from the priests. Thus, *e.g.*, Professor H. P. Smith, following Wellhausen, disposes of the testimony in 2 Sam. xv. 24. That passage reads: "And lo Zadok also, and all the Levites that were with him, bearing the ark of the covenant of God." This will not do, so the comment is: "The present text inserts 'and all the Levites with him.' But as the Levites are unknown to the Books of Samuel [they had been mentioned before in 1 Sam. vi. 15], this is obviously a late insertion. Probably the original was 'Zadok and Abiathar.'"[3] On this subject, it can scarcely be held to be a contradiction that in some of the above passages it is the "priests" who bear the ark, while the Levitical law assigns that duty to the "Levites." The carrying of the ark by the Levites on ordinary occasions, and as servants of the priests,[4] does not preclude the bearing of it by priests on special occasions, as in Josh. iii., iv. It was the priests who were at all times primarily responsible for its right conveyance.[5]

3. A point of some importance in its bearings on the descriptions of the ark in the Priestly Code, which, however, we do not remember having seen adverted to, is the

[1] This, as will be seen below, is a question of some real difficulty. It is not clear whether the ark was always, or only on special occasions, borne in front of the host; or whether it was not borne usually in front of the tabernacle in midst of the host, still with the idea of leadership. In either case, as the passages cited show, it was the movement of the ark, or of the guiding pillar, which determined that of the camp.

[2] "It is more than probable," says Kuenen, "that the cherubim were not mentioned by the author himself, but were inserted by a later writer."—*Rel. of Israel*, i. p. 259.

[3] *Samuel* ("Internat. Crit. Com."), p. 344. In defence of these passages (also in LXX), see Van Hoonacker, *Le Sacerdoce Lévitique*, p. 199.

[4] Num. iv. 15, etc.

[5] Num. iv. 19. In 1 Sam. iv. 4, Hophni and Phinehas (priests) are said to be "there *with the ark* of the covenant of God" (not, apparently, its bearers).

relation of the ancient ark to that of the Solomonic temple. It is not denied, as we have seen, that there was an old Mosaic ark; but the fact is perhaps not always sufficiently attended to that, according to every testimony we have, it was this identical ark which was brought up and deposited in Solomon's splendid house. The Mosaic tabernacle, on Graf's view, is a "fiction"—a "copy" of the temple: it is the temple made "portable," and projected back into Mosaic times. But the ark, at all events, was not a new thing in the temple. It was the *old* ark that was brought into it;[1] the same old ark that can be traced back to the times of the Judges, and of Moses, and had experienced so many vicissitudes. It was an ark, therefore, which continued to exist, and whose character and structure could be verified, down to late historical times. It follows that, if the ark of the law is a "copy" of the ark of the temple, it must, in its general character, form, and structure, be pretty much a "copy," likewise, of the *real* ark of the pre-Solomonic age. Exilian priests would hardly invent an ark totally different from that which had perished within quite recent memory.

Another reflection is suggested by the pre-Solomonic history of the ark. No one disputes the sacredness of the ark in the eyes of the Israelites. It was in a sense the centre and core of their religion. They had the most undoubting belief in the manifestations of God's presence in connection with it, and in the importance of its possession, and of worship before it, as a pledge of God's favour and protection. Yet after its return from the Philistines, and the judgment at Beth-shemesh, we find this holiest of objects taken to the house of a private Israelite, Abinadab, and allowed to remain there till David's time, *i.e.*,[2] during the whole reign of Saul, guarded by this man's son; apparently, therefore, without Levitical ministration, neglected and almost forgotten by the people.[3] Then again

[1] 1 Kings viii. 6 ff. "The ark was guarded," says Dr. Driver, "till it was transferred by Solomon to the temple."—*Introd.* p. 138.

[2] The twenty years of 1 Sam. vii. 2 do not denote the whole duration of the ark's stay at Kirjath-jearim, but the period, apparently, till the time of Samuel's reformation.

[3] 1 Sam. vii. 1, 2. Cf. below, p. 178. The ingenious suggestion of Van Hoonacker (*Le Sacerdoce*, p. 192) that "Eleazar his son" should be "son of Eleazar" (a priest) is without sufficient warrant.

we find it raised to highest honour by David and Solomon. We ask—Would it be safe to argue from the seeming neglect, at least intermission of religious use, of this sacred object for so long a period, to the denial of its earlier high repute, and established place, in the worship of the people? Or, if so extraordinary an irregularity must be admitted in this confused time, must we not, in consistency, admit the likelihood of many more?

IV. The Tabernacle

An initial difficulty in the Mosaic account is the richness and splendour of the "tent of meeting," said to be reared by command of God in the wilderness. This of itself, however, is not insuperable. Neither the resources nor the skill of the people in leaving Egypt were so slender as the critics represent,[1] and the rearing of a sanctuary was an object for which they would strip themselves of their best. If the ark was as fine an object as its description implies, we should expect that the tabernacle made for its reception would have some degree of splendour as well. Much more radical is the position now taken up by the Graf-Wellhausen critics. Such a tabernacle as the Priestly Code describes, they tell us, never existed. The tent of the wilderness is a pure creation of the post-exilian imagination. In Wellhausen's language: "The temple, the focus to which the worship was concentrated, and which was not built until Solomon's time, is by this document regarded as so indispensable even for the troubled days of the wanderings before the settlement, that it is made portable, and in the form of a tabernacle set up in the very beginning of things. For the truth is, that the tabernacle is the copy, not the prototype, of the temple at Jerusalem."[2] The critical and other difficulties which inhere in such a conception are left over for the present; we look only at the facts.

1. Our starting-point here, as before, is the admission of the critics that *a tabernacle of some sort* did exist, as a

[1] Cf. Knobel, quoted by Dillmann, *Exod.-Lev.* pp. 268–70.

[2] *Hist. of Israel*, pp. 36–37. In these expressions about the sanctuary being "made portable," and the tabernacle being "the copy," not the prototype, of the temple, Wellhausen but repeats Graf, *Geschicht. Bücher*, pp. 53, 55, 61, etc.

covering for the ark and a place of meeting with Jehovah, at least as far back as they will allow the history to go. Graf may be quoted here, though his concessions are ampler than those which Wellhausen would be disposed to make. "The presence of the ark in the field (1 Sam. iv. 3 ff.)," he says, "presupposes also that of a tent, of however simple a character, which might serve as a protection and lodging for the ark and for the priests with the sacred utensils; and it lies likewise in the nature of the case that before this tent, where sacrifice was offered by the priests, and the will of Jehovah inquired after, meetings and deliberations of the host were also held; hence the tent was the *ohel moed* (tent of meeting)."[1] But then, it is contended, this is not the tabernacle of the Priestly Code, and reference is made in proof to "the tent" which, in Ex. xxxiii. 7, Moses is said to have pitched (R.V. "used to pitch") "afar off" without the camp, and to have called "the tent of meeting," when as yet the tabernacle of the law was not erected. Wellhausen goes further, and will have it that the pre-Solomonic tabernacle was not a single tent at all, but a succession of changing tents, staying himself in this contention, of all authorities in the world, on the *Chronicler*,[2] whose words—"have gone from tent to tent, and from one tabernacle to another"—are made to bear a sense which that writer assuredly never dreamt of.

Now it is the case, and is an interesting fact, that after the sin of the golden calf, before the Sinaitic tabernacle was made, Moses is related to have taken—strictly, "used to take"—"the tent," and pitched it "without the camp, afar off from the camp," and to have called it "the tent of meeting." The mention of "*the* tent" comes in quite abruptly, and may fairly suggest that we have here, as the critics say, part of an originally independent narrative—the same to which also Num. xi. 16 ff., and xii. 4 ff. (cf. Deut. xxxi. 14, 15) belong. As it stands in the context, however,

[1] *Geschicht. Bücher*, pp. 57–58.

[2] *Hist. of Israel*, p. 45: "The parallel passage in 1 Chron. xvii. 5 correctly interprets the sense" (cf. 2 Sam. vii. 6). How the Chronicler could be supposed to say this, in Wellhausen's sense, not only of the "tent" (*ohel*), but of the "tabernacle" (*mishkan*), is not explained. "The passage says no more," remarks Delitzsch, "than that the ark of Jehovah wandered from place to place, so that He abode in it, sometimes here and sometimes there."—Luthardt's *Zeitschrift*, 1880, p. 63.

the impression distinctly produced is, that the withdrawal of the tent or tabernacle from the camp is *penal* in character (cf. vers. 3–5: "I will not go up in the midst of thee"), and that the tabernacle itself is a provisional one, meeting a need till the permanent "tent of meeting" is got ready. The tenses, indeed, imply usage; but duration of usage is limited by the writer's thought, and need not cover more than the period of alienation, or at most the interval—the greater part of a year—till the erection of the new tabernacle.[1] The critics, however, will not admit this; and, comparing the passages above mentioned, maintain that there are the clearest points of distinction between this JE tent or tabernacle and that of the Priestly Code. The former, it is said, is always represented as pitched *without* the camp; the latter is as invariably pitched *in the midst* of the camp. The one is a place of *revelation* (Jehovah descends in the pillar *to the door* of the tabernacle); the other is a place of divine service or *worship*. The one has *Joshua* as its attendant;[2] the other is served by *priests and Levites*. On this last objection—the absence of Levites—it is enough to remark that, at the time referred to in Ex. xxxiii., Levites had not yet been appointed; the ark itself had not yet been made. The other two objections deserve more consideration. They rest on grounds which have a degree of plausibility, though closer examination, we are convinced, will bring out the essential harmony of the accounts.

2. The first question relates to the *place* of the tabernacle. Is there real contrariety here between the JE and the P accounts? When we examine the evidence for the contention that all through the wanderings, in the JE narrative, the place of the tabernacle was without the camp—"afar off"—we are struck, first, with its exceeding meagreness. It consists of the two passages in Numbers above referred to, concerning which it may be observed that, while their language, taken alone, will agree with this hypothesis, it certainly does not necessitate it. It is not

[1] Cf. Ex. xxxv. 30 ff.; xl. 1 ff.

[2] Wellhausen says: "Thus Moses has Joshua with him as his *æditwus*, who does not quit the tent of Jehovah."—*Hist. of Israel*, p. 130. Cf. Addis *in loc.*, *Hex.* i. p. 155: "The tent of meeting is outside the camp; it is not guarded by Levites, much less by the sons of Aaron, but by Joshua, the 'minister' of Moses" But see Deut. xxxi. 9, etc.

conclusive that we are told on one or two occasions that persons "went out" from the camp to the tent,[1] or that Moses "went out" from the tent to the people;[2] for the same language would be as appropriately used of going out from any particular encampment to the open space in the centre where the sanctuary stood; just as it is said of Dathan and Abiram that they "came out" and stood in the door of their own tents.[3] The question requires to be decided on broader grounds. Even in Ex. xxxiii. 7, the natural suggestion of the statement that Moses, in particular circumstances, took the tent—assumed as known—and pitched it "without the camp, afar off from the camp," would seem to be that the original and proper place of the tent was *within* the camp; and there are not wanting in the narratives indications that this was the real state of the case. Both in the JE and the P sections the region outside the camp is regarded as a region of exclusion from Jehovah's presence; it would be passing strange if His tabernacle, surmounted by the cloudy pillar, were thought of as pitched "afar off" in this region. It requires much faith, for instance, to believe that when Miriam, smitten with leprosy, was "shut up outside the camp seven days,"[4] she was nearer the tabernacle of Jehovah than the people who were within; or that, when quails were sent, the tabernacle was in such a position as to be certainly smothered by them when they fell;[5] or that, when Balaam, looking on Israel, testified, "Jehovah his God is with him, and the shout of a king is among them,"[6] the tabernacle of Jehovah was really beheld by the seer as far apart from the people. But there are other and more crucial JE passages. When, in particular, it is declared in Num. xiv. 44 that "the ark of the covenant

[1] Num. xi. 24–30; xii. 4, 5.

[2] Num. xi. 24. Cf. Strack's remarks on these passages in his *Commentary, in loc.*

[3] Num. xvi. 27.

[4] Num. xii. 14, 15. It should be noted that this JE narrative implies the leprosy law of Lev. xiii. (P).

[5] Num. xi. 31, 32. Van Hoonacker, in his *Le Sacerdoce Lévitique* (pp. 145–46), has an ingenious way of explaining these passages, in comparison with Ex. xxxiii. 7 (where, as he points out, "the tent" is assumed as already known), by the supposition of a series of transpositions in the narrative; but we do not feel this to be justified or necessary.

[6] Num. xxiii. 21. Balaam, in chap. xxiv. 2, sees "Israel dwelling according to their tribes," which implies the orderly encampment of P.

of Jehovah, and Moses, departed not out of the camp," it cannot be supposed that the ark was, before starting, already outside of the camp—"afar off"; the words imply as plainly as may be that its resting-place was *within* the camp. When, again, Moses is related in Num. x. 36 to have said at the resting of the ark, "Return, O Jehovah, to the ten thousands of Israel,"[1] his formula has hardly any meaning if the ark did not return from going before the people to a resting-place within the camp. In the same direction point such allusions as "the cloud of Jehovah was *over* them by day, when they set forward from the camp"[2]—"and Thy cloud *standeth over* them[3]—allusions which those who adopt the hypothesis we are criticising think it necessary to relegate to P or a redactor;[4] together with instances of an immediate acting, speaking, or calling of Jehovah from the tabernacle[5] (were Moses, Aaron, and Miriam, *e.g.*, "afar off" when they heard Jehovah call "suddenly" to them, as in Num. xii. 4?), or of direct transactions with the officials of the sanctuary.[6] Taken together, these things show that, while there may be divergences in the mode of representation, there is no essential disagreement in the accounts as to the *place* of the tabernacle.

3. Neither, when we take the history as a whole, does there appear to be any better basis for the statement that in JE the tabernacle is a place of *revelation* only, whereas in P it is peculiarly a place of *worship*. In P also, as in

[1] Cf. Dillmann and Strack, *in loc.* Professor Gray's comments on this passage, Num. x. 33–35, are a good example of the new method. "Here," he says, "if we may judge from so fragmentary a record, it [the ark] is conceived as moving of itself (!) . . . 35. Here, as in ver. 33, the ark starts of itself, and the words that follow ['Rise up, O Jehovah,' etc.] may be taken as addressed to it. . . . 36. Such words could be suitably addressed to the ark returning from battle to its fixed sanctuary . . . after the people were settled in Canaan. It is less clearly suitable to the circumstances of the march through the wilderness: the people overtake the ark, the ark does not return to them" (?)—*Numbers* ("Inter. Crit. Com."), p. 97. How would Dr. Gray apply his canon to Ps. cxxxii. 8?

[2] Num. x. 34.

[3] Num. xiv. 14.

[4] Thus Dillmann, Gray, the Oxford *Hex.*, etc. (not Addis). On the ground that "E nowhere describes it [the pillar] as 'over' it" [the tent]—the thing to be proved—the Oxford annotator arbitrarily makes the word *over* in Num. xii. 10 bear a different sense from what it ordinarily has in this connection. The phrase is identical with that in Ex. xl. 36; Num. ix. 17 (P).

[5] *E.g.*, Num. xi. 1, 10, 16; xii. 4.

[6] *E.g.*, Deut. xxxi. 9, 25, 26.

JE, the tabernacle is a place of revelation; in JE, and in pre-Solomonic times, as in P, it is a place of worship, with its altars and sacred furniture, its priestly ministrants, its assemblies at the feasts, etc. Only by isolating one or two special passages, in which the aspect of revelation in JE is prominent,[1] can it be made to appear otherwise. In certain respects there is obvious resemblance from the first. In P, as well as in JE, the tabernacle is called *ohel moed* (tent of meeting):[2] in P this alternates with the name *mishkan* (dwelling). A curious fact here, and one puzzling to the critics, is that in certain sections of P (Ex. xxv.–xxvii. 19) only *mishkan* is used; in others (chaps. xxviii.–xxxi.) only *ohel moed*; in others the names intermingle.[3] In both JE and P Jehovah manifests His presence in a cloud of fire;[4] the fact that in JE the cloud is spoken of as a "pillar" is no contradiction. If in JE Jehovah descends in the pillar to the *door* of the tabernacle to speak with Moses, this mode of communication is also recognised in P ("At the door of the tent of meeting . . . where I will speak with you," Ex. xxix. 42, 43);[5] elsewhere Jehovah speaks from between the cherubim.[6] The tabernacle in both JE and P contains the ark of the covenant; a Levitical priesthood in its service is implied in the JE notices in Joshua,[7] and in Deuteronomy.[8] A tabernacle existed, and was set up in Shiloh, in Joshua's time, as Josh. xviii. 1, ascribed to P,[9] declares: this reappears under the name "the house of God" in Shiloh, in Judg. xviii. 31.[10] In this connection it should not be

[1] Num. xi., xii.; Deut. xxxi. 14, 15. These are the only passages after Ex. xxxiii. 7–11: a narrow basis for an induction.

[2] In JE, *e.g.*, in Num. xi. 16; xii. 4; Deut. xxxi. 14.

[3] Cf. Oxford *Hex.* ii. p. 120. In consistency different authors ought to be assumed.

[4] Numbers and Deut. for JE; in P, Ex. xl. 34–38; Num. ix. 15–23, etc. It should be noted that in the narrative of the dedication of the temple in 1 Kings viii., vers. 10, 11 are modelled directly on the *P passage*, Ex. xl. 34–35.

[5] Cf. Oxford *Hex.* ii. p. 120.

[6] Ex. xxv. 22; Num. vii. 89.

[7] Josh. iii.–vi.

[8] Deut. x. 6, 8; xxxi. 9, 25, 26.

[9] On the critical analysis here, cf. Van Hoonacker, *Le Sacerdoce*, p. 177.

[10] Cf. Judg. xix. 18, "to the house of Jehovah," where, however, the LXX has "my (the man's own) house" (R.V. marg.). The "house of God" in Judg. xx. 26 is more correctly "Bethel," where either the tabernacle was for a time (cf. chap. ii. 1, in LXX), or where the ark was temporarily taken for the war.

overlooked that the Book of the Covenant (JE) already provides for offerings being brought to "the house of Jehovah thy God."[1] At the sanctuary at Shiloh an annual feast, described as "a (*or* the) feast of Jehovah,"[2] is held, which is most naturally identified with one of the three prescribed feasts[3] (cf. 1 Sam. i. 3). The notices of the ark,[4] again, and the custom of "inquiring of Jehovah,"[5] attest the existence of a stated priesthood, of sacrifices—the offering of "burnt offerings and peace offerings before Jehovah"[6]—and of the priestly ephod. In face of all this, Wellhausen's assertion that in the Book of Judges "there is no mention of the tabernacle . . . it is only in preparation, it has not yet appeared,"[7] can only excite astonishment.

When we pass to the Books of Samuel, we get fresh and valuable light on the tabernacle, and its place in the religion of Israel. At the end of the period of the Judges, it is still at Shiloh, with Eli, of the house of Aaron, as its principal priest. It bears the old name—"the tent of meeting"—to which no suspicion need attach;[8] contains the ark with its cherubim;[9] is the centre of worship for "all Israel";[10] in its furniture and ritual suggests the prescriptions of the Levitical Code. "The lamp of God" burns, as directed, all night;[11] from the later incidental mention of the shewbread, and of the regulations connected with it, at Nob,[12] we may infer the presence of the table

[1] Ex. xxiii. 19. It is one of the astounding statements in Wellhausen that "house of God" always means "house of an image."—*Hist. of Israel*, p. 130.

[2] Judg. xxi. 19.

[3] According to Bertheau, the word *ḥag* is almost without exception used of the three great feasts.—*Exeg. Handb.* p. 278.

[4] Judg. xx. 27, 28.

[5] Judg. i. 1; xx. 18, 23, 28.

[6] Judg. xx. 26.

[7] *Hist. of Israel.* Graf also says that there is no mention of "a sacred tent" in the time of the Judges, but remarks that this is not to be wondered at, as the ark of the covenant is also not mentioned (p. 58). The critics in both cases reach their results by rejecting what does not please them. "The house of God" and "the ark of the covenant" are both mentioned in Judges.

[8] See next page.

[9] 1 Sam. iv 4; cf. above, p. 137.

[10] 1 Sam. ii. 14, 19; iii. 19, 21.

[11] 1 Sam. iii. 3; cf. Ex. xxvii. 20–21.

[12] 1 Sam. xxi. Dr. Driver objects that these allusions do not prove that the institutions "were observed *with the precise formalities prescribed in P.*"—*Introd.* p. 142. How much does one expect in a historical allusion?

with the shewbread. Elkanah goes up yearly to worship,[1] and his sacrifice for his vow is according to the law.[2] In 1 Sam. ii. 22, there is allusion to "the women who did service at the door of the tent of meeting"—the only other mention of these women being in Ex. xxxviii. 8. (P). The genuineness of this important passage, the second half of which, for reasons that may be guessed, is omitted in the LXX (Vat. Cod.), has been disputed, but, it seems to us, without sufficient reason.[3]

Thus far the resemblance of "the house of God" in Shiloh to the tabernacle of the law must be admitted. But objections, on the other hand, are urged, which, it is thought, disprove the identification.[4] It is pointed out that the sanctuary is described, not as a tent, but as a "temple" (*hēkal*), with doors and posts, which implies a permanent structure;[5] that Samuel is represented as sleeping in the room where the ark of God was;[6] that the sons of Eli were within their Levitical rights in demanding uncooked flesh, etc.[7] But there is needed here not a little forcing of the text to make out a case in favour of the critics. "*Everywhere else* in 1 Sam. i.–iii.," says Wellhausen, arguing against the name *ohel moed*, "the sanctuary of Shiloh is called *hēkal*":[8] the "everywhere else" being simply twice. And it does not prove his point. Whatever structures or supports may have grown up about the sanctuary (for safety, stability, protection, convenience) during its century-long stay at Shiloh—and from its age such were to be expected —it was still essentially, as 2 Sam. vii. 6 shows, "a tent and a tabernacle," nor did Israelitish tradition ever know of

When the Chronicler expands, it is taken as a proof of non-historicity. See below, p. 300.

[1] 1 Sam. i. 3, 7. Professor W. R. Smith allows that the yearly feasts were observed (*O.T. in J. C.*, p. 345).

[2] 1 Sam. i. 21, 25; cf. Lev. vii. 16; Num. xv. 8–10.

[3] The name *ohel moed* is, as we have seen, an old, well-attested name of the tabernacle (cf. Graf, p. 58), and is found again, in both Heb. and LXX, in 1 Kings viii. 4. As regards the women, even on the supposition, which we do not accept, of a post-exilian composition of Ex. xxxviii., it is inconceivable that there should occur *this single mention* of the women at the tabernacle in the Code, if there was not old, well-established tradition behind it.

[4] Cf. in Wellhausen, Kuenen, W. R. Smith, and the critics generally See the very dogmatic statements in *O.T. in J. C.*, pp. 269–70.

[5] 1 Sam. i. 9; iii. 3.

[6] 1 Sam. iii. 3.

[7] 1 Sam. ii. 15.

[8] *Hist. of Israel*, p. 41 (italics ours).

ny other kind of habitation of Jehovah. The further supposition that Samuel slept literally in the shrine of the ark s, from the point of view of an Israelite, an outrage on all robability; neither does the language of the text compel ny such meaning.[1] Samuel and Eli slept in contiguous hambers of some lodgment connected with the sanctuary, uch as may be presumed to have been provided for the riests and others engaged in its service. The sin of the sons f Eli consisted in their greed and violence, and in the approriating of such portions as their "flesh-hooks" laid hold of, efore the fat was burned on the altar, as the law required.[2] 'he Levitical dues are presupposed: not contradicted.

What remains to be said on the tabernacle may be briefly ummed up. Ark and tabernacle, as above noted, were eparated during the long period that the former was at Kirjath-jearim. When David brought the ark to Zion, he tabernacle, probably then old and frail, and unfitted for emoval, was at Gibeon.[3] Thence it was brought up with ts vessels, and preserved, apparently, as a precious relic, in Solomon's temple.[4] The supposition that the *ohel moed* f 1 Kings viii. 4 was not this historic tabernacle, but the emporary tent set up by David on Zion, is contradicted by he name,[5] which is not given to that tent, by the mention f the vessels, and by the unlikelihood that a temporary ent would have such honour put upon it, while one can vell understand why the old tabernacle should.

V. The Unity of the Sanctuary

We now approach a subject of cardinal importance—robably the one of most importance—in this discussion: *he unity of the sanctuary*, and the conflict alleged to exist n the *centralisation of the cultus* between Deuteronomy and he earlier law and practice in Israel. The point of the

[1] Delitzsch says: "That he should sleep *beside the ark* would certainly e a colossal contradiction of the law, but Wellhausen reads this *into* the xt."—Luthardt's *Zeitschrift*, 1880, p. 232. Cf. Wellhausen, p. 130. On he alleged *priesthood* of Samuel, see below, pp. 189–90.

[2] Lev. iii. 1 ff.; vii. 28 ff.

[3] 1 Kings iii. 4; viii. 4; cf. 1 Chron. xvi. 39, 40; 2 Chron. i. 3 ccording to 1 Chron. xvi. 39, Zadok ministered at Gibeon.

[4] 1 Kings viii. 4; 2 Chron. v. 5. If this be admitted, then the tabernacle, s well as the ark, was there for inspection till late times.

[5] Cf. Delitzsch, as above, p. 63.

critical position on this head, briefly, is, that, while in Deut. xii.—placed in or near the age of Josiah—we have the law of a central sanctuary at which alone sacrifices are lawful, in the earlier history we have not only no trace of this idea of a central sanctuary, in which all lawful worship is concentrated, but, in the absolute freedom of worship that prevailed, convincing proof that such a law was neither observed nor known. The older law in Ex. xx. 24, on which the people acted in that earlier time, granted, it is alleged, unrestricted liberty of worship; as Professor W. R. Smith interprets it—"Jehovah promises to meet with His people and bless them at the altars of earth or unhewn stone which stood in all corners of the land, on every spot where Jehovah has set a memorial of His name."[1] The idea of the central sanctuary was, it is contended, the outcome of the great prophetic movement which resulted in the reign of Josiah in the suppression of the *bamoth*, or "high places," till then regarded as lawful. The relation of the Deuteronomic to the Priestly Code—assumed to be still later—on this subject is thus expressed by Wellhausen: "In that book (Deuteronomy) the unity of the cultus is *commanded*; in the Priestly Code it is *presupposed*. . . . In the one case we have, so to speak, only the idea as it exists in the mind of the lawgiver, but making no claim to be realised till a much later date; in the other, the Mosaic idea has acquired also a Mosaic embodiment, with which it entered the world at the very first."[2] The case, however, is not nearly so strong as these statements would imply, as many critical writers are coming themselves to perceive.[3] Reserving, as before, what is to be said on the purely critical aspects, we proceed to look at the subject in its historical relations.

The Priestly Code may be left out of consideration at this stage, for it will scarcely be denied that, if there was a sacrificial system in the wilderness at all, it would be a system centralised in the sanctuary, as the Code represents. The question turns then, really, on the compatibility of the law in Deuteronomy with the enactment in Ex. xx. 24, and

[1] *Prophets of Israel*, p. 109. [2] *Hist. of Israel*, pp. 35, 37.

[3] This point is emphasised in an interesting lecture by Dr. S. A. Fries delivered to a Scientific Congress at Stockholm in 1897, entitled *Modern Vorstellungen der Geschichte Israels* (Modern Representations of the History of Israel). See below, pp. 176, 273.

with the later practice. And the first condition of a satisfactory treatment lies, as the lawyers would say, in a proper adjustment of the issues.

1. We do well to begin by looking at the precise form of the *fundamental law* in Ex. xx. 24 itself. The passage reads: "An altar of earth thou shalt make to Me, and shalt sacrifice thereon thy burnt offerings, and thy peace offerings, thy sheep and thine oxen: in every place where I record My name, I will come to thee and I will bless thee." The law is general in form, but it must be observed that there is nothing in it warranting the worship "at the altars of earth and unhewn stones in all corners of the land," which Professor W. R. Smith reads into its terms. It is addressed to the nation, not to the individual; and it does not speak of "altars," but only of "an altar." It is not a law in the least giving unrestricted liberty of worship; its scope, rather, is carefully limited by the clause, "in every place where I record My name."[1] It would be unduly narrowing the force of this law to confine it, with some, to the *successive* places where the sanctuary was set up during the wilderness wanderings and in Canaan; it must at least include all places sanctified to their recipients by special appearances or revelations of God. This fully explains, and legitimises, *e.g.*, the cases of Gideon,"[2] of Manoah,[3] of David,[4] of Solomon,[5] of Elijah.[6] Neither is there anything here that conflicts with Deuteronomy. The law in Deut. xii. gives the general rule of worship at the central sanctuary, but is not to be understood as denying that circumstances might arise in which, under proper divine authority, exceptional sacrifices might be offered. The clearest proof of this is that Deuteronomy itself gives directions for the building of an altar on Mount Ebal. precisely in the manner of Ex. xx. 25.[7]

[1] Professor W. R. Smith, replying to Dr. Wm. H. Green, seems to insist that these words can only bear the meaning, "in all places" in the sense of a number of co-existent sanctuaries.—*Prophets*, p. 394. On this see Note B on the Force of Ex. xx. 24.

[2] Judg. vi. 25, 26.

[3] Judg. xiii. 16.

[4] 2 Sam. xxiv. 18.

[5] 1 Kings iii. 4, 5.

[6] 1 Kings xviii. 31.

[7] Deut. xxvii. 5, 6.—Van Hoonacker advocates the view that there were two systems of worship—a private and a public—and supposes that the law in Exodus refers to the former, and the law in Deuteronomy to the latter. See his ingenious discussion in his *Le Lieu du Culte dans la Legislation*

2. With this, in the next place, must be taken the fact, which the critics too much ignore, that, even in the earliest period, *the rule and ideal in Israel is that of a central sanctuary*, as the legitimate place of worship. It has just been seen that the fundamental law itself speaks of "an altar," not of "altars," and no countenance is given anywhere to a multitude of co-existing altars.[1] It is not questioned that the Priestly Code—the only Code we possess for the wilderness—"presupposes" unity of worship; neither, in the history, is there trace of any other than centralised worship of a lawful kind during the wanderings. The Book of the Covenant—the same which contains the law of the altar—has plainly the same ideal of the unity of the sanctuary. It takes for granted "the house of Jehovah thy God," and requires that three times in the year all males shall present themselves there before Jehovah.[2] The idolatrous shrines in Canaan are to be broken down.[3] It is in keeping with this, that, in prospect of entering Canaan, Deuteronomy relaxes the law requiring the slaying of all oxen, lambs, and goats at the door of the tabernacle,[4] and permits the slaying of animals for food at home.[5] In the Book of Joshua, the incident of the altar *Ed*—the narrative of which, in a way perplexing to the critics, combines peculiarities of P and JE[6]—is a striking testimony to the hold which this idea of the one altar had upon the tribes. We have already seen that the tabernacle at Shiloh was the recognised centre of worship for "all Israel" in the days of

rituelle des Hébreux, and in his *Le Sacerdoce Lévitique* (pp. 5 ff.). Similar views are advocated by Fries, referred to above (p. 174), in his work, *Die Zentralisation des israelitischen Kultus*. The hypothesis is probably not without its elements of truth, and would explain certain anomalies, but we have not felt it necessary to adopt it.

[1] Ex. xx. 24; xxi. 14. Cf. Robertson's *Early Religion*, pp. 405–13. "It is remarkable," says Professor Robertson, "that we do not find in all the Old Testament such a divine utterance as 'My altars'; and only twice does the expression 'Thy altars,' addressed to God, occur. It is found in Elijah's complaint, which refers to Northern Israel, at a time when the legitimate worship at Jerusalem was excluded; and in Ps. lxxxiv., where it again occurs [on the critical view, post-exilian], no inference can be drawn from it. On the other hand, Hosea says distinctly, 'Ephraim hath multiplied altars to sin' (Hos. viii. 11)" (p. 112).

[2] Ex. xxiii. 14–17.

[3] Ex. xxiii. 24.

[4] Lev. xvii. 1 ff. The object of the law is to prevent promiscuous sacrificing to demons (vers. 5, 8).

[5] Deut. xii. 20. See below, pp. 276, 314.

[6] Josh. xxii. 9–34. On the criticism, cf. Oxf. *Hex.*, Driver, etc.

Eli.[1] In Judges, legitimate sacrifices are offered at the sanctuary,[2] or before the ark,[3] or where God has "recorded His name" in a special revelation;[4] all others are condemned as transgressions.[5] The period succeeding the captivity of the ark is considered below.

3. When we turn, next, to Deuteronomy, we discover *another* fact of great importance in this connection, viz., that there also, as Wellhausen says, the unity of the cultus is an "idea" which makes "no claim to be realised till a much later date."[6] The law in Deut. xii., in other words, is *not given as a law intended to come into perfect operation from the first.* It has just been seen that the *principle* of centralisation of worship was involved in the Mosaic system from the commencement, but the realisation of the idea was, and in the nature of the case could only be, gradual. The law of Deuteronomy, in agreement with this, bears on its face that it was not intended to be put strictly in force till certain important conditions had been fulfilled—conditions which, owing to the disobedience of the people, who, during the time of the Judges, so often put back the clock of their own history, were not fulfilled till as late as the days of David and Solomon. The law reads thus: "When ye go over Jordan, and dwell in the land which Jehovah your God causeth you to inherit, and He giveth you rest from all your enemies round about, so that ye dwell in safety: *then* shall it come to pass that the place which Jehovah your God shall choose to cause His name to dwell there," etc.[7] In point of fact, the unsettled state of things here described lasted till the reign of David.[8]

[1] See above, p. 171. Cf. Jer. vii. 12. [2] Judg. xxi. 19.

[3] Judg. xx. 26, 27; xxi. 2–4 (for "house of God" read "Bethel").

[4] Gideon, Manoah, as above, p. 175. Cf. Judg. ii. 1–5. It has been inferred, and is not improbable, that Gideon's altar in Judg. vi. 24, to which he gave the name "Jehovah-Shalom," was a monumental altar, like the altar "Ed" in Josh. xxii. This would explain why he was required next day to build a new altar beside it (ver. 26).

[5] Judg. viii. 27, xvii. 5, 6, etc. Dr. W. R. Smith appears to assume that the phrase "before Jehovah" (Judg. xi. 11, etc.) always implies sacrifice. That, however, is not so. Cf. Gen. xxvii. 7; Ex. vi. 12, 30; Deut. iv. 10; ix. 25; 1 Sam. xxiii. 18. See Graf, *Geschicht. Bücher*, p. 58.

[6] See above, p. 174. [7] Deut. xii. 10, 11.

[8] 2 Sam. vii. 1. Professor W. R. Smith allows that Deuteronomy "puts the case as if the introduction of a strictly unified cultus was to be deferred till the peaceful occupation of Palestine was accomplished."—*O.T. in J. C.*, p. 272. Where then is the contradiction?

Accordingly, in 1 Kings iii. 2, it is not urged that the law did not exist, or that it was not known, but the excuse given for irregularities is that "there was no house built for the name of Jehovah until these days."[1] This principle alone solves many difficulties, and goes a long way to bring the history and the law into harmony.

4. This leads, finally, to the remark that, in the interpretation of these laws, large allowance needs to be made for the *irregularities* incident to times of political confusion and religious declension. It is not fair to plead, as contradictory of the law, the falling back on local sanctuaries in periods of great national and religious disorganisation, as when the land was in possession of enemies, or when the ark was in captivity, or separated from the tabernacle, or when the kingdom was divided, and the state-worship in the Northern division was idolatrous. In particular, the period following the rejection of Eli and his sons was one of unusual complications, during which Samuel's own person would seem to have been the chief religious centre of the nation.[2] It is here that the critical case finds its strongest support, and there are undoubted difficulties. How could it be otherwise, after "the capture of the ark, the fall of Shiloh, and the extension of the Philistine power into the heart of Mount Ephraim"?[3] We are reminded, however, that even after the ark had been brought back, and settled in the house of Abinadab, Samuel made no attempt to remove it to Nob, but "continued to sacrifice at a variety of shrines"[4] —Bethel, Gilgal, Mizpah, Ramah. It is a sweeping and unwarranted inference to draw from this that "Samuel did not know of a systematic and exclusive system of sacrificial ritual confined to the sanctuary of the ark."[5] Samuel evidently knew something of it as long as Shiloh stood; for we read of no attempt *then* to go about the shrines

[1] Cf. 1 Kings viii. 29; ix. 3; 2 Chron. vi. 5, 6.

[2] Shiloh had probably fallen. Cf. Jer. vii. 12, xxvi. 6, with subsequent mention of Nob, 1 Sam. xxi.

[3] *O.T. in J. C.*, p. 271.

[4] *Ibid.* p. 272. Professor Smith, as usual, overshoots the mark in his statement that "Eleazar ben Abinadab was consecrated its *priest.*" There is no mention of a "priest" in 1 Sam. vii. 1. Eleazar was sanctified for the custody of the ark. Samuel's apparent neglect of the ark has to be accounted for on *any* theory (see above, p. 164).

[5] *Ibid.* p. 274.

sacrificing.[1] The ark and Shiloh had been rejected; the former had been taken to Kirjath-jearim under judgment of God; Israel felt itself in a manner under bereavement, and "all the house of Israel lamented after Jehovah."[2] The age was truly, as Professor Smith says "is generally argued," "one of religious interregnum";[3] are we, in such circumstances, to judge Samuel by the law of an orderly and settled time? He fell back naturally, as even the law in Deuteronomy permitted him to do, on local sanctuaries until such time as Jehovah would give the people rest. The law had its place; but even under the law, "the letter killeth, but the spirit giveth life;[4] and in no age were prophetically-minded men the slaves of the mere letter of the commandment to the degree that the critics suppose.[5] Samuel acted with a measure of freedom, as his circumstances demanded; and writers who suppose that priests and prophets were perpetually engaged in changing and modifying laws believed to be divine should be the last to challenge his right to do so.

5. When all is said, it is plain from the statement in the Book of Kings that, in the beginning of Solomon's reign, there was a widespread resort of the people to *high places* for worship, and that even the establishment of Solomon's great temple, with its powerful centralising influence, was not effectual to check this tendency. The compiler of Kings looks on worship at "high places" before the temple was founded as irregular, but excusable;[6] after that it is condemned. The history of these "high places" has yet to be written in a fairer spirit than is generally manifested in notices of them. Much obscurity, in reality, rests upon them. In Judges the word does not occur, and the defections described are mostly of the nature of worship at the Canaanitish shrines of Baal and Ashtoreth.[7] The few allusions in Samuel are connected with Samuel's own city

[1] The statement that Samuel regularly sacrificed at all the places mentioned is an importation into the text. The special mention of his building an altar at Ramah (1 Sam. vii. 17) would suggest that he did not. Professor Smith's list of "sanctuaries" needs a good deal of sifting.

[2] 1 Sam. vii. 2. [3] *O.T. in J.C.*, p. 272. [4] 2 Cor. iii. 6.

[5] See Note C on Freedom under the Law. Cf. Num. x. 16–20; 1 Sam. xv. 22; xxi. 1–6; 2 Chron. xxix. 34; xxx. 17, 19.

[6] 1 Kings iii. 2, 3.

[7] Allusions to Canaanitish "high places" are found in Lev. xxvi. 30; Num. xxi. 28; xxii. 41; xxxiii. 52.

of Ramah, and with the residence of the band of prophets at Gibeah:[1] elsewhere in Samuel they are unnoticed. It may be inferred from the toleration accorded to it that the greater part of what worship there was at "high places" prior to the founding of the temple was directed to Jehovah; afterwards, partly through Solomon's own evil example,[2] idolatry found entrance, and rapidly spread. What the "high places" became in the Northern Kingdom, latterly in Judah also, we know from the prophets. It is, however, a perversion of the facts to speak of the prophets as ever sanctioning, or approving of, this style of worship. If it is replied that it is *idolatrous* worship which the prophets so strongly reprobate, not worship at the "high places" as such, it may be pointed out that they never make such a distinction, or use language which would suggest the acceptableness of the *bamoth* worship in any form.[3] That Elijah mourned the breaking down of the altars of Jehovah in Northern Israel is readily explicable from the peculiar circumstances of that kingdom. To Amos and Hosea, Micah and Isaiah, not less than to Jeremiah and Ezekiel, the one legitimate sanctuary is that of Zion at Jerusalem.[4]

The conclusion we reach on this subject of the unity of worship is, that the history is consistent with itself, *provided we accept its own premises,* and do not insist on forcing on it an alien theory of religious development. The reformations of Hezekiah and Josiah then fall into their proper places, without the necessity of assuming the invention of *ad hoc* "programmes."

VI. The Aaronic Priesthood and the Levites

Ark and tabernacle imply a priesthood, and the notices already cited from Joshua, Judges, 1 Samuel, and Deuteronomy, abundantly show that from the days of Moses such

[1] 1 Sam. ix., x. [2] 1 Kings xi. 7, 8.

[3] Dr. W. H. Green says: "The people are never told that they may sacrifice on the high hills and under green trees, or at Bethel and Gilgal and Beersheba, if only they sacrifice to the Lord alone, and in a proper manner. They are never told that God will be pleased with the erection of numerous altars, provided the service upon them is rightly conducted."—*Moses and the Prophets*, p. 157.

[4] Cf. Amos i. 2; Isa. ii. 2; Mic. iv. 2; Hos. iii. 5. See Robertson, *Early Rel.* p. 405.

a priesthood existed, and that it was *Levitical.* But was it *Aaronic?* And was there from early times such a distinction between *priests* and *Levites* as the Priestly Code represents?

1. It is a fundamental contention of the new school that a *distinctively Aaronic priesthood* was unknown before the exile. Till Ezekiel, in his sketch of the new temple arrangements (chaps. xl.–xlviii.), initiated a distinction between Zadokite priests and other Levites—a theory considered in a later chapter[1]—there was no distinction in principle between priests and Levites: all Levites are *possible* priests. In particular, a high priest of Aaronic descent was unknown. The question of the relation of the priests to other Levites is considered below; we inquire at present whether it is the case that the earlier books give no traces of an Aaronic priesthood. We affirm that they do, and believe that the proof of this can only be set aside by the usual circle method of first *assuming* that the Aaronic priesthood is late, then, on that ground, disallowing the passages which imply it.

Wellhausen has some wonderful constructive history on this subject, on which we need not dwell. The Levites of history, he affirms, have nothing to do with the old tribe of Levi: in the J narrative in Exodus, Aaron was not originally mentioned at all; it is the line of Moses, not of Aaron, that gives rise to the clerical guild.[2] As an instance of the critical procedure, we may take the case of the high priest. It is, as just said, an essential part of the Wellhausen theory that this functionary is a creation of the exile. He is, we are told, still "unknown even to Ezekiel."[3] Unfortunately for the theory, the high priest is expressly mentioned in at least four places in 2 Kings, viz., in chaps. xii. 10, xxii. 4, 8, xxiii. 4[4]—the last two chapters being those relied on as furnishing one of the main pillars of the critical theory, the finding of "the book of the law" in the reign of

[1] See below, Chap. IX.

[2] *Hist. of Israel*, pp. 142–43. "Aaron," he says, "was not originally present in J, but owed his introduction to the redactor who combined J and E into JE." Precisely the opposite view is taken by Dillmann, *Exod.-Lev.* p. 437. See also Kuenen below.

[3] *Ibid.* pp. 148–49.

[4] It occurs earlier in 2 Sam. xv. 27, if Wellhausen's amended reading of that text is accepted.

Josiah. The texts are sustained by the parallel passages in Chronicles and by the LXX. What is to be done with them? They are simply *struck out* as interpolations, though it is unaccountable why a redactor should have inserted them in just those places, when so many more invited his attention.[1]

If, on the other hand, we let the history speak for itself, we get such notices as these, which are sufficiently unambiguous. Deut. x. 6, attributed by the critics to E,[2] informs us that, after Aaron's death, "Eleazar his son ministered in the priest's office in his stead."[3] Josh. xxiv. 33 carries this a step further by narrating the death of Eleazar, the son of Aaron, and his burial in the hill of Phinehas, his son. This is continued in Judg. xx. 27, 28, where we read that "Phinehas, the son of Eleazar, the son of Aaron, stood before it [the ark] in these days." From some cause unexplained, the high priesthood became transferred from the line of Eleazar to that of Ithamar, and in the opening of 1 Samuel, Eli, of this younger branch,[4] is found in office. For the sins of his sons it is announced to Eli that his house shall be deprived of its pre-eminence.[5] This took place in the reign of Solomon, when Abiathar was deposed,[6] and Zadok, of the older line, obtained the sole high priesthood.[7] Thus far the case is exactly that described in the words of the "man of God" to Eli in 1 Sam. ii. 27, 28: "Thus saith Jehovah, Did I reveal myself unto the house of thy father, when they were in bondage to Pharaoh's house? And did I choose him out of all the tribes of Israel to be

[1] Graf does not challenge the earlier mention of the "high priest" (*Geschicht. Bücher*, p. 4, etc.). Delitzsch (*Zeitschrift*, 1880, p. 228); Dillmann (*Num.-Jos.* p. 645); Baudissin (*Dict. of Bible*, iv. p. 73); Van Hoonacker, etc., defend the passages. Kautzsch removes 2 Kings xii. 10 as a gloss, but lets the others stand. See below, p. 306. Cf. Professor H. P. Smith's treatment of the Levites in Samuel, above, p. 163.

[2] Thus Oxf. *Hex.*, Addis, etc.

[3] Van Hoonacker draws attention to the harmony of JE and P in passing by Nadab and Abihu; see below, p. 354.

[4] Thus 1 Chron. xxiv. 3, but in 1 Sam. ii. 27, 28 also, Eli is assumed to be of the house of Aaron. Wellhausen's idea that in this passage Moses, not Aaron, is intended scarcely deserves notice. Cf. W. R. Smith, *O.T. in J. C.*, p. 268.

[5] 1 Sam. ii. 27–36.

[6] 1 Kings ii. 26, 27.

[7] 1 Kings ii. 35. Owing to the political division in the reign of David there was for a time a double priesthood. On Wellhausen's denial of the Aaronite descent of Zadok, see Note D on the Genealogy of Zadok.

My priest, to go up unto Mine altar, to burn incense, to wear an ephod before Me?"[1] In using here the term "high priesthood," we do not forget that it is held that the high priest is an exilian creation. But is that so? It has just been pointed out that the title is repeatedly used in the history of the kings. How, in fact, can we otherwise express the undoubted position of supremacy or dignity held by priests like Eleazar, Phinehas, Eli, Abiathar, Zadok? But there is another point of much interest. If the high priesthood was a creation of the exile, we should expect that the title would be one frequently met with in the Levitical Code—at least more frequently than elsewhere. Yet it occurs there only *three times* altogether—twice in Num. xxxv. (vers. 25, 28), and once in Lev. xxi. 10—the last a passage which many take to be very old.[2] The term ordinarily used in the Code is simply "the priest."

The priesthood was Aaronic, but was it *exclusively* so; or even exclusively Levitical? This is contested, but without real force, on the ground of certain notices in the historical books, as where the king is represented as taking a lead in religious celebrations, offering sacrifices, blessing the people,[3] etc., or where David's sons and others are spoken of as "priests."[4] A peculiar place is accorded, certainly, to the king, as representative of Jehovah, in the arrangements and conduct of worship,[5] but this as much in Chronicles and Ezekiel[6] as in the Books of Samuel or Kings. Nor is the king permitted to usurp functions strictly sacerdotal.[7] It is not to be supposed that Solomon offered with his own hand the 22,000 oxen and 120,000 sheep mentioned in 1 Kings viii. 63, to the exclusion of the

[1] Kuenen differs from Wellhausen in allowing in his *Religion of Israel* a Levitical and *originally* Aaronic priesthood. "Levi was one of the twelve tribes from the first . . . Moses and Aaron were Levites; Aaron's family discharges the priestly office at the common sanctuary," etc.—ii. p. 302. Baudissin argues for an Aaronic priesthood at least older than Josiah's reform.—*Dict. of Bible*, iv. p. 89.

[2] On this subject see more fully below, Chap. IX. Cf. also Delitzsch, Luthardt's *Zeitschrift*, 1880, p. 228.

[3] David, 2 Sam. vi. 17, 18; Solomon, 1 Kings iii. 4; viii. 62–64.

[4] 2 Sam. viii. 18 (R.V.); xx. 26 (R.V.); 1 Kings iv. 5 (R.V.).

[5] See the admirable remarks on this in Van Hoonacker, *Le Sacerdoce*, pp. 256 ff.

[6] 1 Chron. xv. 27; xvi. 2; 2 Chron. vi. 3, 12 ff.; vii. 4 ff., etc.; Ezek. xliv. 3; xlv. 7, 16, 17, 22, etc.

[7] Cf. the judgment on Uzziah, 2 Chron. xxvi. 16 ff.; cf. 2 Kings xv. 5.

priests mentioned in vers. 3, 6, 10;[1] or that David, earlier, slew for himself the numerous offerings of 2 Sam. vi. 17, 18, from which "a portion" was given to the whole multitude (also with his own hand?). The priesthood of the sons of David, however that difficult passage and related texts are to be understood,[2] was evidently something different from the ordinary service of the altar, and cannot outweigh the very full testimony to the Levitical character of the latter.

2. This brings us to the second question—that of the relations of *priests and Levites.* The subject will come up at an after stage, and we need not do more here than inquire whether the representation of a special order of Aaronic priests, in distinction from other Levites, is really, as alleged, in conflict with Deuteronomy, and with the facts of the earlier history. The general position of critical writers is that the view of the priesthood in the Levitical Code is irreconcilable with the representation in Deuteronomy, and with the earlier practice. In the Code a strong distinction is made between "the sons of Aaron," who are the only lawful priests, and the ordinary Levites, who are servants of the sanctuary. In Deuteronomy, it is held, this distinction has no place. The tribe of Levi as a whole is the priestly tribe. As Professor W. R. Smith puts it: "Deuteronomy knows no Levites who cannot be priests, and no priests who are not Levites. The two ideas are identical."[3] The phraseology in this book, accordingly, is not "sons of Aaron," but "sons of Levi." It speaks of "the priests the Levites," not of "priests and Levites." This also, it is pointed out, is the phraseology of the older historical books—so far as not revised. The distinction between "priests" and "Levites" is held to be due to a later degradation of priests of the "high places," as sketched by Ezekiel.[4]

[1] Wellhausen says that doubtless Solomon with his own hands offered the "first" sacrifice (*Hist. of Israel*, p. 133), on which Van Hoonacker remarks: "If the 21,999 oxen that remained can be said to be offered by Solomon, when in reality they have been offered by others in his name, the first may have been so also; the text knows nothing of an offering of the first" (p. 259).

[2] Cf. the discussion in Van Hoonacker, pp. 268 ff., and see Note E on David's Sons as Priests. On other questions in the historical books bearing on the priesthood, see pp. 358, 363 ff., 388 below.

[3] *O.T. in J. C.*, p. 360.

[4] See below, Chap. IX. p. 315 ff. The older theory was that Deuteronomy implies an *elevation* of the Levites from their original lower status, and

What is true in this contention is to be frankly acknowledged. The difference in point of view and mode of speech in Deuteronomy must be apparent to every reader; and it may at once be conceded to an able writer on the subject[1] that, if we had only Deuteronomy, we should never be able to arrive at a knowledge of the sharp division of the tribe of Levi into the superior and subordinate orders with which the Levitical law makes us acquainted. But it does not follow that the distinction is not there, and is not presupposed throughout.

(1) We do well, in the first place, to look with some closeness into *the phraseology* on which so much—practically the whole case—is based. When this is done, we discover that the phenomena are not quite so simple as the above statement would suggest. The expression "the priests the Levites," occurring in Deut. xvii. 9, 18, xviii. 1, xxiv. 8, xxvii. 9—*not earlier* in the book,—of itself, it will be allowed, decides nothing: it means simply "the Levitical priests." It is not found, indeed, in the Priestly Code; but as little is the other expression, "priests *and* Levites." That is peculiar to the later books,[2] and even in Chronicles is sometimes interchanged with "the priests the Levites."[3] The Book of Joshua, likewise, has "the priests the Levites":[4] never "priests and Levites." On the other hand, the Priestly Writer occasionally uses "Levites," as in Deuteronomy, to cover *both* priests and Levites:[5] this is the case also in Chronicles.[6] Finally, it is true that "sons of Aaron" is not used in Deuteronomy to describe the priests, though there is the recognition of the Aaronic high priest. But it is very noticeable that, even in the Levitical

the late date of the book was argued for on the ground that it must have taken a long time to bring this change about. The newer criticism gives up the premises, but retains the conclusion.

[1] Van Hoonacker, *Le Sacerdoce*, p. 170. The theory of this writer is, that the distinction existed, but in popular usage the name "priests" came to be applied to *all* Levites, whether of the higher or lower grade (cf. Dillmann on Deut. xviii. 1). The theory, while containing suggestive elements, does not seem to us in this form tenable.

[2] Chronicles, Ezra, Nehemiah; once in 1 Kings viii. 4, where the parallel passage in 2 Chron. v. 5 has "the priests the Levites."

[3] 2 Chron. v. 5; xxiii. 18; xxx. 27.

[4] Josh. iii. ff. (or "priests" simply).

[5] *E.g.*, Num. xxxv. 2, 6, 8; Josh. xiv. 4; xxi. 8 (cf. Van Hoonacker).

[6] 1 Chron. xvi. 4, 37; 2 Chron. xxix. 5 ff. In Malachi also (chap. iii. 3) the priests are "the sons of Levi."

Code, "sons of Aaron" is by no means the only, or universal, designation for the priests; there are considerable sections of the Code in which it either does not occur at all, or occurs only sparingly.[1] It is, moreover, chiefly in the laws and narratives of the *earlier* part of the wilderness sojourn that this usage is found; it is not characteristic of the later chapters of Numbers. Nor can this change from a narrower to a more general designation, on the assumption of the truth of the history, be regarded as strange. At first the priests, "the sons of Aaron," stood out from the people with sharp distinctness as alone invested with sacred office. The case was greatly altered after the separation of the tribe of Levi,[2] when the designation "sons of Aaron" seems to have been gradually dropped for another identifying the priests more directly with their tribe.[3] Priests and Levites had more in common with each other than either class had with the general body of the people; and, besides, the priests *were* Levites. The rise of such a designation as "the priests the Levites" is therefore quite natural, and the view in Deuteronomy of the tribe of Levi as, collectively, a priestly tribe, is entirely in keeping with the situation in which the discourses are supposed to have been delivered. To the popular eye, the tribe of Levi stood apart, forming, as a whole, one sacred body, engaged in ministering in holy things to God.

(2) It does not surprise us, then, to find in Deuteronomy the functions of the priestly ministry—even to the "Urim and Thummim," which was the peculiar prerogative of the high priest—ascribed to the tribe of Levi as a whole.[4] The question of real importance is—Does the book contain any indication of such a distinction as we have nevertheless assumed to exist between the different orders in this tribe, or does it exclude such distinction? We believe there *is* evidence of such distinction; the newer critics deny it.[5] The question belongs more properly to the discussion of Deuteronomy,[6] but, in the

[1] For details see Kittel, *Hist. of Hebs.* i. p. 120.

[2] Num. i. 47 ff.; iii. 5 ff.; viii. 5 ff., etc.

[3] After Numbers the phrase occurs only in Josh. xxi., where discrimination is necessary in the appointment of the cities.

[4] Deut. x. 8; xxxiii. 8.

[5] Dillmann, Delitzsch, Kittel, etc., Van Hoonacker also from his own point of view, hold that distinctions are *not* excluded.

[6] See below, Chap. VIII

interest of the history, we may be permitted thus far to anticipate. We would draw attention first, then, to the fact, that in Deuteronomy the terms "priest" and "Levite" are, after all, not quite synonymous. There are "the priests the Levites," but there are also "Levites" who are not priests. Even allowing them to be "possible" priests, though we do not believe this to be the meaning of the book, they have still to be distinguished from those who, in the sense of the writer, are *actual* priests. It is a perfectly unwarranted assumption that, wherever the term Levite is used we have a synonym for priest. A distinction is already indicated, and the fact of at least certain gradations within the tribe established, by the statement in chap. x. 6 that "Aaron died, and Eleazar his son ministered in the priest's office in his stead."[1] The clearest indication, however, is in chap. xviii. 1–8, where an obvious distinction is made between the "priest" serving at the sanctuary (vers. 3–5), and the "Levite" not thus serving[2] (vers. 6–8); the only intelligible reason for the more general designation being, either that ordinary non-priestly Levites are meant, or at least that they are intended to be *included.* It is a reading into the text what is not there to assert that every "Levite" going up to the sanctuary is a "possible" priest in the stricter sense. This rules the meaning to be attached to the opening sentence: "The priests the Levites, all the tribe of Levi."[3] The second designation includes the first: in apposition it cannot be, since, in the writer's sense, all Levites are not actual priests. To us it seems most evident that when he speaks of "the priests the Levites," he has a definite class in view, and by no means the whole body of the tribe.[4] This view of the passage,

[1] Cf. chap. xxxiii. 8. To what again can the separation in chap. x. 8 refer, if not to the setting apart of the sons of Aaron, and afterwards of the whole tribe of Levi, recorded in the P sections of the history? Critics suppose an *omitted* narrative of this separation in JE (cf. Driver, *Deut.* p. 121).

[2] Thus, *e.g.*, Dillmann, *Num.–Jos.*, *in loc.* It is to be remembered that it is only in the few passages above cited that priests are mentioned at all.

[3] Chap. xviii. 1.

[4] Dr. Driver refers to the frequency of explanatory appositions in Deuteronomy, and gives examples (*Deut.* p. 214). The case seems rather analogous to those in which the lawgiver *expands* his original statement by enlarging additions; *e.g.*, "Ye shall eat . . . ye and your household" (chap. xii. 7); "Ye shall rejoice . . . ye, and your sons, and your daughters," etc. etc. (chap. xii. 12); cf. chap. xii. 18; xv. 11, etc.

we are aware, the critical school meets with a direct negative, assigning as a reason that the terms used in ver. 7 to describe the Levites' services ("to minister in the name of Jehovah," "to stand before Jehovah") are those regularly used of priestly duties. We believe this is far from being really the case; but the question is a little intricate, and had better be discussed apart.[1]

(3) A word may be said before leaving the subject on the difficulty arising from the representations in Deuteronomy of the *dispersed and needy condition* of the Levites. The objection is urged that, instead of being furnished with cities and pasturages, and enjoying an independent income from tithes, as the Priestly Code provides, the Levites appear in this book as homeless and dependent, wandering from place to place, and glad to be invited, with the stranger, the widow, and the fatherless, to share in charitable feasts.[2] Here, in the first place, it must be remarked that the legal provision is not ignored, but is, on the other hand, expressly alluded to in chap. xviii. 1, 2 (cf. chap. x. 9), "And they shall have no inheritance among their brethren; Jehovah is their inheritance, as He hath spoken to them," where the reference seems unmistakable to the law in Num. xviii. 20, 23, 24. Dillmann says: "The corresponding law stands in Num. xviii."[3] But, waiving this, may we not suggest that, if a time is sought when these exhortations to care for the Levite would be suitable, no time is so fit as that when they are supposed to have been delivered, before the tithe-laws had come into regular operation,—when in truth there was little or nothing to tithe,—and when the Levites would be largely dependent on the hospitality of individuals. The Levites were dependent then, and might from very obvious causes

[1] See Appendix to Chapter—"Priests and Levites." Cf. also the case of Samuel, considered below, pp. 189–90.

[2] Deut. xii. 12, 19; xvi. 11, etc.

[3] *Num.-Jos., in loc.* Dr. Driver argues against this on the ground that in Num. xviii. 20 "the promise is made expressly to the *priests* (Aaron) alone, as distinguished from the Levites (vers. 21–24), whose 'inheritance' is specified separately (ver. 24); here it is given to the whole tribe without distinction."—*Deut.* p. 125 (on chap. x. 9). But surely it is obvious that the whole passage in Numbers (xviii. 20–24) goes together, and that the principal part of the "inheritance" of the priests is the tenth of the tithe they are to receive from the Levites (ver. 26). Let the reader compare the passages for himself.

come to be dependent again. Their state would not be greatly bettered in the unsettled times of the conquest.[1] Nothing could be more appropriate in itself, better adapted to create kindly sympathies between Levites and people, or more likely to avert neglect of the tribe by the withholding of their just dues, than the perpetuation of these primitive hospitalities. It is to be remembered that no tribunal existed to enforce payment of the tithes: all depended on the conscientiousness of the individual payer. It is easy to see that an income of this kind was in the highest degree precarious, and that, in times of religious declension, the body of the Levites would be reduced to great straits. The Levites no doubt suffered severely in the days of the Judges, and under bad kings; under good kings, like David, and Solomon, and Hezekiah, the order, we may believe, experienced considerable revivals. At other times it sank in the general corruption, and Levites were content to earn a doubtful livelihood by irregular ministrations at the "high places." There is no evidence we know of that their condition in the later days of the kingdom was so deplorably destitute as the critics represent.

(4) It will be seen later how little can be inferred from the general silence of the history about the Levites;[2] yet that silence, as has already been hinted, is not altogether unbroken.[3] Two instances, at least, of mention occur in 1 Sam. vi. 15, and 2 Sam. xv. 24; perhaps also the presence of Levites may be inferred where Hophni and Phinehas are spoken of as "*with* the ark of Jehovah."[4] A case of special interest is that of the youthful Samuel, who is described as "ministering unto," or "before" Jehovah at Shiloh,[5] though his duties were the subordinate ones of the Levite.[6] The words "ministered before Eli" also show that this was his position.[7] The attempt, on the other hand, sometimes made to prove Samuel to be a *priest*

[1] Cf. König, art. "Judges," *Dict. of Bible*, ii. p. 816: "Further, we see a Levite wandering about, ready to settle down wherever he found office and bread (Judg. xvii. 8 ff.; xviii. 19 ff.; xix. 1). This situation of the members of the tribe of Levi was an actual one as long as a number of the Levitical cities were not yet conquered [König accepts the historicity of these], such as Gezer, and those remarks of the Book of Judges would have possessed no probability if they had proceeded from a period when Jeroboam selected priests from among the people at large," etc.

[2] See below, Chap. IX. p. 304.

[3] Cf. p. 163.

[4] 1 Sam. iv. 4.

[5] 1 Sam. ii. 11, 18; iii. 1.

[6] 1 Sam. iii. 15.

[7] 1 Sam. iii. 1.

(in contradiction of the law) from the mention of his "linen ephod" and "little robe," must be regarded as another instance of forcing the text.[1] It is inexcusable exaggeration when Professor W. R. Smith writes: "As a child he ministers before Jehovah, wearing the ephod which the law confines to the high priest, and not only this, but the high priestly mantle (*me'il*)."[2] The high priestly ephod, as every reference to it shows,[3] was something distinctive, and different from "the linen ephod," which was worn by ordinary priests,[4] but not by them exclusively.[5] The *me'il*, or robe, again, was a long sleeveless tunic, "worn," says Gesenius, "by women of rank (2 Sam. xiii. 18), by men of rank and birth (Job i. 20; ii. 12), by kings (1 Sam. xv. 27; xviii. 4; xxiv. 4, 11)"[6] —therefore no peculiar property of the high priest. The usurpation of high priestly or even of ordinary priestly functions by Samuel is on a par with his sleeping in the inner temple beside the sacred ark.

NOTE.—*The Ark*: In connection with the discussions, pp. 137–38 and 161–65, the author would draw attention to the searching Essay by Professor Lotz, of Erlangen, *Die Bundeslade* (1901), which did not fall into his hands till this chapter was printed. It lends valuable support to the contentions in the text. See especially the discusssion of the *names* of the ark (pp. 28 ff.).

[1] Thus Wellhausen, W. R. Smith, etc. Wellhausen's note should be quoted: "*House of God* is never anything but the house of an image. Outside the Priestly Code, *ephod* is the image; *ephod bad* (the linen ephod), the priestly garment."—*Hist. of Israel*, p. 130. Was Abiathar's ephod then (p. 132) an image?

[2] *O.T. in J. C.*, p. 270.

[3] Cf. Ex. xxviii. 6; 1 Sam. ii. 28; xxiii. 6, 9; xxx. 7.

[4] 1 Sam. xxii. 18. It was not, however, a *prescribed* part of the dress.

[5] 2 Sam. vi. 14

[6] *Lexicon, in loc.*

APPENDIX TO CHAPTER VI

Priests and Levites

Dr. Driver gives a reason for rejecting the view of the relation of priests and Levites indicated in the text, which, if it were valid, would be fatal; but which, as it stands, seems to us, we confess, an example of that overstraining which plays so large a part in these discussions. He writes: "The terms used in [Deut. xviii.] 7 to describe the Levite services are those used regularly of *priestly* duties. *To minister in the name*, as xviii. 5 (of the priest; cf. xvii. 12; xxi. 5); *to stand before—i.e.*, to wait on (see, *e.g.*, 1 Kings x. 8)—*Jehovah*, as Ezek. xliv. 15; Judg. xx. 28; cf. Deut. xvii. 12; xviii. 5. (The Levites 'stand before'—*i.e.*, wait upon—*the congregation*, Num. xvi. 9; Ezek. xliv. 11*b*. In 2 Chron. xxix. 11, *priests* are present; see v. 4)."[1] We should not, of course, presume to differ from Dr. Driver on a question of philology or grammar; but this is a question of palpable fact, and invites examination. All Hebrew scholars, besides, are far from agreeing with Dr. Driver in the above *dicta*. The statement made, we venture to think, needs much qualification. It is not denied that the terms employed are appropriate to priestly duties; the question is whether they are used of these duties "regularly" and *only*. And this it is difficult to admit. The exact phrase "to minister in the name" is, so far as we know, found nowhere else than in vers. 5, 7, of this passage; but the verb itself, "minister" (*sharēth*) is used constantly in the law and in Chronicles of *Levitical* as well as of priestly service.[2] The Levites, we read, shall be appointed over the tabernacle of the testimony, "and they shall minister

[1] *Introd.* p. 83 (note); cf. W. R. Smith, *O.T. in J.C.*, p. 361.

[2] Num. i. 50; iii. 6, 31; iv. 9, 12, 14; viii. 26; xvi. 9; xviii. 2; 1 Chron. xv. 2; xvi. 4, 37.

to it";[1] aged Levites "shall minister with their brethren in the tent of meeting,"[2] but shall do no service; the Levites "are chosen to carry the ark of God and to minister unto Him for ever";[3] they "minister before the ark of the covenant of Jehovah,"[4] etc. *In fact, the only use of the word "minister" in the Book of Numbers*, if we are not mistaken, *is with reference to the service of the Levites.*[5] With this may be compared Dr. Driver's own note in his *Deuteronomy*, where the facts are stated more fully, but still, as we think, onesidedly. "*To minister*," he there says, "is a less distinctive term, being used not only of priests, but also of Levites (Num. viii. 26), and other subordinate attendants, as in 1 Sam. ii. 11, 18; iii. 1 (of Samuel)."[6] [We gather from this that Dr. Driver does not adopt Wellhausen's theory that Samuel was a "priest."] But then, what becomes of its peculiar force in Deuteronomy? For Samuel also ministered "to Jehovah"; so in 1 Chron. xv. 2, etc. It does not fare better with the expression "to stand before Jehovah." Apart from the passage quoted, it is used in Deuteronomy *once* of the tribe of Levi,[7] and *once* of the Levitical priest.[8] In the Levitical law *it does not occur at all*—a curious instance of "regularly." On the other hand, in Chronicles, the Levites "stand every morning to thank and praise Jehovah, and likewise at even,"[9] and "priests and Levites" are addressed together as "chosen to stand before Jehovah."[10] In Nehemiah also "priests and Levites" are spoken of together as those who "stood."[11] Can it be claimed that the case is made out?[12]

[1] Num. i. 50.
[2] Num. viii. 26.
[3] 1 Chron. xv. 2.
[4] 1 Chron. xvi. 4, 37.
[5] The note on the word as found in P in the Oxf. *Hexateuch* is: "Of priests in the sanctuary, or of Levites attending on priests" (i. p. 216).
[6] *Deut.* p. 123.
[7] Deut. x. 8.
[8] Deut. xvii. 12.
[9] 1 Chron. xxiii. 30.
[10] 2 Chron. xxix. 11; cf. xxxv. 5. Dr. Driver says that here "*priests* are present." The important point is that *Levites* also are present, and that *both* are addressed.
[11] Neh. xii. 44 (Heb.).
[12] In Lev. ix. 5, and a few places in Deuteronomy (iv. 10; xix. 17, etc.), "stand before Jehovah" is used of Israel generally. "To stand before the congregation" (used of the Levites) occurs *once* (Num. xvi. 9; cf. Ezek. xliv. 11).

CHAPTER VII

Difficulties and Perplexities of the Critical Hypothesis: I. The JE Analysis

"He His fabric of the Heavens
Hath left to their disputes; perhaps to move
His laughter at their quaint opinions wide
Hereafter, when they come to model Heaven
And calculate the stars; how they will wield
The mighty frame;—how build, contrive
To save appearances;—how gird the sphere
With centrick and eccentrick scribbled o'er,
Cycle and epicycle, orb in orb."—MILTON.

"To base a determination of age on bare peculiarities of language, especially in things that concern legal relations, in which the form of expression is not arbitrarily employed by the writer, is precarious. When the relationship of certain sections is assumed on perhaps insufficient criteria, and then other sections are added to them because of some similar linguistic phenomena, and from these again further and further conclusions are drawn, one easily runs the risk of moving in a vicious circle."—GRAF.

"The history of critical investigation has shown that far too much weight has often been laid on agreement in the use of the divine names—so much so that it has twice led the critics wrong. It is well therefore to utter a warning against laying an exaggerated stress on this one phenomenon."
—KUENEN.

"No intelligent observer, however, will deny that the work of investigation has gone onwards, and not moved in a circle."—DELITZSCH.

CHAPTER VII

DIFFICULTIES AND PERPLEXITIES OF THE CRITICAL HYPOTHESIS: I. THE JE ANALYSIS

THUS far we have been content to proceed on the assumption of the correctness of the ordinary critical analysis of documents in the "Hexateuch," and, without challenging either documents or dates, have endeavoured to show that, even on this basis, the essential facts of the history, and the outstanding features in the Biblical picture of the religion and institutions of Israel, remain unaffected. We now take a further step, and go on to inquire whether the critical theory of documents, as usually presented, is valid, and, if at all, how far. Here we part company with many, of whose help, in defending the truth of supernatural revelation, we have hitherto gladly availed ourselves, but who, we are compelled to think, have unnecessarily hampered themselves, and weakened their contentions, by assent to critical positions which are far from being solidly established. We shall still seek, as far as may be, common ground with these writers, and hope to show that, if we break with them, our doubts are born, not from an obstinate wedding of the mind to obsolete traditions, but from a sincere regard to the facts, as we are constrained to apprehend them.

It is not uncommon to find the course of criticism during the last century represented as purely a work of unbelief, resulting in hopeless error and confusion. That, however, is not altogether our opinion. If it cannot well be denied that, as before stated, what is called "Higher Criticism" was cradled in, and received its characteristic "set" from the older rationalism,[1] and if, unfortunately,

[1] That this statement is not too strong may be seen from the names of its founders as given in Cheyne and other writers. Cheyne himself censures the early excesses of criticism. "In the previous age" (before Gesenius), he

this vice of its origin has clung to it, more or less, in all its subsequent developments, it would be unreasonable not to acknowledge that it is also, in large part, the product of a genuinely scientific temper, and of a true perception of phenomena which are *there* in Scripture, and, on any theory, require explanation. Its course, too, has been marked by a real and continuous advance in the apprehension of these phenomena, and, with whatever mingling of error, has tended to an ever closer definition of the problem to be solved. A brief glance at the principal *stadia* in the history of the development will illustrate what we mean.

I. Stadia of the Critical Development

The chief stages in the development of the critical hypothesis have been the following:—

1. The beginning of the critical movement is usually associated with the French physician Astruc,[1] who, in his *Conjectures*, in 1753, drew attention to the presence of Elohistic and Jehovistic sections in Genesis, and on this based his theory of the employment of distinct documents in the composition of the book. The fact thus founded on is a highly interesting one, and, once pointed out, cannot be ignored. It is the case that some chapters, and portions of chapters, in Genesis are marked by the use, exclusively or predominatingly, of the divine name "Elohim" (God), and others by a similar use of the divine name "Jehovah" (E.T. Lord). This distinction continues till Ex. vi., when God reveals Himself by His name Jehovah, then (mainly) ceases. A considerable part of Genesis, accordingly, can really, by the use of this criterion, be divided into

says, "there had been an epidemic of arbitrary emendation in the department of textual criticism, and a tendency (at any rate among some 'higher critics' of the Pentateuch and Isaiah) to break up the text into a number of separate pieces, which threatened to open the door to unbounded caprice." —*Founders of Criticism*, p. 63. [What will a future critic say of Dr. Cheyne?] The result is described by Tholuck in his inaugural lecture at Halle in 1821: "For the last twenty or thirty years the opinion has been generally prevalent, that the study of the Old Testament for theologians, as well as the devotional reading of it for the laity, is either entirely profitless, or at least promises little advantage" (*Ibid.* p. 67).

[1] One of the best accounts of Astruc is that by Dr. H. Osgood in *The Presbyterian and Reformed Review* for January 1892. It shows that Astruc's personal character was deeply marred by the vices of French society.

Elohistic and Jehovistic sections.[1] A fact to be placed alongside of this, though its full bearings do not always seem to be perceived, is that in the Psalter we have an arrangement of psalms into Jehovistic and Elohistic groups by a similar distinction in the use of the divine names.[2]

2. A further step was taken when Eichhorn (1779),[3] to whom is due the name "Higher Criticism," and who seems to have worked independently of Astruc, pointed out that the Elohistic and Jehovistic sections in Genesis were distinguished, not simply by the use of the divine names, but by certain other literary peculiarities, which furnished aid in their discrimination. The Elohistic sections in particular—not all of them, as came afterwards to be seen—were found to be characterised by a vocabulary and style of their own, which enabled them, on the whole, to be readily distinguished. This result also, whatever explanation may be offered of it, has stood the test of time, and will not, we believe, be overturned. The long lists of words and phrases customarily adduced as characteristic of the Elohist (now P), need, indeed, much sifting,[4] but enough remains to justify the critic in distinguishing a P hand in Genesis, different from that of JE.[5]

3. It was at this point that De Wette struck in with his thesis (1805–6) that Deuteronomy, shown by him to have also a style and character of its own, could not have been

[1] As examples of Elohistic sections in this sense, cf. Gen. i.–ii. 3; v.; xvii.; xxiii.; xxv. 7–17, etc.: in the story of the flood, vi. 9–22; vii. 11–16; ix. 1–18, etc. As specimens of Jehovistic sections, cf. Gen. ii. 4–iv.; xi. 1–9; xii.; xiii. (mainly); xviii., xix., etc., with the alternate sections in the flood story.

[2] The Psalter is divided into five Books, each concluding with a doxology (Pss. xli. 13; lxxii. 18, 19; lxxxix. 52; cvi. 48). In the first three of these books the psalms are grouped according to the predominant use of the divine names: Book I. (i.–xli.), *Jehovistic*, ascribed to David; Book II. (xlii.–lxxii.), *Elohistic*, ascribed to sons of Korah, Asaph (one psalm), David; Book III. (lxxiii.–lxxxix.), *Jehovistic*, ascribed to Asaph, sons of Korah, etc. The last two books are mainly Jehovistic. See below, pp. 277 ff., on these groups of psalms, and their significance. For details, cf. W. R. Smith, *O.T. in J. C.*, pp. 195–96, etc.

[3] Eichhorn was a rationalist of the Paulus type, giving a naturalistic explanation of the miracles.

[4] See below, pp. 336 ff.

[5] Astruc and Eichhorn did not carry the analysis beyond Genesis, though Eichhorn suggests such extension (cf. De Wette, *Introd.* ii. p. 150). Both regarded Moses (wholly or mainly) as the compiler. Their position may be compared with that of Principal Cave in his *Inspiration of the O.T.*, who, however, makes Moses also the probable author of both documents.

composed earlier than the reign of Josiah. This he inferred mainly from the law of the central sanctuary in Deut. xii., and from the breaches of that law in the older history, considered in last chapter. Westphal has declared that "Deuteronomy is the Ariadne's thread in the labyrinth of the historical problem of the Pentateuch,"[1] and we are not sure that we are not disposed to agree with him, if in a sense different from what he intended. Meanwhile, as was inevitable, the question arose as to whether the Elohistic and Jehovistic documents did not extend beyond Genesis into the remaining books of the Pentateuch, and, further, into Joshua (Bleek, 1822), with which the earlier books are so closely connected. In this extension, the criterion of the divine names failed,[2] but the other linguistic phenomena, and relations with acknowledged J and E sections, were relied on to establish the distinction. Thus, mainly under the guidance of Bleek, Ewald (1831), and Stähelin (1835),[3] the criticism of the "Pentateuch" passed definitely over into that of the "Hexateuch"—the Pentateuch *and* Joshua.

4. The next step is connected with *Hupfeld* (1853), and marks again a distinct advance. Ilgen (1798) had preluded the discovery, but Hupfeld, with more success, drew attention to the fact that the assumed Elohistic document in Genesis was not all of one cast. Certain sections—all, indeed, up to chap. xx.—had the well-marked characteristics now attributed to P; but other portions, agreeing in the use of the name Elohim, were quite dissimilar in style, and closely resembled the Jehovistic parts—were, in fact, indistinguishable from the latter, save in the difference of the divine names.[4] Hupfeld's solution was that we have here a document from a *third* writer—named by him the 2nd Elohist (E), who agreed with the older in the use of

[1] *Sources du Pent.* ii. p. xxiv. De Wette, with most scholars of that age, regarded the Elohistic document as the *older*, and partly *on that ground* argued for the lateness of Deuteronomy (to give time for development). Modern scholars, *reversing* the relations of age, yet held by De Wette's conclusion.

[2] Colenso to the last (in published works) broke off the Elohistic narrative at Ex. vi.; Cave, attributing it to Moses (or earlier writer), does the same—a curious instance of extremes meeting.

[3] Stähelin made important contributions in *Stud. und Krit.*, 1835 and 1838.

[4] Examples are Gen. xx.; xxi. 6.–xxii.; xxxi.

the name Elohim, but whose style, vocabulary, and mode of representation were akin to, and nearly identical with, those of the Jehovist. This observation, again, in substance corresponds with facts; for it is the case that in the sections in question there is little or nothing to distinguish the Elohist from the Jehovist, beyond the use of the divine names.[1] A natural solution would seem to be that, despite the difference in names, the documents are not really two, but one;[2] but modern critics generally adhere to Hupfeld's distinction of J and E, and evolve a number of other peculiarities which are thought to distinguish the two writers. The theory had its disadvantages, which kept many of the older scholars, *e.g.*, Bleek, from assenting to it; for, while explaining certain stylistic phenomena, it destroyed, in doing so, the previously boasted unity of the Elohistic narrative,[3] and created in the latter great and unaccountable hiatuses: left in fact, as we shall see, only a few fragments and lists for P after Gen. xxiii. to the end of the book![4]

5. The final stage in the development—if that can be termed development which is more properly *revolution*—outstrips in importance all the preceding. Hitherto, with some little regarded exceptions,[5] the universal assumption had been that the Elohistic Writer, or 1st Elohist—was the oldest of all, and his date was variously fixed in the time of the Judges, or in the reigns of Saul or David. The order was assumed to be: 1st Elohist—Jehovist and 2nd Elohist—Deuteronomy. Then came the somersault of Graf, who, in his *Historical Books of the Old Testament,* in 1866,

[1] Colenso, who only partially accepted Hupfeld's analysis, says: "The style of the two writers is so very similar ,except in the use of the divine names, that it is impossible to distinguish them by considerations of style alone."—*Pent.* v. p. 59.

[2] Colenso favours this solution for the parts he accepts of E: so Klostermann. Cf. below, p. 218.

[3] Cf. De Wette, *Introd.* ii. p. 77: "The Elohistic fragments form a whole which can be reduced to a form almost perfect." (See below, pp. 333, 341.) On the other hand, writers like Bleek (more recently Cave), who accept the Elohistic narrative in its integrity, are in this dilemma, that they destroy their own grounds for distinguishing the Elohist from the Jehovist. For it has to be admitted that considerable sections of the Elohistic document are in every respect of style (except the names) indistinguishable from the Jehovistic. Those again who, like Colenso, in parts identify E with J, have to own that the names are not an infallible criterion.

[4] See below, pp. 341 ff. [5] See below, p. 204.

propounded the view,[1] which he owed to Reuss,[2] that the legislation of the middle books of the Pentateuch (the Levitical law) was not earlier, but later, than Deuteronomy —was, in fact, a product of the age of the exile. Graf, however, was not yet of the opinion that all the Elohistic sections of the Pentateuch were late: he accepted the ordinary view that the Elohistic writing was the oldest for the *historical* sections, but contended that the priestly *laws* were a later, and post-exilian, insertion.[3] Kuenen and Riehm, from opposite sides, wrote to show that this was an untenable position. History and laws go together, and either the whole is early, or the whole is late.[4] Graf before his death acknowledged the force of Kuenen's arguments for the late date of the (P) history as well as of the legislation,[5] while not admitting that the P writing constituted an independent document. Owing mainly to the powerful advocacy of Wellhausen,[6] the more thoroughgoing view has prevailed, and, as formerly stated, it is now held to be one of the "settled" results of criticism[7] that the Priestly element is the very latest constituent in the Hexateuch, and is of exilian or post-exilian date. Yet in one respect

[1] See above, p. 160. An earlier work in 1855, *De templo Silonensi*, preluded the idea of his chief work.

[2] Cf. Kuenen, *Hex.* pp. xxxiv–v. Reuss's own work, *L'Histoire Sainte et la Loi*, was published in 1879.

[3] This also was Colenso's position in his published works, after he had come round to Graf's standpoint (*Pent.* Pts. v. and vi.)—*history* early, *laws* late. See below, p. 334.

[4] Kuenen puts it thus: "Must the laws stand with the narratives, or must the narratives fall with the laws? I could not hesitate for a moment in accepting the latter alternative."—*Hex.* p. xxii.

[5] *Ibid.* pp. xxviii, xxx. Professor Robertson properly says: "To say bluntly that the narratives must go with the laws, is no more a process of criticism than to say that the laws must go with the history. It is therefore inaccurate to describe the position of Graf as a conclusion of criticism. It was simply a hypothesis to evade a difficulty in which criticism had landed him."—*Early Rel.* pp. 418–19.

[6] Wellhausen tells us: "I learned through Ritschl that Karl Heinrich Graf placed the law later than the prophets; and, almost without knowing his reasons for the hypothesis, I was prepared to accept it."—*Hist. of Israel*, p. 3.

[7] Professor W. R. Smith names "Kuenen and Wellhausen as the men whose acumen and research have carried this inquiry to a point where nothing of importance for the historical study of the Old Testament still remains uncertain."—*Rel. of Semites*, p. vii. There can be "no doubt," says a recent able writer, that "all this part of the Hexateuch is, in its present form, post-exilic."—McFadyen, *Mess. of Historians*. See Note A on Self-Confidence of Critics, p. 240.

even this theory, which we shall have occasion to oppose very decidedly, appears to us to mark an advance. In so far as a documentary hypothesis is to be accepted at all—on which after—it is difficult to resist the conviction that P must be regarded as relatively later than JE, for whose narratives, in Genesis at least, it furnishes the "framework,"[1] and that it is not, as former critics held, a separate older work. In agreement with Graf,[2] however, we do not suppose that *at any period* it ever formed a separate, independent writing.

As supplementing this sketch of the chief stadia in the critical development, a glance may be taken at the views which have been held on the *relation of the elements* of the Pentateuch in the course of this long history. These may be roughly divided into the *fragmentary*, the *supplementary*, and the *documentary*.

(1) At an early stage Vater (1805) and others developed the idea that the Pentateuch was made up, not of continuous documents, but of a great number of smaller *fragments*. This view was vigorously contested, especially with respect to the Book of Genesis, by Stähelin, Ewald (1823), Tuch (1838), etc., as well as by the thoroughgoing defenders of the Mosaic authorship, who, till the middle of the century, formed an influential group.[3] The fragmentist view was regarded as overcome; but it will be seen as we advance that the newer criticism, with its multiplication of documents (P^1 P^2 P^3 etc.), its substitution of "schools" for individual authors, and its minute tesselation of texts, represents largely a return to it.[4]

(2) The theory which superseded the fragmentary was that of an Elohistic groundwork, or fundamental document (*Grundschrift*), *supplemented* at a later time by Jehovistic additions. This was the view of Bleek, and of most of the above-named writers: later representatives of it are Knobel,

[1] Cf. Klostermann, *Pentateuch*, p. 10. On P as "framework," see below, pp. 215, 340.

[2] Graf adhered to this till his death, cf. Kuenen, *Hex.* p. xxx. See below, Chap. X.

[3] The best known names in this conservative school are those of Ranke, Drechsler, Hengstenberg, Hävernick, Keil.

[4] For examples, cf. text and notes in Oxford *Hexateuch*, which hardly leaves a paragraph, verse, or even clause untouched.

Schrader, and Colenso.[1] It was a theory which, granting its initial assumption, had much to recommend it. Its advocates based on the fact that the Jehovistic narrative as it stands, is incomplete, and presupposes the Elohistic *e.g.*, it has no command to build the ark (cf. Gen. vii. 1) and contains no notices of the deaths of the patriarchs "It is still more unmistakable," argued Bleek, "that those Elohistic portions in the first part of our book refer to one another, presuppose one another, and follow one another in due course, whilst they take no notice of the Jehovistic passages lying between them."[2] Its opponents reply that it is impossible that the Jehovist could have filled in passages which, as they hold, are contradictory of the main narrative.[3] Hupfeld's theory of the 2nd Elohist weakened this view and it fell to the ground altogether when the Graf theory came to prevail, that P (=the Elohist) was not the earliest, but the latest, of the sources.

(3) The *documentary* hypothesis—earliest of all—afterwards revived by Hupfeld, rose again to favour, and since Graf's time has generally been held in the form already described, viz., JE and P as independent documents, which have been combined with each other, and with Deuteronomy (D), by a redactor, or series of redactors. So stated, the theory seems simple: its enormous difficulties are only revealed when the attempt is made to work it out in detail. We advance now to the consideration of these difficulties, with a view to the attainment of a more positive result.

II. Difficulties of the Critical Hypothesis in General

The course of criticism, we have granted, has been in a very real sense onward, so far as the discovery of phenomena is concerned. As the outcome, the critics are justified in saying that on certain leading points there is very general agreement in their ranks. It is agreed that four main sources are to be distinguished in the Pentateuch (or Hexateuch)—J E D P—and that these have been com-

[1] Colenso maintained his supplementary theory to the close against Hupfeld and Kuenen. See below, p. 334.

[2] *Introd.* i. p. 275.

[3] Cf., *e.g.*, Dillmann, *Genesis*, i. pp. 14, 15; Kuenen, *Hex.* p. 160.

bined by one or more hands to form the present work. It is also very generally believed (not, however, by Dillmann), that J and E were combined, if not before the time of Deuteronomy (Kittel, Addis, and others think *after*), at least before their final union with that book (D) and with P. Beyond these very general results,[1] however, it is, as will immediately be seen, highly misleading to speak, as is sometimes done, of unanimity. Agreement in main features of the critical division there is, especially with regard to P, — the original premises being granted, there is little alternative,—but whenever the attempt is made to carry the analysis into details, or to establish a consistent theory of the relations of the documents, or of their mode of combination, divergences wide and deep reveal themselves, complications thicken at every step, and inevitable doubt arises as to the soundness of the premises which lead to such perplexity in the results. Two unimpeachable witnesses may be cited at the outset in general corroboration of what is said as to the absence of unanimity. Kautzsch, the author, with Socin, of one of the best typographical analyses of the Book of Genesis, makes this remarkable statement: "In the Pentateuch and the Book of Joshua, it is only with regard to P that something approaching to unanimity has been reached."[2] Kuenen, again, says with special reference to JE: "As the analysis has been carried gradually further, it has become increasingly evident that the critical question is far more difficult and involved than was at first supposed, and the solutions which seemed to have been secured have been in whole or in part brought into question again."[3] These words might be taken as the text of nearly everything that follows.

1. With every allowance for what may be said of progress, inevitable doubt is awakened in regard to the soundness of the critical process by the *conflicts of opinion* which the

[1] Westphal reduces the results on which there is agreement to three: "(1) The existence, henceforth established, of four sources in the Pentateuch: the 1st Elohist, or Priestly Code, the 2nd Elohist, the Jehovist, and the Deuteronomist; (2) the admission of the fact that each of these sources, before its entrance into the composition of our Biblical books, existed as an independent writing; (3) the unanimity of scholars as to the manner in which it is necessary to reconstruct, at least in their great lines, the four sources indicated."—*Sources du Pent.* ii. p. xxvi. We shall see that even this statement requires considerable modification.

[2] *Lit. of O.T.*, p. 226.

[3] *Hex.* p. 139.

history of criticism itself discovers. It is to be remembered in discussing this subject, that the J E D P of the critics—so far as not simply symbols for the supposed documents themselves—with their serial duplicates, to be immediately referred to, and the numerous retinue of redactors, are, though spoken of so familiarly, purely hypothetical entities—postulated beings, of whom history or tradition knows nothing. Moses, Joshua, Samuel, we know, or think we do; but these shadows have left no trace of themselves, save, if it be so, in their work, now taken to pieces again by the critics. When we desire to know something more of their time or their relations, we are in a region in which, the history of criticism being witness, the agreements are far overborne by the disagreements. Do we ask when they lived? the dates assigned to P (the 1st Elohist), we have found, range from the days of Samuel (Bleek, Colenso, older writers generally), through the period of the kings (Riehm, Dillmann, Nöldeke, Schrader, etc.), to the time of the exile, or later (Graf school). The dates of JE run from the time of the Judges (König, Köhler, etc.) to the tenth, ninth, eighth centuries, with, in the view of Kuenen, "Judæan editions" after. The composition of Deuteronomy is commonly placed in the reign of Josiah, or of Manasseh; but many able critics (Delitzsch, Oettli, Klostermann, etc.) hold it to be much older, and in kernel Mosaic; while others divide it up, and put extensive portions later than Josiah. Do we inquire as to dependence? The older view was, as we saw, that J and E are supplementary to P; the newer theory is that P is later than JE and presupposes them. J is held by many (Dillmann, Nöldeke, Schrader, Kittel, etc.) to be dependent on E and to have borrowed from him; Wellhausen, Kuenen, Stade, etc., as confidently reverse the relation, and make E dependent on J;[1] others treat the documents as practically independent (*e.g.*, Woods).[2] One set of critics (Dillmann, Riehm, etc.) hold that the marks demonstrate E to be about a century older than J; the prevailing tendency at present is to make J about a century older than E. Addis says that this question of priority "is

[1] Wellhausen points out that E "has come down to us only in extracts embodied in the Jehovist narrative," and appears to doubt its independence. *Hist. of Israel*, pp. 7, 8. See below, p. 217.

[2] Art. "Hexateuch" in *Dict. of Bible*.

;ill one of the most vexed questions in the criticism of the Iexateuch."[1] The interesting point in the discussion is the ogency with which each critic refutes the reasonings of his eighbours, and shows them to be nugatory. All this would ıatter little, if it were, as is sometimes said, mere variation n the surface, with slight bearing on the soundness of the ıeory as a whole. But it is far from that. The criteria 'hich determine these judgments are found on inspection go deep into the substance of the theory, and afford valuable practical test of the principles by which it is uilt up.[2]

2. These perplexities are slight, however, in comparison ith those arising from another cause now to be mentioned -the excessive *multiplication of sources.* The matter is :latively simple when we have to deal only with a J E D r P, and when the critic honestly abides by these. But, s the analysis proceeds, we find it impossible to stop ere. As the old Ptolemaic astronomer discovered that,) explain the irregularities in the visible motions of the eavenly bodies, he had to add epicycles to his original ycles, then fresh epicycles to these, till his chart became huge maze of complications—and incredibilities; so the ritic finds that the application of the same criteria 'hich guided him in the severance of his main documents, ecessitates, when pushed further, a continuance of the rocess, and the splitting up of the documents into yet ıinuter parts. Hence new divisions, and the gradual :solution of the original JE, etc., into the nebulous series, $^1J^2J^3$; $E^1E^2E^3$; $P^1P^2P^3P^4$; $R^1R^2R^3$, etc., or equivalents; ll of which have now become part of the recognised pparatus of the critical schools.[3] Can we wonder that

[1] *Hex.* i. p. lxxxi.

[2] *E.g.*, Driver says on the opposite views of Dillmann and Wellhausen bout J and E: "The difference turns in part upon a different conception of ıe limits of J. Dillmann's 'J' embraces more than Wellhausen's 'J' . . . illmann's date, *c.* 750, is assigned to J largely on the ground of just those assages which form no part of Wellhausen's J."—*Introd.* p. 123. Kittel, gain, upholding Dillmann's view, says: "When Wellhausen finds E to be closer contact than J with the specially prophetic spirit . . . this arises, at ıy rate in part, from his altogether peculiar analysis of J; an analysis hich, again, is based on this character assigned to J by him."—*Hist. of 'ebs.* i. p. 80. Again: "Kuenen will not admit any reference [in Amos ıd Hosea] to E, but only to J; Dillmann cannot see any acquaintance with , but only with E. I cannot assent to either view."—*Ibid.* p. 83.

[3] Cf. Oxford *Hexateuch*, or any of the text-books. **As a popular book,**

even a tolerably advanced critic like Dillmann should write: "with a $Q^1Q^2Q^3$ [= P], $J^1J^2J^3$, $E^1E^2E^3$ I can do nothing, and can only see in them a hypothesis of perplexity."[1] Assume such multiples to have existed, does anyone with a modicum of common sense believe it possible for a twentieth century critic to pick their handiwork to pieces again, and assign to each his proper fragment of the whole? These processional Js and Es, however, should not be scoffed at as arbitrary. They are really indispensable parts of a critical stock-in-trade *if the original principles of the theory are to be consistently carried out.* In that respect they serve again as a test of the value of these principles. The critic thinks he observes, for instance, within the limits of the same document, a discrepancy, or a new turn of expression, or a duplicate incident—the denial of a wife, *e.g.*, in Gen. xii. xxvi., both in J,[2] or a seeming intermingling of two stories—in Korah's rebellion, *e.g.*, in Num. xvi. 2–11, P,[3]—or a reference in J (older writer) to E (younger): what is to be done except to assume that there is here a trace of a distinct source, or of a redactor?[4] The hypothesis is as essential to the critic as his epicycle was to the Ptolemaic star-gazer.

3. The matter becomes still more complicated when, finally, the problematical J E D P lose all individuality, and are frankly transformed, as they are by most of the newer writers, into *schools*.[5] When these "schools" are made to extend over a very long period, as from the statements made, and the work attributed to them, we must suppose them to have done, the problem of maintaining for them the identity of character and style with which the investigation started becomes insoluble. Obviously, if the writers are to be regarded as "schools," it will be impossible, as before, to insist on minute criteria of language often descending to single words, and the finest *nuances* of expression, as infallible means of distinguishing their several

see Bennett's *Genesis*, Introd. pp. 23, 32, 37, 52, etc. Kuenen has a P^4 with redactors (*Hex.* pp. 86 ff.).

[1] Pref. to *Exod.-Lev.*

[2] Cf. Oxford *Hexateuch*, ii. p. 19.

[3] *Ibid.* p. 212. Cf. Dillmann, *in loc.* See below, p. 358.

[4] For a longer example, see Note B on Cornill's Decomposition of J, and compare in full Cornill's *Einleitung*, pp. 52–53.

[5] See Note C on the Views of J and E, etc., as "Schools." See also below on P, Chap. X p. 335.

contributions. It is possible to argue, however unreasonably, that an individual author must be rigidly bound down to one style, one set of phrases, one idea or circle of ideas; but this will hardly apply to "schools," lasting for centuries, where, within the limits of a general tradition, there must, with difference of minds, inevitably be wide diversities of culture, thought, and speech. We may properly speak, *e.g.*, of an "Anglican," a "Ritschlian," or a "Cobdenite" school, and may mark how in each the influence of dominant ideas stamps a general resemblance on the style and speech of the members, but none the less individual idiosyncrasies will assert themselves in each writer. If, further, the writers are to be regarded as "schools," the question of date assumes a new aspect. How far may or do these "schools" go back? Why must J and E be any longer forced down to the ninth or eighth century?"[1] Why must the priestly narratives be of the same age as the priestly laws? Delitzsch was of opinion that "the literary activity of the Elohistic pen reaches far back to ancient times nearly approaching the time of Moses."[2] Why, on this hypothesis should it not be so?

There is, one cannot help feeling, something essentially mechanical in this idea of "schools" of writers continuously engaged for centuries in patching, revising, tesselating, resetting, altering and embellishing, the work of their predecessors. We are here back, in fact, by another route, and under another name, to the old "fragmentary" hypothesis, thought so long ago to have been exploded.[3] But the striking thing about the labours of these manifold unknowns is that the product shows so little trace of this excessive fragmentariness of its origin. The Pentateuch—pre-eminently the Book of Genesis, but even the legal part[4]—is undeniably a well-planned, massively-compacted work. Apart from the "firmly-knit" character of its story, it is marked by a unity of thought and spirit, is pervaded by

[1] Carpenter allows that the question of the date of J (so of the others) has become "increasingly complex" under the influence of this new idea (*Hex.* i. p. 106).

[2] *Genesis*, p. 49.

[3] Carpenter says with reference to this newer theory of "schools": "This was the truth that lay behind the fragment-hypothesis of the older criticism: is it possible to re-state it in more suitable form?"—*Hex.* i. p. 108.

[4] See below, pp. 294, 325–26.

great ideas, is instinct with a living purpose, as no oth book is. Its organic character bespeaks for it a high origin than a concourse of literary atoms.[1]

III. Special Problems of JE: Place of Origin and Extent

It is now necessary, in order that the value of the curre critical theories may be thoroughly tested, to investigate t analysis and other questions connected with the differe documents more in detail; and first we consider *the problem involved in the relations of J and E.* These problems, in o view, all converge ultimately into one—Are the critics rig in distinguishing two documents at all? To set this questi in its proper light, and reveal more clearly the serio differences that emerge on fundamental points, it will advisable to look, first, at the views entertained as to t *place of origin* of the assumed documents, and as to the *extent.* Some hint of the range of these differences h already been given.

1. Much light is cast on critical procedure by observi the methods employed to determine *the place of origin* the documents, with the implications as to their *age.* W saw before that it has become customary to take for grante though without real proof,[2] that J and E first originated, t one (*which* one is in dispute) in the ninth century, the oth about the middle of the eighth century B.C. It is also ve generally held, and is confidently stated, that E was a nati of the Northern Kingdom, while J, probably, was a nati of the Southern, or Judæan Kingdom.[3] The chief reaso given for localising E in Ephraim are his peculiar intere in the sacred places of Northern Israel (Bethel, Sheche etc.), his exaltation of the house of Joseph, and his preferen in the story of Joseph for Ephraim over Judah. Ho shadowy and assumptive all this is, and how inadequa as a ground of separation of the documents, will be evide from the following considerations:—

(1) In the first place, there are eminent critics (*e.*

[1] See further in Chap. X.

[2] See above, p. 73.

[3] Cf. Dillmann, Driver ("*relatively* probable," *Introd.* p. 123), Add Carpenter, etc.

chrader, Reuss, Kuenen, Kautzsch), who *place J also in* *'orthern Israel*, and for precisely the same reason of his ıpposed interest in Ephraimitic shrines.[1] The two writings, ıerefore, it may be concluded, cannot really stand far part in this respect. Kautzsch, *e.g.*, thinks it inconceivable that a Judahite, at a time when the temple of Solomon 'as already in existence [note the assumption on date], rought the sanctity of Shechem, Bethel, and Peniel into ıe prominence they have at Gen. xii. 6, xxviii. 13 ff., and xxii. 30 ff."[2] Yet the Judæan origin of J is one of the ıings which Dillmann, among others, regards as "demon-;rable with certainty."[3]

(2) In the next place, the whole reasoning proceeds on ıe assumption that the writings are as late as the ninth or ighth century, and that the *motive* for recording the move-ıents and residences of the patriarchs is to glorify existing ıcred places, or exalt one branch of the divided kingdom bove the other. The *naïveté* of the narratives might save ıem from this charge of "tendency," which has really othing tangible to support it. There is no trace of the ivided kingdom,[4] or of partiality for one side or the other, ı the patriarchal narratives. The history of Joseph is ecorded with fulness and freshness by *both* writers. unkel takes strong ground on this point. "There can," e says, "be no talk of a party-tendency in the two collec-ions for the North or for the South Kingdom: they are too ıithful."[5] Even Kuenen writes: "It would be incorrect ɔ say that the narratives in Genesis exalt Joseph at the xpense of his brothers, and are unfriendly to Judah. This

[1] "The data," says Carpenter, "do not appear to be decisive, and each ossibility finds eminent advocates. . . . Critical judgment has consequently een much divided."—*Hex.* i. pp. 104–5. Hommel also places J in Northern srael (*Anc. Heb. Trad.* pp. 289–90).

[2] *Lit. of O.T.*, p. 38. Kittel also thinks it "*impossible* to assert that J riginated in Northern Israel" (p. 85). Kautzsch and Kuenen explain ecalcitrant phenomena by the hypothesis of a later Judæan redaction vhich Kittel rejects, i. p. 85).

[3] *Genesis*, p. 10.

[4] Cf. Gunkel, *Genesis*, p. lx, and see above, p. 111. The older writers ıstly laid stress on this in evidence of date (*e.g.*, Bleek, *Introd.* pp. 291 ff., 98 ff.). It is curious how little stress, for different reasons, critics are isposed to lay on the one passage which might be regarded as an exception -the reference to the subjection of Edom in Gen. xxvii. 40. De Wette rged this as proof of a late date, but the inference is rejected by Bleek, ittel (i. p. 88), Kautzsch (*Lit.* p. 39), etc.

[5] *Genesis*, p. lx.

would contradict their ever present idea that all the tribes have sprung from a single father, and on the strength of this common descent are a single people. . . . Neither J nor E takes sides with any one of the tribes, or specifically for or against Joseph or Judah; for both alike occupy the Israelitish position, in the widest sense of the word."[1] The real reason why the sojournings of the patriarchs are followed with such interest in J and E is simply that, in the old Israelitish tradition, Hebron, Beersheba, Bethel, Shechem, were *believed to be the real spots* where these patriarchs dwelt, and built their altars.[2]

(3) When, further, we look into the narratives, we *do not find, in fact, that they bear out this idea* of a special favouritism in E for localities in the North, and in J for places in the South. Addis remarks on J's "large-hearted interest in the myths (?) and sacred places both of Northern Israel and of Judah."[3] Abraham's home in J is at Hebron, but his first altar is built near Bethel.[4] Latterly, in both J and E, he lives at Beersheba (in South).[5] Isaac also, in both sources, lives at Beersheba. J narrates the vision of Jacob at Bethel (with E),[6] his wrestling with the angel at Peniel,[7] his residence at Shechem (with E and P),[8] etc. E also has his stories about Bethel, Shechem, and Beersheba, but he records Jacob's residence in "the vale of Hebron" (South),[9] as, earlier, he had shared in the story of the offering of Isaac on Mount Moriah.[10] As little are we disposed to

[1] *Hex.* pp. 230–32. He thinks he finds significance, however, in the fact that Joseph was "crowned" of his brethren, etc.

[2] "In weighing these accounts," says Kuenen, "for our present purpose, we must remember that the writers were not free to choose whatever spots they liked. Hebron was Abraham's 'territorial cradle,' and Beersheba Isaac's. It needs no explanation or justification, therefore, when they make the two patriarchs dwell respectively in these two places"; but, he adds, "we have to give some account of why Abraham is transplanted to Beersheba."—*Hex.* p. 231. But why? if, as both J and E declare, he actually went there? The lives of Abraham and Isaac were mainly spent in the South, that of Jacob in the middle of Palestine.

[3] *Hex.* i. p. liv. [4] Gen. xii. 8. [5] Gen. xxi. 33; xxii. 19.

[6] Gen. xxviii. 10 ff. [7] Gen. xxxii. 24 ff. [8] Gen. xxxiv.

[9] Gen xxxvii. 14. Though it is clear from the context that Jacob's home was not at Shechem (vers. 12, 13), yet simply on the ground that it mentions Hebron, this verse is treated by Kuenen, with others, as an interpolation (*Hex.* pp. 230, 231). Carpenter says flatly: "Of Hebron, which belonged peculiarly to Judah, no notice is taken."—*Hex.* i. p. 116.

[10] Gen. xxii.

trust the critic's "feeling" for an "Ephraimitic tinge" in E, when we find, *e.g.*, one authority on this "tinge" (Kautzsch) declaring that "it [E] no longer conveys the impression of a triumphant outlook on a glorious future, but rather that of a retrospect on a bygone history, in which were many gloomy experiences;"[1] and another (Kittel) assuring us that "the whole tone of E bears witness to a certain satisfaction of the national consciousness, and joy over what has been won."[2]

(4) Finally, if anything were lacking to destroy our confidence in this theory of tendencies of J and E, it would be supplied by the *interpretations* that are given of particular incidents in the narrative. It strains our faith to breaking-point to be asked to believe that the interest of a prophetic writer like E, of the days of Amos and Hosea, in Bethel and Beersheba, arose from the fact that these places were the then famous centres of (idolatrous) worship (cf. Amos v. 5; viii. 14; Hos. iv. 15);[3] or that Gen. xxviii. 22 is intended to explain and sanction the custom of paying tithes at the calf-shrine at Bethel;[4] or that Hebron was preferred as Abraham's residence because it was "the ancient Judæan capital" (Kittel),[5] or had become "the great *Judaic* sanctuary" (Driver).[6] In the view of one set of critics, Gen. xxxviii. is a bitter mockery of Judah (J therefore is Northern);[7] according to another, it is a tribal history written expressly to *favour* Judah (J therefore is Southern).[8] Kautzsch is of opinion that "at Ex. xxxii. 1 ff. there is in all probability a Judahite condemnation of the Ephraimite bull-worship";[9] others see in the narrative an *Ephraimitic* condemnation of the same practice;[10] Kuenen thinks it glances at a claim of the Northern priests to a

[1] *Lit. of O.T.*, p. 44.
[2] *Hist. of Hebs.* i. p. 88.
[3] Carpenter, *Hex.* i. p. 116; cf. Driver, *Introd.* p. 118.
[4] Driver, *ibid.* p. 122; Dillmann, Kittel, Bennett, etc. See above, p. 135. What of *J's* motive in the references to Bethel and Beersheba?
[5] *Hist.* i. p. 83.
[6] *Introd.* p. 118.
[7] Thus Reuss, Schrader, Renan, etc.
[8] Thus Kittel (i. p. 83), etc. Cf. Kuenen, *Hex.* p. 232: Westphal, *Sources*, ii. p. 259; Carpenter, *Hex.* i. p. 105.
[9] *Lit. of O.T.*, p. 38.
[10] Dillmann thinks a North Israelite could not have framed this protest against Jeroboam's bull-worship (*Exod.-Lev.* p. 332); Kittel differs (i. p. 89). It should be noticed that Kautzsch, Dillmann, Kittel, etc., ascribe the main story in Ex. xxxii. to J; others, as Westphal, as confidently give it to E.

descent from Aaron.[1] So *ad libitum*. When one remembers that it is chiefly on the ground of these supposed "mirrorings" of later events that the narratives are placed where they are in date,[2] one begins to see the precariousness of this part of the critical structure. Thus far nothing has been established as to place or time of origin, or distinct authorship of the documents.

2. A second problem of much importance in its bearings on the possibility of a critical distinction of J and E is that of the *extent* of the supposed documents. The consideration of Genesis may be reserved. There is agreement that the J narrative in Genesis begins with chap. ii. 3*b*, and, in union with other sources, continues throughout the book, and into Exodus. E, on the other hand, though some find traces of its presence earlier,[3] is understood to enter clearly first in chap. xx. With Exodus iii., the criterion of the divine names fails, after which it is allowed, on all hands, that the discrimination is exceedingly difficult, and often impossible. In the words of Addis, "In other books of the Hexateuch [after Genesis] the Jahvist and the Elohist are rather fused than pieced together, and discrimination between the two documents is often impossible."[4] In their union, however, it is commonly agreed that the presence of the two documents can be traced, not only through Exodus and Numbers (in small measure in Deuteronomy) but through Joshua—that Joshua, in fact, is an integral part of the total work now called the "Hexateuch." The validity of this conclusion will occupy us immediately.

Beyond this rises another question, now keenly exercising the minds of scholars, viz., whether there must not be

[1] *Hex.* p. 245; cf. Van Hoonacker, *Le Sacerdoce*, p. 136. See above, p. 122.

[2] Cf. Carpenter, *Hex.* i. p. 107; Kuenen, *Hex.* p. 226. See above, p. 74; also Gunkel, *Genesis*, p. lxii.

[3] See below, p. 217.

[4] *Hex.* i. p. xxxi. McFadyen says similarly: "After Ex. vi. it is seldom possible to distinguish with much confidence between the Jehovist and the Elohist, as they have so much in common."—*Mess. of Historians*, p. 18. The impossibility is owned by critics (as Kautzsch and Socin) in considerable parts of Genesis as well. Strack says generally: "Since J and E are on the whole (*im Grossen und Ganzen*) similar to one another, it is often no longer possible to separate what originally belongs to E and what originally belongs to J."—*Die Bücher Genesis, etc.* ("Handkommentar," i., ii.), *Introd.* p. xviii.

recognised a still further continuation of these documents—J and E—into the Books of Judges, Samuel, and even Kings. Such a possibility was early hinted at,[1] but the newer tendency to resolve J and E into "schools" has led to a revival of the idea,[2] and to its adoption by many critical scholars. Cornill and Budde have no doubt about it; Moore adopts it in his Commentary on Judges; Westphal goes so far as to make it a chief ground in his determination of the dates of the documents.[3] *E.g.*, Cornill discerns J in 1 Kings "with perfect certainty";[4] the traces of E, he thinks, are slight after the story of the death of Saul. These conclusions, with good reason, do not commend themselves to other scholars, so that the camp remains here also divided.[5] The hypothesis has a value as showing the precarious grounds on which writers often build their critical "certainties."

Returning to Joshua, we may briefly test the assertion that the J and E documents are continued into this book, and that Joshua forms with the Pentateuch a single larger work. The question of "Pentateuch" or "Hexateuch" need not be discussed at length; we touch on it only as far as relates to our subject. Addis, however, speaks far too strongly when he declares that the unity of Joshua with the other five books "is acknowledged by all who admit the composite character of the Pentateuch."[6] This is by no means the case. Even Cornill says: "Many now speak of a Hexateuch. Joshua, nevertheless, presents an essentially different literary physiognomy from that of the Pentateuch, so that it appears to me more correct to treat the latter by itself, and the Book of Joshua as an appendix to it."[7] There are, in fact, tolerably strong indications of a tendency among recent critics to separate Joshua again from the Pentateuch, and regard it as a more or less

[1] Gramberg (1830); Schrader (1869).

[2] Cf. Westphal on the views of Ed. Meyer (1884) and Bruston (1885) in *Sources du Pent.* ii. pp. 255 ff. Stade thought he discovered traces of E in above works; Böhme traces of J, etc.

[3] *Sources*, ii. p. 256.

[4] *Einleitung*, pp. 117, 121.

[5] Kittel acutely criticised the theory in *Stud. und Krit.* 1891 (pp. 44 ff.); cf. his *Hist.* ii. pp. 16 ff. Kuenen, Kautzsch (*Lit. of O.T.*, pp. 27, 237–39). Driver (*Introd.* pp. 171, 184), König, H. P. Smith (*Samuel*, p. xxii), etc., reject it.

[6] *Hex.* pp. xiv, xxxi.

[7] *Einleit.* p. 86.

independent work.[1] For such a view also there are many cogent grounds. Cornill gives as one reason that the sources are quite differently worked up in the Book of Joshua from what they are elsewhere. In the narrative portions they are fused together so as to be ordinarily inseparable. The language, too, presents peculiarities. Even in the P parts, as will be seen immediately, it is doubtful if the sections are from the same hand or hands as in the other books. The book has, also, according to the critics, been subjected to a Deuteronomic revision,[2] which curiously, was not extended (or only slightly) to the earlier books.[3]

It is beyond doubt, at least, that, in the separation of the sources in Joshua, the critics continually find themselves involved in inextricable difficulties. With respect particularly to J and E, it has become not simply a question of whether J and E can be severed (admittedly they can not), but *of whether J and E are present in the book at all.* Wellhausen came to the conclusion that J was wholly absent,[4] and Steuernagel more recently has affirmed the same opinion.[5] "The original scope and significance of E" are admitted by Carpenter to be "hardly less difficult to determine."[6] The high-water mark of his

[1] Cf. the views of Wellhausen, *Compos. d. Hex.* pp. 116–17; Carpenter, *Hex.* i. pp. 178–79; Bennett, *Primer of Bible*, p. 90; cf. his *Joshua* ("Polychrome Bible"), p. 44: "Perhaps the Joshua sections of JED and P were separated from the preceding sections before the latter were combined to form the Pentateuch" (or perhaps never formed part of them).

[2] That is, if "revision" is the proper word, and not rather "invention." If, *e.g.*, the incident of the reading of the law on Mount Ebal in Josh. viii. 30–35 did not happen, it was simply invention on the basis of Deut. xxvii. The Deuteronomic reviser is called D^2 to distinguish him from the author of Deuteronomy (D^1). He belongs to the D "school," and writes a similar style.

[3] On supposed Deuteronomic traces in the earlier books, see below, pp. 254–55.

[4] *Comp. d. Hex.* p. 116. Kittel's view of the matter is: "The comparatively few traces which point at all decisively to J frequently allow of the assumption that they have no longer precisely the same form as when they came from the author's pen. E is in almost the same case: of this source, too, there are only a few remnants in the Book of Joshua."—*Hist. of Hebs.* i. p. 263.

[5] Carpenter notes that Steuernagel's *Das Buch Josua* invites comment, "for his results vary very widely from those already set forth. . . . In regard to J, Steuernagel returns to the view of Wellhausen and Meyer that it recognised no Joshua," etc.—*Hex.* ii. p. 318. Thus theories chase each other like clouds in the sky.

[6] *Ibid.* ii. p. 308.

assurance is reached in the statement: "Budde, Kittel, Albers, and Bennett have all concurred in believing that the main elements of J and E *are not disguised beyond recognition*, though their results do not always run side by side."[1] The separation of the P sections in Joshua at first sight seems easier, but in detail the difficulties are nearly as insuperable, and of a kind that set theorising at defiance. "The inquiry" (as to "the relation of the P sections to the rest of the book"), Carpenter admits, "is full of difficulty, and the seemingly conflicting facts have been differently interpreted in different critical schools."[2] The language, as already said, is markedly different. "In chaps. i.–xii., xxiii., xxiv.," says Professor Bennett, "there are only a few short paragraphs and sentences in the style of P, and most of these are rather due to an editor than derived from the Priestly Code."[3] Still more instructive is the fact, pointed out by Professor G. A. Smith, that "in the Book of Joshua P does not occupy the regulative position, nor supply the framework, as it does in the Pentateuch."[4] As Wellhausen puts it: "Without a preceding history of the conquest, these [P] sections are quite in the air: they cannot be taken as telling a continuous story of their own, but presuppose the Jehovistic-Deuteronomic work. . . . We have already shown that the Priestly Code in Joshua is simply the filling up of the Jehovistic-Deuteronomic narrative."[5] As interesting illustrations of the stylistic perplexities, reference may be made to the two important chapters—xxii. and xxiv. The phraseology in chap. xxii. 9–34, "is in the main that of P," says Dr. Driver ("almost a cento of P's phrases," says

[1] *Hex.* ii. p. 306 (italics ours).

[2] *Ibid.* p. 315. *E.g.*, "If xvi. 1–3 is rightly assigned to J, a probability is established that it may have contained other geographical descriptions, now perhaps absorbed into P's more detailed survey. But it appears to be beyond the power of any critical method to discover the clues to their separation" (pp. 307–8).

[3] *Primer*, p. 90. The P sections, Carpenter says, "show several curious features, and doubts have consequently been expressed concerning their original character (*e.g.*, by Wellhausen)."—*Hex.* i. p. 178.

[4] Art. "Joshua" in *Dict. of Bible*, ii. p. 784. Similarly Bennett says: "In the Pentateuch P is used as framework; in Joshua JED."—*Book of Joshua* ("Polychrome Bible"), p. 45.

[5] *Hist. of Israel*, pp. 357, 385. As shown later (Chap. X.), Wellhausen regards the "main stock" of the Priestly narrative as ceasing with the death of Moses.

Carpenter), "but the narrative does not display throughou the characteristic style of P, and in some parts of it ther occur expressions which are not those of P." He proceeds "Either a narrative of P has been combined with element from another source in a manner which makes it difficult t effect a satisfactory analysis, or the whole is the work c a distinct writer, whose phraseology is in part that of I but not entirely."[1] Wellhausen, on the other hand, think it is P's wholly (but not the P of the earlier books). Addi with Kuenen, assumes that "it is a late production in th school and after the manner of P."[2] Chap. xxiv., i turn, is assigned generally to E; yet, says Dr. Driver, "i might almost be said to be written from a standpoin approaching (in this respect) that of D^2."[3] Addi assumes a Deuteronomic revision, and abundant inter polation.[4] What, one is tempted to ask, can such criteri avail?

Not much support, we think it will be felt, is to be go from the Book of Joshua for an original distinction of J an E—if for their existence in that book at all. When it i added that the Samaritans seem from the beginning to hav had, in Buhl's words, "outside of the Canon an independen reproduction of the Book of Joshua,"[5] it may be realise that the reasons for affirming a "*Hex*ateuch" are not s conclusive as is generally assumed.

IV. Are J and E two or one? Difficulties of Separation

The decisive grounds for the separation of J and E mus be sought for, if anywhere, in the Book of Genesis, wher the divine names are still distinguished. It is importan

[1] *Introd.* pp. 112–13. [2] *Hex.* ii. p. 473. [3] *Introd.* p. 115.

[4] *Hex.* i. p. 233. It is a curious observation of Carpenter's that "th Deuteronomic editors of the national histories during the exile were con temporary with the priestly schools of Ezekiel and his successors, and som interchange of phraseology would be only natural" (this to account f occasional appearances of P in D passages).—*Hex.* ii. p. 315. It i interesting to see how the theory of JED and P schools extending into th exile tends to work round to a theory of *contemporary* authorship for muc of the matter. But may not the same thing be assumed for *early* co-opera tion in the production of the book? See below, pp. 375–6.

[5] *Canon of O.T.*, p. 41. On the historicity of Joshua, see Appendix t chapter.

for the purpose of our inquiry here to remember how the discrimination of J and E was originally brought about. It will be recalled[1] that, till the time of Hupfeld, E was commonly regarded as an integral part of P—a proof that, notwithstanding their differences, even these documents are not so far apart as many suppose.[2] Then E was separated from P on the ground of its greater literary affinities with J, and, not unnaturally, in view of the difference in the divine names, continued to be regarded as a distinct writing from the latter. Now the question recurs—Is it really distinct? The only actually weighty ground for the distinction is the difference of usage in the names, and that peculiarity must be considered by itself. Apart from this it is our purpose to show that the strongest reasons speak for the *unity* of the documents, while the hypothesis of distinction is loaded with improbabilities which amount, in the sum, well-nigh to impossibilities.

1. In the first place, then, there is no clear proof that E ever *did* exist as a continuous independent document. It has a broken, intermittent character, which excites doubts, even in Wellhausen.[3] Roughly, after Gen. xx.–xxi., where the document is supposed abruptly to enter,[4] we have only fragments till chap. xxxi., then again broken pieces till

[1] See above, p. 196.

[2] Bleek, Cave, Lange, Perowne, etc., retained the older view. An interesting series of equations might be drawn up along this line, based on the axiom that things that are equal to the same thing are equal to one another, weakening somewhat the force of the ordinary documentary theory. If, *e.g.*, E resembles P sufficiently to have been regarded by most critics till Hupfeld, and by many since, as part of P, and E is at the same time practically indistinguishable stylistically from J, an obvious conclusion follows as to the relations of J and P. So in other places approximations may be shown to exist between E and D, D and J, and even between JE and P, D and P. See below, pp. 253 ff.

[3] Wellhausen says: "Not merely is the Elohist in his matter and in his manner of looking at things most closely akin to the Jehovist; his document has come down to us, as Nöldeke was the first to perceive, only in extracts embodied in the Jehovist narrative." And in a note: "What Kuenen points out is, that certain elements assigned by me to the Elohist are not fragments of a once independent whole, but interpolated and parasitic additions. What effect this demonstration may have on the judgment we form of the Elohist himself is as yet uncertain."—*Hist. of Israel*, pp. 7, 8.

[4] Traces of E are thought by some to be found in chap. xv. (Wellhausen, Dillmann, etc.). Dillmann would attribute to E part of the material in chaps. v. (17 ff.); vi. (1–4) and xiv.; but he is not generally followed in this. Cf. Kuenen, *Hex.* p. 149.

chaps. xl.–xlii., in the life of Joseph, and a few portions thereafter, chiefly in chaps. xlv. and l.[1]

2. Next, doubt, and more than doubt, is awakened by the *thoroughly parallel* character of the narratives. As was shown at an earlier stage,[2] the two supposed documents are similar in character, largely parallel in matter, and, as proved by their complete interfusion in many places, must often have been nearly verbally identical. A few testimonies on this important point may not be out of place.

"In the main," says Wellhausen, "JE is a composition out of these two parallel books of history," adding, "We see how uncommonly similar these two history books must have been."[3]

"The two books," says Addis, "evidently proceeded in parallel lines of narrative, and it is often hard—nay impossible—to say whether a particular section of the Hexateuch belongs to the Jahvist or the Elohist."[4] "Two accounts of Joseph's history, closely parallel on the whole, but discordant in important details (?)[5] have been mingled together."[6]

"It [JE]," says Kautzsch, "must have run in almost unbroken parallelism with the Jahwist in the patriarchal histories, the history of the Exodus, and of the conquest of Canaan."[7]

"In the history of the patriarchs," says Dillmann, "especially in that of Jacob and Joseph, it [E] shows itself most closely related to [J]; so much so that most of its narratives from chap. xxvii. onwards have their perfect parallels in [J]."[8]

After this, it does not surprise us that an able scholar like Klostermann—at one time a supporter of the usual critical hypothesis—was so impressed with the similar character and close relation of these "throughout parallel" narratives as to be led to break with the current theory

[1] Colenso, so far as he accepted Hupfeld's E, did not regard it as independent, but identified it with J. See above, p. 199.

[2] See above, p. 71.

[3] *Comp. d. Hex.* p. 22. It has already been seen that Wellhausen extends this parallel, as regards matter, to P (*Hist. of Israel*, pp. 295, 318). Cf. above, p. 107; but specially see below, pp. 344 ff.

[4] *Hex.* p. liii. [5] See below, p. 237. [6] *Hex.* p xlix.

[7] *Lit. of O.T.*, p. 43.

[8] *Genesis*, p. 11. In a similar strain Driver, König, Strack, Gunkel, etc.

altogether, and to recast his whole view of the origin of the Pentateuch.[1]

3. Again, the marked *stylistic resemblance* of J and E speaks strongly against their being regarded as separate documents. On this point it may be sufficient at present to quote Dr. Driver. "Indeed," he says, "stylistic criteria alone would not generally suffice to distinguish J and E; though, when the distinction has been effected by other means, slight differences of style appear to disclose themselves."[2] *How* slight they are will be afterwards seen.

4. The force of these considerations is greatly enhanced when we observe the *intimate fusion* and *close interrelations* of the documents, and the impossibility of separating them without *complete disintegration* of the narrative. The facts here, as elsewhere, are not disputed.[3] "The mutual relation of J and E," Kuenen confesses, "is one of the most vexed questions of the criticism of the Pentateuch."[4] "It must," he says again, "be admitted that the resemblance between E and the narratives now united with it is sometimes bewilderingly close, so that when the use of Elohim does not put us on the track, we are almost at a loss for means of carrying the analysis through."[5] "There is much difference of opinion," acknowledges Addis, "on the contents of J and E considered separately: the problem becomes more difficult when we pass beyond Genesis to the later books of the Hexateuch, and to a great extent the problem may prove insoluble."[6] The close interrelation of the several narratives is not less perplexing. This interrelation appears all through—*e.g.*, the very first words of Gen. xx., "And Abraham journeyed *from thence*," connect with the preceding narrative; the difficulties of chap. xxi. 1–7 (birth of Isaac), in which J, E, and P are concerned, can only be got over by the assumption that "all three sources, J, E,

[1] Cf. his *Der Pentateuch*, pp. 10, 52–53. On Klostermann, see further below, pp. 227–29, 345.

[2] *Introd.* p. 126; cf. p. 13: "Other phraseological criteria (besides the names) are slight." Cf. Colenso, quoted above, p. 199; and Hupfeld, below, p. 234. Dr. Driver himself speaks on the duality of the documents with considerable reserve, though "he must own that he has always risen from the study of JE with the conviction that it is *composite*" (p. 116).

[3] The notes to Kautzsch and Socin's analysis of *Genesis* are here very instructive.

[4] *Hex.* p. 64. [5] *Ibid* p. 144. [6] *Hex.* p. xxxiv.

and P seem to have contained the account of the birth of Isaac"[1]—but it is at its maximum in the history of Joseph.[2] Illustrations will occur as we proceed.[3] The usual way of dealing with these difficulties is by assuming that sections in J parallel to E, and sections in E parallel to J, once existed (so of P), but were omitted in the combined work. This, if established, would immensely strengthen the proof of parallelism—would, in fact, practically do away with the necessity for assuming the existence of two histories; but the hypothesis, to the extent required, is incapable of proof, and its assumption only complicates further an already too complicated problem.[4]

5. Finally, the argument for unity is confirmed by the *violent expedients* which are found necessary to make the opposite hypothesis workable. We have specially in view here the place given, and the functions ascribed, to that convenient, but most unsatisfactory, appendage of the critical theory — the *Redactor*. The behaviour of this remarkable individual—or series of individuals (R^1, R^2, R^3, etc.)—is one of the most puzzling features in the whole case. At times he (R) puts his sections side by side, or alternates them, with little alteration; again he weaves them together into the most complicated literary webs; yet again he "works them up" till the separate existence of the documents is lost in the blend.[5] At one time, as Klostermann says, he shows an almost "demonic art"[6] in combining and relating; at another, an incapacity verging on imbecility. At one moment he is phenomenally alert in smoothing out difficulties, correcting mistakes, and interpolating harmonistic clauses; at another, he leaves the most glaring contradictions, in the critics' view, to stand

[1] Oxf. *Hex.* ii. p. 29; see below, p. 352.

[2] Cf. Addis and Dillmann above.

[3] Cf., *e.g.*, on the analysis of Gen. xxii. and Gen. xxviii. 10. ff., below, pp. 234–35.

[4] Cf. below, Chap. X. pp. 343, 348–9, 362.

[5] It is customary to speak of the Hebrew writers as if they were scrupulously careful simply to *reproduce* the material at their disposal—combining, re-arranging, but not *re-writing*. That, if the critics are right, can only be accepted with much qualification. P, on Wellhausen's theory, must have re-written the history. According to Kuenen, the "legends" have "been worked up in one way by one writer and another by another . . . so often as to be notably modified, or even completely transformed.—*Hex.* p. 38 (on the process in Joshua, cf. p. 158).

[6] *Pentateuch*, p. 36.

side by side. Now he copies J's style, now D's, now P's.[1] A serviceable, but somewhat unaccountable personage!

V. The Problem of the Divine Names in J and E

The *crux* of the question of the distinction of documents lies, it will be admitted, in the use of the divine names in Genesis, and this problem, so far as it concerns J and E—P stands on a somewhat different basis[2] — must now seriously engage our attention.

1. The first thing to be done is to *ascertain the facts*, and here, once more, we believe, it will be found that the case is not quite so simple as it is ordinarily represented to be. The broad statement is not to be questioned that there are certain sections in the narrative attributed to JE in which the divine name "Jehovah" is preponderatingly used, and certain other sections in which the name "Elohim" (God) is chiefly used. It is this which constitutes the problem. We must beware, however, of exaggeration even here. When, *e.g.*, Dr. Driver says that in the narrative, Gen. xii. 10–20, "the term Jehovah is uniformly employed,"[3] it would not readily occur to the reader that "uniformly" in this instance means *only once*. The truth is, as we soon discover, that *no absolute rule about the use of the names can be laid down.* Even eliminating those instances in which the "redactor" is invoked to interpolate and alter, there remains a not inconsiderable number of cases to show that the presence of the divine names is not an infallible test. Kuenen himself says—and the admission is striking—"The history of critical investigation has shown that far too much weight has often been laid on agreement in the use of the divine names [it is the pillar of the whole hypothesis]. . . . It is well, therefore, to utter a warning against laying an exaggerated stress on this one phenomenon."[4] There are grounds for this warning.

(1) There can be no doubt whatever that the name "Elohim" is sometimes found *in J passages.* In the narrative of the temptation in Gen. iii. (J), *e.g.*, the name

[1] Cf. Dillmann, *Genesis*, p. 21: "The redactor R often writes the language of A [=P]," etc. See later on "imitations" of D, P, etc.

[2] See below, p. 226.

[3] *Introd.* p. 13; *Genesis*, p. xi.

[4] *Hex.* p. 61.

"Jehovah" is not put into the mouth of the serpent, but, instead, the name "Elohim":[1] "Yea, hath Elohim said," etc. Similarly, in the story of Hagar's flight (J), the handmaid is made to say: "Thou Elohim seest me."[2] In such cases one can easily see that a principle is involved. In the story of the wrestling at Peniel, again, in Gen. xxxii. (J), we have "Elohim" in vers. 28, 29. In the life of Joseph, Gen. xxxix. is assigned by Dillmann, Kuenen, Kautzsch, and most to J (as against Wellhausen), despite its "linguistic suggestions" of E, and the occurrence of "Elohim" in ver. 9; and Kuenen writes of other passages: "*Elohim* in chaps. xliii. 29, xliv. 16, is no evidence for E, since Joseph speaks and is spoken to as a heathen until chap. xlv."[3]

(2) Examples of the converse case of *the use of Jehovah by E* are not so numerous, but such occasionally occur. Addis, indeed, says roundly: "The Elohist . . . always speaks of Elohim and never of Yahweh, till he relates the theophany in the burning bush."[4] But Dr. Driver states the facts more cautiously and correctly. "E," he says, "prefers *God* (though not exclusively), and *Angel of God*, where J prefers *Jehovah* and *Angel of Jehovah*."[5] *E.g.*, in Gen. xxii. 1–14 (E) "Angel of Jehovah" occurs in ver. 11, and "Jehovah" twice in ver. 14. Similarly, in Gen. xxviii. 17–22 (E), Jacob says: "Then shall Jehovah be my God."[6] When the use of the divine names is taken from the former exclusive ground, and reduced to a "preference," it is obvious that new possibilities are opened. We ask that it be noted further that isolated Elohistic sections occur *after* Ex. iii.,[7] *e.g.*, in Ex. xiii. 17–19, xviii. —a singular fact to be afterwards considered.

(3) We would call attention, lastly, to the lengths which criticism is prepared to go in acknowledging the principle of *discrimination* in the use of the divine names. Kuenen, with his usual candour from his own point of

[1] Gen. iii. 1, 3, 5.
[2] Gen. xvi. 13.
[3] *Hex.* pp. 145–46.
[4] *Hex.* i. p. liv. Thus most critics.
[5] *Genesis*, p. xiii. Cf. *Introd.* p. 13.
[6] Ver. 21. A redactor is here brought in, as elsewhere, but unwarrantably. What caprice should lead a redactor to change these particular expressions, when so many others are left untouched?
[7] But note the use of "Jehovah" in this chapter *before* the revelation (vers. 2, 4).

view, allows to this principle considerable scope. "The original distinction between Jahwe and Elohim," he says, "very often accounts for the use of one of these appellations in preference to the other."[1] (Dr. Driver allows it "only in a comparatively small number of instances.")[2] He gives in illustration the following cases. "When the God of Israel is placed over against the gods of the heathen the former is naturally described by the proper name Jahwe (Ex. xii. 12; xv. 11; xviii. 11). When heathens are introduced as speaking, they use the word Elohim (Gen. xli. 39). . . . So, too, the Israelites, when speaking to heathens, often use Elohim, as Joseph does, for instance, to Potiphar's wife, Gen. xxxix. 9; to the butler and baker, Gen. xl. 8; and to Pharaoh, Gen. xli. 16, 25, 28, 32 (but also in vers. 51, 52, which makes us suspect that there may be some other reason for the preference of Elohim); so, too, Abraham to Abimelech, Gen. xx. 13 (where Elohim even takes the plural construction). Where a contrast between the divine and the human is in the mind of the author, Elohim is at anyrate the more suitable word (*e.g.*, Gen. iv. 25; xxxii. 28; Ex. viii. 15; xxxii. 16, etc.)."[3]

2. What now, we go on to inquire, is the *explanation* of these phenomena?

(1) We have already seen the difficulties which attend the critical solution of *distinct sources* in the case of documents so markedly similar and closely related as J and E. There can be no objection, indeed, to the assumption of the use by the writer of Genesis of an older source, or older sources, for the lives of the patriarchs; such, in our opinion, *must* have been there. But such source, or sources, would, if used, underlie *both* J and E sections, while the general similarity of style in the narratives shows that, in any case, older records were not simply copied. It may be further pointed out that the supposition of two or more documents (JEP, etc.), combined by a redactor, does not in reality relieve the difficulty. We have still to ask—On what principle did the redactor work in the selection of his material? What moved him, out of the several (parallel) narratives at his disposal, here to choose J, there to choose E, in another place to choose P, at other times to weave in stray sentences or clauses from this

[1] *Hex.* p. 56. [2] *Introd.* p. 13. [3] *Hex.* pp. 58–59.

or that writing? Did he act from mere caprice? If he did not, the difficulty of the names seems only shifted back from the original authors to the compiler.

(2) Shall we then say, sustaining ourselves on such admissions as those of Kuenen above, that the alternation of names in JE narratives in Genesis is due to the fact that these names are always used *discriminatively*? This has been the favourite view of writers of a conservative tendency,[1] and there is assuredly a deep truth underlying it, though we do not think it can be carried through to the full extent that these writers desire. It is the case, and is generally admitted, that there is a difference of meaning in the two names of God,—"*Elohim* and *Jahweh*," as Dr. Driver puts it, "represent the divine nature under different aspects, viz., as the God of nature and the God of revelation respectively,"[2]—and it will also be allowed that to some extent this is the principle governing their selection in particular passages. But is it the principle of distinction throughout?

In this connection it is necessary to consider the important fact, on which the critics rightly lay much stress, that in the case of E the distinction in the use of the divine names ceases (not *wholly*, as we saw, but *generally*) with the revelation in Ex. iii. What does this fact mean? The critical answer is simple: a new name of God—the name Jehovah—is here revealed, and with the revelation of the new name the use of the older name is discontinued. This explanation, however, as a little reflection shows, is not quite so satisfactory as it seems. For, *first*, it is not a distinction between E and J that the one knows of a revelation of God to Moses by His name Jehovah, and the other does not. Both, as we find, are aware of, and describe in nearly the same terms, the commission to Moses. In both Moses was to tell the children of Israel that "Jehovah, the God of [their] fathers" had sent him, Ex. iii. 15 (E); 16 (J); iv. 5 (J). And, *second*, while it is E who records the words of revelation "I AM THAT I AM" (ver. 14), it is not E, but P, who later has the declaration: "I appeared unto Abraham, unto Isaac, and unto Jacob, as El-Shaddai, but by My name Jehovah I was not known to them."[3] There is thus no indication that E regarded

[1] *E.g.*, Hengstenberg, Keil, Green, Rupprecht, etc.
[2] *Introd.* p. 13.
[3] Ex. vi. 3.

the revelation to Moses in any other light than J did:[1] therefore, no apparent reason why E, any more than J, should draw in his narrative so sharp a distinction between the period before and that after the revelation in Exodus. Nor, in fact, did he; for we have seen that Elohistic sections are found later in the book, and many able critics hold the view that originally the E document had this name Elohim till its close.[2]

The general sense of the revelation to Moses is evidently the same in all the three supposed sources, and this helps us in determining the meaning of the words above quoted from P—"By My name Jehovah I was not known to them." Do these words mean, as most critics aver, that the name Jehovah was up to that time absolutely unknown? Was the revelation merely a question of a new vocable? Or, in consonance with the pregnant Scriptural use of the word "name,"—in harmony also with the declarations of J and E that the God who speaks is "Jehovah, the God of your fathers,"[3]—is the meaning not, as many have contended, that the God who in earlier times had revealed Himself in deeds of power and mercy as El Shaddai, would now reveal Himself, in the deliverance of Israel, in accordance with the grander character and attributes implied in His name Jehovah—the ever-abiding, changeless, covenant-keeping One?[4] For ourselves we have no doubt that, as this is the deeper, so it is the truer view of the revelation; any other we have always felt to be a superficialising of it.[5]

There is, therefore, good ground for laying stress on the distinction of meaning in the divine names. This, probably,

[1] E, in point of fact does, as we saw, occasionally use "Jehovah" in Genesis.

[2] Cf., *e.g.*, Dillmann, *Num.-Jos.* p. 617; Addis, *Hex.* i. p. liv. See below, p. 226.

[3] That the name Jehovah was probably really older, as J, certainly, and probably both J and E, assume, is shown in Note B to Chap. V. above.

[4] The "name" denotes in general the revelation-side of God's being. Jehovah, as we understand it, denotes the God of the Covenant as the One who remains eternally one with Himself in all that He is and does: the *Self-Existent* and therefore the *Self-Consistent* One. Kautzsch takes the name as meaning the "eternal and constant."—*Dict. of Bible* (Extra Vol.), p. 625.

[5] It is interesting to notice that Colenso, who at first tenaciously resisted this view, came round latterly to regard it as admissible—even suggests it as an explanation of how J might use the sacred name in Genesis without a sense of discrepancy with P. "Whereas," he says, "if it means (as some explain it) that it [the name Jehovah] was not fully *understood* or *realised*, the contradiction in terms would disappear altogether," etc.—*Pent.* vi pp. 582–83.

—so far we go with the critics,—is the real reason of the predominating usage in the P parts prior to Ex. vi. The usage in this writing is ruled by the contrast of two stages of revelation, which the writer desires to emphasise. Still we think that, while this explanation of discriminative use is perhaps not *impossible* for JE, and often has real place,[1] it is highly *improbable* that the same author should designedly change the name in so marked a fashion through whole chapters, as is done in this narrative, without more obvious reason than generally presents itself. Only, as formerly remarked, the critics themselves cannot wholly get away from this difficulty. If not the author, then the redactor, must have had some principle to guide him in choosing, now a Jehovistic, now an Elohistic section. He is too skilful a person to have worked at random; the distinction of names in his documents must have been as obvious to him as to us; he is supposed to have often changed the names to make them suit his context; it is difficult, therefore, to think that he had not some principle or theory to guide him.

3. This leads to another, and very important question—Is it so certain that in the case of JE there has been no *change* in the names? The question is not so uncalled for as it may seem. We do not need to fall back on the redactor of the critics to recognise that the Pentateuch has a *history*—that, like other books of the Bible, it has undergone a good deal of revision, and that sometimes this revision has left pretty deep traces upon the text. The differences in the Hebrew, Samaritan, and LXX numbers in Gen. v. and xi. are a familiar example. But in the use of the divine names also suggestive facts present themselves. It has been mentioned above as the conjecture of certain critics that the E document had originally "Elohim" till its close, and was designedly changed to "Jehovah" after Ex. iii. (but why then not wholly?). A plainer example is in Gen. ii.-iii. (J), where the two names are conjoined in the form "Jehovah Elohim" (LORD God). It is generally allowed that this is not the original form of writing,[2] and that the

[1] As in Gen. iii. above, p. 222. Cf. also below, pp. 234–35. As analogous, the usage in the prologue and close of the Book of Job may be compared with that in the body of the book.

[2] Gunkel, however, following Budde, actually thinks that we have here also the working together of two stories of Paradise—an Elohistic and a Jehovistic.—*Genesis*, p. 4.

names are intentionally combined to show the identity of the "Elohim" of chap. i. (P) with the "Jehovah" of the subsequent narratives. If we may believe Klostermann, the ancient Hebrews could never have used in speech such a combination as "Jehovah Elohim," and would read here simply "Elohim."[1] The LXX is specially instructive on this point, for it frequently reads "God" simply (chap. ii. 5, 7, 9, 19, 21), where the Hebrew has the double name. So in chap. iv. 1, for "I have gotten a man by the help of Jehovah," the LXX reads "God" (conversely in ver. 25, for "God" in the Hebrew it reads "Lord God"); and in ver. 26, for "call on Jehovah," it has "Lord God." This raises the question, more easily asked than answered—Did this combination of the names stop originally with chap. iii.? Or if not, how far did it go? The LXX certainly carried it a good way further than our present text—at least to the end of the story of the flood.[2]

There is, however, yet another class of phenomena bearing closely on our subject—which has, in fact, furnished Klostermann with the suggestion of a possible solution of our problem well deserving of consideration. We refer to the remarkable distribution of the divine names in the *Book of Psalms*. It was before pointed out that in the first three of the five Books into which the Psalter is divided, the psalms are systematically arranged into Jehovistic and Elohistic groups: Book I. is Jehovistic (Davidic); Book II., Elohistic (sons of Korah, Asaph, David); Book III., Jehovistic (sons of Korah, etc.).[3] Here, then, in the Pentateuch and in the Psalter are two sets of phenomena sufficiently similar to suggest the probability of a common cause. What is the explanation in the case of the psalms? Is it, as Colenso thought, that David wrote Elohistic psalms

[1] *Pentateuch*, p. 37. "Only in the temple, according to Jacob (*Zeit. d. Alttest. Wissenschaft*, 1896, p. 158), was the sacred name JHVH pronounced." —Kirkpatrick, *Psalms*, p. 57.

[2] The compound expressions "Jehovah, God of Shem" (Abraham, etc.), Gen. ix. 26; xxiv., etc., also deserve consideration. Is it, besides, certain that the divine names in the oldest script were always written in full, or as words, and not represented by a sign? Dillmann, it may be observed, thinks that, conversely, Elohim in E is frequently changed into Jehovah (*Num.–Jos.* p. 52), a statement which proves rather the uncertainty of his hypothesis than the necessity of the change.

[3] Cf. above, p. 197. For details see W. R. Smith, *loc. cit.*; Kirkpatrick, *The Psalms*, pp. lv ff., etc.

at one period of his life, and Jehovistic psalms at another? Few critics at the present day would accept this solution; besides, it does not explain the phenomena of the other groups. The real key, it is generally allowed, is furnished in the fact that, in a few cases, the same psalms (or parts of psalms) appear in different groups—in one form Jehovistic, in the other Elohistic. Thus Ps. liii. is an *Elohistic* recension of the *Jehovistic* Ps. xiv.; Ps. lxx. is an *Elohistic* recension of the *Jehovistic* Ps. xl. 13–17 (in the remaining case, Ps. cviii. = Ps. lvii. 7–11, and lx. 5–12, both versions are Elohistic). As the psalmist cannot well be supposed to have written the psalm in both forms, it is clear that in one or other of the versions the name has been designedly changed. This also is the nearly unanimous opinion of modern scholars.[1] Facts show that there was a time, or were times, in the history of Israel, when in certain circles there was a shrinking from the use of the sacred name Jehovah,[2] and when, in speech, the name "Elohim" or "Adonai"[3] was substituted for it. Not only was the name changed in reading, but versions of the psalms apparently were produced for use with the name *written* as it was to be read—that is, with Elohim substituted for Jehovah.[4] Klostermann's suggestion, in brief, is that precisely the same thing happened with the old Jehovistic history-book of Israel, which corresponds with what we call JE. There was an *Elohistic* version of this work in circulation alongside of the original *Jehovistic*—a recension in which the divine name was written "Elohim," at least up to Ex. iii., and possibly all through. When the final editing of the Pentateuch took place, texts of both recensions were employed, and sections taken from one or the other as was thought most suitable.[5] In other words, for the J and E

[1] Cf. W. R. Smith, *O.T. in J. C.*, p. 119; Driver, *Introd.* p. 372; Kirkpatrick, *Psalms*, as above, *Library of O.T.*, p. 39; Klostermann, *Pentateuch*, p. 36; König, *Hauptprobleme*, p. 28, etc.

[2] Cf., *e.g.*, *Ecclesiastes*, and the preference for "Elohim" in Chronicles. "The compiler of Chronicles," says Driver, "changes conversely *Jehovah* of his original source into *God*," etc.—*Introd.* p. 21; cf. p. 372.

[3] It is well known that the Jews change "Jehovah" in reading into "Adonai" or "Elohim," and that the vowels of "Jehovah" itself are really those of "Adonai." The name, we have seen, is properly Jahweh.

[4] Cf. Klostermann, as above.

[5] Evidently on this theory the need remains of finding a *reason* for the preference of the divine names as much as ever. This brings us back, as at

documents of the critics, Klostermann substitutes *J and E recensions of one and the same old work.*[1] To him, as to us, the piecing together of independent documents in the manner which the critical theory supposes, appears incredible. If hypothesis is to be employed, this of Klostermann, in its general idea, seems to us as good as any.[2]

VI. Linguistic and other alleged Grounds for Separation

It has been shown that the strongest reasons exist, despite the distinction in the divine names, for believing that J and E never had currency as separate documents; it is now to be asked whether these reasons are overborne by the remaining grounds ordinarily alleged to prove that J and E were originally independent. The long lists of marks of distinction adduced by Dillmann and other critics[3] have at first sight an imposing appearance. On closer inspection, however, they reduce themselves to much scantier dimensions. They were, for the most part, not obvious to the earlier critics, and, as proofs of independence, can be shown to be largely illusory. Such, *e.g.*, are all the marks, formerly adverted to, supposed to show a superior interest of E in Ephraimitic localities and in the house of Joseph. It turned out that J displayed at least as warm an interest in Northern places, while E dwells also on Beersheba, the one Southern locality that comes prominently into the part of the history he narrates. Indeed, "the South country" is adduced as one of his favourite phrases.[4] The chief remaining grounds of dis-

least the main reason, to the feeling of a superior appropriateness of one name rather than the other in a given context.

[1] Cf. *Pentateuch*, pp. 10, 11, 27 ff.

[2] We do not gather that Klostermann supposes his Elohistic recension to be necessarily late—the same causes probably operated at earlier periods—or to be inconsistent with a union of JE with P. His own theory is that such a union goes far back (*Pent.* p. 185). The fault of Klostermann's treatment is the excessive scope he allows for variations of the text in course of transmission. The well-marked physiognomy of the JE and P text is an argument against such wide change.

[3] Cf. Dillmann, *Num.-Jos.* pp. 617 ff.; more moderately, Driver, *Introd.* pp. 118–19. *Genesis*, p. xiii.

[4] E mentions also Hebron (see above, p. 210), and, if his hand is really present, as some suppose, in Gen. xv. he must have had an account of the

tinction are alleged linguistic peculiarities, distinctive modes of representation, duplicate narratives, etc. Let us look at these.

1. On the subject of *linguistic peculiarities*, Dr. Driver's statement was formerly quoted that "the phraseological criteria" distinguishing J and E are "slight."[1] They *are* slight, in fact, to a degree of tenuity that often makes the recital of them appear like trifling. In not a few cases words are fixed on as characteristic which occur only once or twice in the whole Pentateuch, or which occur in *both* J and E, or in contexts where the analysis is doubtful, or where the reasoning is of the circular order which first gives a word to J or E, then assigns a passage to that document *because* the word is present in it. Here are a few examples:—

E is credited with "what may be called an antiquarian interest,"[2] on the ground, among other things, that he *once* uses in Genesis (xxxiii. 19), in narrating a purchase, the word *Kesitah* (a piece of money)—found elsewhere in the Bible only in Josh. xxiv. 32 (E?) and Job xlii. 11.

"Land of the South," above referred to, occurs only three times in the Pentateuch—in Gen. xx. 1 (E), in Gen. xxiv. 62 (which Delitzsch says cannot be referred to E), and in Num. xiii. 29 (doubtful); and once in Josh. xv. 19 (J).

The phrase "after these things," said to be a mark of E (Well.), is found first in Gen. xv. 1 (J)—E's presence in this context is contested, and the analysis is declared to be at best "only probable"—then in three passages given to E (Gen. xxii. 1; xl. 1; xlviii. 1); but also in two J passages (Gen. xxii. 20; xxxix. 7), and in Josh. xxiv. 29 (possibly P, as giving an age).

The word *Koh* (in sense of "here") in Gen. xxii. 5, assigned as a mark of E, is found elsewhere *once* in Genesis (xxxi. 37 E), in Num. xxiii. 15 (mixed), and besides in Ex. ii. 12, assigned by Wellhausen to J, and in Num. xi. 31, given by Kuenen to J.

When we turn to instances which may be judged more important, we are in hardly better case. One observes that

covenant with Abraham at Mamre. If otherwise, it is not easy to see how E can be expected to speak of localities which belong to a period before his own narrative begins.

[1] *Introd.* pp. 13, 126; see above, p. 219. [2] Addis, *Hex.* i. p. lv.

where other writers indulge in the customary "always" and "invariably," Dr. Driver frequently uses the safer word "prefers."[1] The following are a few principal examples, and the extent of the "preference" may be gauged from them:—

"The Jahvist," we are told, "calls a female slave or concubine *Shiphḥah*, the Elohist invariably *Amah*."[2] Dr. Driver says in the case of E, "prefers"—and prudently. *Amah* is used by E some half-dozen times in Genesis (xx. 17; xxi. 10, 12, 13; xxx. 3; xxxi. 33), but *Shiphḥah* occurs nearly as often in E or in inseparably interwoven contexts (Gen. xx. 14; xxix. 24, 29, assigned to P; xxx. 4, 7, 18).[3] Whether *Amah* is used by E or J in Ex. ii. 5, xx. 10 (Fourth Com.), xxi. (Book of Covenant—repeatedly), depends on the accuracy of the analysis which assigns these parts to E, and on this critics are quite divided.[4] Ex. xxi.–xxiii., *e.g.*, are given by Wellhausen, Westphal, etc., to *J*.

We are told again that "the Jahvist speaks of 'Sinai,' the Elohist of 'Horeb.'" E's usage reduces itself to three passages (Ex. iii. 1; xvii. 6; xxxiii. 6)—the last two determined mainly by the presence of the word; J employs Sinai *solely* in chaps. xix. (cf. ver. 1; xxiv. 16, P) and xxxiv. 2, 4, in connection with the actual giving of the law.[5] The related expression "mountain of God" seems common (Ex. iii. 1, E; iv. 27, J; xxiv. 13?).

"The Jahvist," it is said, "calls the aborigines of Palestine 'Canaanites,' the Elohist 'Amorites.'" This, on examination, breaks down entirely. E has no monopoly of "Amorite" (cf. Gen. x. 16; xiv. 13; xv. 21),[6] and the

[1] *Genesis*, p. xiii.

[2] Addis, i. p. lvi. The quotations that follow are also from Addis, pp. lvi, lvii.

[3] It is pure arbitrariness and circular reasoning to change this single word in chap. xx. 14 and xxx. 18, on the ground that "the regular word for women slaves in E is *Amah*," and that "J on the other hand always employs *Shiphḥah*" (Oxf. *Hex.* ii. pp. 29, 45)—the very point in dispute. In chap. xxix. 24, 29, the verses are cut out and given to P; chap. xxx. 4, 7 are similarly cut out and given to J (p. 45).

[4] Ex. ii. 5 is confessedly given to E because "the linguistic conditions in vers. 1 and 5 [*i.e.*, this word] point to E rather than J" (Oxf. *Hex.* ii. p. 81). Jülicher, however, gives the verse to J. The assignment of the Decalogue and the Book of the Covenant are matters of much controversy. Delitzsch remarks on the latter: "Such words as *Amah* . . . are no marks of E in contradistinction to J and D."—*Genesis*, i. p. 32.

[5] Possibly Horeb is a wider designation.

[6] Oxf. *Hex.* itself says: "Otherwise in lists." Cf. Kuenen on Gen. x., *Hex.* pp. 140, 149.

two instances assigned to him in Genesis (xv. 16; xlviii. 22) are in passages of most doubtful analysis.[1] Similarly with the few instances of 'Canaanite' in J (Gen. x. 18; xii. 6; xiii. 7, etc.; cf. xv. 21, "Amorite and Canaanite," given to R).

One other instance must suffice. "The Jahvist calls Jacob in the latter part of his life 'Israel'; the Elohist retains the name 'Jacob.'" Dr. Driver more cautiously says "prefers"; Kuenen says "generally."[2] Here, again, the case is only made out by tearing asunder the web of what is evidently a closely-connected narrative, and by liberal use of the redactor. It will be observed that it is only in the "latter part" of Jacob's life that this peculiarity is said to be found. J had recorded the change of name from Jacob to Israel in chap. xxxii. 24–32,[3] but from some eccentric motive he is supposed not to commence his use of "Israel" till xxxv. 21. Yet, as the text stands, "Jacob" is found in a J narrative later (chap. xxxvii. 34), and "Israel" in a long series of E passages (Gen. xxxvii. 3; xlv. 27, 28; xlvi. 1, 2; xlviii. 2, 8, 10, 11, 14, 21). There is no reason for denying these verses to E *except that this name is found in them.* The logician could find no better example of the *circulus vitiosus* than in the critical treatment of Gen. xlviii It may be noted that in Exodus J has "the God of Abraham, of Isaac, and of *Jacob*" (chap. iii. 16), and E in both Genesis and Exodus has "sons of *Israel*."

2. Connected with these alleged peculiarities of language are others which turn more on general style, "tone," *mode of representation* of God, and the like. E has a more elevated idea of God; J is more vivid and anthropomorphic, etc. Much depends here on subjective impression,[4] and on the view taken of the relation sustained by E to J—whether

[1] Gen. xv. 16 is attributed by Wellhausen, Budde, Kuenen, etc., to another hand (not to E).

[2] "At present we can only say that in the E sections after Gen. xxxii. the patriarch is *generally* called 'Jacob,' whereas the J passages *generally* speak of Israel," but "in our mongrel state of the text numerous exceptions occur" (*Hex.* p. 145).

[3] If, with some critics, as Dillmann, we assign Gen. xxxii. 24–32 to E, we have, as Dr. Green points out, "this curious circumstance," that "P (xxxv. 10) and E (xxxii. 28) record the change of name to Israel, but never use it; J alone makes use of it, and, according to Dillmann, he does not record the change at all."—*Genesis*, p. 450.

[4] Cf. the illustration given on p. 211.

earlier or later. Two examples may be selected of these alleged differences, and one or two illustrations given of the analysis of passages resulting from the theory.

We take examples universally accepted. "The God of whom he [E] writes," we read, "appears in dreams, or acts through the ministry of angels."[1] "His angel calls out of heaven."[2] The "dream" criterion is one much insisted on, and for various reasons deserves attention. As the "dream" is a lower form of revelation, and is generally employed in connection with secular personages—Abimelech, Laban, Joseph (dreams of secular pre-eminence), the butler and baker, Pharaoh, etc.—it is not wonderful that it should commonly appear in passages of a prevailingly Elohistic cast. But the attempt to make out this to be a peculiar criterion of E proves, on inspection, to be an exaggeration. The passages adduced in its support, indeed, frequently prove the contrary. Thus, Gen. xv. 1, given by Driver, is on the face of it Jehovistic.[3] Gen. xx. 3, and most of the other instances (Abimelech, Laban, Pharaoh), fall under the above rule of fitness, and in some of the cases are assigned to E simply because a "dream" is recorded. Gen. xxviii. 10–22—Jacob's vision at Bethel (cf. chap. xlvi. 2)—is divided between E and J (arbitrarily, as shown below), but the dream is implied in both. In E, Jacob sleeps and dreams (ver. 12); in J, he awakes (ver. 16). In J also God reveals Himself to Isaac in a night vision (chap. xxvi. 24: cf. E passage above, xlvi. 2). Further, it is not the case that in E God reveals Himself *only* in dreams or by angels, as on the theory He ought to do. God speaks directly with Abraham in chaps. xxi. 12 (contrast with case of Abimelech), xxii. 1; and with Jacob in chap. xxxv. 1. He "appears" to Jacob at Bethel in E, chap. xxxv. 7, just as He does in P (ver. 9). Finally, Wellhausen himself concludes from chap. xxxvii. 19, 20 that the "Jahvist" also must have related Joseph's dreams;[4] and Professor Bennett, who adduces this very criterion of E,[5] follows suit and

[1] Addis, i. p. lv; cf. Driver, *Genesis*, pp. xx, xxi; McFadyen, *Mess. of Hist.*; "In the Elohist He usually appears in a dream" (p. 19).

[2] Driver, *ibid.* p. xxi; cf. Addis, i. p. 36; McFadyen, p. 19, etc.

[3] There is certainly no agreement that chap. xv. 1 is E's. This refutes also the exclusive right of E to a "coming" of God in a dream (Driver)—twice elsewhere in Genesis. Why, it may be asked, if the dream is so peculiar a mark of E, is it not carried into the other books?

[4] *Comp. d. Hex.* p. 54.

[5] *Genesis*, p. 31.

says: "Perhaps J had also an account of Pharaoh's dream."[1] So falls this hypothesis of "dreams"—itself a dream.

The argument based on the calling of the Angel of God "out of heaven" is not more successful. The expression occurs once in an E passage, in Gen. xxi. 17, then *twice* in chap. xxii. (11, 15), but in both the latter cases in a Jehovistic form, "the Angel of *Jehovah* called out of heaven." Even if the redactor be called in to change the word to "Elohim" in ver. 11, because of the E context, this is inadmissible in the second case, where the context is Jehovistic. There is, in truth, no warrant for changing it in either case. Yet on this infinitesimally slender basis an argument for the distinction of E is reared.

This leads us to say that no stronger proof for the inadmissibility of the partition hypothesis in the case of J and E could be desired than the two passages just referred to—Gen. xxii. 1–19 (the sacrifice of Isaac), and Gen. xxviii. 10–22 (Jacob at Bethel). We would almost be willing to stake the case for the unity of the alleged documents on these narratives alone. Each, on its face, is a single story, which needs both the parts ascribed to E and those ascribed to J to constitute it in its completeness, and for the dividing of which nothing of importance but the variation in the divine names can be pleaded. The E and J portions, on the other hand, are unintelligible, if taken by themselves. Even on the basis of the divine names, the analysis presents great difficulties, and critics are far from agreed in their ideas of it. Thus, in Dr. Driver's scheme, Gen. xxii. 1–14 is given to E, though "Jehovah" occurs in ver. 11 and twice in ver. 14; in Gen. xxviii. 21, "Jehovah" occurs in the E part, and has to be forcibly excised. The unity of the story in both cases is destroyed by the partition. In Gen. xxii. vers. 1–14 are given, as said, to E, vers. 15–18 to J (others give vers. 14–18 to a Jehovistic "redactor"), ver. 19, again, is given to E. But each of these parts is evidently complementary to the others.[2] If we break off

[1] *Genesis*, p. 29.

[2] Hupfeld, to whom is due the 2nd Elohist, has a remarkable admission of this. "I cannot conceal the fact," he says, "that the entire narrative seems to me to bear the stamp of the Jehovist; and certainly one would never think of the Elohist, but for the name Elohim, which here (as in part of the history of Joseph) is not supported by the internal phenomena, and embarrasses criticism" (*Quellen*, p. 178). Knobel also says: "Apart from

with E at vers. 13 or 14 (still more, with the older critics, at ver. 10), the sequel of the story is clearly lacking. It is the same with Gen. xxviii. 10–22. E begins with vers. 10–12; vers. 13–16 are given to J; vers. 17, 18 again fall to E; ver. 19 is credited to J; and vers. 20–22 are once more E's.[1] Is such a patchwork credible, especially when "redactors" are needed to help out the complicated process?[2] It is clear that both documents must have had the story, yet neither, it appears, is able to tell it completely. Jacob, as already pointed out, falls asleep in the one document, and awakes in the other. Even as respects the names, it is difficult not to see an appropriateness in their distribution, whether that is supposed due to an original writer, or to a later editor combining Elohistic and Jehovistic recensions. In both narratives the story begins on a lower level and mounts to a higher—the "crisis" in each case being marked by the change of name. Hengstenberg,[3] but also Knobel, Delitzsch, and others,[4] have pointed this out in the case of the sacrifice of Isaac. "Elohim" tempts Abraham, and the name continues to be used till the trial of faith is complete; it then changes—ascends—to "Jehovah" with the new revelation that arrests the sacrifice, and confirms the covenant promise. So in Gen. xxviii. 10 ff., Jacob, leaving his father's house, is practically in a state of spiritual outlawry. As befits this lower level, he receives his revelation in a dream ("angels of Elohim ascending," etc.); but "Jehovah" appears to him above the mystic ladder, and renews the covenant. It was a revelation of grace, wholly undeserved and unexpected, designed to set Jacob on his

Elohim nothing in this narrative reminds us of the Elohist; on the contrary, everything speaks for the Jehovist" (quoted by Green, *Genesis*, p. 483).

[1] There are variations among the critics here as elsewhere, several, *e.g.*, give ver. 10 to J.

[2] Orelli says: "Gen. xxviii. is probably Yahwistic, at least the splitting up of the narrative is in the highest degree arbitrary."—*O.T. Prophecy*, p. 105.

[3] *Gen. of Pent.* i. p. 348.

[4] Knobel, who gives the whole narrative to J, says: "We have to assume that the Jehovist here uses Elohim so long as there is reference to a human sacrifice, and only introduces Jehovah (ver. 11) after setting aside such a sacrifice, which was foreign to the religion of Jehovah" (as above). The change to the divine name, says Delitzsch, "is in its present state significant, the God who commands Abraham to sacrifice Isaac is called '(Ha)-Elohim,' and the divine appearance that forbids the sacrifice, 'the Angel of Jehovah.'"—*Genesis*, ii. pp. 90–91.

feet again, and make a new man of him. Only the higher name was suited to such a theophany.

3. One of the strongest of the evidences—because not depending on single words—relied on to prove the distinction of J and E, and the validity of the documentary hypothesis generally, is the occurrence of "duplicate" narratives of the same event ("doublets"), and to this subject we may now finally refer. Duplicates, or what are held to be such, are pointed out in the case of JE and P, as in the two narratives of creation, Gen. i.–ii. 3 (P), ii. 3 ff. (J), and the twice naming of Bethel, Gen. xxviii. 19 (J), xxxv. 15 (P), cf. ver. 7 (E); but also between J and E, as in the twice naming of Beersheba, Gen. xxi. 31 (E), xxvi. 33 (J), the two flights of Hagar, Gen. xvi. 4–14 (J), xxi. 9–21 (E), and specially in the stories of the denials of their wives by Abraham and Isaac, Gen. xii. 10–20 (J), xx. (E), xxvi. 6–11 (J).[1] Similar duplications are thought to be found in the Mosaic history. The presence of such differing and so-called contradictory accounts is held to prove distinct sources.

On these alleged "duplicate" narratives the following remarks may first be made *generally*:—

(1) Narratives of the same event may be different in point of view and detail, without being necessarily, as is constantly assumed—"contradictory" or "discordant" (creation, flood, etc.[2]).

(2) Similar acts may be, and frequently are, repeated under new circumstances. *E.g.*, in the cases of Bethel and Beersheba above, the second narrative expressly refers back to the first (Gen. xxxv. 9, cf. on E below; xxvi. 15, 18). This close interrelation of the different parts of the narrative (JEP) is one of the most striking facts about it.

(3) It weakens the argument that "duplications" do not always occur in *different* documents—as on the theory they ought to do—but in no inconsiderable number of cases fall within the limits of the *same* document. Thus E has a second visit to Bethel as well as P (Gen. xxxv. 6, 7); J has two denials of wives — see below; alleged duplicate accounts of the Korahite rebellion are found in Num. xvi.

[1] See a list of duplicates in Kuenen, *Hex.* pp. 38 ff. De Wette laid great stress on this argument in his *Introduction.*

[2] See below, pp. 346 ff.

-10 (P),[1] etc. Criticism is driven here to further disntegrations.

(4) This suggests, lastly, that, even were the similarity f incidents as clear as is alleged, it would not necessarily rove different authorship. The same author might find arying narrations in the traditions or sources from which e drew, and might *himself* reproduce them in his history. uppose, to take a favourite instance, that the narrator f the life of Joseph found the merchants to whom Joseph vas sold described in one of his sources as Ishmaelites and n another as Midianites, is it not as likely that he would imself introduce both names (Gen. xxxvii. 27, 28, 36; xxix. 1), as that a later "redactor" should weave together he varying histories of J and E?[2] Even this hypothesis is ot necessary, for we have independent evidence that Ishmaelites" was used as a wide term to include Midianites" (Judg. viii. 24). In Hagar's flights (in econd case an expulsion),—one before the birth of Ishmael, he other when he was grown up to be a lad,—it seems lain that tradition had preserved the memory of *two* ncidents, connected with different times and occasions, and ach natural in its own place.[3]

Without delaying on other instances, we may take, as test-case, the most striking of all these "doublets"—the enial of their wives by Abraham and Isaac—and subject hat, in closing, to a brief analysis. The results will be

[1] Cf., *e.g.*, McFadyen's *Mess. of Hist.* p. 7, where this case is founded on. ee below, pp. 358–59.

[2] The critics evolve from the narrative two discrepant histories of oseph, according to which, in the one case (E), Joseph is, unknown to the rothers, taken out of the pit by passing *Midianites*, and sold to Potiphar, aptain of the guard, in Egypt; in the other (J) he is sold by the brothers no pit) to a company of *Ishmaelites*, who sell him in turn to an unnamed gyptian (no Potiphar). The "they" in ver. 28 is referred to the lidianites. In chap. xxxix. 1, indeed, Potiphar is expressly said to have ought him from the Ishmaelites, but this is excised as an interpolation. he whole thing seems to us an exercise of misplaced ingenuity, refuted by he narrative, which hangs together as it is, but not on this theory.

[3] A difficulty is created about the *age* of Ishmael in the second story. he critics adopt the reading of the LXX for chap. xxi. 14, "put the child on er shoulder," and find a discrepancy with the representation of him as a lad f some fourteen years of age (cf. Addis, *Hex.* i. p. 34). But the story itself escribes him as a "lad" (vers. 12, 17, 18, 19, 20), and the "mocking" of saac (ver. 9) implies some age. Colenso, for once, is not stumbled by the "carrying," and cites a curious Zulu parallel (quoted in Quarry, *Genesis*, . 456). The LXX reading has no claim to supersede the Hebrew (cf. elitzsch, *in loc.*). See further below, p. 352.

instructive, as throwing light on critical methods, and showing how far from simple this matter of "duplicates really is.

(1) We have first, then, to observe that what we hav here to deal with is not *two*, but *three* incidents (not *dupli cates*, but *triplicates*)—one denial in Egypt (Gen. xi Abraham), and two in Gerar (chap. xx. Abraham, xxv Isaac). Of these narratives, *two* are classed as Jehovisti (Gen. xii. xxvi.), and *one* is classed as Elohistic (chap. xx. In strictness, therefore, on the duplication theory, we seen bound to assume for them, not two, but *three* authors; an this, accordingly, is what is now commonly done. It i allowed that "the narrative in chap. xii. shows the genera style and language of J,"[1] *but* "it can hardly be suppose that the story of Abram passing off Sarai as his sister a Pharaoh's court, and that of Isaac dealing similarly wit Rebekah at Gerar, belonged originally to the same series o traditions."[2] The former story, therefore, must be given t some later representative of the J "school."[3] We hav here the critical process of disintegration in a nutshell.

(2) We have next to look at the phenomena of th divine *names*. In Gen. xii. 10–20, Dr. Driver, in word formerly quoted, tells us that "the term *Jehovah* is uniforml employed."[4] In point of fact, it is employed only *onc* (ver. 17), and, strikingly enough, it is employed *once* also i the Elohistic narrative (chap. xx. 18) in a similar connection In the third narrative (Gen. xxvi. 6–11), the divine nam does not occur *at all*, though the context is Jehovistic (vers 2, 12). So uncertain, indeed, are the criteria, that, accordin to Dillmann,[5] Wellhausen actually at first gave Gen. xi 10–20 to E (same as in chap. xx.). Now, he gives th section, as above hinted, to a later writer on the ground for one thing, that Lot is not mentioned as accompanyin Abraham to Egypt (Lot's presence, however, is plainl assumed, cf. chap. xiii. 1). As respects the third narrativ (Gen. xxvi.), so far from there being disharmony, the openin verse of the chapter contains an express reference to th going down of Abraham to Egypt in the first narrativ (Gen. xii. 10); but the whole text of this passage (vers. 1–5

[1] Carpenter, *Hex.* ii. p. 19.
[2] *Ibid.* i. p. 108.
[3] See Wellhausen, below.
[4] *Genesis*, p. xi.
[5] *Genesis*, ii. p. 17.

s made a patchwork of by the critics.[1] Finally, in chap. x. it remains to be explained how a Jehovist verse comes o stray into the story of E at ver. 18. It is easy to say "redactor"; but one desires to know what moved a redactor o interpolate into his E context the mention of a fact for which he had no authority, and to employ in doing so a livine name out of keeping with his context.

(3) The facts as they stand may be *summed up* thus. All three scenes are laid in heathen courts. In the first nd third stories, the divine name is not used in the body of he narrative (in the third is not used at all); in the first nd second, the name "Jehovah" is used towards the close chaps. xii. 17; xx. 18) in connection with the divine action n inflicting penalty. As two of the narratives are allowed y the more moderate critics (*e.g.*, Dillmann, Driver) to be y the same writer (J), there is no need, on the mere round of duplication, to assume a different writer for he third story. All three stories may well have belonged o the original tradition. Nor do the conditions require us o treat the stories as simply varying traditions of the *same* ncident. There are resemblances, but there are also great lifferences. From both chaps. xii. and xx. it appears that t was part of Abraham's *settled policy*, when travelling n strange parts, to pass off Sarah, still childless, as his ister (chap. xii. 13; xx. 13: on the half-truth by which his was justified, cf. chap. xx. 12).[2] This of itself implies hat the thing was done more than once (cf. "at every lace," etc.); if, indeed, chap. xx. 13 is not a direct glancing ack to the former narrative. What Abraham was known o have done, Isaac, in similar peril, may well have been empted to do likewise. In the story about Isaac there is, n fact, as above noticed, a direct reference to his father's arlier visit to Egypt (chap. xxvi. 1).[3]

[1] Cf. Oxf. *Hex. in loc.*

[2] See above, p. 109.

[3] It would obviously be easy, on similar lines to the above, to make out a eries of "demonstrable" duplicates in, say, British history, as in Spanish vars, Chinese wars, Afghan wars, mad Mullahs, etc.: so in history enerally.

APPENDIX TO CHAPTER VII

THE HISTORICITY OF THE BOOK OF JOSHUA

THE historical character of the Book of Joshua is assailed, partly on the ground of discrepancies in the narrative, as in the chapters on the crossing of Jordan (chaps. iii., iv.), where two accounts apparently blend; but chiefly because of an alleged difference in the mode of representation of the conquest. On the so-called discrepancies we have no need to deny the use of separate sources,[1] if these are not held to be contradictory. In the above instance, Köhler remarks that the notices of the two monuments (of twelve stones, one in Jordan, the other at Gilgal), while belonging to distinct sources, do not exclude each other, and are both to be held fast:[2] so in other narratives.

As regards the conquest, it is urged that, according to one representation, that derived from the Deuteronomic redactor and the still later P, the conquest under Joshua was rapid, continuous, and complete; while older notices in separate passages,[3] and in Judg. i., show that it was in reality only achieved gradually, by the efforts of the several tribes, and never completely. There is, however, if the book be taken as a whole, and allowance be made for the generalising tendency peculiar to all summaries, no necessary contradiction in the different representations of the conquest,[4] while the circumstantiality, local knowledge, and evidently full recollection of the narratives, give confidence in the truth of their statements. On the one hand, the uniform assumption in all the JE history, from the

[1] Probably not, however, the J and E of the previous books. See above, p. 214.

[2] See his *Bib. Geschichte*, i. pp. 473–74.

[3] *E.g.*, chaps. xiii. 13; xv. 13–19, 63; xvi. 10; xvii. 12 ff.; xviii. 2 ff.

[4] Cf. König's criticism of Budde in his article on Judges in *Dict. of Bible*, ii. pp. 818–19.

original promise to Abraham of the possession of the land to the actual conquest, in the Deuteronomic discourses, and generally in the tradition of the people, is, that the tribes under Joshua *did* take effective possession of the land; and this is borne out by the fact that in Judges it is not the Canaanites chiefly by whom they are molested (an exception is the temporary oppression by Jabin[1]), but surrounding and more distant peoples (*e.g.* Chushan-rishathaim, king of Mesopotamia,[2] Moab,[3] Ammon,[4] Midianites,[5] Philistines[6]). With this agrees the picture given of the conquest, beginning with the taking of Jericho and Ai, advancing to the defeat of the confederacy of the kings at Bethhoron, and destruction of their cities,[7] then to the defeat of the greater confederacy in the North under Jabin, and conquests there,[8] afterwards, in more general terms, to further campaigns in the middle, South, and North of Palestine, till the whole land has been overrun.[9] The course of conquest is what might have been expected from the terror described by Rahab (JE ?),[10] and accords with the retrospect of Joshua in his last address (E ?).[11] On it the division of the land, described with so much topographical minuteness, naturally follows.[12]

On the other hand, the Book of Joshua itself gives many indications that, notwithstanding these extensive, and, as respects the main object, decisive conquests, there still remained much land to be possessed, which the tribes could only conquer gradually.[13] Much detail work had to be done in the several territories; and there is no difficulty in the supposition that, after the first sweeping wave of conquest, the Canaanites rallied, and regained possession of many places, *e.g.*, Hebron, from which they had been temporarily expelled. An instance of this we have in Jerusalem, which had been taken by the Israelites,

[1] Judg. iv.
[2] Judg. iii. 8 ff.
[3] Judg. iii. 12 ff.
[4] Judg. x. 7 ff.
[5] Judg. vi. 1 ff.
[6] Judg. xiii. 1 ff.
[7] Josh. x.
[8] Josh. xi. 1–14.
[9] Josh. xi. 15 ff., xii.
[10] Josh. ii. 9; cf. ver. 24.
[11] Josh. xxiv. 11, 18.
[12] Chaps. xii. ff. On the historicity of this, see below, pp. 379–80, and cf. König on Judges in *Dict. of Bible*, ii. p. 820. It is noted below (p. 242) that a division of the land is implied in Judg. i., as Budde himself admits (cf. König, *loc. cit.*).
[13] Josh. xiii. 1, 2; see passages cited on p. 240.

and burnt with fire, and the population destroyed,[1] but which the Jebusites regained, and held till the time of David.[2] These facts do not really contradict the other narrative:[3] indeed, it is hard to see how a Deuteronomic redactor could have incorporated them unchanged in his narrative, if he believed they contradicted it. The language in Joshua about the conquest is not more sweeping than that in the Tel el-Amarna tablets about the Khabiri. In the letters of Abdi-Khiba, king of Jerusalem, *e.g.*, to Amenophis IV. of Egypt, we have such expressions as the following: "The cities of my lord, the king, belonging to Elimelech, have fallen away, and the whole territory of the king will be lost. . . . The king has no longer any territory. . . . If no troops come, the territory of my lord, the king, is lost." "Bring plainly before my lord, the king, these words: 'The whole territory of my lord, the king, is going to ruin.'" "The Khabiri are occupying the king's cities. There remains not one prince to my lord, the king: every one is ruined." "The territory of the king has fallen into the hands of the Khabiri."[4]

There is no feature in the conquest better attested than that Joshua was the leader of the tribes in this work, and that they advanced and acted under his single leadership till the first stages of the conquest were completed. This was not a thing done at once, but probably occupied several years. Kittel, who defends in the main the truth of the historical recollections in the narrative, and emphasises this point about Joshua,[5] thinks that a partition of the land (which he finds implied in Judg. i., etc.[6]) must have taken place before the conquest began, and supposes that, after the general crossing of Jordan under Joshua, and capture of

[1] Judg. i. 8; cf. Josh. x.

[2] 2 Sam. v. 6–8.

[3] König says: "It is a groundless assertion that the record of Judg. i. 'excludes' the narrative of the Book of Joshua" (p. 820).

[4] See Bennett's *Book of Joshua* ("Polychrome Bible"), p. 55. The Khabiri are supposed by some to have been the Hebrews. See further below, Chap. XI. p. 421.

[5] *Hist. of Hebs.* i. p. 274. He points out that the view of Meyer, Stade, etc., that J did not know Joshua, is impugned by Kuenen, Dillmann, and Budde.

[6] The summary in Judg. i., he says, begins with the question, "Who shall begin the fight?" and the territory of each tribe is called its "lot"—"two facts which clearly enough presuppose a previous common agreement," etc.—*Ibid.* p. 275.

Jericho, Judah and Simeon separated from the main body to act for themselves in the south. Joshua was thereafter leader of the Joseph tribes alone.[1] The view seems artificial, and no improvement on that in the book. The course of events is, we may believe, correctly represented in Josh. xxiv.

[1] *Hist. of Hebs.* pp. 272-77.

CHAPTER VIII

Difficulties and Perplexities of the Critical Hypothesis: The Question of Deuteronomy

"The Book of Deuteronomy in and for itself teaches nothing new. . . . How could Josiah have been so terrified because the prescriptions of this book had not been observed by the fathers, and the people had thereby incurred the wrath of Jahweh, if he had not been aware that these commands were known to them?"—GRAF.

"I am still certain that the finding of the book of the law in the eighteenth year of Josiah is neither meant, nor is, to be understood of the first appearance of the Book of Deuteronomy, originating about that time." —DELITZSCH.

"Our review of sources has convinced us that it [Deuteronomy] draws from old Mosaic tradition, which in fact in many places goes back demonstrably into the Mosaic time, and *par excellence* to the person of the lawgiver. It goes so far as to incorporate such ordinances as no longer suited the writer's own time, but only suited the time of the conquest and settlement in Canaan."—OETTLI.

"Leaving out of account isolated passages, especially the close, Deuteronomy is a whole proceeding from one and the same hand."—RIEHM.

CHAPTER VIII

IFFICULTIES AND PERPLEXITIES OF THE CRITICAL HYPOTHESIS: THE QUESTION OF DEUTERONOMY

'HE questions we have been engaged in discussing with elation to J and E, while interesting as an object-lesson in riticism, and, in their bearing on dates, important, are econdary in comparison with those which yet await in-estigation—the age and origin of Deuteronomy and of the o-called Priestly Code. It will be remembered that the raf-Wellhausen school does not pretend to settle the age nd relations of documents or codes by critical considera-ions alone. Criticism is to be guided, and its conclusions re to be checked, at every step, by history. A parallel, it s alleged, can be traced between the course of the history nd the successive stages of the legislation. Up to the time f Josiah, it is held, no trace can be discovered of the ex-stence and operation of any body of laws but that of the ook of the Covenant in Ex. xx.–xxiii. With the finding of the book of the law" in Josiah's reign,[1] there enters a nanifold influence of the spirit and teaching of the Book of euteronomy, strongly reflected in the later literature—or instance, in Jeremiah; but no sign is yet shown of the eculiar institutions of the Levitical Code. These first egin to be visible in the sketch of the restored temple and ts ordinances in Ezekiel (chaps. xl. ff.), and emerge as a efinitely completed system in the law-book which Ezra rought with him from Babylon, and gave to the post-exilian ommunity in Jerusalem.[2] Thenceforth they rule the life f the nation. The ingenuity of the new scheme is un-oubted, and the acceptance it has won is sufficient evidence

[1] 2 Kings xxii.

[2] Ezra vii.; Neh. viii. For a popular statement of the theory of the hree Codes see Professor W. R. Smith's *O.T. in J. C.*, Lects. viii., ix.

of the skill with which it has been expounded and defende
But is it really tenable? Many reasons—not the lea
cogent of them derived from the course of criticism itself-
convince us it is not. We shall deal in this chapter wi
the application of the theory to the Book of Deuteronomy.

I. State of the Question and General View

The Book of Deuteronomy, in its main part, consists,
is well known, after a slight introduction, and with son
connecting notes, of three hortatory discourses purporti
to have been delivered by Moses in the *Arabah*[2] of Moa
shortly before his death (chaps. i. 6–iv. 40, v.–xxviii.; xxix.
xxx.). To these discourses are appended an account
certain closing transactions of Moses (chap. xxxi.), the So
and Blessing of Moses (chaps. xxxii., xxxiii.), and a narrati
of Moses' death on Mount Nebo (chaps. xxxii. 48–52; xxxiv
The longest of the discourses (chaps. v.–xxviii.) embraces a r
hearsal (chaps. xii. ff.), in the form of popular address, of t
principal laws given by God to Moses at Horeb, as the
were to be observed by the people in their new settleme
in Canaan. There is general agreement that the laws
which reference is made in this recapitulation are chiefly-
though, as will be seen after, by no means *exclusively*—tho
contained in the Book of the Covenant (Ex. xx.–xxiii.
but they are handled by the speaker, not literally, b
in free reproduction, with rhetorical amplification
abbreviation, and occasionally modification to suit ne
circumstances.

Deuteronomy is the one book of the Pentateuch whi
might seem on the face of it to make claim to direct Mosa
authorship. "Moses," it is declared, after the rehearsal
completed, "wrote this law."[3] This view of its orig
modern criticism decisively rejects; will hardly allow ev

[1] Graf makes the Book of Deuteronomy his starting-point. His wo
opens: "The composition of Deuteronomy in the age of Josiah is one of t
most generally accepted results of the historical criticism of the Old Test
ment, for all who do not simply ignore these results."—*Geschicht. Büch*
p. 1; cf. p. 4.

[2] "That is, the deep valley running north and south of the Dead Se
(R.V.). Usually (in P) *Arboth*, the steppes or plains of Moab. See
interesting description in an article on *The Steppes of Moab* by Professor G.
Gray in *Expositor*, January 1905.

[3] Deut. xxxi. 9, 24–26; see below, pp. 262 ff.

be discussed.[1] It was De Wette's achievement in criticism, s we saw, that he relegated Deuteronomy to the age of osiah; and in this judgment the great majority of critics ow follow him, only that a few carry back the composition f the book a reign or two earlier—to the time of Manasseh r of Hezekiah. Views differ as to how the book is to be egarded—whether as a pseudograph ("forgery"), or as a ee composition in the name and spirit of Moses without itention to deceive; but it is generally agreed that, in its resent form, it is a production of the prophetic age, and as for its leading aim the centralising of worship at the anctuary at Jerusalem. The reasons given for this view re its prophetic tone and standpoint, its obvious connection ith the work of reformation, the irreconcilability of its law f the central sanctuary with the older history, inconistencies with earlier legislation, etc. A main objection of he older critics was its alleged incompatibility with the evitical legislation, then believed to be in substance Iosaic:[2] but the newer criticism has taken the ground rom this objection by putting the Levitical laws still later han Deuteronomy—in the exile.

What weight is to be allowed to these opinions is conidered below. The composition of a book of exhortation or nstruction in the form of addresses by Moses—provided his is *only* literary dress, with honest motive in the writer —is not *a priori* to be ruled out as inadmissible, or incomatible with just views of Scripture.[3] The only question is vhether Deuteronomy is a book of this character, or, if it is o, in what sense and to what extent it is so, and to what ge it belongs. On the other hand, we cannot shut our eyes o certain far-reaching consequences of the acceptance of he critical view. If Deuteronomy is a work of the age f Josiah, then, necessarily, everything in the other Old 'estament books which depends on Deuteronomy — the)euteronomic revisions of Joshua and Judges, the Deutero-

[1] Cf. Graf, above. Wellhausen says: "About the origin of Deuteronomy here is still less dispute; in all circles where appreciation of scientific esults can be looked for at all, it is recognised that it was composed in the ame age as that in which it was discovered, and that it was made the rule f Josiah's reformation, which took place about a generation before the detruction of Jerusalem by the Chaldeans."—*Hist. of Israel*, p. 9.

[2] Cf. Bleek, *Introd.* i. pp. 328 ff.

[3] Ecclesiastes, *e.g.*, put into the mouth of Solomon, is generally admitted, ven by conservative critics, to be a work of this kind.

nomic allusions and speeches in the Books of Kings,[1] narratives of facts based on Deuteronomy—*e.g.*, the blessings and cursings, and writing of the law on stones, at Ebal,[2] all must be put later than that age. If, again, it be the case that the Levitical laws are later than Deuteronomy, this requires the carrying of these down to where the critics place them—at or near the exile. The very gravity of some of these conclusions is our warrant for raising the question—Is the critical view correct? The course of criticism itself, as just hinted, despite the apparent unanimity, forces this question upon us. For, as we soon come to discover, even on the subject of Deuteronomy, the critical school is rent within itself by divisions which raise the greatest doubts as to the soundness of the original premises. The mania for disintegration—the appetite for which seems to grow with what it feeds on—has been at work here also. In the Oxford *Hexateuch*, *e.g.*,—so far to anticipate,—the unity of Deuteronomy with which criticism started—that even of the Code in chaps. xii.–xxvi.—is lost in a sort of dissolving view.[3] There are, however, in our judgment, other and far stronger reasons for scepticism than even these critical vagaries. We hear much of the reasons for putting the book late, many of them, we shall find, sadly overstrained; but we hear little or nothing of the enormous difficulties attaching to the critic's own hypothesis. These are either ignored completely, or are toned down and minimised till they are made to appear trifling. We are content, when the case has been presented, to let the reader judge on that matter for himself. The time, at all events we venture to think, has fully come, when a halt should be called, and the question should be boldly put for reconsideration—Is the Josianic origin of Deuteronomy a result

[1] *E.g.*, Solomon's prayer, 1 Kings viii., or Amaziah's sparing the children of murderers, 2 Kings xiv. 5, 6.

[2] Josh. viii. 30 ff.

[3] Cf. *Hex.* i. pp. 92–96; ii. p. 246. On the Code it is said: "The Code and its envelopments, homiletic and narrative, hortatory or retrospective, must thus be regarded as the product of a long course of literary activity to which the various members of a great religious school contributed, the affinities with the language and thought of Jeremiah [not Jeremiah's affinities with Deuteronomy] being particularly numerous." To this group it is added, "other additions were made from time to time, involving further dislocations"; to these again final additions when J E D were united with P (ii. p. 302).

of scientific criticism which the impartial mind is bound to accept?

II. Unity and Style of Deuteronomy

As clearing the way for the discussion of date, a few words may be said, first, on the subject of *unity* and *style*.

1. No book in the Bible, it may be safely affirmed, bears on its face a stronger impress of *unity* than the Book of Deuteronomy. It is not disputed that, in the form in which we have it, the book shows traces of editorial redaction. The discourses are put together with introductory and connecting notes,[1] and the last part of the work, with its account of Moses' death, and in one or two places what seem unmistakable indications of JE and P hands,[2] points clearly to such redaction. This suggests the possibility that such archæological notices as occur in chap. ii. 10–12, 20–22, and perhaps slight annotations elsewhere, may come from the same revisional hand. But these minor, and in general readily distinguishable, traces of editorial labour only throw into more commanding relief the general unity of the book in thought and style. The most ordinary reader cannot peruse its chapters without perceiving that, as one has said, "the same vein of thought, the same tone and tenor of feeling, the same peculiarities of thought and expression," characterise it throughout. Accordingly, up to a comparatively recent period—till Graf's time—the unity of Deuteronomy, as respects the discourses, was recognised on nearly every hand as one of the surest results of criticism.[3] It

[1] These, however, differ little in style from the rest of the work.

[2] Chap. xxxii. 48–52 is generally given to P, and chap. xxxi. 14, 15, 23, to JE; both are found in chap. xxxiv.

[3] "By far the greater part," says De Wette, "belong to one author."—*Introd.* ii. p. 131.

"These" (the discourses), says Bleek, "are so homogeneous in their language and whole character that we may assume as certain—and on this point there is scarcely a conflicting opinion—they were on the whole composed in the shape in which we now have them, by one and the same author."—*Introd.* i. p. 320.

In 1864 Colenso wrote: "There can be no doubt that Deuteronomy is throughout the work of the same hand, with the exception of the last chapter . . . the book is complete in itself and exhibits a perfect unity of style and subject."—*Pent.*, Pop. edit. p. 185. By 1871, in Pt. vi. of his large work, he had come to believe that that which admitted of "no doubt" earlier was wrong, and that the original Deuteronomy began with chap. v.

was not doubted that the book found in the temple and read to Josiah was substantially the Deuteronomy we possess.

This can no longer be affirmed. The fine art of distinction acquired in the dissection of the other Pentateuchal "sources" soon led, as it could not but do—as it would do with any book in existence—to the discovery of abundant reasons for dividing up Deuteronomy also, first, into a number of larger sections of different ages, then into a variety of smaller pieces,[1] till, latterly, as indicated above, the unity tends entirely to disappear in the flux of the labours of a "school." Kuenen, who, in this point, is relatively conservative, extends the length of what he calls "the Deuteronomic period, which began in the year 621[2] B.C., and which called the additions to D^1 into existence," beyond the beginning of the Babylonian captivity.[2] Broadly, however, two *main* opinions on division may be distinguished, in regard to which we are happy in being able to leave it with the critics to answer each other. (1) There is the view of Wellhausen, Cornill, and others, who would limit the original Book of Deuteronomy (its "kernel") to chaps. xii.–xxvi.; but this, as Dr. Driver justly says, "upon grounds which cannot be deemed cogent."[3] Even Kuenen contests the reasons of Wellhausen on this point, and upholds the unity of chaps. v.–xxvi.[4] He gives also chap. xxviii. to the author of these chapters, as against Wellhausen.[5] (2) Kuenen, however, following Graf,[6] here draws a new line, and, "with the majority of recent critics," says Dr. Driver, "declares chaps. i.–iv. to be the work of a different hand."[7] The resemblance of style cannot be denied, but, says Kuenen, "the great similarity of language must be explained as the result of imitation."[8] To Dr. Driver himself there seems "no conclusive reason" for questioning the unity of

[1] See Note A on the Breaking up of Deuteronomy.

[2] *Hex.* p. 225.

[3] *Deut.* p. lxv.

[4] *Hex.* pp. 113 ff.

[5] *Ibid.* pp. 126 ff.

[6] Cf. Graf, *Geschicht. Bücher.* pp. 4, 5. It is interesting to notice the reasons given by Graf, as a pioneer in this division. He does not base it on style. He thinks, indeed, that in parts a greater "diffuseness" may be detected, but this "may perhaps seem too subjective." His objective reason is that, through the first four chapters, Deuteronomy is "closely bound with the preceding books," even as "the last four chapters contain the continuation of the historical narrations of those books." This does not suit his hypothesis that the Pentateuch as a whole did not exist in Josiah's day.

[7] *Deut.* p. lxvii; cf. Kuenen, *Hex.* pp. 117 ff.

[8] *Hex.* p. 117.

chaps. i.–iii. with the body of the work, and he doubts whether "the only reason of any weight" for questioning chap. iv. 1–40 is conclusive either.[1] Oettli, another witness, says on chaps. i.–iv.: "The usage of speech is the same as in chaps. v.–xi."[2]

For ourselves, the broad argument from unity of thought, language, and style throughout the book seems overwhelming against all these attempts at disintegration. Dr. Driver is mainly with us here. He points out how "particular words, and phrases, consisting sometimes of entire clauses, recur with extraordinary frequency, giving a *distinctive colouring* to every part of the work."[3] Almost more important is his statement that "the majority of the expressions noted occur seldom or never besides; others occur only in passages modelled upon the style of Deuteronomy, and representing the same point of view."[4] As respects the opinions of other critics, Dillmann, Westphal, Kittel, Oettli, Delitzsch and others, defend, like Dr. Driver, the general unity of Deuteronomy. Dillmann and Westphal, however, have hypotheses of transpositions, etc., which Dr. Driver, with good reason, rejects as "intrinsically improbable."[5] The unity of Deuteronomy, it may be concluded, is likely to survive the attacks made upon it.

2. An interesting question arises here, with considerable bearings on later discussions—How does the *style* of Deuteronomy stand related to that of the other Pentateuchal books, and to those passages said to be "modelled" on it in other Old Testament writings? There are marked differences between the Deuteronomic and the JE and P styles, but it is important that these should not be exaggerated, and that affinities also should be noted.[6] Delitzsch, in his *Genesis*,

[1] *Deut.* p. lxxii. [2] *Com. on Deut.* p. 9.

[3] *Deut.* p. lxxvii. Dr. Driver's words on chaps. v.–xxvi., xxviii. are worth quoting: "There is no sufficient reason for doubting that the whole of these chapters formed part of the law-book found by Hilkiah; all are written in the same style, and all breathe the same spirit, the only material difference being that, from the nature of the case, the parenetic phraseology is not so *exclusively* predominant in chaps. xii.–xxvi., xxviii. as it is in chaps. v.–xi. . . . Chaps. v.–xxvi. may thus be concluded, without hesitation, to be the work of a single author; and chap. xxviii. may be included without serious misgivings."—Pp. lxv, lxvii.

[4] *Ibid.* p. lxxxv.

[5] *Ibid.* p. lxxv. Kittel sympathises with Dillmann and Westphal. See his *Hist. of Hebs.* i. pp. 53 ff.

[6] See Note B on Deuteronomic and Priestly Styles.

made an interesting attempt, from comparison of the Decalogue and Book of the Covenant with Deuteronomy (which he took to be Mosaic in kernel), to arrive at an idea of the mode of thought and language of Moses. He found many Deuteronomic assonances in the above writings, and concluded that there was "an original Mosaic type," which he termed "Jehovistic-Deuteronomic."[1] It is at any rate certain that comparison with the other Pentateuchal books reveals some curious relations. Of all styles, that of the so-called P is furthest removed from Deuteronomy; yet in Lev. xxvi., which is of the P type, the language rises to a quite Deuteronomic strain of hortatory and admonitory eloquence. The resemblance is in fact so remarkable that it is commonly allowed that a close relation of some kind subsists between Lev. xxvi. and Deuteronomy, whether of priority or dependence on the part of Leviticus remains yet to be considered.[2] The affinities of Deuteronomy with JE are much closer.[3] Such are clearly traceable in the Decalogue and Book of the Covenant,[4] whether we ascribe the latter, with some critics, to J, or, with others, to E.[5] More generally, "there are," says Dr. Driver, "certain sections of JE (in particular, Gen. xxvi. 5; Ex. xiii. 3–16; xv. 26; xix. 3–6; parts of xx. 2–17; xxiii. 20–23; xxxiv. 10–26), in which the author (or compiler) adopts a parenetic tone, and where his style displays what may be termed an approximation to the style of Deuteronomy; and these sections appear to have been the source from which the author of Deuteronomy adopted some of the expressions currently used by him."[6] Not, it will be observed, *borrowed* from Deuteronomy,—a proof, surely, of an early Deuteronomic type.

[1] *Genesis*, pp. 29–32.

[2] Cf. Colenso, *Pent.*, Pt. vi. pp. 4 ff.; and see on Law of Holiness below, Chap. IX. pp. 308 ff. On P phrases in Deuteronomy, see below, p. 277.

[3] Some older critics, as Stähelin, even attributed the composition of Deuteronomy to the Jehovist. De Wette writes of Deuteronomy: "By far the greater part belongs to one author, and, as it appears, to the Jehovistic, of which it has numerous characteristic marks."—*Introd.* ii. p. 131.

[4] Cf. Delitzsch above. Wellhausen—Dillmann also—explains the references by a "back-current" from Deuteronomy. But the Decalogue, whether provided with "enlargements" or not, must in its present form, as incorporated in the JE history, have been older than Deuteronomy (on critical date of that book). So with the Book of the Covenant.

[5] See above, p. 231; below, p. 276.

[6] *Deut.* pp. lxxvii–lxxviii; cf. pp. lxxxv–vi. Delitzsch also finds Deuteronomic traces occasionally in Genesis (*e.g.*, chap. xxvi. 5). Colenso

Still more interesting in this connection are certain passages in Joshua, Judges, and Samuel, described by Dr. Driver as "pre-Deuteronomic" (*i.e.*, pre-Josianic), and "allied to E," yet which have affinities in thought and expression to Deuteronomy.[1] And a last interesting and curious fact, as bearing on the alleged "modelling" on Deuteronomy, is that, if Dr. Driver is correct, the purity of the Deuteronomic revisers' style seems to *diminish* as we recede further in the history from the Mosaic age. It is, he tells us, most "strongly-marked" in Joshua and Judges, hardly appears in Samuel at all, is mingled with other forms of expression in Kings. "It is interesting to note," he observes, "what is on the whole an interesting accumulation of deviations from the original Deuteronomic type, till in, *e.g.*, 2 Kings xvii. it is mingled with phrases derived from the Book of Kings itself, Judges, and Jeremiah."[2] The inference we are disposed to draw from these facts is not quite that of the learned author. They appear to us to point to a much earlier dating and influence of Deuteronomy than he would allow.

III. Difficulties of Critical Theory on Age and Origin

We now approach the central problem of the *age* and *origin* of the book. Was the Book of Deuteronomy, as the critics, with nearly united voice, allege, a production of the age of Josiah, or of one of his immediate predecessors? If not, what were the circumstances of its origin? It is extremely important to observe that for most of the critics this question is already settled before they begin. Deuteronomy is universally allowed to presuppose, and to

finds the hand of the Deuteronomist traceable from Genesis to 2 Kings (*Pent.*, Pt. vi. p. 28). He finally finds 117 Deuteronomic verses in Genesis, 138½ in Exodus, and 156½ in Numbers (Pt. vii. pp. i–vi; App. pp. 145 ff.). Kuenen points out that Wellhausen approaches the positions of Stähelin and Colenso "when, from time to time, he notes a relationship between JE, *i.e.*, the redactor of the two works J and E, and the Book of Deuteronomy, and even asks whether JE may not have been revised by a deuteronomic redactor."—*Hex.* p. 137.

[1] *Ibid.* p. lxxxvi. Cf. *Introd.* pp. 106, 107, etc. Such passages are parts of Josh. xxiv. 1–26; Judg. vi. 7–10; x. 6–16; 1 Sam. ii. 17–36; parts of 1 Sam. vii.–viii.; x. 11–27, etc.

[2] *Ibid.* p. xcii.

be dependent on, the laws and history contained in JE, and, these writings being brought down by general consent to the ninth or eighth century B.C., a later date for Deuteronomy necessarily follows.[1] We decline to bind ourselves in starting by this or any similar assumption. It may well be that the result of the argument will rather be to push the date of JE farther back, than to make Deuteronomy late. Reasons for the late date are found in the narrative of the finding of "the book of the law" in 2 Kings xxii., in statements of Deuteronomy itself, and in the character of its laws, compared with the earlier code, and with the history.[2] It seems to us, on the other hand, that, under these very heads, insoluble difficulties arise, which really amount to a *disproof* of the critical theory. Reversing the usual procedure, it will be our aim, first, to set forth these difficulties which call for a revisal of the current view, then to weigh the force of the considerations adduced in its support.

1. Investigation naturally begins with the narrative of the *finding of "the book of the law"* in the eighteenth year of the reign of Josiah (B.C. 622), which criticism holds to be the first appearance of Deuteronomy. The story, in brief, is that, during repairs in the temple, Hilkiah the high priest found a book, identified and described by him as "the book of the law." He announced his discovery to Shaphan the scribe, who, after reading the book himself, presented and read it to the king. Josiah was extraordinarily moved by what he heard, confessed the guilt of the "fathers" in not hearkening to the words of this book, sent to inquire of Jehovah at the prophetess Huldah, finally, after the holding of a great assembly, and the renewal of the nation's covenant with God on the basis of the book, instituted and carried through the remarkable "reformation"

[1] "Of course," remarks Dr. Driver, "for those who admit this [viz., that JE is long subsequent to Moses], the post-Mosaic authorship of Deuteronomy follows at once; for, as was shown above, it is dependent upon, and consequently later than, JE."—*Deut.* p. xlii. Thus one part of the theory rules another.

[2] Dr. Driver again says: "As a work of the Mosaic age, Deuteronomy, I must own, though intelligible, if *it stood perfectly alone,—i.e.*, if the history of Israel had been other than it was,—does not seem to me intelligible, when read in the light shed upon it by other parts of the Old Testament."—*Ibid.* Pref. p. xii. This seems to show that it is the *history* (or view taken of it) which really decides the late date.

connected with his name.[1] There is no reason to doubt that the book which called forth this reformation, embraced, if it did not entirely consist of, the Book of Deuteronomy.[2] The critical theory, in its usual form, is, that the book was composed at or about this time, and was deposited in the temple, with the express design of bringing about just such a result. Is this credible or likely?

(1) Now, if anything is clear on the face of the narrative above summarised, it surely is, that this finding of the book of the law in the temple was regarded by everybody concerned as the *genuine discovery of an old lost book*, and *that* the "book of the law" of Moses. This is evident as well from the terms in which the book is described ("the book of the law,"[3] "the book of the covenant,"[4] "the law of Moses"[5]), as from the profound impression it produced on king and people, and from the covenant and reformation founded on it. Hilkiah, who announced its discovery in the words, "I have found the book of the law in the house of Jehovah,"[6] the king, who was vehemently distressed "because our fathers have not hearkened to the words of this book,"[7] Huldah the prophetess, who confirmed the threatenings of the book,[8] had no other idea of it. There is not a whisper of doubt regarding its genuineness from any side—from priests at the temple, whose revenues it seriously interfered with, from prophets, on many of whom it bore hardly less severely, from the people, whose mode of life and religious habits it revolutionised, from priests of the high places, whom it deposed, and whose worship it put down as a high crime against Jehovah. The critics

[1] 2 Kings xxii., xxiii.; cf. 2 Chron. xxxiv., xxxv. The credence accorded to this narrative in 2 Kings by the critics contrasts singularly with their free treatment of other parts of the later history of Kings, *e.g.*, the reforms of Hezekiah (2 Kings xviii. 4 ff.) questioned by Wellhausen, Stade, Smend, etc.), and the deliverance from Sennacherib (chap. xix.; cf. H. P. Smith, *O.T. Hist.* p. 245).

[2] The narrative in Kings generally does not require, though at points it suggests, more (*e.g.*, chap. xxiii. 21); the Chronicler's account of the great Passover implies the Mosaic ordinance.

[3] 2 Kings xxii. 8. [4] Chap. xxiii. 2. [5] Chap. xxiii. 24, 25.

[6] Chap. xxii. 8.

[7] Chap. xxii. 13; cf. Jer. xxxiv. 13 ff. Professor W. R. Smith could persuade himself that "it was of no consequence to him [Josiah] to know the exact date of the authorship of the book"—*O.T. in J. C.* Not its *exact date*, perhaps, but its antiquity?

[8] Chap. xxii. 16.

themselves do not dispute, but freely allow, that it was taken for a genuinely Mosaic book, and that it was this fact which gave it its authority. The last thing, we may be certain, that would enter the minds of Josiah or of those associated with him, was that the book which so greatly moved them was one newly composed by prophetic or priestly men of their own circles. This was a point, moreover, on which we may be sure that king and people would not be readily deceived. People at no time are easily deceived where their own interests or privileges are concerned, but in this case there were special difficulties. A new book, after all, does not look like an old one; and if high priest, scribe, king, prophetess, were misled into thinking that they were dealing with an old Mosaic book, when the parchment in their hands was one on which the ink was hardly dry, they must have been simpletons to a degree without parallel in history. On the other hand, assume the book to have been old, mouldy, defaced, and what are we to say of its recent origin? Did its authors, as Oettli asks, disfigure the book to make it look old?[1]

(2) To these objections, there is but one plain answer, if the Josianic origin of the book is to be upheld, and that is an answer which the more influential leaders of the new school do not hesitate to give—the book was a result of *pious fraud*, or of a deliberate intention to deceive. It was a "pseudograph"; in popular speech, a "forgery." This, without any disguise, is the view taken of the matter by Reuss, Graf, Kuenen, Wellhausen, Stade, Cornill, Cheyne, etc.,[2] as by Colenso,[3] and many older critics. Many believing scholars, to their credit, repudiate it, but their scruples are treated by the real masters of the school as the result of timidity and weak compromise. Yet, as Klostermann says, in criticising it, "What a swallowing of

[1] *Deut.* Introd. p. 19.

[2] One of Reuss' propositions (endorsed by Wellhausen) is: "Deuteronomy is the book which the priests *pretended* to have found in the temple in the time of Josiah."—Wellhausen, *Hist. of Israel*, p. 4. For the views of other scholars, see Note C on Deuteronomy as *Fraus Pia*.

[3] Colenso, who thinks it likely that Jeremiah was the *falsarius*, writes: "What it [the inner voice] ordered him to do, he would do without hesitation, as by direct command of God; and all considerations of morality or immorality would either not be entertained," etc. (*Pent.* Pop. edit. 1864, p. 201; cf. pp. 196 ff.).

camels is here!"[1] It is a view which, despite the excuse attempted to be made for it by talk about the "less strict" notions of truth in those days,[2] shocks the moral sense, and is not for a moment to be entertained of a circle to which the prophet Jeremiah, with his scathing denunciations of lying and deceit, and of the "false pen of the scribes" that "wrought falsely,"[3] belonged. Not that even on this supposition the difficulty of the transaction is removed. Hilkiah might be a party with prophets and priests in an intrigue to palm off a "book of the law" on the unsuspecting king;[4] but how should he be able to use such language to Shaphan as, "I have found *the* book of the law"? or how should Josiah speak of the disobedience of the "fathers" to commandments which he must have been aware were not known to them? Is it not apparent that, though "the book of the law" had long been neglected, disobeyed, and allowed to become practically a dead letter, men still knew of the existence of such a book, and had sufficient idea of its contents to be able to recognise it when this old temple copy, which had evidently been left to lie covered with its dust, one does not know how long, in some recess, was suddenly brought to light. It is nothing to the point to urge, in answer, that, had Deuteronomy existed earlier, there could not have been that long course of flagrant violation of its precepts which Josiah deplores. The whole condition of Jerusalem and Judah at this time, as described in 2 Kings xxiii., was in flagrant violation of far more fundamental statutes than that of the central sanctuary in Deuteronomy. Let one read, *e.g.*, the account of the state of things under Manasseh, or in Josiah's time, alongside of such a sentence as the following from Dr. Driver: "Now if there is one thing which (even upon the most strictly critical premises) is certain about Moses, it is that he laid the greatest stress upon Jehovah's being Israel's only God, who tolerated no other God beside Him, and who claimed to be the only object of the Israelite's

[1] *Pent.* p. 97.
[2] Kuenen, *Rel. of Israel*, ii. p. 19. See Note C.
[3] Jer. viii. 8; cf. chaps. v. 30, 31, vi. 3–8, etc. See below, p. 294.
[4] The extreme improbability of Hilkiah being a party to the forgery of a work which (on the theory) seriously infringed on the privileges of the Jerusalem priesthood, is pointed out by many writers (W. R. Smith, Dillmann, Kittel, Driver, etc.).

allegiance."[1] And are there no parallels in history, both to the condition of neglect into which the book of the law had fallen, and to the startling effect of the timely rediscovery of a book long forgotten?[2]

(3) In light of these facts, it is not a little singular that Dr. Driver, in repelling the charge that "if the critical view of Deuteronomy be correct, the book is a 'forgery,' the author of which sought to shelter himself under a great name, and to secure by a fiction recognition or authority for a number of laws 'invented' by himself"[3]—should not make it clearer than he does that this opinion—represented by him as a groundless "objection" of opponents—is, so far as the pseudographic character of the work is concerned, precisely and explicitly that of the heads of the school with which "the critical view" he defends is specially associated. It is the theory also, we cannot help agreeing, to which we are logically brought, if it is assumed that Deuteronomy is really a product of the age of Josiah, in which it was found.[4] Dr. Driver himself, however, and, as already said, most believing scholars, separate themselves from this obnoxious hypothesis of deceit, and, to explain the "discovery" of the book by Hilkiah, commonly suppose that it belongs to a somewhat *earlier* period[5]—*e.g.*, to the reign of Manasseh, or that of Hezekiah, or the age immediately *before* Hezekiah.[6]

[1] *Deut.* p. lix.

[2] The general neglect of the Scriptures in the age before the Reformation, and the effect on Luther's mind and work of the discovery of a complete copy of the Bible at Erfurt, offer a partial illustration. For a remarkable instance of the total oblivion of a noted code of laws in the Middle Ages, see Note D on Oblivion of Charlemagne's Code.

[3] *Deut.* p. lxi. Dr. Driver refers to the plot theory on p. liv. Even as regards "invention," it may be noticed that this was the view of De Wette, who first set the ball a-rolling. The book may be proved, De Wette thought, "to rest entirely on fiction, and indeed so much so that, while the preceding books amidst myths contained traditional data, here tradition does not seem in any instance to have supplied any materials."—*Beiträge*, ii. pp. 385 ff.; cf. i. p. 268.

[4] Cf. Kittel, *Hist. of Hebrews*, i. pp. 64 ff.

[5] Dr. Driver says that "the narrative of the discovery certainly supports the view that the book which was found was one which had been lost for some time, not one which had just been written" (p. liv). His own mind leans to an origin in the *childhood* of Josiah. But does this answer to the idea of a book "lost" for some time, and, apart from fraud, what would be the appearance of such a book?

[6] So Ewald, Bleek, W. R. Smith, Kittel, Kautzsch, etc. (Manasseh); Delitzsch, Riehm, Westphal, Oettli, König, Klostermann, etc. (Hezekiah or before).

The moral qualms which lead to these theories are to be respected, but those who adopt them now labour under the disadvantage that, having cut themselves away from the age of Josiah, they have no fixed principle to go by, and, apart from *a priori* assumptions in regard to the course of development, there is no particular reason why they should stop where they do, and not carry the date of Deuteronomy much higher still. They find themselves exposed also to the attacks of the advocates of the Josiah date, who point out the unsuitability of Deuteronomy to Manasseh's gloomy reign ("the calm and hopeful spirit which the author displays, and the absence even of any covert allusion to the special troubles of Manasseh's reign"[1]); but, above all, urge what Kuenen calls "the great, and in my opinion fatal objection," "that it makes the actual reformation the work of those who had not planned it, but were blind tools in the service of the unknown projector."[2] It would, indeed, be strange procedure on the part of anyone composing a work in the spirit of Moses, yet not desiring to pass it off as other than his own, to deposit it secretly in the temple, there to lie undiscovered for perhaps a century—finally, in the irony of history, on its coming to light, to be accepted as a work of Moses, and continuously regarded as such by the Jewish and Christian world for over two millenniums! "Fatal" objections thus seem to lie at the door of all these hypotheses, and we are driven to ask whether some other explanation is not imperative.

(4) It may be added that the critics are seriously at variance on another point, viz., whether the author of Deuteronomy in Josiah's—or an earlier—age is to be sought for among the *prophets* or the *priests*. It seems a curious question to ask, after starting with the view that Deuteronomy was a "prophetic" programme; yet it is one of no small importance in its bearings on origin, and the reasons against *either* view, on the critical premises, seem extremely strong. If a prophet, why, unlike the practice of other prophets, did he adopt this device of clothing his message in the form of addresses of Moses,

[1] *Deut.* p. liii.

[2] *Hex.* p. 219. Kuenen adds: "The *rôle* assigned to D himself is almost equally improbable; for he is made to commit his aspirations to writing, urge their realisation with intense fervour—and leave the result to chance (p. 220). Cf. Carpenter, *Hex.* i. pp. 96–97.

and whence the strength of his interest in the sanctuary, its worship, and its feasts? As Kuenen, who favours the view of the *priestly* origin, points out: "It is obvious from Deut. xxiv. 8, and still more from chaps. xvii. 18, xxxi. 9, that the Deuteronomist had relations with the priesthood of Jerusalem. In chap. xiv. 3–21 he even incorporates a priestly *torah* on clean and unclean animals into his book of law."[1] But then, on the other hand, if a priest, how account for the remodelling of the older laws in a direction inimical to the prerogatives of the Jerusalem priesthood?[2] The last thing one would look for from a priest would be the concocting of ordinances which meant the sharing of his temple perquisites with all Levites who chose to claim them. The idea, again, of a *joint* composition by prophets and priests is not favoured by the conditions of the age, and is opposed to the unity of style and spirit in the book. This apparent conflict of interests, so difficult to harmonise with the time of Josiah, seems to point to an origin far nearer the fountainhead.

2. The next natural branch of inquiry relates to *the testimony of the book itself* as to the circumstances of its own origin. To the ordinary reader it might seem as if no doubt whatever could rest on this point. The book would appear in the most explicit fashion to claim for itself a Mosaic origin. Not only are the discourses it contains affirmed to have been delivered by Moses in the *Arabah* of Moab—this *might* be accounted for by literary impersonation—but at the close there are express attestations that Moses *wrote* his law, and delivered it into the custody of the priests for safe preservation. "And Moses wrote this law," we read, "and delivered it unto the priests, the sons of Levi. . . . When Moses had made an end of writing the words of this law in a book, until they were finished, Moses commanded the Levites, which bare the ark of the covenant of Jehovah, saying, Take this book of the law, and put it by the side of the ark," etc.[3] In view of these declarations, one does not well know what to make of the remarkable statement of Dr. Driver that, "though it may appear paradoxical to say

[1] *Hex.* p. 273. It is to be remembered that Hilkiah was a priest.

[2] Cf. Kautzsch, in criticism of this view, *Lit. of O.T.*, pp. 64–65.

[3] Deut. xxxi. 9, 24–26. The Song and the Blessing of Moses are also said to be from Moses—the former to have been written by him (chaps. xxxi. 22, xxxiii. 1).

so, *Deuteronomy does not claim to be written by Moses.*"[1] The paradox Dr. Driver defends is, at all events, not one accepted by the leaders of the critical school, who lay stress upon the fact that the writer obviously *intended* his book to be received as genuinely Mosaic, and in that way sought to gain authority for its teachings.[2] It was undoubtedly as a genuine work of Moses—subject, of course, to any necessary revisional processes—that it was received by Josiah and his contemporaries.

There is, however, the possibility of a mediating view, which must in justice be taken account of, though it is not one, it seems to us, which greatly helps the newer critics. First, we should say, as respects the *scope* of the above testimony, we entirely agree that the words, "Moses wrote this law," cannot, in the connection in which they stand, be fairly extended, as has sometimes been attempted, to cover the whole Pentateuch.[3] On the other hand, we see no fitness or probability in confining them, with Delitzsch[4] and many others, to the "kernel" of the Mosaic law in chaps. xii.–xxvi. The word *torah* must be taken here in its widest sense as covering the hortatory and admonitory parts of the book, not less than its strictly legal portions.[5] The godly of later times, who found their souls' nourishment and delight in

[1] *Introd.* p. 89. The fact that the above statements are made in the third person does not alter their purport. Dillmann's explanation of the notice of authorship is singularly roundabout and lame. "The statement," he says, "is satisfactorily explained by the fact that the writer was convinced of the antiquity and Mosaic character of the law [represented as] expounded by Moses, and it was precisely for one who wished to give out the old Mosaic law in a renewed form that an express statement of the writing down and preservation of that law was indispensable."—*Num.–Jos.* p. 601. "Indispensable" to assert that as a fact which existed nowhere but in his own imagination!

[2] De Wette says: "The author of Deuteronomy, as it appears, would have us regard his whole book as the work of Moses."—*Introd.* ii. p. 159. Cornill instances Deuteronomy as "an instructive proof that only under the name of Moses did a later writer believe himself able to reckon on a hearing as a religious lawgiver."—*Einleit.* p. 37.

[3] Thus Hengstenberg, Hävernick, etc.

[4] *Genesis*, i. pp. 36–37.

[5] Cf. chap. i. 5: "began Moses to declare this law." There is little force in the objection drawn from the command to write the law on plastered stones on Mount Ebal (Deut. xxvii. 3). The recently discovered Code of Hammurabi shows what was possible to ancient times in the way of writing on stones. It is stated by Dr. Green that "the famous Behistun inscription of Darius in its triple form is twice as long as this entire Code (Chaps. xii.–xxvi.), besides being carved in bold characters on the solid rock, and in a position difficult of access on the mountain side."—*Moses and Prophets*, p. 53

the "law of Jehovah" (cf. Pss. i., xix. 7 ff., cxix., etc.), had, we may be sure, other material before them than the bare legal precepts of either the Deuteronomic or the Priestly Code.[1] The notice can only fairly be understood as meaning that Moses put in writing, and delivered to the priests, the substance, if not the letter, of what he had just been saying; and such a statement, once and again repeated in the book (cf. in addition to the above, chap. xvii. 18), must, for those who recognise its honesty of intent, always have the greatest weight. But, this being granted, the question remains whether the words "this law" necessarily apply to the discourses *precisely as we have them, i.e.*, in their present literary form. Assuming that Moses, as Delitzsch conjectures, "before his departure left behind with the priestly order an autograph *torah* to be preserved and disseminated,"[2] may we not reasonably suppose that, in the book as we possess it, we have, not a literal transcription of that *torah*, but a "free literary reproduction" of its contents, in the form best adapted for general instruction and edification, with occasional developments and modifications suited to the time of its origin? So again Delitzsch and not a few others think. "The Deuteronomian," he says, "has completely appropriated the thoughts and language of Moses, and from a genuine oneness of mind with him reproduces them in the highest intensity of divine inspiration."[3]

There will be little doubt, we think, as to the *admissibility* of this "reproduction" theory, if the circumstances are shown to require it. It implies no purpose to deceive, and stands on a different footing from theories which, under the name "development," assume the attribution to Moses of ideas, laws, and institutions, not only unknown to him, but, if the critical hypothesis is correct, actually in conflict with his genuine legislation. Perhaps, also, in a modified degree,

[1] See below, pp. 376–77. [2] *Genesis*, i. p. 35.

[3] *Ibid.* Cf. also art. in Luthardt's *Zeitschrift*, 1880, pp. 503–5. For related views, cf. Oettli, *Deut.* Introd. pp. 16–18; Ladd's *Doct. of Sac. Scripture*, i. p. 527–29; Robertson, *Early Religion*, etc., pp. 420–25. Dr. Driver approximates to this view. "Deuteronomy," he says, "may be described as the *prophetic reformulation, and adaptation to new needs, of an older legislation.* It is probable that there was a tradition, if not a written record, of a final legislative address delivered by Moses in the steppes of Moab; the plan followed by the author would rest upon a more obvious motive, if he thus worked upon a traditional basis" (p. lxi). This too much ignores the strong *positive* testimony that Moses *did* write his last discourses.

some recasting in form and language, in the sense of this hypothesis, *must* be admitted, if we suppose—what is very probable—that the script which Moses used was other than the ancient Hebrew, or grant that the discourses were written out rather in substance than in full detail—leaving it to the transcriber or interpreter to fill out, and give the living impression of scene and voice. If this was done (as we believe it must have been) when the remembrance or tradition of Moses and his time was still vivid and reliable, it would give us a book such as we have in Deuteronomy. On the other hand, if so much is admitted about Moses, the question which must always recur regarding this theory, even to the very limited extent indicated, is—*Cui bono?* If, as Delitzsch supposes, the contents of Deuteronomy are *substantially* Mosaic,—if Moses really delivered testamentary discourses, and in some form wrote them down for posterity,—whence the necessity for this literary "double" to re-write and improve them? Why should the form in which Moses spoke and wrote them not be substantially that in which we have them? Shall we suppose that the actual discourses were less grand and sustained in style—less tender, glowing, and eloquent—than those we possess,—that they contained less recitation of God's dealings,[1] less expostulation, exhortation, and affectionate appeal,—or were less impressive in their counsels and warnings? Or that Moses, when he came to write them down—"till they were finished," says the text—was not able to make as noble and powerful a record of them as any inspired man of a later date? We, at least, have a less mean idea of Moses, the man of God, and of his literary capabilities. We have a full and vivid picture of him, and specimens of his style of thought and pleading, in the history; we can judge of his lofty gifts, if the Ode at the Red Sea, or the Song in Deuteronomy,[2] are from his pen; and we may well believe that, of all men living, he was the one most capable of giving worthy literary form to his own addresses.[3] If the book, in substance, is from Moses, very

[1] If so, what dealings? Those in the JE history? It is to be remembered that, wherever we place Deuteronomy, the JE history, in substance at least, stands behind it.

[2] Nothing necessitates us," says Delitzsch, "to deny the Song to Moses."—Luthardt's *Zeitschrift*, 1880, p. 506; cf. *Genesis*, i. p. 45.

[3] "In presence," says Delitzsch, "of the Egyptian and Babylonian-Assyrian written monuments, which likewise contain great connected

cogent reasons must be shown for putting it, even in its literary form, at a much later date.

In reality, however, so far as critics of the newer time are concerned, such a hypothesis as we have been considering is wholly in the air. Possessed of quite other ideas of what *must* have been, these writers will hardly entertain even the possibility, either of Moses having written these discourses, or of his being able to write them. For them the Mosaic age is literally, as Duhm says, "wiped out."[1] Underlying their refusal of Deuteronomy to Moses will generally be found the denial that we know anything definitely at all about Moses, or of his literary capabilities. or that he delivered any testamentary discourses, or that any of the laws or institutions ordinarily attributed to him —even the Ten Commandments—are actually of his age.[2] In that case, Delitzsch's hypothesis, with other mediating views, falls, and we are brought back essentially to the old alternative. The thorough-paced critic will have nothing to say to a hypothetical or traditionary basis for a book admitted to belong in its present shape to the age of the kings.[3] Kuenen will allow no alternative between "authenticity" and "literary fiction."[4]

3. When, finally, from the external attestation, we turn to the *internal character* of the book—and it is here the strength of the critical position is held to lie—we find a series of phenomena which, so far from supporting, throw very great, if not insuperable, obstacles in the way of its ascription to the age of Josiah. On these the minifying end of the critical telescope is persistently turned, while the

oratorical pieces, and represent a form of speech which remained essentially the same during 1000 years, one need not be disturbed by the high antiquity of a written production of Moses."—Luthardt's *Zeitschrift*, 1880, p. 506. See his testimony to Moses as a poet in *Genesis*, i. pp. 44–45.

[1] *Theol. d. Proph.* p. 19. See below, p. 286.

[2] It is not advanced writers alone that fall into this arbitrary style of reasoning. Such a reason, *e.g.*, as that assigned even by a believing critic like Riehm for refusing the Deuteronomic discourses to Moses—"the spiritual apprehension of the law, as seen in the demand for a circumcision of the heart" (*Einleit.* i. pp. 245–46)—belongs to the same *a priori*, subjective system of judging of a past age, which scientific investigation is increasingly discrediting.

[3] "The opinion," said De Wette long ago, "that these latter passages (Deut. xxxi. 9, etc.) refer to a short treatise which has been worked over in Deuteronomy is quite arbitrary."—*Introd.* ii. p. 159.

[4] *Hex.* p. 219.

magnifying end is brought to bear in its full power on any difficulties that seem to tell against an earlier date. We have to remember that the book, on the critical view, was composed with the express design of calling into being such a reformation as that which followed its "discovery" in the reign of Josiah.[1] The proof of its origin in that age is held to be its suitability to the conditions of the time, and the stress it lays on the demand for centralisation of worship. When, however, we open the book itself, we are forcibly struck by the *absence* of clear evidence of any such design on the part of the author, and by the numerous indications of *un*suitability to the age in which it is believed to have been composed. The book and the history, in a word, do not fit each other.

(1) It is extremely doubtful if "centralisation of worship," in the critical acceptation of that phrase, was *the dominant motive* in Josiah's reformation at all. The idea of the unlawfulness of worship—even of Jehovah—on high places need not have been absent; it had, we believe, been in the background of men's minds ever since the founding of Solomon's temple. But it was not that which so strangely moved Josiah to alarm and action. His reformation from beginning to end was a crusade against the *idolatry* which had everywhere infected Church and state—central sanctuary included,[2]—and the "high places" were put down as part of this stern suppression of *all* idolatrous and heathenish practices. Of a movement for unity of worship as such the narrative gives not a single hint. On the other hand, when we look to Deuteronomy, we find little or nothing that points directly to a consuming zeal against the "high places"—in Josiah's time the crying sin, because the chief centres of idolatry, in Judah. There are warnings against falling into the idolatries and other abominations of the *Canaanites*, when the land should be possessed,[3] and in chaps. vii. 5, 25, xii. 2–4, injunctions to "utterly destroy" the sanctuaries, altars, pillars, Asherahs, and graven images of these former inhabitants. But there is nothing peculiarly

[1] "It was not by accident," Kuenen says, "but in accordance with the writer's deliberate purpose, that it became the foundation and norm of Josiah's reformation."—*Hex.* p. 215. Cf. Wellhausen, ***Hist. of Israel***, p. 33.

[2] Cf. 2 Kings xxiii. 4, 7, 11, 12, etc.

[3] Cf. especially chap. xviii. 9 ff.

Josianic in this—it is all there already in the older Book of the Covenant.[1] Still further, while Deuteronomy gives prominence to the idea of the centralisation of worship at the sanctuary, it is far from correct to say that this is the dominating idea of the book—the one grand idea which inspires it.[2] It has its place in chap. xii., and recurs in the regulations for feasts, tithing, and priestly duty; but the *preceding* discourses have nothing to say of it, and in the Code it appears with a multitude of other laws, some of them more fundamental than itself. The bulk of the laws in the book, as will appear below, are taken from the Book of the Covenant; others are from a priestly source yet to be investigated.

(2) Here already is a puzzling problem for the critics—to account for the relevancy of this wide range of laws, many of them dealing with seemingly trivial matters, in a book assumed to be specially composed to effect a reformation in *worship*.[3] The irrelevancy of the greater number of the precepts for such a purpose is obvious at a glance. But the incongruity of the Code in structure and contents with the supposed occasion of its origin appears in other respects. The most favourable view of the book is that it is a *corpus* of old laws reproduced in a hortatory setting with special adaptation to the circumstances of a late time. Yet in

[1] Ex. xx. 3 ff.; xxii. 18, 20; xxiii. 13, 24, 32, 33; cf. xxxiv. 14–17. The exception is the sun, moon, and "host of heaven" in Deut. iv. 19, xvii. 3, founded on by Riehm (i. p. 245) and others. But the worship of sun, moon, and other heavenly bodies goes far back beyond Moses, and is alluded to in the Old Testament long before the time of Josiah (Isa. xvii. 8, R.V.; Amos v. 26). Cf. Beth-shemesh in Josh. xv. 10, etc.

[2] Oettli says: "It rests on an unusual onesidedness in the mode of consideration, if, as now mostly happens, the aim of Deuteronomy is restricted to the centralisation of the cultus, and the ordinances of worship connected with this. That is one of its demands, but it is neither the most original nor the weightiest, but only an outcome of its deepening of the thought of the covenant."—*Deut.* Introd. p. 21.

[3] This is in fact made the starting-point by the newer critics for their hypothesis of "gradual accretion." "There is no apparent appropriateness," we read, "so far as the programme of the Deuteronomic reforms is concerned, in the historical retrospect, i. 6–iii. But neither is there, for example, in the laws which regulate birds'-nesting or parapets upon a roof in xxii. 6–8. With what feelings [one may well ask it] could Josiah have listened to these details? . . . It is plain that the contents of the Code, at least in its later portions, are very miscellaneous."—Carpenter, *Hex.* i. p. 93. But then, instead of recasting the theory of "programmes" which thus has the bottom taken out of it, the law-book of Josiah is reduced practically to chaps. xii.–xix. (p. 95).

int of form everything is thrown back into the age of oses. The standpoint of the speaker is the East of Jordan,[1] ith the prospect of the people's immediately entering naan; Israel is treated *in its unbroken unity as a nation* all Israel"), and there is not a hint anywhere of the great vision that, centuries before Josiah's time, had rent the ngdom into twain, and had ended in the destruction of e of its branches (Ephraim). What is even more remark- le, the laws frequently are, not only long obsolete, but of character ludicrously out of place in a reforming Code of e end of the seventh century. We need not dwell at ngth on these anachronisms of the Code, which have been often pointed out,[2]—the law, *e.g.*, for the extermination the Canaanites,[3] when no Canaanites remained to be terminated; the injunction to destroy the Amalekites;[4] e rules for military service (inapplicable to the later ne),[5] for besieging of foreign cities,[6] for arrangements in e camp;[7] the warnings against choosing a foreigner for a ng, and causing to return to Egypt,[8] the friendly tone wards Edom,[9] so strangely in contrast with the hostile irit of the prophets;[10] and the like. These things may em as the small dust of the balance to the critic,[11] but ey may not appear so insignificant to others. Dr. river's answer, that the injunctions against the Canaanites d Amalekites are repeated from the older legislation, and n a recapitulation of Mosaic principles addressed *ex pothesi* to the people when they were about to enter naan, would be naturally included,"[12] only corroborates

[1] On the expression "the other side Jordan," see below, p. 281.
[2] Cf. Delitzsch, *Genesis*, p. 38; Oettli, *Deut.* Introd. pp. 11, 12, 17 ff.
[3] Chaps. vii. 1, 2, xx. 10–18.
[4] Chap. xxv. 17–19. Dr. Green speaks of these injunctions as being as terly out of date as would be at the present day "a royal proclamation in eat Britain ordering the expulsion of the Danes."—*Moses and the Prophets*, 63.
[5] Chap. xx. 1–9.
[6] Chap. xx. 9–15, 19, 20.
[7] Chap. xxiii. 2–9. Imagine these provisions in a Code seven centuries er Moses.
[8] Chap. xvii. 15–16. See Note E on the Law of the King.
[9] Chap. xxiii. 7, 8.
[10] Jer. xlix. 17, 18; Obadiah; Joel iii. 19; Isa. lxiii. 1–6.
[11] Cf. Kuenen, *Hex.* pp. 218–19. Kuenen has no difficulty, because he nkly attributes to the author the design to deceive.
[12] *Deut.* p. lxii. Dr. Driver's suggestion that the injunctions against the naanites would have an *indirect* value as a protest against heathenish actices in Judah is without support in the text, which evidently

our point, that they were suitable to the times of Moses, but not to those of Josiah. The difficulty is not touched why a writer in that age should go out of his way to includ them, when they did not bear on his purpose, and had n relevancy to existing conditions. But even in the matte of reformation of worship, it is important to observe tha the laws in Deuteronomy were not of a kind that could be or were, enforced by Josiah in their integrity. In the Code e.g., it is ordained that idolaters of every degree, with all wh secretly or openly entice to idolatry, are to be unsparingl put to death.[1] Josiah, it is true, slew the priests of th high places of Samaria upon their altars. But he did no attempt any such drastic measures in Judah. He brough up, instead, the priests of the high places to Jerusalem, an allowed them to "eat of the unleavened bread among thei brethren."[2] It is one of the most singular instances o the reading of a preconceived theory into a plain text, whe in face of the law ordaining death for all idolatry, thes "disestablished priests" of the high places are regarded a the Levites of Deut. xviii. 8, for whom provision is mad out of the temple dues.[3] Of course, there is not a syllabl hinting at "disestablished priests" of the high places in th provisions of Deuteronomy for the Levites. The latte besides, were permitted to minister at the sanctuary, whi Josiah's priests were not.

IV. Critical Reasons for Late Dating of the Book: Validity of these

It is now incumbent on us, having indicated th difficulties which seem to us decisive against a late datin of Deuteronomy, to consider the reasons ordinarily adduce in favour of that late dating, or at least of the origin of th book in times long posterior to Moses. We have alread seen that, of those who reject the substantially Mosa

means them to be taken quite seriously, and does not apply to t Amalekites, etc.

[1] Deut. xiii. [2] 2 Kings xxiii. 9.

[3] Thus Dr. Driver connects—as if it were a matter of course—De xviii. 8 with "Josiah's provision made for the support of the disestablish priests out of the temple dues."—*Deut.* p. xlv. Cf. Wellhausen: "He [t Deuteronomist] provides for the priests of the suppressed sanctuarie etc.—*Hist. of Israel*, p. 33.

origin of the book, a *few* place the book earlier than Hezekiah, *some* put it in the reign of Manasseh, *most* put it in the reign of Josiah. It may be found that several, at least, of the reasons for this late dating turn, on examination, into arguments for the opposite view.

It cannot be too constantly borne in mind, what was before said, that, with the majority of critics of the Graf-Wellhausen school, the really determining grounds for the late dating of Deuteronomy lie outside the region of properly critical discussion altogether, viz., in the completely altered view taken of the age of Moses, and of the subsequent course of the religious history of Israel. If the accounts we have of Moses and his work are, as Kuenen says, "utterly unhistorical,"—if it is inconceivable that he should have had the elevated conceptions or the prophetic foresight attributed to him in these discourses,—then it needs no further argument to prove that Deuteronomy must be late. The date of Deuteronomy is, in this case, no longer *merely* a literary question, and the critics are not wrong in speaking of it, as they have sometimes done, as the pivot of the Pentateuchal question. It does not, indeed, follow, as we formerly sought to show, that the Mosaic history and religion are subverted, even if a late date is accepted for the present form of the book. But very important conclusions certainly *do* follow, if the book is admitted to be early. If Deuteronomy, in its present form, be even *substantially* Mosaic,—if it conveys to us with fidelity the purport of discourses and laws actually delivered by Moses to the people of Israel before his death,—then we must go a great deal further. For Deuteronomy undeniably rests in some degree on the JE history embodied in our Pentateuch; on the Code of laws which we call the Book of the Covenant, incorporated in that history; as well as on priestly laws from some other source. The effect of the acceptance of an early date for Deuteronomy, therefore, is to throw all these writings back practically into the Mosaic age, whatever the time when they were finally put together. We should like to be more sure than we are that it is not the perception of this fact which is at least one motive in leading the critics to put down Deuteronomy as far as they do, in the age of the kings.

1. It is important, in this connection, to observe how

much is *conceded* by the more moderate advocates of the critical hypothesis themselves. These concessions are very considerable—so extensive, in fact, that they really amount in our view, to the giving up of a large part of the critical case for the late dating. We have seen how Delitzsch postulates written "testamentary discourses" and laws of Moses; but critics like Oettli and Driver also go a long way in allowing, in the words of the latter,[1] "a continuous Mosaic tradition," reaching back to Moses' own time, and "embracing a moral, a ceremonial, and a civil element." When particularly, the object is to vindicate Deuteronomy against the charge of "forgery" and "invention," stress is strongly laid on the fact that the great bulk of the legislation is old and that the few laws which are really new are but "the logical and consistent development of Mosaic principles." So far, indeed, is this insistence on the antiquity and genuinely Mosaic character of the legislation carried—in striking and favourable contrast with the more radical tendency to deny *all* legislation to Moses—that one begins to wonder where the contradictions with earlier law and practice come in which are to prove indubitably that the book *cannot* be Mosaic. Thus we are bid remember "that what is essentially new in Deuteronomy is not the *matter* but the *form*."[3] Dillmann is quoted as testifying that "Deuteronomy is anything but an original law-book." "The new element in Deuteronomy," it is said, "is not the laws, but their *parenetic* setting. . . . [The author's] aim was to win obedience to laws, or truths, which were already known, but were in danger of being forgotten."[5] "It was felt to be (in the main) merely the re-affirmation of laws and usages which had been long familiar to the nation though in particular cases they might have fallen into neglect."[6] Most significant of all is a sentence quoted from Reuss: "The only real innovation . . . was the absolute prohibition of worship outside of Jerusalem."[7]

Here at length we seem to come to a definite issue. The "only real innovation" in Deuteronomy is *the law of the central sanctuary*. We are not unjustified, therefore, in

[1] *Deut.* p. lvii. Cf. Oettli, *Deut.* Introd. pp. 17, 18. Delitzsch may be quoted again: "The claim of Deuteronomy to a Mosaic origin is justified on internal grounds."—Luthardt's *Zeitschrift*, 1880, p. 503; cf. p. 504.

[2] *Ibid.* p. lvi. [3] *Ibid.* [4] *Ibid.*

[5] *Ibid.* p. lxi. [6] *Ibid.* p. lvi. [7] *Ibid.*

egarding this as the *fundamental pillar* which upholds the ase for the late dating of Deuteronomy. Even this aw, moreover, it is conceded, is only "relatively" new; it vas a genuine development from Mosaic principles, and ocalising of tendencies which had long been in operation.[1] 'he natural inference one would draw from this is, that it annot be *really* incompatible with the law in Ex. xx. 24, vith its supposed permission of unlimited freedom of vorship.[2] The subject was discussed in an earlier chapter, o which it is sufficient here to refer.[3] The conclusion there rrived at was that there is nothing in this Deuteronomic aw essentially at variance with the altar-law in Exodus, or vith the later religious practice, if allowance is made for imes of religious backsliding and neglect, and for the omplete disorganisation of an age like Samuel's, when cclesiastical and every other kind of laws were necessarily n large part in abeyance. One fact which should lead riticism to pause before giving too narrow an interpretation f the law is that, as before noted, in Deuteronomy itself a ommand is given for the building of an altar for sacrifice n Mount Ebal, in harmony with the law in Exodus.[4] We narked also a tendency in the newer criticism itself to break vith the Wellhausen "dogma" of an absolute centralisation f worship in Deuteronomy, and a consequent conflict with he older law in Exodus.[5]

2. If this fundamental prop of the Wellhausen theory ives way, as we are persuaded it does, most of the *other* con- iderations adduced in favour of the late date of Deuteronomy nay fairly be treated as of subordinate importance. They esolve themselves, partly into alleged discrepancies between he Deuteronomic *laws* and those of the Book of the Covenant, and of the Levitical Code; partly into alleged

[1] *Deut.* p. lvi.

[2] See above, pp. 173 ff.

[3] Chap. VI. pp. 173 ff.

[4] Deut. xxvii. 5–7.

[5] See above, Chap. VI. pp. 174, 176. Fries, in his *Moderne Vorstellungen ler Geschichte Israels*, speaks of this "dogma" as playing well-nigh the same art in the Wellhausen criticism as did formerly "the opposition between ewish and Pauline Christianity in the school of Baur in the New Testa- nent domain" (p. 15); and Van Hoonacker, in his *Le Sacerdoce Lévitique*, ays: "The whole historical and critical system of the school of Wellhausen ests in effect on the pretended first promulgation of the principle of the nity of the sanctuary in the seventh century" (p. 14). This writer points ut that the unity of the sanctuary is not so much enacted as *presupposed* n Deuteronomy (p. 13).

discrepancies with the *history* of the preceding books; and partly into a few *expressions* in the book thought to imply a later date than that of Moses. On none of these classes of objection will it be found necessary to spend much time; a few typical examples may be examined.

(1) The subject of *laws* may be glanced at first. In a previous chapter we endeavoured to show that there is nothing in Deuteronomy necessarily incompatible with the Aaronic priesthood and Levitical arrangements of the middle books of the Pentateuch[1]—arrangements now held, however, by the critical school to be *later* than Deuteronomy; and we shall see as we proceed that, while it was no part of the design of the speaker in these farewell addresses to dwell on details of ritual, chiefly of interest to the priests, yet Levitical regulations are presupposed, and in some instances are referred to, in his recital.[2] As to the Book of the Covenant, it is allowed on all hands that the bulk of its provisions are taken up, and reiterated and enforced in the discourses.[3] In such hortatory recapitulation, where much is left to be understood by the hearer, points of difficulty in comparison with other Codes may be expected to arise; but, considering the number of the laws, the seeming discrepancies must be pronounced very few. In some cases it may be that we do not possess all the elements for a complete solution, but there is no reason to suppose that, if we had them, a solution would not be forthcoming.

A chief example of discrepancy between Deuteronomy and the Priestly Code—*the* chief, perhaps, after that of the priests and Levites[4]—is in the tithe-laws in chaps. xii. 6, 17–19, xiv. 22–29, xxvi. 12–15, which certainly present a different aspect from those in Num. xviii. 21–31.[5] In the latter case the tithe is devoted in fixed proportions to the maintenance of Levites and priests; in the former, it is used by the worshippers for two years out of three in

[1] Cf. Chap. VI. pp. 180 ff.

[2] See below, pp. 311 ff. On the relation of Deuteronomy to the so-called "Law of Holiness," see next chapter.

[3] Lists of comparison of the laws in the Book of the Covenant and in Deuteronomy may be seen in Driver (*Deut.* pp. iv ff.), Westphal, Oettli, or any of the text-books.

[4] See above, pp. 184 ff.

[5] Cf. on the discrepancy, Kuenen, *Hex.* pp. 28, 29; Driver, *Deut.* pp. 168 ff.

easts at the sanctuary, to which the Levites are invited, and n the third year is given up wholly, at home, to the evites, orphans, widows, and strangers. Apart, however, om the fact that the Levitical provision seems clearly ndeed, verbally) referred to in chap. xviii. 1, 2,[1] it appears, better solution does not offer,[2] a not unreasonable explanation that, in accordance with later Jewish practice, the estal tithe of Deuteronomy is different from, and additional o, the ordinary tithe for the maintenance of the Levites (a second tithe").[3] We may perhaps venture the suggestion hat it is really this Deuteronomic tithe which was the old nd traditional one, and the Levitical tithe which was the econd and additional impost. The tithe devoted to ehovah probably goes back in pious circles to remotest imes (cf. Gen. xiv. 20; xxviii. 22), and then can only be upposed to have been used in a religious feast, or in charity. 'his was the old and well-understood voluntary tithe; the evitical had a different object. But if the Deuteronomic ithe creates difficulty, what is to be said of the countertheory of the critics? Is it really to be credited—for this s the alternative supposition—that a tithe-law for the naintenance of the Levites, unknown in the days of Josiah, irst came in with Ezra, yet, though previously unheard of, was unmurmuringly submitted to by everybody as a law iven in the wilderness by Moses?[4]

Minor examples of discrepancies, as those which relate o firstlings (chap. xv. 19, 20; cf. Num. xviii. 17, 18), to riestly dues (chap. xviii. 3, 4), to the treatment of bond-

[1] See above, p. 187.

[2] Van Hoonacker has here an ingenious, but, as it seems to us, untenable heory, based on the expression in Deut. xxvi. 12, "the third year, which s the year of tithing," compared with Amos iv. 4, that the Levitical tithe of Num. xviii. was not an annual, but a *triennial* one, and that the yearly estal tithe of Deuteronomy was a secondary and less strict taxing of produce, which only improperly got the name tithe (*Le Sacerdoce*, pp. 384 ff.).

[3] Thus in Tob. i. 7; Josephus, *Antiq.* iv. 8. 22; LXX in Deut. xxvi. 12. The explanation does not remove all difficulties, especially the absence of allusion to the primary tithe. It is to be noticed, however, that the speaker is here evidently alluding to a custom already established, not (as Dr. Driver has it), instituting a second tithe for the first time.

[4] See below, pp. 296, 319. Seeing that in Deuteronomy also the tribe of Levi is set aside for sacred service, and has therefore no inheritance with the other tribes, is it conceivable that no provision should be made for the tribe but these rare feasts at the sanctuary, or every third year? Does chap. xviii 1, 2 not suggest a different view?

servants (chap. xv. 12; cf. Ex. xxi. 1–6), to the law of carrion (chap. xiv. 21; cf. Lev. xvii. 15), seem capable of reasonable explanation.[1] A few modifications on older laws are made in view of the altered circumstances of settlement in Canaan, notably the permission to kill and eat flesh at home (Deut. xii. 15), in room of the wilderness requirement that all slaying for food should be at the door of the tabernacle (cf. Lev. xvii. 3 ff.).

(2) There are alleged, next, certain *historical* discrepancies, some of them, we cannot but think, instructive examples of that *Widerspruchsjägerei*—"hunting for contradictions"—which Delitzsch not unjustly ascribes to the school of Wellhausen.[2] The opponents of the unity of Deuteronomy find numerous inconsistencies in the different parts of the book itself (*e.g.*, between chaps. v.–xi. and xii.–xxvi., or between chaps. i.–iv. and v.–xxvi.); but these the critical *defenders* of the unity find means of satisfactorily explaining.[3] A slight extension of the same skill, we are persuaded, would enable them to dispose as satisfactorily of most of the others. On the general relation to the preceding history it is agreed on all hands that the retrospects in Deuteronomy presuppose the narratives of JE, and reproduce them with substantial fidelity.[4] The Wellhausen school, in accordance with its principles, denies any similar dependence on the P sections of the history;[5] but this it is difficult to maintain in view of the considerable number of references to particulars, and turns of expression, found only in P. Only in P., *e.g.*, is there mention of Moses and Aaron being debarred from Canaan as a punishment;[6] of "seventy" as the number who went down to Egypt;[7] of "twelve" as the number of the

[1] See Note E on Minor Discrepancies in Laws.

[2] Luthardt's *Zeitschrift*, 1880, p. 623.

[3] Cf. Kuenen (against Wellhausen), *Hex.* pp. 113 ff.; Driver, *Deut.* pp. lxviii ff. etc.

[4] Driver represents the general view in saying that Deuteronomy "is demonstrably dependent upon JE" (p. xix; cf. p. xv). Some assume a closer dependence on E than on J, but this depends on what is attributed to E, and what to J. Westphal, *e.g.*, as before noticed, gives the Book of the Covenant to J; Dillmann and Kuenen give it to E. Dillmann, on the other hand, gives the story of the golden calf (Ex. xxxii.) to J; Westphal and others give it to E.

[5] *Ibid.* p. xvi.

[6] Num. xx. 12; xxvii. 13 ff.; Deut. xxxii. 50 ff. Cf. Deut. i. 37; iii. 26; iv. 21.

[7] Gen. xlvi. 27; Ex. i. 5. Cf. Deut. x. 22.

pies;[1] of the making of the ark of acacia wood.[2] The vords, "Since the day that God created man upon the arth," in chap. iv. 32, seem a verbal reference to Gen. i. 26, 27; and there are numerous phraseological assonances with P in this fourth chapter,—"belonging usually to P," says Carpenter,—"suggesting occasional contact with the school hat produced P,"[3]—and later, as "horses and chariots," hard bondage," "stretched-out arm," etc. (only in P).[4] In o case, however, is there slavish dependence on the letter of the history.[5] The speaker deals with his materials with he freedom and intimate knowledge of one who had been a chief actor in the events he recounts; amplifies, abbreviates supplies fresh details; groups according to subject rather han time; passes by swift association to related topics. It s this which in a few instances gives rise to the appearance of what the critics are pleased to call "contradictions." Instead of telling against the genuineness of the book, they constitute, to our mind, one of the most convincing internal evidences of its genuineness. For what later composer, with the JE history before him, would have allowed himself hese freedoms, or have wilfully laid himself open to the charge of "contradiction" of his sources?[6]

But what, taken at their utmost, do these "contradictions" amount to? We shall glance at a few of the chief cases. It is to be borne in mind that the question here is not, whether Moses wrote personally the JE or P sections of the Pentateuch, but whether there is such contradiction with these as to forbid us ascribing the discourses in Deuteronomy to Moses as their speaker. We do not disprove, *e.g.*, the Mosaic character of the discourses by

[1] Num. xiii. 2–10. Cf. Deut. i. 23. See below, p. 279.

[2] Ex. xxxvii. 1. Cf. Deut. x. 3. The critical view is that JE also had a story of the making of the ark.

[3] *Hex.* ii. p. 254.

[4] Deut. xi. 4; xxvi. 6 (cf. Ex. i. 14); iv. 34, etc. Cf. Driver, *Deut.* pp. xvii, lxxi.

[5] Graf concludes from the freedom of reproduction that the author draws from oral tradition and not from written sources. *Geschicht. Bücher*, p. 13.

[6] Unless, indeed, the reader is prepared to accept for the Deuteronomist the patronising apology of Colenso: "He treats them [the statements of the older narrative] often with great freedom, and sometimes in a way which shows that, though generally familiar with that document, he was not so thoroughly at home with it as a devout English reader of the Pentateuch would be."—*Pent.* Pt. vi. p. 27.

showing, *e.g.*, that the P sections are not directly, or at all, from Moses' pen.

A first instance of discrepancy is, that in Deuteronomy (i. 9 ff.) Moses reminds the people how, with their consent, he appointed judges over them; in Ex. xviii. we are told that this plan was originally suggested to Moses by Jethro. We submit that there is not here the shadow of a real difficulty? Can it be supposed that the composer of the book, whoever he was, imagined that there was any conflict? Yet this is one of two "discrepancies" which Dr. Driver allows "are not absolutely incompatible"[1] with Moses' authorship. The other is, that in Deuteronomy (i. 22, 23) the people *ask* that spies be sent to search the land, while in Num. xiii. 1 (P), Jehovah gives the *order* for the mission. "Not *absolutely* incompatible"!

As an example of a discrepancy held to be *irreconcilable* with Mosaic authorship, we take the passages relating to Jehovah's anger against Moses, and the prohibition to enter Canaan. "In Num. xx. 12 (cf. xxvii. 13 ff.; Deut. xxxii. 50 ff.)," we are told, "Moses is prohibited to enter Canaan on account of his presumption in striking the rock at Kadesh, in the thirty-ninth year of the Exodus; here (Deut. i. 37, 38; iii. 26; iv. 21), the ground of the prohibition is Jehovah's anger with him *on account of the people*, upon an occasion which is plainly fixed by the context for the second year of the Exodus, thirty-seven years previously."[2] We invite the reader to compare carefully the passages, and judge for himself whether there is any real basis for this assertion. In three places in his address, Moses refers to his exclusion from Canaan, and in one of them tells of his pleading with Jehovah (fixed in the fortieth year, chap. iii. 23) to have the sentence reversed. The narrative of this exclusion is given at length in Numbers, with the rebellion of the people that led to it, and the permission to view the land alluded to in Deut. iii. 27 (cf. Num. xxvii. 12, 13). It is surely only the hyper-acute sense of a critic that can see in the words "for your sakes," which evidently refer to the provocation of the people that occasioned the offence of Moses (Num. xx. 2 ff.), a "contradiction" of the statement that he, with Aaron, personally sinned at Meribah (Num. xx. 10); while the assertion that the

[1] *Deut.* p. xxxvii.

[2] *Ibid.* p. xxxv.

incident is "plainly fixed" in Deut. i. 37 in the second year of the Exodus is a "plain" misreading of the text. Moses is speaking in the context of the exclusion of that older generation from Canaan, and by a natural association he alludes in passing to how the rebellious spirit of the living generation had brought a similar sentence of exclusion on himself. The discourses are full of such rapid transitions, determined not by chronology, but by the connection of the thought. Cf., *e.g.*, chap. i. 9, where the discourse turns back to events a year before the command in ver. 6; chap. ii. 1, 2, where there is a leap over thirty-seven or thirty-eight years; chaps. ix., x., where x. 1 resumes, with the words "at that time," the transactions at Horeb, left far behind in chap. ix. 22 ff.

The mission of the spies, alluded to above, is itself a fruitful source of "contradictions," occasioned, however, mainly by the merciless way in which the narrative in Numbers is torn up.[1] The incident will be examined in detail in a future chapter;[2] only the main point, therefore, need be anticipated here. Deuteronomy, it is said, following JE, knows nothing of Joshua as one of the spies, and represents the search party, in contrast with P, as proceeding only as far as Eshcol (chap. i. 24, 25). Yet Deuteronomy knows of the choosing of "twelve" spies, "one of a tribe," as in Num. xiii. 2 (P), where Joshua is included in the list (ver. 8); and the statement in Deut. i. 38 that Joshua (as well as Caleb, ver. 36) would enter the land, connects most naturally with the promise given in Num. xiv. 30.[3] If the letter in JE is pressed to mean that Caleb only was to enter the land, it would seem to exclude Joshua, not only from the number of the spies, but from Canaan, which cannot be the meaning. In the JE narrative also it is clearly implied, as will be afterwards

[1] The critical analysis of Num. xiii.–xiv. certainly results in a mass of contradictions (see below, pp. 356 ff.). Addis says of the JE parts: "Attempts have been made to separate the component documents. . . . But the task seems to be hopeless, and there is nothing like agreement in results."—*Hex.* i. p. 165.

[2] Cf. Chap. X. pp. 356 ff.

[3] Dillmann and Kittel take Joshua to be included among the spies in the J narrative, but not in the E narrative—a distinction that falls, if JE are one, and at any rate is an acknowledgment of the inclusion of Joshua in the combined JE story. Cf. Dillmann, *Num.–Jos.* p. 69, and on Num. xxvi. 65; xxxii. 12, pp. 177, 195; Kittel, *Hist. of Hebs.* p. 201. See below, p. 357.

seen, that the spies, or some of them (for there surely wer *several* parties; they did not all march in a body), wer through the whole land (Num. xiii. 28, 29).

The last-named instance is one of several involving th question of the possibility of an acquaintance of Deutero nomy with the P history. The denial of such acquaintanc is founded in part on the mention of Dathan and Abiram and the silence about Korah, in chap. xi. 6.[1] Here, it i concluded, the mention of Korah is omitted because h had no place in the JE narration. This, however, w would point out, does not necessarily follow. Apart fro the question of "sources" in Num. xvi., it is evident tha in the combined uprising there narrated, Dathan an Abiram represented the general spirit of murmuring i the congregation (vers. 12–15), while Korah stood for th Levites, in their aspiration after the privileges of the priest hood (vers. 8–11). This of itself is sufficient reason why Mose in his address to the people, should refer only to the former.

A more definite "contradiction"—likewise implicate with intricate questions of analysis—is in the brief notic of Aaron's death, and of the journeyings of the people i chap. x. 6, 7, as compared with the notice in the list o stations in Num. xxxiii. In Deuteronomy, Aaron is state to have died at Moserah, while his death is placed i Numbers (ver. 38) at Mount Hor; in Deuteronomy, fou stations are mentioned in the journeyings (Bene-Jaakan Moserah, Gudgodah, Jotbathah), but in Numbers (vers 31, 32) the first two are named in inverse order. Moserah however, as we discover from comparison, was in th immediate neighbourhood of Hor, and there is evidenc in the list in Numbers itself that after wandering southward to Eziongeber, at the Red Sea, and turning again north wards, the people returned in the fortieth year from Kadesh to the district of Mount Hor, where Aaron died (vers. 35–39 cf. Num. xx.). The old camping spots would then be revisited, as stated in Deuteronomy. The mention o these places may thus be regarded rather as an un

[1] On this incident, see below, pp. 358–9.

[2] It must be allowed that great suspicion attaches to the clause—"o Korah, Dathan, and Abiram"—in Num. xvi. 24, 27, in the connection i which it stands with *mishkan* (dwelling), which everywhere else in thes narratives is the designation of the tabernacle (not of an ordinary tent) Cf. Strack, *in loc.*

esigned corroboration of the accuracy of the list in Numbers.[1]

Finally, a word should perhaps be said on the alleged contradiction" between the law in Ex. xxi. 12–14, nd the Deuteronomic appointment of three cities of efuge (chap. iv. 41–43; cf. xix. 1 ff.). The asylum in the lder law, Wellhausen argues, is the altar; now "in order ot to abolish the right of asylum along with altars [mark he change to the plural], he [the Deuteronomist] appoints pecial cities of refuge for the innocent who are pursued y the avenger of blood."[2] It is a little difficult to understand how anyone could hope to persuade the people of osiah's age that three cities of refuge had been appointed y Moses (three more afterwards) when, *ex hypothesi*, they new perfectly well that up to their day no such cities xisted. The whole objection, however, is largely a creation f the critic's fancy, as shown by the fact that the future ppointment of a place of refuge for the manslayer is rovided for in the very law of Exodus to which appeal is nade (chap. xxi. 13).

3. For the above reasons we cannot allow that a case as been made out on the ground of discrepancies in laws nd history for denying the Deuteronomic discourses to the reat lawgiver with whose name they are connected. When these are set aside, there remain as proofs of post-Mosaic origin chiefly incidental expressions, as "other side f (or beyond) Jordan," "unto this day," and the like. The first of these expressions—"other side of Jordan"—s much relied on, as showing that the standpoint of the uthor of the book was the *Western* side of Jordan.[3] If we ave not hitherto taken notice of this favourite argument, t is principally because, after the fairest consideration we

[1] The supposition that, according to JE, the Israelites stuck immovably ike limpets on a rock to Kadesh for thirty-eight years, is against common ense, and can only be made out by tearing the narrative to pieces. Even then, he command to the Israelites in JE, "Turn ye, and get you into the vilderness by the way of the Red Sea" (Num. xiv. 25), implies intervening vanderings, as in Num. xxxiii. In the beginning of the fortieth year (not he third, as Bleek), the Israelites are found again at Kadesh (chap. xx. 1; f. Dillmann, *in loc.*). Criticism rejects the thirty-eight years' wanderings, but n contradiction to *all* the sources, J E D P. Cf. Kittel's remarks, *Hist. of Hebs.* i. pp. 231–32.

[2] *Hist. of Israel*, p. 33; cf. W. R. Smith, *O.T. in J. C.*, p. 354.

[3] Cf. Driver, *Deut.* pp. xlii ff.

have been able to give it, it seems to us to have extremely little force. So far as the expression occurs in the frame work of the book (*e.g.*, chap. i. 1, 5), it occasions littl difficulty, but it may appear to be different when it is foun in the discourses themselves. It does occur there, but (a also in the framework) with an application both to th *Eastern* (chap. iii. 8), and, more commonly, to the *Wester* (chaps. iii. 20, 25; xi. 30), sides of the Jordan.[1] Very generall there is some determinative clause attached, to show whic side is meant—"beyond Jordan, toward the sunrising" (cha iv. 41, 46), "eastward" (ver. 49), "behind the way of th going down of the sun" (chap. xi. 30), etc. It is most natura to conclude that the phrase "beyond Jordan" was a curren geographical designation for the Moabite side of the river but that, along with this, there went a local usage, deter mined by the position of the speaker.[2] Far more reasonabl may we argue from the minute and serious care of the write in his geographical and chronological notices in the intro duction to the discourses and elsewhere, that he means hi book to be taken as a genuine record of the last utterance of the lawgiver.

It may be serviceable at this stage to sum up th conclusions to which the discussions in this chapter hav conducted us.

1. The discovery of "the book of the law" in Josiah' day was a genuine discovery, and the book then found wa already old.

2. The age of Manasseh was unsuitable for the com position of Deuteronomy, and there is no evidence of it composition in that age. The ideas of Deuteronomy n

[1] Num. xxxii. 19 is a remarkable case of the use of the phrase in bot senses in a single verse. Dr. Driver explains the passage, not very con vincingly, by an "idiom"; and accounts for Deut. iii. 20, 25 by the assume position of the speaker, which, he thinks, by a lapse, is forgotten in ver. 8 where the *real* situation is betrayed. We may, however, pretty safely clea the writer of Deuteronomy from the suspicion of such unconscious "be trayals" of his position.

[2] When Dr. Driver says: "It is of course conceivable that this was habit of the Canaanites, but it can hardly be considered likely that th usage suggested by it passed from them to the Israelites, before the latte had set foot in the land," etc. (p. xliii), he seems to forget that the father of the Israelites had lived for at least two centuries in Canaan, and that th traditions and hopes of the people were all bound up with it (cf. their word for "West," etc.).

doubt lay behind Hezekiah's reformation, but there is no evidence of the presence of the book, or of its composition, at or about that time. Had it been newly composed, or then appeared for the first time, we should have expected it to make a sensation, as it did afterwards in the time of Josiah The question also would again arise as to its Mosaic claim, and the acknowledgment of this by Hezekiah and his circle.

3. From Hezekiah upwards till at least the time of the Judges, or the immediately post-Mosaic age, there is no period to which the composition of the book can suitably be referred, nor is there any evidence of its composition in that interval. Traces of its use may be thought to be found in the revision of Joshua, in speeches like those of Solomon (1 Kings viii.), in Amaziah's action (2 Kings xiv. 5, 6), and in allusions in the early prophets.[1] But this we do not at present urge.

4. The book definitely gives itself out as a reproduction of the speeches which Moses delivered in the *Arabah* of Moab before his death, and expressly declares that Moses wrote his addresses ("this law"), and gave the book into custody of the priests.

5. The internal character of the book, in its Mosaic standpoint, its absence of reference to the division of the kingdom, and the archaic and obsolete character of many of its laws, supports the claim to a high antiquity and a Mosaic origin.

6. The supposition that Deuteronomy is "a free reproduction," or elaboration, of written addresses left by Moses, by one who has fully entered into his spirit, and continues his work, while not inadmissible, if the facts are shown to require it, is unnecessary, and, in view of the actual character of the book, not probable. The literary gifts of Moses were amply adequate to the writing of his own discourses in their present form. This is not to deny editorial revision and annotation.

7. There are no conclusive reasons in the character of the laws or of the historical retrospects for denying the authorship of the discourses, in this sense, to Moses.

8. It seems implied in Deut. xxxi. 9, 24–26, that Deuteronomy originally subsisted as a separate book. It may have done so for a longer or shorter period, and separate copies may have continued to circulate, even after its union

[1] See below, pp. 323 ff.

with the other parts of the Pentateuch.[1] It was probably a separate authentic copy which was deposited in the temple, and was found there by Hilkiah.

9. It is *possible*, as some have thought, that the JE Pentateuchal history may originally have contained a brief account of the testamentary discourses of Moses, and of his death (cf. the fragment, chap. xxxi. 14, 15, 23). This would be superseded when Deuteronomy was united with the rest of the Pentateuch.

10. The historical laws and narratives which Deuteronomy presupposes must, in some form, have existed earlier than the present book, if not earlier than the delivery of the discourses. These also, therefore, are pushed back, in essentials, into the Mosaic age. They need not, however, have been then completed, or put together in their present shape; or may only have furnished the basis for our present narratives.

The relation of Deuteronomy to the Priestly Writing has yet to be considered.

NOTE.—*Steuernagel's Theory of Deuteronomy*: A word should perhaps be said on the novel theory of Deuteronomy expounded by C. Steuernagel in his work, *Deuteronomium und Josua* (1900). Discarding, with much else (as the dependence of Deuteronomy on the Book of the Covenant), the view of a division of the Book into hortatory and legal portions, Steuernagel contends for a division, as it were transversely, into sections, distinguished respectively by the use of the singular ("thou," "thy," etc.) and the plural ("ye," "your," etc.) numbers (Sg and Pl). These sections (Pl being itself highly composite) were united in the pre-Josianic period, and subsequently underwent extensive enlargements and redactional changes. It is difficult not to regard this theory as another instance of misplaced ingenuity. The use of singular and plural affords no sufficient ground for distinguishing different authors. The nation addressed as "thou" was also a "ye," and there is a free transition throughout from the one mode of speech to the other, often within the limits of the same verse or paragraph (cf., *e.g.*, Deut. i. 31; iv. 10, 11; 25, 26; 34–36; vi. 1–3; 17, 18; viii. 1, 2; 19, 20; ix. 7; xi. 12, 13, etc.).

[1] See below, p. 376.

CHAPTER IX

Difficulties and Perplexities of the Critical Hypothesis: The Priestly Writing. I. The Code

"Nothing in fact is simpler than the Grafian hypothesis: it needs only the transference of *a single source*—the collection of laws named commonly the *Grundschrift*, by others the Book of Origins, the Writing of the Older Elohist, or of the Annalist, which we would call the *Book of Priestly Law* or *Religion*—into the post-exilian time, into the period of Ezra and Nehemiah, and at one stroke the 'Mosaic' period is wiped out."—DUHM.

"I have specially drawn attention to the fact that one result of these criticisms must inevitably be that, for all those who are convinced of the substantial truth of the above results, the whole ritualistic system, as a system of divine institution, comes at once to the ground. . . . The whole support of this system is struck away, when it is once ascertained that the Levitical legislation of the Pentateuch is entirely the product of a very late age, a mere figment of the post-captivity priesthood."—COLENSO.

"But, if we place at the head of their whole history [the Hebrew nation's] a great positive act of the will, a legislation by which the natural development is forestalled, and its course prescribed, we account for the rise of that discrepancy [the sense of guilt, consciousness of departure from the known will of God] and the peculiar tone of the national character among the Hebrews."—DE WETTE (against VATKE).

"But again the questioning spirit revives when one is asked to believe that Moses is partly at least a historic figure. Alas! how gladly would one believe it! But where are the historical elements? . . . No one can now be found to doubt that Sargon is a historical personage with mythic accretions. But can one really venture to say the like of Moses?"—CHEYNE.

CHAPTER IX

DIFFICULTIES AND PERPLEXITIES OF THE CRITICAL HYPOTHESIS: THE PRIESTLY WRITING. I. THE CODE

It was indicated in our sketch of the critical development that the greatest revolution in Pentateuchal criticism up to the present has been the acceptance by the majority of scholars of the Graf-Wellhausen contention that the legislation of the middle books of the Pentateuch, instead of being, as was formerly all but universally supposed, the oldest, is in reality the very youngest of the constituent elements in that composite work—not, as it professes to be, a creation of the work of Moses, but a production of priestly scribes in exilian and post-exilian times. Up to the appearance of Graf's work on *The Historical Books of the Old Testament* in 1866, as was then pointed out, though earlier writers like Von Bohlen, George, and Vatke had advocated the idea, and Reuss, Graf's teacher, had been inculcating it in his class-room at Strassburg,[1] the hypothesis of a post-exilian origin of the law had met with no general acceptance. De Wette repudiated it;[2] Bleek declared it to be "decidedly false to hold with Vater, Von Bohlen, Vatke, and George, that Deuteronomy, with the laws it contains, is older than the foregoing books with their legislation";[3] even Kuenen, in 1861, pronounced its grounds to be "not worthy of refutation."[4] Since the publication of Graf's book, the tide has

[1] On Reuss, see below, p. 288.

[2] *Introd.* ii. p. 143. Similarly Ewald.

[3] *Com. on Deut.*, Introd. p. 107.

[4] See quotation from Kuenen in full in Note A. Nearly the only writer who seems to have had a glimpse into the possibilities of George's view was Hengstenberg, who wrote: "The view maintained by De Wette, that Deuteronomy was the latest of all, the topstone of the mythical structure, which at one time seemed to have won universal acceptance, begins now to yield to the exactly opposite opinion, that Deuteronomy is the most ancient

decisively turned, and the previously rejected theory has now become the dominant (though by no means the universally-accepted) hypothesis among critical scholars.

There are many reasons, apart from the skill and plausibility with which its case has been presented, which account for the fascination of this theory for minds that have already yielded assent to the previous critical developments. It is not without justice, as we shall by and by see, that the claim is made for the Wellhausen hypothesis that it is the logical outcome of the whole critical movement of last century. A chief value of the theory is that, by the very startlingness of its conclusions, it compels a halt, and summons to a reconsideration of the long course by which its results have been reached.

I. Graf-Wellhausen Theory of the Priestly Code

We shall best begin by sketching more fully than has yet been done the Graf-Wellhausen position. The problem relates, as said, to the age and character of that large body of laws found in Exodus, Leviticus, and Numbers, which forms the kernel of the writing described by the critics as the Priestly Code. Whereas formerly this Levitical legislation was held to be at least older than Deuteronomy, and probably in its main parts Mosaic,[1] the newer theory supposes it to be the work of scribes in the exile, or after. It is not, indeed, contended, as we shall find, that everything in the Code was absolutely the creation of that time.[2] There had been, of course, a temple, priesthood, religious institutions, sacrificial ritual, priestly rules and *technique.* Still the law, as elaborated in the exile, was practically a new thing. What belonged to the practice of a previous age was taken up, transformed, had a new meaning put into it, was brought under new leading ideas, was developed and

among all the books of the Pentateuch."—*Gen. of Pent.* i. p. 58 (he refers to George's work).

[1] Thus, *e.g.*, Bleek, *Introd.* i. pp. 212 ff.

[2] Cf. Graf, as above, p. 93; Kuenen, *Rel. of Israel*, ii. pp. 96, 192. (But see below, p. 291.) Reuss, on this point, does not go so far as some of his successors. He says: "It is self-evident that the existence of a Levitical tradition in relation to ritual, as early as the days of the kings, cannot be denied; we cannot speak, however, of a written, official, and sacred codex of this kind."—*Geschichte der Heil. Schriften A.T.* i. p. 81 (in Ladd, i. p. 530). See below, pp. 300 ff.

enlarged by new rites and institutions. Above all, in order to clothe it with a Mosaic character, and secure for it the necessary authority, old and new alike were thrown back into the age of Moses and the wilderness, and were represented as originating and being put into force there. This Mosaic dress was a fiction. The elaborate descriptions of the tabernacle and its arrangements, the dispositions of the camp in the wilderness, the accounts of the consecration of Aaron and his sons, of the choice and setting apart of the Levites, of the origin of the passover, etc.—all was a "product of imagination."[1]

The idea of the Code was not wholly original. The first conception and sketch of a Priestly Code was in Ezekiel's vision of the restored temple in the closing chapters of his book.[2] The scheme of the scribes, however, was not that of Ezekiel, but was independently wrought out. A chief feature borrowed from the prophet's programme was the idea of the Levites as a class of temple servants subordinate to the priests. It will be seen below[3] how, in Ezek. xliv., the law is laid down that the priests who had gone astray into idolatry were to be degraded from their priestly office, and made servants in the sanctuary. Only the Zadokites, who had remained faithful, were to retain their priestly dignity. This, according to the theory, is the origin of the class of Levites. The priests thus degraded were, it is contended, the "disestablished priests" of the high places, for whom some sort of provision had to be made. We are called to trace here a development. Deuteronomy had, it is alleged, allowed such "disestablished priests" the full rights of priesthood when they came up to the temple; Ezekiel degrades them to the rank known afterwards as Levites: now the Priests' Code gives them a permanent standing in the sanctuary, and represents them as always having had this secondary position, and as having been originally honourably set apart by Jehovah for His service in the wilderness. The Israelites being thus organised as a hierarchy—"the clergy the skeleton, the high priest the head, and the tabernacle the heart"[4]—liberal provision is

[1] Cf. Kuenen, *Rel. of Israel*, ii. pp. 171, etc.

[2] Ezek. xl. etc.

[3] See below, pp. 315 ff.

[4] Wellhausen, *Hist. of Israel*, p. 127. Cf. p. 8: "The Mosaic theocracy, with the tabernacle at its centre, the high priest at its head, the priests and Levites as its organs, the legitimate cultus as its popular function."

made for the sacred body. Tithes, hitherto unknown for such a purpose, are appointed for the support of the priests and Levites, and the priestly revenues are otherwise greatly enlarged. Forty-eight cities, with pasturages,[1] are—only, of course, on paper—set apart for the Levitical order. The sacrificial system, now centralised in the tabernacle, is enlarged, and recast in its provisions. Sin- and trespass-offerings (the sin-offering is held by Wellhausen to appear first in Ezekiel)[2] are introduced; a cycle of feasts is established, with new historical meanings; an annual day of atonement—previously unheard of—is instituted. Sacrifice loses its older joyous character, and becomes an affair of the priesthood—a ritual of atonement, with associations of gloom.[3]

Still better to facilitate the introduction of this novel scheme, a *history* is invented to suit it. In its preparatory part in Genesis, this history goes back to the creation, and is marked in the patriarchal period by the rigid exclusion of all sacrifices;[4] in the Mosaic part, there is the freest indulgence in the invention of incidents, lists, genealogies, numbers, etc. All this, if we accept Wellhausen's view, was, some time before the coming of Ezra to Jerusalem in 458 B.C., put together in Babylon; was afterwards combined with the previously existing JE and D, which knew nothing of such legislation, and indeed in a multitude of ways contradicted it; finally, in 444 B.C., as related in Neh. viii., was produced and read by Ezra to the people, was accepted by them, and became thenceforth the foundation of post-exilic religion. Precisely at this crucial point, however, a serious divergence of opinion reveals itself in the school. According to Wellhausen, it was the *completed Pentateuch*, substantially, that was brought by Ezra to Jerusalem, and read by him to the people;[5] according to perhaps the majority of his followers, it was only the *Priests' Code* that was then made known, and the combination with JE and D

[1] The Levitical cities are held by Wellhausen to be a transformation of the old *bamoth* or high places.—*Ibid.* pp. 37–38, 162.

[2] *Ibid.* p. 75.

[3] *Ibid.* p. 81: "No greater contrast could be conceived than the monotonous seriousness of the so-called Mosaic worship." Delitzsch and others have shown the groundlessness of this allegation.

[4] See above, p. 156.

[5] "Substantially at least Ezra's law-book must be regarded as practically identical with our Pentateuch."—*Ibid.* p. 497. Cf. p. 404.

did not take place till later, after new redactions and developments of the Code.[1] Wellhausen, who retains his opinion, argues convincingly that the narrative (cf. Neh. ix.) clearly requires that the book should be the whole Pentateuch;[2] the others as triumphantly ask how Codes of laws, which *ex hypothesi* were in flat contradiction of each other, could simultaneously be brought forward with any hope of acceptance! We agree that neither set of critics succeeds in answering the others' reasons.

Such, in barest outline, is the nature of the scheme which is to take the place of the "traditional" view of the Mosaic origin of the Levitical legislation. It will, we venture to predict, be to future generations one of the greatest psychological puzzles of history how such a hypothesis, loaded, as we believe it to be, with external and internal incredibilities, should have gained the remarkable ascendency it has over so many able minds. It is a singular tribute to the genius of Wellhausen that he should have been able to secure this wide acceptance for his theory, and to make that appear to his contemporaries as the highest wisdom which nearly all his predecessors scouted as the extreme of folly. His feat is hardly second to that of Ezra himself, who, on this new showing, succeeded in imposing on his generation the belief that a complex system of laws and institutions had been given by Moses, and had been in operation since the days of that lawgiver, though, till the moment of his own promulgation, nothing had been heard of them by anyone present![3]

[1] For a sketch of these supposed developments after 444 B.C., cf. Kuenen, *Hex.* pp. 302 ff.; Professor W. Robertson Smith, *O.T. in J. C.*, Note F. Professor Smith differs again in thinking that "the Priestly Code has far too many points of contact with the actual situation at Jerusalem, and the actual usage of the second temple [?], to lend plausibility to the view that it was an abstract system evolved in Babylonia, by someone who was remote from the contemporary movement at Jerusalem; but, on the other hand, its author must have stood . . . outside the petty local entanglements that hampered the Judæan priests" (pp. 448–49). He holds that to conjecture "that Ezra was himself the author of the Priests' Code is to step into a region of purely arbitrary guesswork" (p. 449). Thus the theories eat up each other.

[2] Professor H. P. Smith gets rid of Ezra and the narrative altogether. Cf. below, p. 295.

[3] "They were not," says Kuenen, "laws which had been long in existence, and which were now proclaimed afresh and accepted by the people, after having been forgotten for a while. The priestly ordinances were made known and imposed upon the Jewish nation *now for the first time*. As we have

II. Initial Incredibilities of the Theory

There are, it seems to us, *three huge incredibilities* which attach to this theory of the origin of the Levitical legislation, and to these, at the outset, as illustrative of the difficulties in which the modern criticism involves itself, we would refer.

1. There is no mistaking in this case the serious nature of the *moral* issue. In the case of "the book of the law" brought to light in Josiah's reign, there is at least always open the assumption of a literary artifice which involved no dishonest intention on the part of the writer. Here, on the other hand, there can be no evading of the meaning of the transaction. What we have is the deliberate construction of an elaborate Code of laws with the express design of passing it off upon the people in the name of Moses. It is not a sufficient reply to urge that much in the law was simply the codification of pre-exilian usage. A codification of ancient law—if that were all that was meant—even though it involved some degree of re-editing and expansion, is a process to which no one could reasonably take exception, provided it were proved that it had actually taken place.[1] But though this notion is, as we shall see, a good deal played with, the Wellhausen theory is assuredly not fairly represented, when, with a view to turn the edge of an objection, it is spoken of as mainly a work of "codification." The very essence of the theory, as Kuenen and Wellhausen expound it, is, that in all that gives the Priestly Code its distinctive character, it is something entirely new.[2] There never, *e.g.*, existed such an ark or tabernacle as the Code describes with minute precision. The tabernacle is

seen, no written ritual legislation yet existed in Ezekiel's time," etc.—*Rel of Israel*, ii. p. 231. Cf. Wellhausen, *Hist. of Israel*, p. 408.

[1] Few of the critics of the Wellhausen hypothesis object, within reasonable limits, to a theory of codification, but treat it as a question of evidence. Cf. Robertson's *Early Religion of Israel*, p. 394. It already goes beyond codification when the object is to stamp pre-existing usage with a divine sanction.

[2] According to Wellhausen, the Code was not only not in operation, but "it did not even admit of being carried into effect in the conditions that prevailed previous to the exile."—*Hist. of Israel*, p. 12. "The idea that the Priests' Code was extant before the exile," says Kautzsch, "could only be maintained on the assumption that no man knew of it, not even the spiritual leaders of the people, such as the priests Jeremiah and Ezekiel."—*Lit. of O.T.*, p. 116.

a pure fiction, obtained by halving the dimensions of the temple, and making it portable.[1] There never was a choice of Aaron and his sons to be priests, or a separation of the Levites to be ministers to the priests. There never was a tithe system for the support of priests and Levites; there never were Levitical cities; there never were sin- and trespass-offerings, or a day of atonement, such as the Code prescribes; there never were feasts having the historical origin and reference assigned to them in the law. These institutions were not only not Mosaic, but they never existed at all; and *the constructors of this Code knew it*, for they were themselves the inventors. This cannot be evaded by saying, as is sometimes done, that it was a well-recognised custom to attribute all new legislation to Moses. For first, apart from the singular problem which this raises for the critics who attribute *no* laws to Moses, such a custom simply did not exist;[2] and, second, this is not a case of mere literary convention, but one of serious intention, with a view to gaining a real advantage by the use of the law-giver's authority. The nearest parallel, perhaps, that suggests itself is the promulgation in Europe in the ninth century of our era of the great collection of spurious documents known as the Isidorian Decretals, carrying back the loftiest claims of the mediæval Papacy to apostolic men of the first century. No one hesitates to speak of these spurious decretals, which gained acceptance, and were for long incorporated in the Canon law, by their rightful name of "forgeries."[3] Can we help giving the same designation to the handiwork of these exilian constructors of a pseudo-Mosaic Code?[4] It is futile to speak, in excuse, of the

[1] See above, pp. 165 ff.

[2] *E.g.*, Ezekiel did not attribute his laws to Moses; the Chronicler did not attribute the elaborate ordinances in 1 Chron. xxiii. to Moses but to David; Ezra and Nehemiah themselves did not attribute their modified arrangements to Moses. Circumcision was not attributed to Moses, etc. We do not know of any laws being attributed to Moses which were not *believed* to be Mosaic.

[3] Hallam says of these in his *Middle Ages*: "Upon these spurious decretals was built the great fabric of papal supremacy over the different national Churches; a fabric which has stood after its foundation crumbled beneath it; for no one has pretended to deny, for the last two centuries, that the imposture is too palpable for any but the most ignorant ages to credit" (*Student's Hallam*, p. 295).

[4] "Such procedure," says Riehm, "would have to be called a fraud."—*Einleit.* i. p. 217.

different standards of literary honesty in those days. It is not overstepping the mark to say, as before, that men like Jeremiah, Ezekiel, and Ezra, were as capable of distinguishing between truth and falsehood, as conscious of the sin of deceit, as zealous for the honour of God, as incapable of employing lying lips, or a lying pen, in the service of Jehovah, as any of our critics to-day.[1] We simply cannot conceive of these men as entering into such a conspiracy, or taking part in such a fraud, as the Wellhausen theory supposes. For it was undeniably as genuine Mosaic ordinances that it was meant to pass off these laws upon the people. Let only the effect be imagined had Ezra interpolated his reading with the occasional explanation that this or that principal ordinance, given forth by him as a law of Moses in the wilderness, was really a private concoction of some unknown priest in Babylon—perchance his own!

2. Besides the moral, there confronts us, in the second place, a *historical* incredibility. We do not dwell on the peculiar taste of these exilian scribes, of whose very existence, it must be remembered, we have not a morsel of evidence, who, out of their own heads, occupied themselves with tireless ingenuity in elaborating these details of tabernacle, encampments, and ceremonial, planning new laws, festivals, and regulations for imaginary situations—devising everything with such care, and surrounding it with so perfect an air of the wilderness, that, as Wellhausen owns,[2] no trace of the real date by any chance shines through. Neither do we dwell on the singular unity of mind which must have pervaded their ranks to enable them to concert so well-compacted and coherent a scheme as, on any showing, the Levitical law is.[3] We shall assume that some peculiarly constituted minds might delight in evolving these fanciful things, and might even, at a sufficient distance of time, get their romance by mistake accepted as history.

[1] See above, p. 259. Cf. Jer. viii. 8; xiv. 14; xxiii. 32; Ezek. xiii. 6, 7, 19, etc.

[2] "It tries hard to imitate the costume of the Mosaic period and, with whatever success, to disguise its own. . . . It guards itself against all reference to later times and a settled life in Canaan. . . . It keeps itself carefully and strictly within the limits of the situation in the wilderness."—*Hist. of Israel*, p. 9. Riehm says: "Nowhere are any anachronisms found in the Levitical legislation."—*Einl.* i. p. 217.

[3] Cf. Note B on Unity of the Law.

reading of the law was in 444 B.C. But nearly a century earlier, in 536 B.C., at the time of the first return under Zerubbabel, we find no inconsiderable part of the law *already in operation*. Priests and Levites are there; the high priest is there;[1] a complete organisation of worship is there, morning and evening sacrifices are there, set feasts are there, etc.[2] Even if details are challenged, the central facts in this narrative, *e.g.*, the presence of priests and Levites, and of an organisation of worship, cannot be overthrown.[3]

3. There is yet, however, a third incredibility arising from the *unsuitability* of the Code itself. We found the Code of Deuteronomy to be in many respects unsuitable to the age of Josiah. But the unsuitability of Deuteronomy is slight compared with the lack of agreement in the Levitical Code with the state of things in the days of Ezra and Nehemiah. From the point of view of the theory, the Code was designed to be put in force after the return from the exile. The return, therefore, even in the exile, must have been confidently expected. Yet, when the Code is examined, nothing could seem less suitable for its purpose. The whole wilderness framework of the legislation was out of date and place in that late age. The sanctuary is a portable tabernacle, whereas the circumstances of the time demanded a temple. Many of the laws, like that requiring that all sacrifices should be offered at the door of the tabernacle, with the reason for this regulation,[4] were quite out of keeping with the new conditions, had, indeed, no relevancy from the time when the people entered on a settled life in Canaan. Suitable in its place, if it precedes the relaxing rule of Deut. xii. 15, it is unintelligible after. Other parts of the Code had to be dropped or changed, as inapplicable to the post-exilian order of things. There was, *e.g.*, no ark, or priestly Urim or Thummim, in the second

p. 408. We contend, on the contrary, that the narrative of this introduction is a conclusive *disproof* of Wellhausen's view of its date.

[1] Cf. Zech. iii. 1.

[2] Ezra iii. 2 ff.

[3] Delitzsch says: "It is a fact as credibly attested as possible that the distinction of ranks of priests and Levites existed already in B.C. 536, and long before B.C. 444; and indeed so uncontested, so thoroughly established, so strictly maintained, that it must be dated back beyond the exile, in which it cannot have originated, as one regulated by law and custom in the pre-exilian time."—Luthardt's *Zeitschrift*, 1880, p. 268.

[4] Lev. xvii. 1-4. See below, p. 314.

temple. The tax imposed by Nehemiah was a *third* part of a shekel, instead of the *half*-shekel of the law.[1] The law, in one place, prescribes twenty-five years as the age for the Levites entering on service, and in another place thirty years.[2] We find, however, that, after the return, neither of these laws was adopted, but, in accordance with a rule ascribed in Chronicles to David, the Levites commenced their duties at the age of twenty.[3] A more striking example of unsuitability to contemporary conditions is found in the tithe-laws, declared to be a direct creation of the exile. The Levitical law in Numbers is based on the assumption of a large body of Levites, and a relatively small body of priests. The tithes are to be paid directly to the Levites, who are then required to give a tenth of what they receive to the priests.[4] But these provisions were absolutely unsuitable to the times succeeding the exile, when, as we see from the Book of Ezra, the number of Levites who returned was very small, while the number of priests was large.[5] Instead of ten Levites for every priest, the proportion may have been about twelve or thirteen priests for every Levite. This rendered completely nugatory the arrangements of the Code, and made readjustment inevitable. Wellhausen calls this discrepancy "a trifling circumstance,"[6] but fails to explain why a law should have been promulgated so entirely unsuited to the actual situation. The history, besides, has no mention of the tithing of cattle under Nehemiah as prescribed by the law—only of tithes of field produce.[7] As if to render the contrast more striking, while we have in the Code these rules about tithes, so absolutely unsuitable to the circumstances of the exile, with its numerous priests and handful of Levites, we have, on the other hand, mention in the history of an extensive *personnel* connected with the service of the temple—porters, Nethinim, children of

[1] Ex. xxx. 11–16; cf. Neh. x. 32.

[2] Num. iv. 23, 30, etc.; cf. viii. 24. The LXX makes both passages thirty years. This is one of those unessential variations in laws, which, if the ordinary harmonistic explanation is not accepted, viz., that the one law (Num. viii.) refers to the lighter service of the tabernacle itself, the other (Num. iv.) to the harder work of transportation, points to a liberty of varying the strict letter of the law, provided its spirit or principle was adhered to. See above, p. 179.

[3] Ezra iii. 8; cf. 1 Chron. xxiii. 24, 27.

[4] Num. xviii. 24–26.

[5] Ezra ii.; viii. 15 ff.

[6] *Hist. of Israel*, p. 167.

[7] Neh. x. 39; xiii. 5.

ıese statements; the one is, in fact, as we shall immediately ›e, destructive of the other. The tendency in writers of ıis school is, in reality, to a kind of *see-saw* between these vo positions; the one that the Priestly Code was in the ıain a simple "codification" of pre-exilic usage—a comıratively innocent hypothesis; and the other that the ıaracteristic institutions of the Priestly Code—ark, bernacle, Aaronic priests, Levites, tithes, Levitical cities, n-offerings, day of atonement," etc., were, one and all, the ee creation of the exilic period—were then, despite Dr. river's disclaimer, "manufactured"[1]—and were absolutely ıknown earlier. If the latter proposition cannot be aintained, the whole hypothesis goes to earth. Here ;ain we are entitled to say that the critics must really ake their choice. They cannot well be allowed at one me to employ arguments which are of no force unless on ıe assumption that the Levitical law is, as a whole, in atter as well as in form, *new*; and at another, to use 'guments based on the contention that the bulk of the gislation is, in practice, *old*.[2]

Let us, however, accept, as we are glad to do, the stateent that "the main stock" of the legislation of P is "based ɔon pre-existing temple usage," and see what follows. The ›servance of this "main stock" before the exile either ›pears in the history, or it does not. If it does *not*, what ›comes of the argument from silence against the other .stitutions? If it *does*, what becomes of Wellhausen's atement that "no trace can be found of acquaintance ith the Priestly Code, but, on the other hand, very clear .dications of ignorance of its contents?"[3] It is nothing to ıe purpose to reply, as is commonly done, that before the ɛile there was indeed *praxis* — usage — but no written

ɔn before the exile, even though a system of priestly legislation was ınting at that time" (p. 192).

[1] We may take in illustration the law of the passover in Exodus, ferred to further below, pp. 320–21. Graf treats Ex. xii. 1–28 as a pure eation of the time of the exile, and deduces from the fact of its agreement .th the priestly and sacrificial laws of Leviticus, that these must be ilian or post-exilian also (*Geschicht. Bücher*, pp. 34–36). Wellhausen's ew is that the law has undergone a transformation which inverts the lation of cause and effect. It was the Israelitish custom of offering the stlings which gave rise to the story of the slaying of the firstborn in ɜypt, not *vice versa*.—*Hist. of Israel*, pp. 88, 100, 102, 352.

[2] Cf. Robertson on Wellhausen, *Early Religion*, etc., pp. 393–94.

[3] *Hist. of Israel*, p. 59.

Priestly Code, or Code of ritual law attributed to Mose
For (1) *the very ground on which the existence of a writt Code is denied is that there is no proof of the practice*; and if the practice is allowed, who is to certify that a writt law, regulating the practice, was not there? Against t existence of a written law, we have only Wellhause dogmatic *dictum*, repeated by other critics, that, so lo as the cultus lasted, people would not concern themselv with reducing it to the form of a Code.[2] It was only wh it had passed away that men thought of reducing it writing. That, however, Wellhausen certainly cannot pro and his view is not that of older and of a good ma recent scholars.[3] Nor has it probability in itself. A written Codes—especially in the light of modern knowled —so entirely unknown to antiquity as to warrant anyone saying *a priori* that, even where an elaborate ritual acknowledged to be in operation, a Code regulating cannot have existed?[4]

2. There is an admitted "pre-existing temple usag constituting "the main stock" of the priestly law; reflecti may next convince us that this "pre-existing usage mu have covered a much larger part of the Levitical Code th is commonly realised. There existed at least a splen temple, with outer and inner divisions; a sacred a temple furniture and utensils; a hereditary priestho The priests would have their sacred vestments, prescrib duties, ritual lore, their *technique* in the manipulation the different kinds of sacrifices, their recognised rules the discernment and treatment of leprosy, their rules ceremonial purification, their calendar of sacred festiva etc. These things *existed*; assume the laws relating to th

[1] *Ibid.*; cf. Kuenen, as above, p. 96. [2] *Ibid.*

[3] Cf. Bleek, *Introd.* i. pp. 221 ff.; Dillmann, *Exod.-Lev.* Pref. p. (see above, p. 160); p. 386.

[4] Analogy and discovery furnish strong grounds for believing that Is would have a written law. Kittel says on this point: "Israel came out and always continued to be connected with, a country where exter prescriptions and rules played their part in all ages. As in Egypt, s Babylonia and Assyria, rules were laid down for sacrificial worship at early period. The Marseilles Table of Offerings has brought the same fac light as regards the Phœnicians. Is it to be believed that with all t scrupulosity on the part of the surrounding priesthoods, a primit informalism, of which there is no other example, prevailed in Israel al until the days of the restoration?"—*Hist. of Hebs.* i. p. 113. Cf. Dillma *Num.-Jos.* p. 647.

to be written down, what ground have we for supposing that they would have differed greatly from the laws preserved to us in Leviticus and Numbers? Yet how little of all this obtrudes itself in the history? Nothing, we have again to point out, is gained by the substitution of *praxis* for written law; for it is not the written law, usually, but the practice, that history takes cognisance of, and, if silence in the history is compatible with the *practice*, it must also be compatible with the existence of any *Code* that regulates it. How far this reaches will appear more clearly if we look at specific instances.

Wellhausen speaks repeatedly of the splendour and elaboration of the pre-exilic cultus. There was a cultus "carried on," he tells us, "with the utmost zeal and splendour"[1]—"splendid sacrifices, presumably offered with all the rules of priestly skill."[2] "Elaborate ritual may have existed in the great sanctuaries at a very early period."[3] He correctly infers "that Amos and Hosea, presupposing as they do a splendid cultus and great sanctuaries, doubtless also knew of a variety of festivals."[4] But he has to add, "they have no occasion to mention any one by name." To the same effect Isaiah is quoted: "Add ye year to year, let the feasts go round."[5] But where shall we look in history for any notice of these feasts? It is allowed that the three feasts of the Book of the Covenant were observed from early times; yet, says Wellhausen, "names are nowhere to be found, and in point of fact it is only the autumn festival that is well attested, and this, it would appear, as the only festival, as *the* feast."[6] Still the critic has no doubt that "even under the older monarchy the previous festivals must also have already existed as well."[7] As particular examples, let the reader take his concordance, and note the exceeding paucity of the allusions in the historical books to such institutions as the sabbath, the new moon, or even the rite of circumcision. How easy, on the strength of this silence, would it be to say in the familiar way: "Joshua, Judges, the Books of Samuel, know nothing of the sabbath!" Drop one or two incidental references, which might easily

[1] *Hist. of Israel*, p. 56.
[2] *Ibid.* p. 55.
[3] *Ibid.* p. 54.
[4] *Ibid.* p. 94.
[5] *Ibid.*
[6] *Ibid.* It is not the case, however, that no other feasts are named. See below, pp. 321–22.
[7] *Ibid.* p. 96.

not have been there, and the evidence in the history for the above, as for many other institutions, disappears altogether Does it follow that the sabbath, or a law of the sabbath had no existence?

3. The test may be applied in another way. It is urged *e.g.*, that there is no clear reference in pre-exilian literatur to the existence of a class of Levites as distinct from th priests. It has already been seen that this is not altogethe the case,[1] and, at least, as pointed out, the Levites appea quite distinctly at the return, nearly a century before th Priestly Code was promulgated by Ezra. But what of *post* exilian literature? Apart from Ezra and Nehemiah, an the Books of Chronicles, how many references to the Levite could be gleaned from exilian and post-exilian writings The second Isaiah (assuming the critical date), the prophet Haggai, Zechariah, Joel (if he be post-exilian), Malachi,[2] th Psalter—declared to be the song-book of the second templ —*all are silent*, with the possible exception of Ps. cxxxv. 2 The Priests' Code generally finds little reflection in th Psalter. Even in the Priestly Code itself, it is surprising t discover how large a part contains no allusions to th Levites. In Leviticus—the priestly book *par excellence*— with the solitary exception of chap. xxv. 32, 33, they are n so much as named.[3] Equally remarkable is the silence the *New* Testament on the Levites. One stray allusion the parable of the Good Samaritan;[4] one in the Fourt Gospel;[5] one in Acts, where Barnabas is described as Levite[6]—that is all. The Epistle to the Hebrews, eve has nothing to say of them. Priests everywhere, b Levites nowhere. This, surely, is a sufficiently striki object-lesson in silence. Yet it is on the ground of similar silence to this that we are asked to believe th there was no pre-exilian observance of the day of aton ment.[7] Doubtless there is no mention in the history of t yearly day of expiation—any more than there is of t

[1] See above, pp. 163, 189.

[2] The Levites in Malachi are the priests.

[3] Cf. Kittel, *Hist. of Hebs.* i. pp. 120–21. Kittel shows that in large pa of the Priestly Code "there is no contrast between priests and Levites."

[4] Luke x. 32. [5] John i. 19. [6] Acts iv. 36.

[7] We are aware that it is argued that its observance is on certain occasi *precluded* by the narrative. But see Delitzsch's article, Luthardt's *Zeitschr* 1880, pp. 173 ff.

sabbatical year,[1] the year of jubilee,[2] and many other nstitutions which we have good reason to believe were known, even if they were not always faithfully observed.[3] But the argument from silence in the case of the day of atonement proves too much; for, as it happens, *post*-exilian iterature is as silent about it as *pre*-exilian. Important solemnity as it was, it is not mentioned by Ezra, Nehemiah, Chronicles, or any of the post-exilian prophets. The first notice of its observance is in Josephus, who tells us that, in 37 B.C., Herod took Jerusalem on that day, as Pompey had done twenty-seven years before.[4] The Gospels and Acts contain no reference to the day of atonement; yet we know from the Epistle to the Hebrews that it was observed, and that its rites were familiar.[5]

IV. Proof of Earlier Existence of Priestly Legislation

Thus far we have proceeded on the critics' own ssumption of the silence in pre-exilian times regarding he laws and institutions of the Priestly Code. But was he silence really as unbroken as is alleged? We shall now ndeavour to show that it was not. The opposite can only e maintained by the process of circular reasoning which xplains away every testimony to the contrary by the ssumption of late date or interpolation of the notice, or by he convenient distinction between Code and usage. We o on the contrary principle that *praxis*, as a rule, is a estimony in favour of *Code*; but we hope to do something o prove the presence of Code also.

In an earlier chapter we sought to establish the existence n pre-exilic times of many of the characteristic institutions

[1] Ex. xxiii. 10; Lev. xxv. 2 ff.; xxvi. 34, 35. The first mention of the abbatical year is in the time of the Maccabees (1 Macc. vi. 53).

[2] Lev. xxv. Cf. Isa. lxi. 1, 2. Kuenen admits that Ezekiel knew the ubilee year (*Rel. of Israel*, ii. p. 191).

[3] The Wellhausen school deny the observance, but without good reason cf. Dillmann on Lev. xxv. 7, p. 608).

[4] *Antiq.* xiv. 16. 4.

[5] Heb. ix. 7 ff. The list of silences might easily be extended. The east of weeks, *e.g.*, is not mentioned by Ezekiel, who speaks of the assover and the feast of tabernacles. It is alluded to only once in the whole history before the exile (1 Kings ix. 25; 2 Chron. viii. 13). Neither oes Ezekiel allude to the evening sacrifice.

of the Levitical Code, *e.g.*, the ark, the tabernacle, the Aaronic priesthood, the high priest, etc.[1] It adds to the weight of the argument that in many instances we are indebted to quite incidental allusions for a knowledge of facts and observances whose existence might not otherwise have been suspected. It is, *e.g.*, only by accident that we came on the notice of "the shewbread" in the sanctuary at Nob in the reign of Saul.[2] Again, from 1 Sam. i., ii., we might hastily conclude that there were at Shiloh no priests but Eli and his two sons; as from chap. xxi. we might infer that there was at Nob only the single priest Ahimelech. Yet Saul's massacre after David's flight discovers to us the presence at Nob of eighty-five priests that wore a linen ephod.[3] If it be replied that the references to ark, tabernacle, priesthood, shewbread, and the like, do not prove the existence of the detailed representations of the Priestly Code,[4] this may be granted, and is only to be expected. But they show at least that these things were *there* to be legislated for, and annul the presumption against laws which have this for their object. It is a curious state of mind that can see a propriety in the codification of laws, *e.g.*, about parapets and fringes,[5] but supposes that everything about sanctuary and sacrifice was left to drift on without authoritative regulation. It is now necessary, however, to come to closer quarters, and to ask whether there is any direct evidence of the existence of priestly laws in written form in pre-exilian times.

1. We turn first to the *Book of Ezekiel*, and specially to chaps. xl.–xlviii., which Wellhausen says have been not incorrectly called "the key of the Old Testament,"[6] and between which and the Priestly Code, at any rate, it is

[1] Cf. above, Chap. VI. [2] 1 Sam. xxi.

[3] 1 Sam. xxii. 18. Wellhausen allows that there must have been a considerable establishment at Shiloh. "The temple of Shiloh," he says, "the priesthood of which we find officiating at Nob a little later." "The office is hereditary, and the priesthood already very numerous."—*Hist. of Israel*, pp. 19, 128.

[4] Thus Dr. Driver, *Introd.* p. 142. See above, p. 171. The regulations for such an establishment must have been pretty detailed, if they existed at all.

[5] Deut. xxii. 8, 12.

[6] *Hist. of Israel*. p. 421. (Cf. p. 25 above.) Smend also says: "The decisive importance of this section for the criticism of the Pentateuch was first recognised by George and Vatke. It has been rightly called the key of the Old Testament. In fact it is only intelligible as an intermediate

llowed on all sides that there exists a close relation.[1] What is the nature of that relation? Is it, as the world as till recently believed, the Levitical Code, with which s a priest he was necessarily familiar, which furnished Ezekiel with suggestion and guidance in the framing of his sketch of a new theocracy, in which older institutions are reely remodelled and changed?[2] Or is it, as the newer ritics allege, that no written priestly laws as yet existed, nd that Ezekiel's sketch was the first rough draft—"programme"—on the basis of which exilian scribes fterwards worked to produce their so-called Mosaic Code.[3] The latter view is necessary to the Wellhausen hypothesis,[4] et it is one against which a powerful note of dissent is aised by an influential company of scholars, many of them vell-nigh as "advanced" as Wellhausen himself.[5] It is ointed out, surely with justice, that the vision of Ezekiel s only conceivable as the product of a mind saturated with he knowledge of temple law and ritual; that the parallels vith the Priestly Code are not confined to chaps. xl.–xlviii., ut go through the whole book;[6] that much is simply lluded to, or left to be understood, which only the Priestly Code can explain;[7] above all, that the scheme of the Levitical Code deviates so widely in conception and detail rom that of Ezekiel as to render it unthinkable that its

ink between Deuteronomy and the Priestly Code, and it thence follows hat the latter is exilian or post-exilian."—*Ezechiel*, p. 312.

[1] "On one point," says Baudissin, "there can be no doubt, namely this, hat the affinity between the law of Ezekiel and the Priests' Code is so reat that it can be explained only by the dependence of one of these upon he other."—*Dict. of Bible*, iv. p. 86.

[2] It seems obvious that the vision is a work of prophetic imagination, nd is not intended to be taken as a literal programme for future realisation. One has only to read the vision of the waters, and the direction for the livision of the land in chap. xlvii. to see that they belong to the region of he ideal—not of fact.

[3] Cf. Kuenen, *Rel. of Israel*, ii. p. 116.

[4] One of the theses on which, from 1833, Reuss based his lectures was this: "Ezekiel is earlier than the redaction of the ritual code, and of the laws, which definitely organised the hierarchy." (Cf. Wellhausen, *Hist.* p. 4.) See above, p. 200. Since the time of Graf, Delitzsch says, "the Book of Ezekiel has become the Archimedean point of the Pentateuchal criticism." —Luthardt's *Zeitschrift*, 1880, p. 279.

[5] Among critics of the theory may be mentioned Delitzsch, Riehm, Dillmann, Schrader, Nöldeke, Baudissin, Kittel, Oettli, etc.

[6] See below, pp. 308–9.

[7] *E.g.*, the sin- and trespass-offerings, chaps. xl. 39; xliv. 29. See Note C on Ezekiel and Earlier Law and Observance.

authors took the temple-vision of Ezekiel as a pattern. How, indeed, if they viewed the vision of Ezekiel as a prophetic revelation, should they presume to ignore or contradict it so directly as they do?[1] We are aware that the objection is retorted: how should Ezekiel presume to alter a divinely-given earlier Code?[2] But the cases are quite different. Ezekiel is not putting forward a code in the name of Moses. He is a prophetic man, avowedly legislating in the Spirit for a transformed land and a transformed people in the future. Not only, however, does the prophesying of Ezekiel *presuppose* an older law, but the references with which his pages are filled to "statutes and judgments," or "ordinances" of God,[3] which the people had transgressed (in their "abominations" at the sanctuary among other things), show explicitly that he had such laws habitually before him.

2. But the subject admits of being brought to a nearer determination. There is at least *one important section* of the Priestly Code which, it is allowed, stands in the closest possible connection with Ezekiel. We refer to "that peculiar little collection of laws," as Wellhausen calls it,[4] embraced in Lev. xvii.–xxvi. (with, according to most, extensive fragments elsewhere), which modern writers, following Klostermann, usually name "The Law of Holiness."[5] The resemblances with Ezekiel here, particu-

[1] "It is," says Delitzsch, "incomprehensible how Ezra and Nehemiah could dare to publish a law-book whose ordinances contradict those of Ezekiel on all sides, and which still, in matter and form, shows itself well acquainted with the latter."—*Zeitschrift*, p. 281. The systematic character of Ezekiel's law, as compared with the *un*systematic character of the Levitical Code, shows that it is not the latter which is dependent on the former, but *vice versa*.

[2] Thus Graf, Kautzsch, etc. Professor Robertson remarks: "Well, on the critical hypothesis, the Deuteronomic law at least existed as authoritative, and yet Ezekiel deviates from it."—*Early Religion*, pp. 432–33. Dr. A. B. Davidson points out: "Inferences from comparison of Ezekiel with the Law have to be drawn with caution, for it is evident that the prophet handles with freedom institutions certainly older than his own time."—*Ezekiel*, Introd. p. liii.

[3] Ezek. v. 6; xi. 12, and *passim*.

[4] *Hist. of Israel*, p. 51 (cf. pp. 75, 86, 376, 384).

[5] Klostermann gave it this name in 1877 in a searching article since reprinted in his *Der Pentateuch*, pp. 368 ff. "The principle," says Dr. Driver, "which determines most conspicuously the character of the entire section is that of *holiness*—partly ceremonial, partly moral—as a quality distinguishing Israel, demanded of Israel by Jehovah."—*Introd.* p. 48. Characteristic of it is the phrase "I am Jehovah."

the Aaronic priesthood,[1] the high priest,[2] sin- and trespass-offerings,[3] the day of atonement,[4] the three historical feasts,[5] the sabbatic year,[6] the year of jubilee,[7] the Levitical cities,[8] etc. We shall think twice, and require strong evidence, before surrendering all this, at the bidding of critical theory, to post-exilian hands.

3. Accepting it as established that the Law of Holiness, and other Levitical laws, were known to Ezekiel, we may now carry the argument a considerable way higher, with fresh confirmation of the result already reached. It is essential to the Wellhausen hypothesis to prove that the Levitical Code is posterior to Ezekiel; it is still more indispensable for its purpose to show that it is later than *Deuteronomy*. But is this really so? The assertion is, no doubt, continually made; but on this point, once more, the critical camp is keenly divided, and there appears the clearest evidence that, as the older scholars all but unanimously maintained, the author of Deuteronomy is familiar with, and in his legislation actually embodies or alludes to, many provisions of the Levitical Code. Here again Dr. Driver will be our witness, though this time, perhaps, against his own intention. At first sight, indeed, this careful scholar seems altogether against us. "The pre-exilic period," he tells us, "shows no indications of the legislation of P being in operation. . . . Nor is the legislation of P presupposed in Deuteronomy."[9] Ere long, however, we discover that here, also, after the critical fashion, we have to distinguish *two* Dr. Drivers (Dr.[1] and Dr.[2], shall we say?)—a first, who contends unqualifiedly that the pre-exilic period "shows *no* indications of the legislation of P," and a second, who admits that it is only "the *completed* Priests' Code" that is unknown before the exile, and that "the contradiction of the pre-exilic literature does not extend to the *whole* of the Priests' Code indiscriminately."[10] Citation is made of Deut. xiv.

[1] Lev. xvii. 2; xxi. 1, 17, 21, etc. [2] Chap. xxi. 10–15.
[3] Chaps. xix. 21, 22; xxiii. 19. [4] Chaps. xxiii. 27–32; xxv. 9.
[5] Chap. xxiii. [6] Chap. xxv. 2–7. [7] Chap. xxv. 8 ff.
[8] Chap. xxv. 32, 33. The notice of the cities is the more valuable that it comes in incidentally in connection with a different subject.
[9] *Introd.* pp. 136, 137. Cf. above, p. 300.
[10] *Ibid.* p. 142 (italics are Dr. D.'s). As statements so discrepant within a short compass can hardly be supposed to come from the same pen, we are

4–20, but in the remarks that follow there is a slight varia tion between the first and the revised editions of th *Introduction* which deserves attention. We quote the firs edition, as better representing the facts, and give the revise form below.[1] "Here," it is said, "is a long passage virtuall identical in Deuteronomy and Leviticus; and that it i borrowed by D from P—or at least from a priestly collec tion of *toroth*—rather than conversely, appears fro certain features of style which connect it with P and no with Deuteronomy. . . . If so, however, one part of P was i existence when Deuteronomy was written; and a presump tion at once arises that other parts were in existence als Now the tenor of Deuteronomy as a whole conflicts wit the supposition that *all* the institutions of the Priests' Cod were in force when D wrote; but the list of passages jus quoted shows that *some* were, and that the terminolog used in connection with them was known to D."[2] Th "list" referred to gives in parallel columns a long catalogu of passages of Deuteronomy corresponding "with P (inclu ing H)," with note of some peculiarities in the mode quotation.[3] On another page it is said: "In Deuteronom the following parallels may be noted," with list again given These are significant admissions, and completely dispose the unqualified statements first quoted. Reduced to i real dimensions, Dr. Driver's argument only is that som of the *characteristic* institutions of P—*e.g.*, the distinctio of priests and Levites—conflict with the tenor of D;[5] an even this contention, resting largely on the argument fro silence, cannot be allowed the weight he attaches to it. A he himself says: "That many of the distinctive institutio of P are not alluded to—the day of atonement, the jubil year, the Levitical cities, the sin-offering, the system

driven back, on critical principles, upon the supposition that the work really the composition of a Driver "school" whose members vary slightly their standpoints—a hypothesis which other indications support.

[1] The 7th edition reads: "Here is a long passage in great measu verbally identical in Deuteronomy and Leviticus, and a critical comparis of the two texts makes it probable that both are divergent recensions of common original, which in each case, but specially in Leviticus, has be modified in accordance with the spirit of the book in which it was i corporated. It is thus apparent that at least one collection of priest *toroth*, which now forms part of P, was in existence when Deuteronomy w written," etc. (p. 145). The rest as above.

[2] *Ibid.* pp. 137–38 (1st edit.).

[3] *Ibid.* pp. 73–75.

[4] *Ibid.* p. 144.

[5] *Ibid.* p. 137.